# The Basque Witch-Hunt

# The Basque
# Witch-Hunt

A Secret History

**Jan Machielsen**

BLOOMSBURY ACADEMIC
LONDON • NEW YORK • OXFORD • NEW DELHI • SYDNEY

BLOOMSBURY ACADEMIC
Bloomsbury Publishing Plc
50 Bedford Square, London, WC1B 3DP, UK
1385 Broadway, New York, NY 10018, USA
29 Earlsfort Terrace, Dublin 2, Ireland

BLOOMSBURY, BLOOMSBURY ACADEMIC and the Diana logo are trademarks of
Bloomsbury Publishing Plc

First published in Great Britain 2024

Copyright © Jan Machielsen, 2024

Jan Machielsen has asserted his right under the Copyright, Designs and Patents Act, 1988,
to be identified as Author of this work.

For legal purposes the Acknowledgements on pp. 239–243 constitute an
extension of this copyright page.

Cover design by Elena Durey
Cover image: *El aquelarre* (Witches' Sabbath), circa 1797–1798. Francisco de Goya y
Lucientes. © The Picture Art Collection / Alamy

All rights reserved. No part of this publication may be reproduced or transmitted
in any form or by any means, electronic or mechanical, including photocopying,
recording, or any information storage or retrieval system, without prior
permission in writing from the publishers.

Bloomsbury Publishing Plc does not have any control over, or responsibility for, any
third-party websites referred to or in this book. All internet addresses given in this
book were correct at the time of going to press. The author and publisher regret any
inconvenience caused if addresses have changed or sites have ceased to exist, but can
accept no responsibility for any such changes.

A catalogue record for this book is available from the British Library.

A catalog record for this book is available from the Library of Congress.

ISBN: HB: 978-1-3504-4150-7
ePDF: 978-1-3504-4151-4
eBook: 978-1-3504-4152-1

Typeset by Newgen KnowledgeWorks Pvt. Ltd., Chennai, India
Printed and bound in Great Britain

To find out more about our authors and books visit www.bloomsbury.com
and sign up for our newsletters.

For Rich,

because he is precious

# Contents

List of figures  ix
List of maps  xi
Naming conventions  xii
Dramatis personae  xiv
Chronology  xviii

Introduction: The summer of 1609  1

## Part One  A Perfect Storm

1  Living on the edge  15
2  Beginnings (1603–1608)  43

## Part Two  Outsiders

3  Judging the judges  67
4  Throwing roosters at lions  77
5  Between a rock and an anchor  87
6  The royal will  95

## Part Three  The Commission (1609)

7  Into the devil's snare  109
8  Of village musicians and dancing queens  119

**9** Child spies 145

**10** Opposition 167

## Part Four Aftermath (1610–1619)

**11** Too many witches 187

**12** Spiritual solutions 207

**13** New witch bottles 219

Epilogue: Acts of remembrance 235

**Acknowledgements** 239
Notes 245
Bibliography 287
Index 311

# Figures

0.1  The title page of the *Tableau de l'inconstance des mauvais anges et démons* 5

0.2  Jan Ziarnko, 'Description et figure du sabbat des sorciers' (description and illustration of the witches' sabbat) in Pierre de Lancre, *Tableau de l'inconstance des mauvais anges et démons* 7

1.1  The Bay of Saint-Jean-de-Luz, with the town to the left and Ciboure to the right (*c*. 1620?) 27

1.2  A Basque sailor at prayer in stormy waters. Painting on wood (late sixteenth century) 33

1.3  A cloud of witches, the central vignette of the 1613 sabbat engraving 34

1.4  A Basque woman wearing traditional headgear. Christoph Weiditz, *Trachtenbuch* (*c*. 1530/1540) 36

1.5  An unmarried Basque woman. Christoph Weiditz, *Trachtenbuch* (*c*. 1530/1540) 37

2.1  The Chateau d'Urtubie 60

3.1  The Palais de l'Ombrière. Nineteenth-century engraving 69

3.2  The devil as goat on a throne, vignette from the 1613 sabbat engraving 74

5.1  Pierre de Lancre's coat of arms 88

| | |
|---|---|
| 6.1 | A 1614 map with the new port of Socoa and the towns of Saint-Jean-de-Luz and Ciboure 100 |
| 8.1, 8.3 | A witch on a broomstick and a salamander, from Jacques de Gheyn II, 'Witches Preparing for Sabbath' (*c.* 1610) 126 |
| 8.2, 8.4–8.15 | Fragments or scenes of the 1613 sabbat engraving 126–141 |
| 9.1 | Posthumous (?) portrait of Antoine II de Gramont (date unknown) 158 |
| 10.1 | Testimony of Marie Du Cornau, signed by Jean d'Espagnet and Pierre de Lancre 178 |
| 10.2 | Portrait of Bertrand d'Echaux (date unknown) 181 |
| 11.1 | The Chateau du Ha, Bordeaux, by Hermann Van der Hem (1638) 193 |
| 11.2 | Engraving of Marc-Antoine de Gourgue (1628?) 201 |

# Maps

0.1   Map of the French-Spanish border region  xiii
0.2   Map of Western Europe  xiii
7.1   Reconstruction of the witchcraft commission's most probable route  115

# Naming conventions

The Basque country is a multilingual and multicultural space, like all contested border regions. This book uses the place names by which towns and communities are primarily known today. In practice, this means the use of Basque rather than Castilian place names south of the border – Pasaia instead of Pasajes, Bera instead of Vera – with the notable exception of Donostia which is too well-known in English as San Sebastián. By the same logic, for place names in the Pays de Labourd (Lapurdi), I have adopted the French version, in recognition of the fact that Basque place names have not gained widespread currency there, both locally and further afield. Referring to Saint-Jean-de-Luz, the town at the epicentre of the Basque witch-hunt and often at the heart of this study, as Donibane Lohizune would confuse rather than clarify.

Similarly, where persons are concerned, I have mostly let myself be guided by the sources. Only when I encountered multiple variants of a name did I choose one option over the others. The result means that we shall encounter persons called María and Marie, Juanes and Jean, and even Pedro, Petry and Pierre within the covers of this book. I trust that such polyphony will not disturb the reader. It is meant to capture both the cultural richness of what was – also then – a vibrant and diverse space and the challenges of living in a border region. Much of this book is an attempt to productively engage with those facets. Translating all names to modern Basque equivalents would only have elided them.

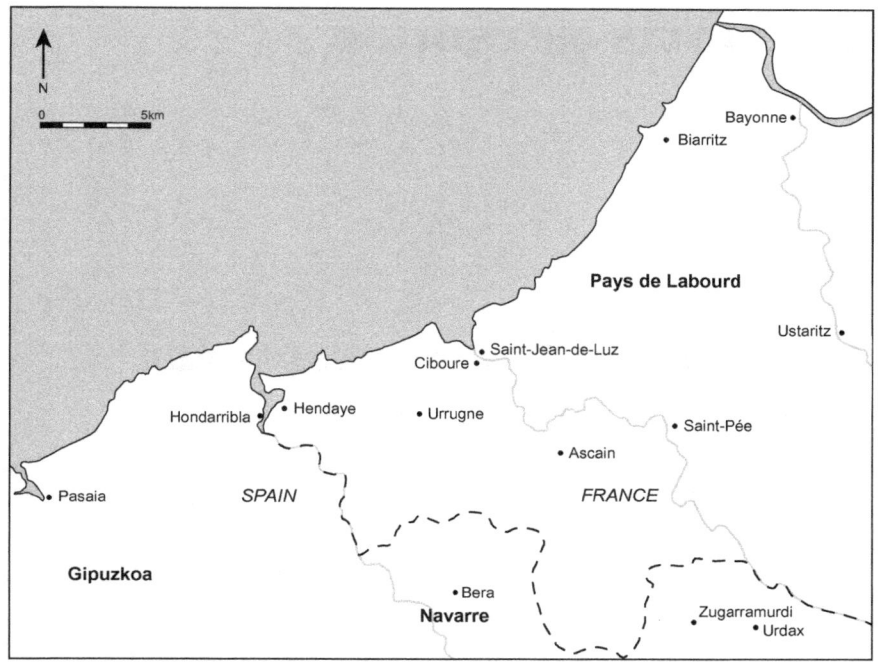

**Map 0.1** Map of the French-Spanish border region.

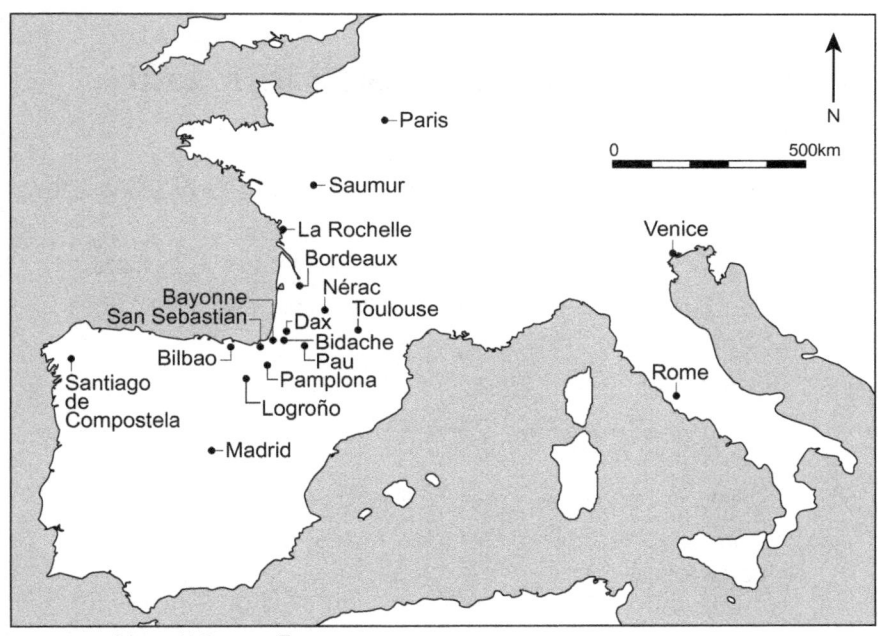

**Map 0.2** Map of Western Europe.

# Dramatis personae

## Saint-Jean-de-Luz merchants and officials

Adam de Chibau
Guiraud de Sanson
Jean de Goyetche
Jean de Haraneder
Joannes de Sanson
Martin de La Masse
Martin d'Oriotz

## Lapurdi and Bayonne officials and noblemen

Antoine II de Gramont (1572–1644), hereditary mayor of Bayonne, count (later duke) of Gramont, and prince of Bidache

Auger de Ségure, self-described *assesseur criminel* of the Pays de Labourd

Bertrand d'Echaux (c. 1556–1641), bishop of Bayonne (1599–1617), later archbishop of Tours (1617–41)

Charles de Sorhaindo, lieutenant mayor of Bayonne

Jean-Paul de Caupenne, Lord of Amou and Saint-Pée, bailli of the Pays de Labourd (1590–1621)

Pierre de Chibau, lieutenant-general of the Pays de Labourd

Tristan de Gamboa d'Alzate, Lord of Urtubie, married to the daughter of a Bordeaux judge

## Observers of the Basque country

Bertrand de Haitze, a young parish priest at Ustaritz

Mathias de Lissalde, a Recollect friar at the monastery of Notre-Dame-de-la-Paix

## Bordeaux judges and officials

Étienne de Cruseau (d. 1616), Bordeaux judge and diarist

Florimond de Raemond (1540–1601), a Catholic apologist and Pierre de Lancre's brother-in-law

Jean d'Espagnet (1564–>1643), an alchemist pursuing the philosophers' stone and Pierre de Lancre's immediate colleague in the Labourd

Marc-Antoine de Gourgue (or Gourgues; 1575–1628), an accidental witchcraft commissioner

Michel de Montaigne (1533–92), a famous philosopher and (witchcraft) sceptic; Pierre de Lancre's relative through marriage

Pierre de Lancre (1556–1631), gleeful executioner of the Pays de Labourd

## Spanish Inquisition officials

Alonso de Becerra (*c.* 1560–1622), Alonso de Salazar Frías (*c.* 1564–1636), Juan de Valle Alvarado (*c.* 1553–1616), inquisitors at the Logroño Tribunal

José de Elizondo, successor to Léon de Aranibar as abbot of the monastery of San Salvador de Urdax

Léon de Aranibar, abbot of the monastery of San Salvador de Urdax (1591–1600, 1607–13), and Inquisition commissioner (from 1609)

Lorenzo de Hualde, parish priest at Bera (from 1605) and Inquisition commissioner (from 1609)

Marcos de Ylumbe, a spectacularly unsuccessful Inquisition spy

## Known Lapurdi witchcraft suspects

The list below includes *all* named individuals from the Pays de Labourd who are known to have been interrogated or tried as witches before, during or after the 1609 witchcraft commission, whether they appear in this book or not. Those whose names only featured in the testimony of others have been omitted. Known executions are marked with a †.

Ansugarlo, a musician †
Arguibel, a priest †
Catalina de Lesalde
Catherine d'Abaustena †
Catherine de Barrendeguy, also known as Cathalin de Bardos †
Catherine de Landalde
Catherine de Moleres †
Catherine de Sonsac
Detsail †
Françoise de Haristeguy, also known as 'Hihy' †
Graci Doihaugaray
Haritourena, a priest
Inesa de Gajén
Jean de Lasson, a priest
Jean Souhardibels, a priest
Jeanne D'Aguerre
Jeanne Dibasson
Jehanne Mondens †
Jehanette de Bardos
Joaneta Motharena
La Masse, a priest
María de Echagaray
Marie Bonne †
Marie de Haristeguy
Marie Dindarte †
Marie Marchant
Marie Martin
Marie Ourdinez
Marierchiquerra de Machinena
Marissans de Tartas †
Martin de Haraneder, a priest
Migalena, a priest †
Necato
Petry d'Aguerre and family †
Pierre Bocal, a priest †
Sansinena, Lady of
Saubadine de Soubiete †

# Known Lapurdi witnesses (accusers of witches)

The list below includes *all* individuals from the Pays de Labourd (mostly but not exclusively teenagers) who accused others of witchcraft before, during or after the 1609 commission and whose names are known.

Aspilevera
Catherine d'Arreioüaque
Catherine de La Masse
Catherine de Naguille
Corneille Brolic
Cristoval de la Garralde
Bertrand de Handuch
Dojartzabal
Isabel García
Janne de Hortilopits

Jeannette d'Abadie
Jeannette de Belloc
Johannés d'Aguerre
Lisalde
Marguerite Hareder
María de Ximildegui
Marie d'Aguerre
Marie d'Aspilcouette
Marie de Gastagnalde
Marie de Marigrane

Marie de Naguille
Marie de la Parque
Marie de la Ralde
Marie de la Rat
Marie du Cornau
Miguel de Sahourspe
Morguy
Petry de Linarre
Sandoteguy

# Chronology

| | |
|---|---|
| **10 October 1603** | The witchcraft trial of Marie de Haristeguy in Saint-Jean-de-Luz |
| **Late 1604/early 1605** | Saint-Jean-de-Luz placed under an interdict by the bishop of Bayonne, Bertrand d'Echaux |
| **1605** | First witchcraft commission sent by the Bordeaux Parlement |
| **1606–7** | Basque witchcraft trials held in Bordeaux |
| **10 June 1607** | Catherine de La Masse, one of the original accusers, denounces in church those who attempted to force her to retract her testimony |
| **14 and 24 June 1607** | Further popular disturbances in Saint-Jean-de-Luz |
| **17 November 1608** | Aldermen from Urrugne, Hendaye and Ciboure approach their colleagues in Bayonne with the plan for a royal witchcraft commission |
| **December 1608** | María de Ximildegui arrives in Zugarramurdi from Ciboure and accuses others of witchcraft, leading to the Spanish Inquisition's intervention |
| **10 December 1608/17 January 1609** | Henry IV signs the letters patent setting up a royal witchcraft commission |
| **2 July 1609** | The two witchcraft commissioners, Jean d'Espagnet and Pierre de Lancre, arrive in Bayonne |
| **22 September 1609** | The first of several waves of Moriscos is expelled from Spain |
| **1 November 1609** | The commission's work ends |
| **14 May 1610** | King Henry IV is assassinated; Marie de' Medici becomes regent for her young son, Louis XIII |
| **7 and 8 November 1610** | The Spanish Inquisition holds an elaborate *auto de fe* in Logroño which features 29 witches |
| **1610–12** | A new commissioner, Marc-Antoine de Gourgue, is sent to sort out the Labourd's problems, including the passage of the Moriscos |

| | |
|---|---|
| **1612** | Pierre de Lancre publishes his *Tableau* |
| **1614–16** | Jesuit missionaries visit the Labourd to reconcile confessed witches to the Catholic church |
| **19 March 1619** | The brutal killing of Catarina de Fernandes |

# Introduction
# The summer of 1609

Witches aside, Pierre de Lancre saw many other strange things as he travelled down the Basque coast during the summer of 1609. At Biarritz, he expressed concern about the 'older girls and young fishermen' whom he saw mix and mingle naked in the waves – a worry shared centuries later by well-to-do parents when the fishing village grew into a luxury seaside resort.[1] At Anglet and Bidart, he observed women and men of all ages entering the rough sea, engaged in some sort of ritual, welcoming the 'thundering' waves and holding on to fishermen's ropes – 'as if', he observed, 'they were presenting themselves to the god Neptune.' But it was the children of Saint-Jean-de-Luz and Ciboure who mesmerized him. The two seafaring communities on opposing banks of the river Nivelle were connected by a new bridge from which the children jumped, seemingly without a care in the world. The Bordeaux judge, who loved exaggerated Baroque metaphors, stood agog as these teenagers disappeared 'a hundred thousand times in these great heaps, which were white like snowflakes, and by their very whiteness were like a headband which blinded us'. So rough was the sea that its movements were 'capable of drowning the strongest courage of the most constant philosopher of the world'.[2] Despite these dangers, some very naked and very fearless teens dived head-down from the bridge in pursuit of some small piece of coin, only to emerge 500 feet from where they went in.

To us, this scene may appear idyllic, but de Lancre saw something very different altogether. There was something dark and sinister stirring underneath the surface, with the children at the heart of an evil, quite literally, Satanic conspiracy, which he had been sent to investigate. Throughout the summer and autumn of 1609, the judge travelled through the Pays de Labourd, a Basque-speaking territory on France's border with Spain. Together with a colleague, Jean d'Espagnet, he interrogated dozens, perhaps even hundreds of children and teenagers who had been forcefully taken to witches' sabbats, nocturnal assemblies where witches allegedly congregated to worship and have sex with demons. At one point, while indulging in his typical exaggerations, de Lancre estimated that 2,000 children in the Labourd had been dedicated to the devil, making the whole territory a 'nursery' for witchcraft.[3]

The witch-hunt of the Pays de Labourd (Lapurdi in Basque) was, in all likelihood, France's deadliest. Unlike other contenders for that dubious honour, sparked by enterprising witch-finders or freewheeling local officials, it was unquestionably legal. A royal decree had empowered de Lancre and Espagnet, members of the Bordeaux Parlement, the highest appeals court for the south-west of the kingdom, to sort out the territory's witchcraft problem, without any oversight or possibility of appeal. The exact death toll before, during and after the commission's work will never be known, but perhaps as many as one hundred Basque women and men lost their lives.[4] There are undoubtedly larger witch-hunts in history – several German ones were larger by factors of ten or even twenty – but it still left an indelible impact not just on the Basque country but also on Pierre de Lancre and, because of him, on the larger history of the European witch-hunt. De Lancre's sensationalist account, by far the most sexually explicit work of early modern demonology, brought him fame and notoriety. The testimony that the Bordeaux judge collected was beyond strange: Basque witches – women and men – did not simply feast on the bodies of dead babies, as they were said to do elsewhere, they dug up the bodies of deceased witches from cemeteries and consumed *those*. They did not simply adore the devil by kissing him on the backside, the devil also sucked *their* blood. And above all, the witches brought their children to the sabbat – the really young ones were playing with toads while their parents were having sex with Satan. Basques, as a result, became known for their sabbats, for dark and demonic tales which, centuries later, inspired the painter Francisco Goya (1746–1828) to create the work reproduced on this book's cover.

*The Basque Witch-Hunt* situates these exceedingly strange stories within the territory from which they emerged. As far as explanations go, this may appear like the obvious trail to follow, but the direction is surprisingly new. The witch-hunt of the Pays de Labourd is by no means an untold story: Pierre de Lancre was the first to tell it, and as a result, the witch-hunt has always started with *him*. In important ways, the traditional account has not changed, except that the judge now plays the role of villain rather than hero. In this book, we will avoid this well-trodden path. With fresh eyes, we will seek out the secret history underneath, starting our journey in the Labourd rather than with de Lancre. But we cannot proceed with our investigation without examining why the traditional narrative, going back, almost by accident, to de Lancre himself, has proven so durable.

## The sound of silence

On 14 November 1609, two weeks after Pierre de Lancre and Jean d'Espagnet left the Pays de Labourd, a secretary in Paris answered a letter from his boss, the Protestant diplomat Philippe de Mornay. Pierre Marbault replied to Mornay, then in Saumur in Western France, that the news the well-connected diplomat had already heard was quite true. Witches had been discovered in Bayonne at the edge of the Basque country: 'I am sorry that I have not been able to obtain a copy of a letter which one of the judges wrote to [the duke of] Sully, which contains some very remarkable particularities.'[5] This passing comment is the only surviving contemporary discussion of the witch-hunt – de Lancre himself would not turn to print until a few years later. Mornay's original letter to his secretary has been lost, just as the judges' letter to Sully, King Henry IV's right-hand man, though de Lancre later implies that he was the one who wrote it.[6]

Given that this letter to Sully was apparently public knowledge, it is remarkable how little attention was paid to it. The Parisian diarist Pierre de L'Estoile, who as the proud owner of a haunted house relished a good ghost story, recorded a great many witchcraft cases in his journal but he never made any mention of the letter or its supposedly remarkable contents.[7] The *Mercure françois*, an early newspaper, recounted quite a few witchcraft trials for the year 1609. Among those reported were an Italian, executed in Grenoble for conjuring up so-called *incubi* and *succubi* (male and female sex demons, respectively), for the gratification of his clients, a Norman priest who was hanged and burnt in Paris for saying a black Mass, various magical treasure hunters who were banished and a Breton gentleman who had bought a fake book of conjurations with which he had hoped to rid himself of an inconvenient neighbour.[8] About the witches of the Basque country, however, there is not a word. Nor is there any trace of a news pamphlet about their fate. Yet, news of the execution in December 1608 of 'a famous thief' in Bayonne – the same city from which de Lancre wrote a year later – was widely disseminated. Throughout the summer of 1608, this criminal had haunted the Basque countryside at night, naked and covered in black body paint, waking sleeping shepherds and scaring them into surrendering their best sheep by pretending to be the devil.[9]

The eerie quiet that envelops the 1609 witchcraft commission is unsettling. The silence of L'Estoile's diaries or the *Mercure françois*, a work that claimed to carry news 'from the four corners of the world', in fact, speaks volumes.[10] The fate of alien and remote Basque women and men, living at the very edge of the French kingdom, simply carried little or no interest, just as terrorist attacks beyond the Western world barely make the headlines today. Even Marbault, our sole contemporary witness, did not think that Basque witches were worth more than two lines. In his report to Mornay, the secretary swiftly moved on to court politics and the latest on the major international crisis of the day, provoked by the death of the mad and childless duke of Jülich-Cleves-Berg.[11]

Silences reveal the marginality of our subjects in the eyes of those who recorded events and preserved archives. The reason why the fate of Basque women and men living at the kingdom's edge went unrecorded was because they were simply not noteworthy.[12] Throughout this book, we shall encounter other instances when potential witnesses turned to look away. But silences are also the discarded remnants of narratives: the tales that did not resonate, the leftovers that did not fit. The stories reported by the *Mercure françois* and the Bayonne pamphlet are compelling: they are humorous, involving gullible shepherds and book buyers, or they appeal to the readers' illicit fantasies, sex with whomever they (we?) fancy. Like almost every other early modern crime story, they end with a clear moral lesson through exemplary punishment (making it a very good thing that we did not give in to those fantasies ourselves). The Basque witch-hunt did not easily fit these moulds, although it has been subject to a great deal of moralizing since.

It is strange but necessary to acknowledge that the person often held responsible for the witch-hunt of the Labourd is the main reason why we know of its existence at all. It was Pierre de Lancre who found the silence intolerable. The contrast with Spain was particularly galling to him. Even before de Lancre's arrival, the panic had spread across the border, and on 7 and 8 November 1610 – almost a year to the day after the French commissioners had ended their work – the Spanish Inquisition held a spectacular public ceremony, called an *auto de fe*, in the northern town of Logroño, which featured twenty-nine convicted witches, six of whom were burnt alive. Unlike the silence that followed the French trials, this *auto* drew massive crowds and gave rise to at least two sensational pamphlets and even a printed ballad.[13] The Venetian ambassador in Madrid, not otherwise given to supernatural fancies, interrupted his dry updates on court politics to report the discovery of 'more than 12,000 souls who adore the devil, dedicate altars to him, and deal with him familiarly in all matters'.[14] One contemporary scholar, Pedro de Valencia, wrote to Spain's Inquisitor General objecting to the publication of all this salacious news, protesting that they would only encourage 'wicked little women' to fornication and adultery because every other sin would seem like mere child's play compared to the crime of witchcraft.[15] For de Lancre, however, these pamphlets were an inspiration. He included one in translation in his eventual book, the *Tableau de l'inconstance des mauvais anges et démons* (*Tableau of the Inconstancy of Evil Angels and Demons*, 1612). The *auto de fe* even featured prominently on the title page, although this was not quite a compliment (Figure 0.1). At a time when Franco-Spanish rivalry dominated European geopolitics, the *Tableau*'s title page proudly promised to show that French justice was superior to that of 'all other empires, kingdoms, republics and states'. Spain's inquisitors had, in de Lancre's view, been much too mild.

In a sonnet that prefaced the *Tableau*, Jean d'Espagnet predicted that de Lancre had granted the Basque witches immortality: 'your pen giving them eternal life'. There is not only an irony here – an executioner causing immortality – but, for historians at least, also an ethical and methodological problem. How can we ever rescue de Lancre's victims from his sordid and solid embrace? After all,

TABLEAV
# DE L'INCONSTANCE
DES MAVVAIS ANGES
ET DEMONS,
OV IL EST AMPLEMENT TRAI-
cté des Sorciers & de la Sorcelerie.
LIVRE TRES-VTILE ET NECES-
saire, non seulement aux Iuges, mais à tous ceux
qui viuent soubs les loix Chrestiennes.
AVEC
Vn Discours contenant la Procedure faicte par les Inquisiteurs d'Espagne
& de Nauarre, à 53. Magiciens, Apostats, Iuifs, & Sorciers, en la ville
de Logrogne en Castille, le 9. Nouembre 1610. En laquelle on voit, com-
bien l'exercice de la Iustice en France, est plus iuridiquement traicté, &
auec de plus belles formes qu'en tous autres Empires, Royaumes, Republi-
ques & Estats.

PAR PIERRE DE LANCRE Conseiller du Roy au
Parlement de Bordeaux.

Maleficos non patieris viuere. Exod. 22.

A PARIS,
Chez NICOLAS BVON, au mont Sainct Hilaire,
à l'enseigne Sainct Claude.

M. DC. XII.
AVEC PRIVILEGE DV ROY.

**Figure 0.1** The title page of the *Tableau de l'inconstance des mauvais anges et démons* (Paris, 1612). (Harry Ransom Center, the University of Texas at Austin, BF 1565 L35 1612.)

de Lancre revived the women and men the judges had killed only so that they could die again: 'you make rise / thousands upon thousands of witches from their ashes / who in order to live again will be ready to suffer the same death.'[16] What should we do when a witchcraft judge is our key witness? Especially one as odd and unusual as de Lancre? The *Tableau* is a disorganized and rambling work, which indulges its author's every whim. De Lancre told his dedicatee, the chancellor of France Nicolas Brûlart de Sillery, that he had composed his account to obtain the 'special recognition' which the commission's hard work deserved.[17] But he was also writing because he was enthralled by what he had found and wanted to share his discoveries with the world. De Lancre was kept spellbound by the witches' sabbat. His portrayal of witches dancing, flying, feasting, and having sex with demons has shaped how historians think about the sabbat and, indeed, witchcraft in general.[18] The result, then, was a rambling work that straddles many genres, among them ethnography and 'scholarly pornography'.[19] A second, 1613 edition included a hallucinatory fold-out engraving, which has dominated discussions of early modern witchcraft's visual culture (Figure 0.2). In fact, de Lancre never lost the 'witchcraft bug' after the Pays de Labourd.[20] The subject kept him busy well into retirement when he published two more lengthy tomes. His last work, *Du sortilège* (*On Witchcraft*, 1627), appeared in a limited print run, solely for its author's 'personal contentment'.[21] All three works taken together, a total of 1,761 pages, make the Bordeaux judge the most loquacious demonologist of the early modern period.

While de Lancre may have shattered the silence and thus preserved valuable information, he does not make the historian's task any easier. Although he offers us something rare and valuable – 'a voyage inside the imagination of a judge'[22] – there are also real risks when we see the witch-hunt solely through his eyes. He was no unbiased observer but an active participant. His *Tableau* was no straightforward chronological account. His silences – those aspects which de Lancre chose to omit or simply failed to notice – must be at least as significant. For instance, there are few examples of the death and destruction caused by witches in the *Tableau*, probably because these were nowhere near as exciting as the sabbat. Reducing the witch-hunt to those aspects that titillated de Lancre, therefore, would be to victimize his victims a second time. Yet, until now, scholars have mostly made do. This is partly because we cannot do what the judge once urged his readers to do: we can no longer consult the original trial documents for ourselves.[23] The Bordeaux court building went up in flames one dark winter night in 1704.[24] But, de Lancre's account has also endured because, like other durable narratives, it resonated with later audiences, though not in ways the author could have foreseen or wanted. With his *Tableau*, de Lancre made himself into the archetype of a cruel and credulous witch-hunter who prosecuted his innocent victims with self-evident glee.

This sort of narrative used to appeal to witchcraft historians, who once saw their research subject as a battle between elite men – superstitious, bigoted

**Figure 0.2** Jan Ziarnko, 'Description et figure du sabbat des sorciers' (description and illustration of the witches' sabbat) in Pierre de Lancre, *Tableau de l'inconstance des mauvais anges et démons* (Paris, 1613). (University of Glasgow Archives & Special Collections, Ferguson Al-x.50.)

theologians and judges *versus* heroic witchcraft sceptics – in which the (mostly female) victims barely featured.[25] This has meant casting de Lancre as the 'gleeful executioner' or the 'butcher' of the Pays de Labourd.[26] The urge to judge – indeed, convict – de Lancre is hard to resist, and other historians have endowed him with an 'infantile credulity' or even 'an attitude bordering on imbecility'.[27] By contrast, on the Spanish side of the border, the witch-hunt was transformed into a celebration of the inquisitor Alonso de Salazar Frías, who (as Lu Ann Homza's important new book shows) was quite wrongly credited for single-handedly causing its end.[28] Such moralizing no longer satisfies historians. It overlooks the impact of wider social, climactic and geopolitical forces and, most concerningly, it deprives the victims of any role or agency they may have had themselves. While the field of witchcraft history has moved on from this preoccupation with denouncing 'baddies', no one has thought to re-evaluate Pierre de Lancre. His gaze and his perspective as an author are just that difficult to escape. For different reasons, the many local historians who *have* written on the subject have maintained versions of the traditional narrative. For them, the witch-hunt was a fundamental injury and injustice, committed by an outsider on an innocent community, and as such, it constitutes a formative part of Basque identity.

## Narratives of Basqueness

Pierre de Lancre was not only a leading European demonologist, he was also the first major observer of the Basque people. One of the first historians of the early modern witch-hunt, Jules Michelet (1798–1874) even suggested that 'the character of the Basques was never better drawn than in [de Lancre's] book *On Inconstancy*'.[29] Basques have chafed at that characterization ever since.[30] And yet, the *Tableau*'s value as the first essentially book-length study of Basque culture is difficult to ignore. One local historian with a penchant for exclamation marks called it 'one of the richest ethnographic resources to describe Basque customs!'[31] Because we have so few contemporary accounts composed by Basques themselves, let alone in their own language, texts like de Lancre's *Tableau* matter.

As a result, the Basque country and its people were mostly seen from the outside: by visiting diplomats, merchants and missionaries, as well as by the many northern European pilgrims who crossed the Pyrenees on the arduous journey to Santiago de Compostela in north-western Spain.[32] De Lancre was not alone in feeling that he entered an alien environment. Comparisons with the New World were commonplace. Visitors reported finding themselves stranded in an unfamiliar territory amidst strangely dressed folk who spoke an indecipherable language.[33] The famous French historian Jacques-Auguste de Thou, on a visit to Bayonne in 1582, described the language spoken, Basque, as 'very peculiar' and 'the dresses of their womenfolk are just as uncommon ... If you saw people wearing their fashion elsewhere, you would think that they were expressly dressed to raise laughter in a theatre or to go to a masque'.[34]

We saw how the witch-hunt itself was neglected and overlooked at the time and how it has led to de Lancre's perspective being privileged. But the Basque country, especially the smaller French side, has long suffered the same fate. We need to move beyond outsider descriptions of wonder, confusion and occasional hilarity. It is not helpful to transform early modern Basques into exotic creatures, as works with titles such as *The Basque Mystery* and *The Basque Mystery Uncovered* have done, and as de Lancre did.[35] We must reverse the gaze and uncover the mostly unwritten and unrecorded Basque side of this cultural exchange. We can undo some of the silences by searching for new sources – these do exist! – with different vantage points. We can even retrieve the voices of de Lancre's victims that are subsumed in *his* writings, if only we listen carefully enough. The judge presented the *Tableau* as the 'written record of the proceedings' and interspersed his ornate prose with long extracts from legal depositions, immediately identifiable by formulaic markers such as 'asked if' and 'said that'. Unbeknownst to its occasionally oddly oblivious author, there are voices of dissent and opposition present in a text which was meant to celebrate the commission's deadly record. And finally, we must zoom out for the bigger picture: the comings and goings of these many outside observers show that the Basque country was no island. It was where French and Spanish kings met, while the Basques themselves travelled the globe. Cod fishing and whaling sent Basque sailors across the North Atlantic and put them in fierce competition with English, Dutch and other French rivals.

The fractured geopolitics of the region facilitated further cultural exchange. Throughout the later Middle Ages and the early modern period, the Basques were divided into six or seven provinces, spread across two or even three different kingdoms, stretching from Bilbao to the western Pyrenees. Two northern provinces on the French side of the Pyrenees – Labourd and Soule (or Lapurdi and Zuberoa, respectively, in Basque) – had been English from the twelfth century until the end of the Hundred Years War.[36] In 1451, Bayonne's citadel was the last English stronghold to fall into French hands.[37] That war was by no means ancient history by 1609 – de Lancre even suggested that the English had introduced witchcraft into France.[38] The fact that the Labourd was not only a border region but also a relatively recent French acquisition added to the geopolitical uncertainties that underpinned this witch-hunt.

The third northern Basque province, Lower Navarre, squeezed in between Labourd and Soule, indirectly plays a significant role in our story as well. It was all that remained of the independent kingdom of Navarre, after the much larger Iberian 'Upper' part had been conquered by Spain in 1512.[39] By 1609, however, Lower Navarre was slowly being integrated into the French kingdom after its monarch, Henry of Navarre, had also become the king of France at the end of a long series of civil and religious wars. The king who, as Henry IV of France, had signed off on the witchcraft commission, thus, came from the region and knew some of the local stakeholders well. The commission was not the result of an accidental royal pen stroke.

The most important actor in this book, however, is not the monarchy, nor even Pierre de Lancre: it is the unstable frontier that separated the three French provinces from Spain.[40] Living on the edge of France changed everyone's calculus. The border emboldened local actors and weakened authorities in Paris, Bordeaux and Madrid because it made the Basques the first line of defence for the two kingdoms. The frontier even imbued witchcraft suspects with agency because even the seemingly powerless could flee across it. Its influence persists: the border also affects us, warping our understanding by determining what we consider marginal and central, and therefore what matters. While de Lancre placed the Labourd at the margins of France (and, by extension, civilization) and worried about its exposure to foreign influences, the territory, on the main route between France and Spain, also played host to key events between the two great powers of the period. While the witch-hunt may have seemed alien and insignificant to the urbane audiences of Paris and Bordeaux, the kings of France overlooked the Labourd at their peril. The release of Francis I, captured by the Spanish at the Battle of Pavia, took place in 1526 on the Bidasoa river that separates the two countries, his two young sons crossing the river in the opposite direction as hostages. The inhabitants of Hendaye and Saint-Jean-de-Luz were the first to welcome the clearly angry and upset king, 'offering themselves as good and loyal subjects to the French crown'.[41] In 1660, Sun King Louis XIV married the Spanish Infante Maria Theresa at Saint-Jean-de-Luz. The door through which the happy couple left the church of St John the Baptist was boarded up and remains a major tourist attraction.

The European Union fundamentally altered what was once a capricious border. The frontier temporarily roared back to life during the Covid pandemic, but crossings are principally marked by petrol stations on the Spanish side where prices are lower. Yet, centuries of living under different rule have placed the Basques living in France and Spain on different political trajectories, which, especially on the Spanish side, have shaped perceptions of the witch-hunt. The twentieth century has had a particularly profound impact, as the fascist regime of General Franco sought to erase Basque language and culture, provoking fierce and, at times, violent opposition. In modern Spain, where regions have considerable autonomy, Basque identity has undergone a resurgence, and it is particularly in the Spanish provinces that the witch-hunt is seen as part of a longer history of cultural genocide.[42] By contrast, place names on the much more sedate French side are still in French first and Basque second. Since the French Revolution, the three ancient Basque provinces north of the Pyrenees have been grouped together with Béarn, a neighbouring territory with its own Gascon language and independent history, to form the single and inconspicuously named *département* Pyrénées-Atlantiques, with department number 64. It is a cunning ploy that frustrates any political aspirations that either the Basques or Béarnais might have.

While de Lancre was doubtlessly an imperfect observer of the Basque country and its people, there are nonetheless reasons beyond the sheer existence of his *Tableau* as to why his writings have taken on the significance that they did. Given this unhappy history, it is not surprising that local historians present the witch-hunt as an injustice carried out by malevolent, outside actors. They have rightly noted how the Bordeaux judge demonized the Lapurdi population, insisting that no place in Europe 'approached the infinite number [of witches] that we found there'.[43] The witch-hunt – 'the fires of injustice', to quote the unsubtle subtitle of one recent local history – was a formative wrong that helped define Basque identity. If not a true 'holocaust' or 'final solution' – a claim that the death toll cannot possibly support – it is nevertheless described as at least an attempted or aborted one.[44] References abound to the 'bloody commission' or 'our blood-soaked Basque soil', while some cling to an older, discredited figure of six hundred deaths.[45] Ulterior motives, ranging from French resentment about Basque maritime competition to fears of alleged political subversion – 'and France was freed from the Basque danger'[46] – are common allegations. They are a powerful example of the politics of grievance, real or imagined, that fuel so much of our contemporary discourse.

Yet, in addition to assigning the roles of wicked witch-hunter and innocent victim, these narratives also claim to reveal a deeper truth about the Basque character, which squares de Lancre's alleged thirst for blood with his status as an ethnographer. These accounts identify a different conception of witchcraft as an original, true, perhaps even natural part of Basque religion and culture, in which female healers and animal spirits play a central role.[47] Fittingly, this was the approach adopted in *La dama de Urtubi* (*The Lady of Urtubie*, 1916) by Pío Baroja, one of the Basque country's (and indeed Spain's) most famous novelists. Baroja's short story represented the witches' sabbat as a festive carnival and witchcraft as the 'remnants of ancient forms of worship mixed with practices of spell-craft brought over from Béarn', neatly divorcing a core of positive natural beliefs from baneful foreign witchery.[48] Such digging for native religion is more than an attempt to explain some of the – even by the standards of other witch-hunts – extremely odd testimony emanating from Basque witchcraft confessions, involving vampirism, sodomy and toads dressed up in velvet. These details could not all have emerged from de Lancre's lurid imagination, and they further transform the witch-hunt into a persecution of not just of Basque people but of their religion and culture as well. If it was de Lancre who first gave the witch-hunt a narrative coherence, it was this revised structure, part-tragedy–part-origin story built on the *Tableau*, that has been told and retold since at least the late nineteenth century.

The witch-hunt of the Pays de Labourd may well have been forgotten, as notable hunts in other parts of France – for instance, in the Champagne region in 1587–8 and in the Languedoc in 1643–4 – have been.[49] The fact that – like the famous hunts of East Anglia and Salem in England and colonial America – it did not fall into oblivion underlines its enduring cultural significance as part of a region's, country's or people's origin story. The pitfalls are obvious. We need to be conscious of narrative spin and ensure, to the best of our abilities, that we do not make the past serve the concerns of the present. Like wagon tracks on a well-trodden path, the traditional narrative, repeated across the ages, is almost impossible to avoid completely. But there is a secret, untold history out there for us to discover, and our own direction should be clear. The original story may have served alternate ends, but it started with de Lancre. If we wish to uncover what really happened, we must start in the Pays de Labourd itself. De Lancre, strangely enough, would have agreed.

PART ONE

# A Perfect Storm

# Chapter 1
# Living on the edge

Is geography destiny? France's most influential post-war historian Fernand Braudel seemed to think so. Braudel dismissed *histoire événementielle*, the history of events, as 'surface disturbances, crests of foam that the tides of history carry on their strong backs'. In his famous *longue durée* history of the Mediterranean, Braudel treated the Basque witch-hunt as one of many 'irresistible outbreaks of diabolism' that swept across the continent. Ever the determinist, Braudel located witch-hunting particularly in Europe's uplands ('whose primitive isolation maintained them in backwardness'), and especially in mountainous regions such as the Pyrenees 'with their violent history and primitive cruelty'.[1] Historians of witchcraft have had little to say about alpine geography, beyond a much derided early comment about the hallucinatory influence of the 'thin' mountain air.[2] Yet, the Alps and Pyrenees certainly saw some of the continent's earliest witch-hunting, while a mountain's magical reputation, as a foreboding site of devil worship, could also cast long shadows. The Blocksberg or Brocken, the highest peak in Germany's Harz mountain range, made it into witchcraft confessions in the port city of Rostock, more than 200 miles away, and it still inspired Goethe centuries later.[3] The Labourd's more humble peak, the 900-metre tall Larrun (or La Rhune), makes the occasional appearance in the surviving testimony – some witches claimed to have jumped off it in a single leap – but looms nowhere near as large.[4]

Pierre de Lancre would not only have heartily approved of Braudel's cresting and foaming Baroque metaphors, he grappled with geography and destiny as well. His account of the witch-hunt was also an ethnography. In it, he argued that the witchcraft epidemic had been the product not only of the 'humour' of its exotic inhabitants but also of 'the location of their country'. As a result, 'there is no space in Europe as far as we know that approaches the infinite number [of witches] that we have found here – it is a marvel'.[5] De Lancre in effect developed a form of demonic determinism, identifying the openings and weaknesses that the devil exploited. He even worried, though not very much, about whether the estimated 30,000 or so inhabitants of the Labourd were culpable as a result.[6] While their geography and livelihoods infected them with all sorts of vices, de Lancre felt that the Labourdins simply should have tried harder: 'if they had been in the grace of God the little that they used to plant would have sufficed, at least for preventing them from hunger.'[7]

Some of de Lancre's arguments from geography are very silly. The judge, for instance, was struck by the fact that the Labourd appeared to produce nothing but apples, and he concluded that the land itself seems to have tempted its women to become earthly Eves: 'the women eat nothing but apples, drink nothing but apple juice ... they lend an ear to every serpent that wants to seduce them.'[8] Yet, Lapurdi, to use the Basque name, really *was* a land of apples. Already in the twelfth century, pilgrims on their way to Santiago de Compostela were warned that the territory was 'lacking in wine, bread, and all sorts of food, but one finds apples, cider, and milk by way of compensation'.[9] An early sixteenth-century diplomat similarly observed that 'they make wine out of apples called cider', while a fifteenth-century Bohemian traveller bemoaned the absence – long since rectified – of beer.[10]

Neither mountains nor apples explain the Basque witch-hunt, but for all his problems as an observer and theorist, Pierre de Lancre's larger claim was not wrong: the witchcraft panic of the Pays de Labourd *was* the product of a particular place and time. Perhaps, we could even call it a perfect storm, a combination of factors that come together and explain why it happened then and there, but afterwards never again, at least not in early modern France. As a result, the question of human agency (and its limits) hovers over this book. Some of the factors that set the 1609 witch-hunt in motion are deeply rooted in geography. Two are of exceptional importance, as the Bordeaux judge already realized: the Labourd's location at the border with Spain and its reliance on the sea.

The Labourd's position as a border territory subjected it to military incursions and the whims of Franco-Spanish diplomacy. Yet, the territory was not simply the victim of outside forces. Its location affected the actions and agency of all participants in the impending witch-hunt in ways that we might not expect. The frontier weakened the position of the French crown, which was forced to rely on local agents with their own agendas, notably the noblemen who would sponsor the witchcraft commission. But these were not the only actors with agency. The border empowered everyone who came near it, including the witchcraft suspects who fled across it and spread the panic still further. In de Lancre's view, even the devil took advantage by holding his infernal meetings in different jurisdictions.[11] Indirectly, life on the edge also encouraged conflicts *inside* the Labourd by frustrating outside intervention.

The territory's reliance on the sea mattered as well, though again not for the reason that de Lancre alleged – because the sea tossed the Basques around so much that it made them as fickle as the 'changeable element' itself.[12] Rather, the maritime economy fed into a wider struggle for resources and fostered conflicts between the Lapurdi communities. The sea was a highly risky and yet potentially very profitable business, and it required a form of collective mobilization that could be refocused elsewhere. Its dangers also permeated witchcraft fears, shaping the specific harms that witches were believed to cause. In turn, the long absences of the men affected gender relations and outside perceptions of the Labourd as an exotic, feminized space ready to welcome the devil's advances. An examination of these two geographic factors – the border and the sea – will help set the scene for the witch-hunting in the chapters to come. Yet, we also need to look what came before. The Basque country had accommodated witches long before Pierre de Lancre discovered them there.

## Basques without borders

As a practical matter, it is difficult to miss the border that separates France from Spain as it leaves the coast. For the first ten miles, it follows the Bidasoa river before diverging. Yet, even when the border was effectively a river, it was more than just a line. Its almost magical properties could grow in strength as one approached it, but they could also barely be felt.[13] The border was visible and invisible at the same time but could also emerge with no notice. Outbreaks of pestilence in the Spanish ports of San Sebastián and Pasaia in 1597 and 1598 prompted Lapurdi authorities to close it until the disease passed.[14] But often, many ordinary people took no note of it. Cross-border marriages were common. When, in 1613, one unhappy union ended in a spousal killing, the family lived in Pasaia, but the murdered wife was from Urrugne and the husband's mother (and accomplice) came from Ascain, both on the French side.[15] Many of the Inquisition's local employees needed dispensations because one or both of their parents had been born in the Labourd.[16]

Economically, Lapurdi was fully integrated into a wider Basque seafaring economy, centred on Bilbao and San Sebastián, and business had a way of muddling through even during times of war. Politically, however, the border could have devastating effects. The Franco-Spanish wars of the 1540s and 1550s had a terrible impact. In 1542, Saint-Jean-de-Luz was pillaged by Spanish forces, and they returned again in the summer of 1558, when troops from Navarre and Gipuzkoa occupied Saint-Jean-de-Luz for nine days, 'destroying the place and razing it to the ground'.[17] While such violence may have been rare, tensions were never far from the surface, especially during the 1590s when Spain openly intervened in France's religious wars. The citadel of Bayonne, with its two impressive castles (the oldest of which is still in use by the French Army), was generally regarded as the 'key to the kingdom'.[18] Fears about Spain capturing the city reached a fever pitch – 1591 was known as the 'year of fear' – and they would persist even after the Peace of Vervins of 1598.[19]

Borders, then, do strange things to people. It would be very easy to cast early modern Basques as the helpless playthings of the great Franco-Spanish rivalry that dominated European geopolitics. Yet, as anthropologists have shown, identities were also generated at and by the border rather than imposed from the centre.[20] A conflict between Hondarribia and Hendaye over access to the Bidasoa river – only the Spanish side was allowed seaworthy vessels – was at least as much about economic opportunity for local Basques as it was about national pride. The inhabitants of Hondarribia literally and figuratively looked down on Hendaye from their impressive fortifications. They were the proud inhabitants of a 'very noble and very loyal city', whereas Hendaye in their eyes was not even a village, just a 'place'.[21] Whenever these not-even-villagers challenged the status quo with their own shallops, Hondarribia's city folk retaliated with force.[22] Both sides lobbied their central authorities, but those seemed less keen to risk war over a few small boats with or without a keel.[23] Even the 1558 sacking of Saint-Jean-de-Luz appears to have been motivated more by local considerations and private gain than by the Spanish war effort.[24] Allegations of foreignness could also be a resource in essentially local conflicts. When, in 1605, the town of Bera in Spanish Navarre opposed the appointment of their new parish priest, Lorenzo de Hualde (who would go on to play a major role in the witch-hunt), they did so on the basis of his 'Frenchness'. Although the son of French parents, Hualde had actually been born and baptized in Bera.[25] As we shall see, the virulent anti-French rhetoric of Spanish opponents to the witch-hunt has also caused its origins to be misunderstood.

The effects of living at the border had a way of making themselves felt, even when people usually crossed it without hindrance. The witch-hunt, too, looks different as soon as we switch the border 'on': when we see it as an event happening at the edge of France, rather than as a Basque story. What seems peripheral depends on where one is standing. Viewed from Paris or Bordeaux, the witch-hunt of the Labourd looks almost unique, apparently coming out of nowhere, the product perhaps of its remoteness. Strange things, after all, happen in far-away places. Dragons and sea creatures populate the edges of Renaissance maps.[26] A Basque vantage point leads to an instant perspective shift: the witch-hunt appears less unexpected and less inexplicable because there had been many such hunts before. Neither position is wrong – this is, after all, also a story about the French wheels of justice – and we will have to toggle between them. But it explains, at least partly, why the territory can seem so contradictory. A Spanish spy characterized Saint-Jean-de-Luz (and implicitly the entire Labourd) as 'a place almost forgotten by the whole world from where there are connections to the whole of Spain, Italy, Low Countries, and France'.[27] He was not wrong. As a space, Lapurdi was both central and remote at the same time. The border casts a peculiar spell. It shaped the lives of the inhabitants of the Labourd; it empowered them but also caused them misery.

Any consideration of the Basque country must foreground its language, which – much more than the political border – contributed to a visitor's sense of difference and remoteness. Basques call their land, *Euskal Herria*, the land of the Basque speakers, and did so already at the time.[28] Most of the inhabitants spoke nothing else. In 1600, about half of the population of Upper Navarre – the larger Spanish part of the ancient mountain kingdom – spoke only Basque, and no Spanish. In the northern regions, the percentage of Basque monoglots was considerably higher; for women, the figure would have been close to 100 per cent.[29] Euskera, as Basques call their tongue, puzzled early modern outsiders. The French Protestant scholar Joseph Scaliger, a polyglot if ever there lived one, struggled with the language, though he proudly owned their Bible. 'It is a strange language, Basque,' he told his students. 'It is an ancient form of Spanish … People say that they understand it, but I don't believe it. Bread and wine are called the same, [*they are not*] but the rest is completely different.'[30] Scaliger was mistaken. Basque is not old Spanish but Europe's only 'language isolate', meaning that it cannot be grouped into any larger language family.[31]

For some, this uniqueness conferred on Basque a special status. By the early eighteenth century, when the language had become more firmly established in written form, the editors of the first dictionaries praised its unrivalled sublimeness; they placed it above Latin and even biblical Hebrew and dated its divine origins to the Tower of Babel, if not the Garden of Eden.[32] Perhaps inevitably, befuddled visitors viewed this extreme linguistic difference much less favourably. One Dutch visitor to Saint-Jean-de-Luz in 1664 found the locals 'arrogant and barely communicative with strangers' – 'they speak a language which is only understood by those in this land, and it is so poor that the same word means several things'.[33] When a French preacher passed through two years later, he ventured into town on his own accord but 'as they did not understand me and I did not understand Basque at all', he had to return to the town's entrance and wait for his guide.[34] Pierre de Lancre never mastered the 'very peculiar' language and relied on interpreters during his interrogations.[35]

Several factors complicate the Lapurdi linguistic landscape, however. French, or rather the prevailing Gascon dialect of the south-west, was making inroads from the north. The French lawyer Pierre Pithou, who visited during the 1590s, observed that 'Bayonne and some villages nearby speak Gascon, the rest … speaks Basque'.[36] The location of Saint-Jean-de-Luz – on the coast and on the main trade route between France and Spain – also made it an ideal base for foreign merchants. The German traveller Henningus Frommeling, who visited in 1614, commented on its 'most beautiful buildings inhabited by wealthy merchants, who not only have gathered from Spain but also from France [*sic*], England and other regions and have taken up permanent residence'.[37] Bayonne was also home to English merchants, some of whom acted as intelligencers for the Elizabethan and Jacobean governments. These men kept a close eye on Franco-Spanish diplomacy, the scheming of English Catholics and the movements of any Spanish Armadas.[38] Iberian merchants would inadvertently play an even greater role in the witch-hunt's aftermath. Many – they are often called 'Portuguese' in the sources – were *conversos* New Christians of Jewish descent whose ancestors had forcibly converted. The nearest Spanish Inquisition tribunal at Logroño was obsessed with their possible 'Judaizing', fretting about them more than they ever worried about witches. Their number was growing during the 1600s and 1610s. Contemporary estimates – 300 households or 'more than' 2,000 people in Saint-Jean-de-Luz around 1619 – are high, probably too high given the figures for the Labourd's overall population and those for similar migrant communities elsewhere.[39] As we shall see at the end of this book, their presence was sizable enough to prompt hostility and conflict inside the Labourd as well.

One marginalized group not marked out by language also needs a mention here. The *cagots* (in French; *agotes* in Spanish) lived in poor, segregated communities at the outskirts of villages throughout the French south-west (where they may have made up around 2 per cent of the population) and Spanish Navarre.[40] Associated with disease – one hostile origin myth ties their origins to medieval leper colonies – the cagots lived at the margins of society, a position that did not improve until the late seventeenth century.[41] Possible differences in appearance – green or blue eyes, lighter skin and hair – once inspired pseudo-scientific racial theories that portrayed them as the descendants of Goths or Vikings.[42] Early modern documents do depict them as coming from elsewhere – Lapurdi sources call them 'Bohemians' – but their presence in neighbouring Béarn is already attested from around the turn of the first millennium onwards.[43] The separate church entrances reserved for them (now bricked in) are a visible reminder of the Labourd's history of discrimination.[44] The Basque witch-hunt would catch out some cagots. One study of the Zugarramurdi trials, just across the border in Spain, identifies some of the women accused as cagots based on the professions of their husbands.[45] This may press rather thin evidence too far, but we will certainly encounter them on the French side. Pierre de Lancre hinted at their presence at the witches' sabbat, calling one of the dances 'Bohemian': 'I am speaking about the long-haired ones without a homeland who are neither Egyptians nor from the Kingdom of Bohemia.'[46]

The roles of the French and Spanish language also nuance the monoglot linguistic picture of the Labourd because politically and economically, the territory was by no means an island either. The local nobility, noted de Lancre (who knew them well), was 'raised in the French manner'.[47] The territory's young noblemen had fought on the side of King Henry IV in the later stages of the French Wars of Religion.[48] Communal records in the Labourd were, by law, in French, and the local officials who kept them were fully conversant in it.[49] Economically, Spanish was nearly as important, given the territory's integration into the wider fishing and whaling trade. In Saint-Jean-de-Luz, notaries also drew up contracts in Spanish, and the merchants who ran the town government of Saint-Jean-de-Luz wrote letters in both languages.[50] These men were surprisingly well connected. After an English captain confiscated a French Basque vessel carrying more than 55,000 *livres* of merchandise (thinking it was Spanish), the ship's owner Jehan de Haraneder (who was elected *abbé* or mayor of Saint-Jean-de-Luz in 1612), pursued the corsair in the English law courts, as well as at the English and French royal court for compensation.[51]

Although the population, then, overwhelmingly spoke only Basque, a multilingual elite connected the Labourd to French political institutions, Spanish Basque trade routes and beyond. While the territory itself was far from a melting pot, it was not quite an unintelligible Tower of Babel either. Basque locals who housed Portuguese refugees during the 1610s were able to communicate with them. Tellingly, witchcraft fears also spread among the foreign merchant community. The son of a Flemish merchant based in Saint-Jean-de-Luz, twelve-year-old Corneille Brolic, was among the children caught up in the witch-hunt. Two Basque women had allegedly taken the boy from his bed at night to a common sabbat location. The household fought the bewitchment with Flemish rather than Basque counter-magic, creating a protective charm from the blood of the suspected witch. A friend tricked the suspected Basque woman into believing that a witch's blood would be 'whitish'. When, intent on proving her innocence, she then pricked herself in the nose, they caught her (obviously red) blood in a handkerchief to create the charm.[52] While Brolic's bewitchment was largely a tale of Flemish self-reliance, it also reveals relations with the wider population. Fear and suspicions were especially contagious, easily spreading across communities.

Inevitably, the prosecution of crime posed perhaps the greatest challenge in these linguistic circumstances. French was also the language of the courts, which even at the time raised questions about fairness.[53] The French humanist Michel de Montaigne, himself a former Bordeaux judge, wondered whether 'in the Basque country or Brittany there are enough competent judges' to ensure correct translations into the local languages.[54] The question proved prescient. The possibility that the witchcraft commissioners may not have understood all that they were told would cause de Lancre, Montaigne's relative by marriage, considerable anxiety.[55] The devil, a preternaturally gifted linguist with a forked tongue, possessed an advantage here, or perhaps he rather resembled the local officials. One witness from Hondarribia claimed that the devil addressed his human allies each in their own language.[56] According to de Lancre, demons made the Labourd their 'principal residence', precisely because it was isolated and peripheral. Chased from Japan and the Indies by triumphant Christian missionaries, they set up shop in 'a small corner of France'.[57] Border and language, then, easily combine to create a mirage of remoteness. Yet, as one of Europe's great seafaring people, Basques were also very much of and in the world. The border and the privileges that accompanied it played a role in making that global story possible, but it caused a great many problems as well.

# Pride and privileges

The Pays de Labourd enjoyed exceptional rights and freedoms by the standards of Old Regime France. These privileges – which were time-limited, so that the inhabitants did at least have to lobby and pay to renew them – freed them from nearly all taxation in exchange for raising a militia of 1,000 men.[58] Exemptions from import duties particularly benefited Saint-Jean-de-Luz, the seaside town that would become the witch-hunt's early epicentre.[59] A memorandum drawn up for the king's confessor Pierre Coton explained the rationale behind them: 'the inhabitants are like a garrison established in these mountains, which serve by chance as their base, and the inhabitants are recognized and paid through the said privileges and exemptions, which serve as their pay.'[60] Because they resided 'at the extremity of the realm and their territory bordered foreign kingdoms and lands', the privileges also permitted the Lapurdi to be armed 'at all times'.[61] Their renewal frequently mentioned the poverty and sterility of the soil but also recognized the hardship that resulted from war. In 1595, towards the end of the war with Spain, they were extended because the Labourd had been 'totally ruined ... reduced to such desolation that having lost its ships and the means that are the sinews of war, it would be impossible for them to resist any incursions that the enemy could attempt'.[62] The real extent of the devastation is impossible to assess, as documents of this sort typically tended to exaggerate. (The letters patent setting up the witchcraft commission would strike a very similar tone of desperation.) In fact, the privileges also show that trade continued even during times of conflict. The Basques were granted so-called *traités de bonne correspondance* (treaties of good relations). These ensured that both sides could continue to engage in commerce even when France and Spain were at war, reflecting the integration of the Basque maritime economy.[63]

Their position at the border also explains the inhabitants' exceptional role in local decision-making. The territory's *Coustumes generalles* permitted the 'residents of every parish ... to assemble to discuss their common needs and those of their community whenever it is necessary'.[64] The communities met regularly, usually in church, to discuss their affairs and to elect their *abbé* (mayor) and aldermen, normally for a two-year term. All male heads of households were entitled to vote – a striking form of direct democracy that was only watered down in the mid-seventeenth century. Again, Saint-Jean-de-Luz was particularly advantaged as it had bought its seigneurial rights from its former overlords, making it a 'noble' town.[65] The territory also possessed an assembly of its own. As an annual gathering of the territory's *abbé*s, the *Biltzar* (Basque for 'meeting of elders') was unique across France for excluding the clergy and nobility from participating.[66] Although its records are fragmentary, it can only have been the *Biltzar* which petitioned the French crown for the creation of the witchcraft commission in late 1608.

For all its democracy, it was the lack of gainful aristocratic employment that proved to be an important cause of the Labourd's difficulties. Only one suitable royal position was available, and the territory's two principal noble families competed for it over the centuries.[67] The Urtubie were finally able to snatch this post out of the hands of the Amou in 1653, when the incumbent died and the eldest son was still underage.[68] The *bailli* or 'bailiff' ('but of much more authoritie than ours', as a 1611 English-French dictionary put it) was the king's representative, in charge of maintaining the peace in a province or territory.[69] In the Labourd at least, the role was mostly a military one, with the administration of justice devolved to a qualified legal professional who acted as his 'lieutenant' or deputy. The nobility would prove to be more a source of lawlessness than justice within the territory.

The territory's extensive privileges reflect the realities of power: its importance as the first line of defence reveals the weak arm of the French state. Paris was several weeks of travel away and, especially at times of war, depended on the loyalty of those who garrisoned the border, the local aristocracy very much included.[70] For those living in its vicinity, the French-Spanish frontier presented opportunities because it was close by while authorities in Paris, Bordeaux and Madrid were far away. As a result, the Labourd was a territory in crisis for two intertwined reasons: it was engulfed in struggles for scarce resources and, far removed from central oversight, it was without any obvious peaceful means to settle them. In time, the witchcraft panic would crystallize into the perfect expression of these conflicts. But the spectre of disorder also provided openings to those willing to exploit them, especially the nobles. Their formal rights were strikingly limited: as the lords of the village of Saint-Pée, the Amou family had the right to appoint the local parish priest, to forage in the communal woods and to cast a tie-breaking vote in elections for *abbé* when the villagers deadlocked.[71] There is a logic to these nobles behaving badly: disorder improved their standing and perhaps also their wealth. For them, peace hardly paid, while war provided them with purpose and profit.[72]

In this context, the rather duplicitous behaviour of the local nobility during the 1590s, when France and Spain were at war, is especially revealing. In May 1592, the viceroy in Pamplona wrote to the Spanish court that Jean-Paul de Caupenne d'Amou, the Lord of Saint-Pée, had reached out to him via the abbot of Urdax, a monastery just within Spain's borders, offering his services to King Philip II on account of the Catholic religion.[73] Amou was a young man on the make; he had only taken over the position of *bailli* from his father two years previously.[74] Someone – whether the young nobleman, the abbot or the viceroy – burnished his credentials, making Amou seem more important than he was. The letter described the Lord of Saint-Pée as holding a high legal office – 'the high justice of the whole territory of Bayonne and Labourd', as well as 'hav[ing] influence and power and estates in the kingdom'.[75] (In reality, the city of Bayonne had been separated from the Labourd as early as 1178.[76]) In 1609, Amou emerged as one of the two 'sponsors' (the descriptor is de Lancre's) of the witchcraft commission, which was, if nothing else, another opportunity to assert his personal authority.[77] Fittingly, the rather spooky ruins of Amou's castle in Saint-Pée are still referred to locally as the *chateau des sorcières*, the witches' castle. The local witchcraft memorial – a grim metal re-construction of a burning at the stake – is prominently placed in front of it.

The witchcraft commission's other sponsor, Tristan de Gamboa d'Alzate d'Urtubie, lacked a royal position altogether and became a proper agent of chaos.[78] The behaviour of the Urtubie clan during the 1590s is, therefore, perhaps still more telling. While Tristan was serving in the royal army, his mother, Aimée de Montreal, sent more than a dozen reports, some of the earliest examples of written Basque, to Juan Velázquez, Spain's chief spy in Hondarribia, in exchange for gifts.[79] Aimée's correspondence, part gossip, part hard military news, ceased in 1598 when Tristan d'Urtubie married the daughter of a Bordeaux judge and France and Spain made peace. Her services to the Spanish crown were more a profitable side hustle than an act of treason, and they were sensible given that the family, originally from Navarre, still possessed property on the Spanish side of the border.[80] Pío Baroja's *La dama de Urtubi*, a short novella set in the midst of the witch-hunt, presented Tristan as a widower in his fifties, a cultured book collector with a passion for Don Quixote and Rabelais.[81] The real Tristan could not have been more different. The few historians to have taken note of Aimée's son have underscored his tendency towards violence.[82] During one such incident, Urtubie's followers attempted to seize a Flemish vessel approaching the port of Saint-Jean-de-Luz. When outraged town officials arrested the culprits, Urtubie led a night-time expedition of several hundred men to break them out of prison. One of the town's officials died in the resulting mêlée.[83] Urtubie was responding to the Lapurdi communities who were chipping away at his rights and influence, but profit as much as pride fuelled the nobleman's discontent. His heir Salvat married the only daughter and heir of a wealthy Ciboure merchant to restore the family's solvency.[84]

Mother and son Urtubie may have taken a page out of the playbook of the region's most influential aristocratic family. The Gramont family held the hereditary mayoralty of Bayonne, the city where (perhaps surprisingly) aristocratic control was strongest. Henry IV's appointment in 1595 of the young Antoine II de Gramont as its military governor gave the family almost unquestioned control over the citadel and, with it, a key part of – indeed, the key to – the kingdom until the French Revolution.[85] Antoine had served in the royal army, with the king personally updating his mother, Diane d'Andoins, on his military valour.[86] Diane had been a famed beauty; she had once even been the king's mistress. But despite her influence and her son's position, Diane also reached out to Spain. In May 1592, she stopped at the monastery of Urdax on her way to witness her son's investiture as mayor of Bayonne and informed the Spanish viceroy in Pamplona of her plans beforehand.[87]

As governor of Bayonne, Gramont would similarly perform a variety of minor services for the Spanish in exchange for handsome payments, even after peace between France and Spain returned.[88] In 1610, for instance, Gramont agreed to return captured Spanish artillery in return for 'two Arab horses and a jewel for his wife' – a considerable sum, but the Spanish Council of State considered the funds well-spent, 'to gain him for the service of His Majesty which would be of great importance'.[89] Like Tristan d'Urtubie, Antoine de Gramont was a violent man. His anger and abuse were directed even at the bishop of Bayonne, Bertrand d'Echaux, who as the king's almoner was as well connected politically as the nobleman.[90] Gramont had the city's gates closed against its bishop, accused him of plotting a murder and had his soldiers verbally insult him. The governor even declared that the bishop 'would not die except by his hand'.[91] Echaux's desperate pleas to Paris – search the entire history of Christianity, he urged in 1611, 'there was never a bishop more horribly and shamelessly persecuted than me' – went unanswered until his elevation to the archbishopric of Tours in 1617.[92] His flock did not have that escape route.

Even contemporaries may have classed Amou, Urtubie and Gramont – all of whom would play crucial roles in the unfolding witch-hunt – as 'bad nobles' who reflected poorly on their peers.[93] But brutality was also a sign of aristocracy, and the French nobility had a reputation for feuding and violence.[94] (Crowds, as we shall see, could be equally violent.[95]) The behaviour of our noblemen made sense within the functioning of the early modern French state, especially given their geographic position. Historians of absolutism have long exposed the illusory nature of the grand – *L'état, c'est moi* – pretensions of Sun King Louis XIV. Rather, they have emphasized the extent to which the old regime was built on 'social collaboration' between the crown and local elites in a shared pursuit of revenue and resources.[96] The border was a major complication to this logic. It furnished everyone, including the Labourd's communities, with extensive privileges. Those rights, tied to finite resources, were often a zero-sum game. Spain's proximity meant that the crown could not simply side with local elites. It could not risk settling disputes without antagonizing one party or another. At the border, unlike elsewhere, both sides mattered, as any conflict could have wider geopolitical repercussions. The French crown likely did not know about the Spanish dalliances we just examined, but it was well aware that such double-dealing was always possible. The crown's weakness is key to understanding why the 1609 witchcraft commission was created – its judges were able to assert *central* royal authority by settling these conflicts *locally* and in person.

This weakness of royal authority provided the nobility with opportunities. In 1613, for instance, Bishop Echaux interceded on behalf of his Lapurdi flock. Observing that on account of the 'very great sterility of the country', they had been exempted from paying import duties, he noted with distress Gramont's claim 'as a result of some exchange made with king Louis XIII or Charles VIII' to receive half the original duties. Echaux reminded the crown that the kings of France had never considered it a good idea to deprive those living at the borders of privileges that were once accorded to them 'for their courage', 'their great dexterity', 'the great number of ships they could furnish for the purpose of war' as well as the impact of any war with Spain.[97] Amou had similar pretensions concerning a tax on newly built homes. Because decisions inevitably alienated the losing side and the crown could not readily impose its will, these disputes could lead to decades of conflict and litigation.[98]

Of the three local noblemen, it was Tristan d'Urtubie whose conflicts with the Lapurdi communities were the most violent. His formal standing in the territory was the weakest, while his involvement in the witch-hunt would become the most extensive.[99] Those three factors worked together: for Urtubie, conflict was good. The nobleman quarrelled with Saint-Jean-de-Luz over rights to communal woods and the construction of a new port. (It was the latter that sparked the seizure of the merchant vessel.[100]) Yet, conflict was also rife with the two communities on the edge of Urtubie's traditional domain. Both Hendaye and Ciboure had belonged to the parish of Urrugne, home to the Urtubie castle (which, though open to tourists and hotel guests in the summer, still remains in the family's hands). In 1598, Hendaye on the Bidasoa river was granted the right to build its own church, meaning that its villagers no longer needed to travel to Urrugne for services.[101] The emancipation of Ciboure was more contentious. Located on the opposing bank of the Nivelle from Saint-Jean-de-Luz, the village's Basque name 'Ziburu' (originally Zubiburu) – 'Bridge-end' – attests to its almost accidental origins in the shadow of the wealthy town across the river.[102] Ciboure's separation from Urrugne was a long-drawn-out affair, which involved the usual levels of violence and litigation. During the 1550s, the village obtained two papal bulls which established it as a separate parish and allowed it to construct a church – which the inhabitants of Urrugne then attempted to tear down at night.[103] Only in 1603 did Henry IV grant the new community the right to elect its own officials, but this merely set the stage for greater conflict. Settling the precise boundaries between Urrugne and Ciboure proved contentious, with Urtubie sending two hundred armed men to intimidate the judge appointed for the task. While the village was willing to respect Urtubie's patronage of its church, Ciboure objected to his right to provide the first alms at the collection during Mass because Urtubie used it only to insult them – he 'made his lackeys and his dog-walker go to the offering'.[104]

The Lapurdi communities also fought amongst themselves. Ciboure's independence set the stage for conflict with its wealthier neighbour Saint-Jean-de-Luz (Figure 1.1). De Lancre observed that the inhabitants were 'enemies', and that a new bridge (completed in 1606) had a drawbridge which could be lifted by either side.[105] The source for such conflicts was the natural harbour the two communities shared, the only safe shelter between Bayonne and Pasaia in

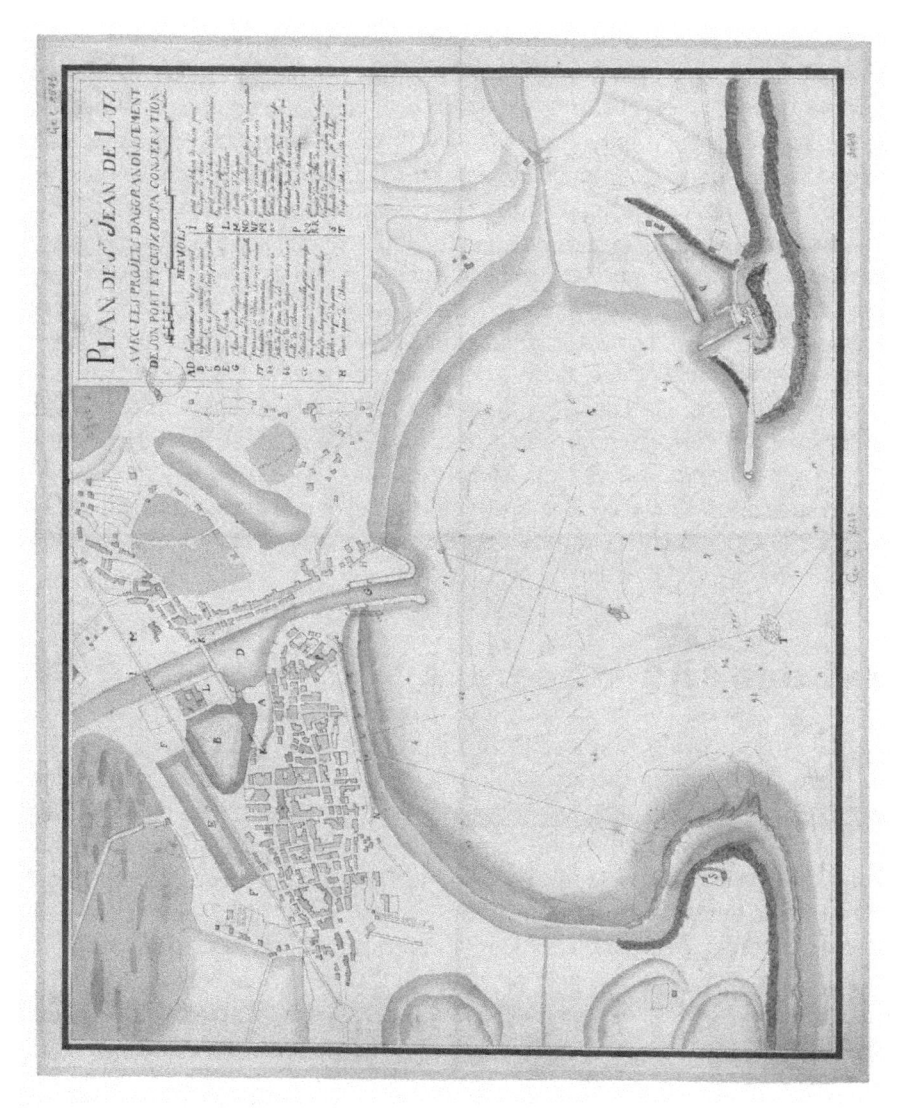

**Figure 1.1** The Bay of Saint-Jean-de-Luz, with the town to the left and Ciboure to the right (*c.* 1620?). (BnF, btv1b531429967.f1.)

Spain. A ruling in 1560 set a strict 3:2 ratio for the number of ships in favour of the wealthier community.[106] Similar commercial competition also existed between Saint-Jean-de-Luz and *its* bigger neighbour, Bayonne. After a *luzien* merchant vessel carrying three barrels of wine violated Bayonne's trading privileges, the town sent a night-time expedition of two hundred men towards Saint-Jean-de-Luz 'where they set fire to one house ... killed two men, profaned the church and took five prisoners whom they are still holding'.[107] (Two hundred appears to be the standard unit for armed men in our history.)

The witchcraft problem, as it developed during the opening decade of the seventeenth century, was both an extension and an expression of the clashes between the communities and noblemen over status, resources and access to the sea. Witches congregated wherever there was conflict. They held their sabbats on the beach of Hendaye in view of Hondarribia and its famous canons, on the bridge that connected the quarrelling neighbours Saint-Jean-de-Luz and Ciboure, inside the castle of one of the bullying noblemen and on the cemetery granted to the 'Portuguese' New Christian merchants.[108] Our fragmentary sources make it difficult to precisely map witchcraft fears onto every social and political tension, but we shall find the same persons lined up against one another with surprising regularity. The same connections were also obvious to contemporaries. De Lancre discussed some of these conflicts but only as openings for the devil to sow further discord. We need to reach neither for the devil nor for cynical ulterior motives for explanations. The politics of our own age already show how easy it is to think the worst of one's enemies. The witch-hunt, as it gathered pace, would in any case soon prove to be beyond any one person's control.

## Sailors and sorcerers

So far, when looking at the Labourd's physical and social geography, we have examined factors that drove its inhabitants often violently apart. Yet, the economic foundations which underpinned the territory also created incentives for communal action. Fishing and commerce were part of daily life, as they were along the Spanish Basque coast as well.[109] Sailors had to work together against the elements and against the whales. In theory, witches posed another potential *communal* threat, responsible for loss of life at sea. Witchcraft could also be a maritime problem. The surviving sources contain many references to weather magic, the sinking of ships and even witches' gatherings across the Atlantic. Neither sailors nor alleged sorcerers played straightforward roles in the Basque witch-hunt as heroes or villains. Yet, we cannot hope to understand the witch-hunt or the stories it generated, without examining the Labourd's life blood: the fishing and navigation which, among other things, sent its men to hunt for whales and fish for cod as far away as Canada. Witches were believed to have followed in their trail.

Fish were a staple of the Basque diet and, on the coast, a key source of local livelihoods. In 1528, the Venetian ambassador Andrea Navagero, whose travel diary offers one of the earliest and most vivid eyewitness accounts of the Labourd, was astounded by 'the greatest abundance of fish' in Bayonne, including 'the most beautiful and best salmon' from its two rivers and the 'infinite' types of other fish from the sea, with whale meat being a particularly 'marvellous thing'.[110] Such bounty was a necessary lifeline because of the Labourd's inhospitable terrain. Most of the male population of the coastal territory found work at sea. A 1638 account of the Basque country noted that 'almost all the inhabitants of Saint-Jean-de-Luz are involved and highly skilled in the business of the sea'.[111] The lawyer Pierre Pithou described Biarritz as a 'village where one only finds fishermen', and he was impressed by the fleets of Saint-Jean-de-Luz and Ciboure.[112] Another witness observed the natural harbour of Pasaia, a stone's throw from the Franco-Spanish border, testifying that all the inhabitants of the village 'are sailors and fishermen with the exception of the clerics, although they sometimes are as well'.[113]

Precise figures of the number of ships and sailors are hard to come by, however.[114] In 1625, Saint-Jean-de-Luz and Ciboure petitioned King Louis XIII, claiming that together they sent 120 ships a year to *Terreneuve*, literally 'Newfoundland' but at the time used to refer to much of the Atlantic coast of Canada. Basque soil being 'barren and sandy', this was their 'sole means to sustain their livelihoods'.[115] (Deforestation, the result of all that ship building, probably also did not help.[116]) The king granted the communities permission to continue their trade with Spain's northern ports during wartime – the *traités de bonne correspondance*, which we already discussed – where French Basque ships would off-load most of their haul of cod and whale oil. 'Depriving them of the liberty of such commerce,' said the letters patent (curiously echoing the language setting up the 1609 witchcraft commission), 'would force them to abandon the land'.[117] Whether 120 vessels are an accurate figure is difficult to determine. The Lapurdi fishing trade continued to show signs of vitality during the early 1600s, after the Spanish Basque fleet had gone in decline as the result of military requisitioning – all those armadas – and heavy losses in war.[118] Account books for the port of Bilbao put the number of French Basque ships arriving at around fifty annually during this period.[119] Moving from ships to sailors is even more difficult, given that vessels also varied in size. The largest on the Spanish Basque side – a *nao* – could carry more than 600 tons and up to 140 crew members when fitted out for transatlantic whaling.[120] Lapurdi vessels, which did not face recruitment into the navy in the same way, were generally smaller, commonly 100 or 200 tons. They still dominated the local economy of the Labourd's coastal communities, directly and indirectly employing thousands of men. The fact that the fisheries are known to have attracted men from Lower Navarre and Soule, the other French Basque provinces, further points to its size.[121]

Of the two activities in which the Basques particularly excelled – cod fishing and whaling – the latter is the more ancient. Basques had been whaling off their own coasts long before there were new-found lands, possibly as early as the tenth century. Outside observers presented their hunt as a noble and dangerous fight. Navagero, the Venetian ambassador, painted a picture (doubtlessly romanticized) of perilous combat in which sailors launch harpoons (or tridents, as he called them) and enraged whales headbutt ships into smithereens: 'in order to capture a whale, one needs to fight it and during these fights one is often injured as a result of the fury with which it defends itself.'[122] When King Charles IX visited Bayonne in 1565, the French court was presented with a re-enactment of an half-hour chase in which 'a large artificial whale was hunted by several small boats full of men who fought it with spears and made every effort at catching it in the same way they use to take them at sea'.[123] Until the early seventeenth century, Basques controlled Atlantic whaling, and with it the lucrative sale of whale oil. Whalebones imported from the Basque country even helped shape English women's dresses.[124] The whaling monopoly was only broken in the 1610s when English and Dutch merchants hired Basque harpooners and crew for their voyages to the North Atlantic.[125]

The hunt for whales took Basques far from their own shores. During the century or so after 1520, they became 'addicted' to the Terreneuve run and, as archaeologists have discovered, they left a profound mark on the coastline of the Canadian Maritimes.[126] The natural harbour on Newfoundland's most south-western tip was identified as 'Port-aux-Basques' as early as 1612 and remains known by this name to this day.[127] This maritime reputation was further cemented by the 1579 publication of *Les voyages aventureux du capitaine Martin de Hoyarsabal, habitant de Cubiburu* (The Adventurous Voyages of Captain Martin de Hoyarsabal, Inhabitant of Ciboure). This work was no gripping memoir but rather a detailed set of sailing instructions for 'every master pilot who goes out to sea' for navigation along Europe's shores and those of Terreneuve.[128] (Tellingly, the printer identified the author as 'not at all French but a Basque from the borders with Spain'.[129]) By the mid-seventeenth century, Basques would claim to have discovered the New World before Columbus, and even suggest that the Genoese explorer had stolen the route from a distressed Basque fishing vessel.[130]

During its heyday, between 1530 and 1620, the Basque fishery near Labrador may have killed between 240 and 360 whales a year.[131] Large vessels, moored in a safe natural harbour, served as living quarters and storage, while the actual hunting was done in small shallops which were better suited for harpooning the whales and giving chase until the wounded prey was exhausted. The French explorer Samuel de Champlain left a graphic eyewitness account of both the collaboration and the dangers involved. A wounded whale would disappear underwater: 'if ... in turning it strikes with its tail the shallop or the men, it crushes them as easily as a tumbler.' When it eventually returned to the surface, several shallops would surround it and 'men with halberds' would attack it, so it would lose even more blood. The floating corpse would then be tied with ropes and dragged to shore.[132] Sailors did not need *Moby-Dick* to teach them the dangers. Devotional works included prayers thanking God for the successful hunting and killing of the whale: 'It is more by Your grace than by our skill that we have wounded the whale with a strike of the harpoon. Accordingly, All-Powerful Lord, ensure that we can quickly immobilize this great fish of the sea.' Whether such printed prayers made it to the lips of sailors is another matter, but the dangers invoked – the whale 'sending the boat's keel towards heaven ... sending [us] with it to the bottom of the sea' – were real.[133]

Basques similarly dominated the trade in medieval cod, even though that fish, unlike whales, never graced their waters. By salting and thus preserving cod, they not only expanded their markets but also extended their own journeys.[134] It was in search of cod that Basques first arrived at Terreneuve – or the *Tierra de los Bacallaos*, the Land of Cod, as it came to be known in Spanish – during the late 1510s or 1520s, in the wake of Portuguese and Breton rivals.[135] Although the two trades clearly differed – cod, after all, did not fight back – they shared important similarities. Both became an annual ritual, akin to a form of temporary mass migration. Ships left every March or April, with cod-fishing ships arriving back usually in September or October, and some whaling ships returning as late as January.[136] The journey across the Atlantic took around a month.[137] During this time, the sailors were reliant on each other and on their provisions, including ship's biscuit and (because it was the Basque country) cider. Sleeping took place, in turns, on the deck. Both cod fishing and whaling also necessitated the setting up of stations on land for processing, for which Basques also made use of native labour.[138] According to a 1622 pamphlet promoting a (doomed) English colony on Newfoundland, the Basques 'who resort thither yeerely for the Whale-fishing, and also for the Cod-fish' reported that the local tribes were 'an ingenious and tractable people ... they are ready to assist them with great labour and patience, in the killing, cutting, and boyling of Whales; and making the Traineoyle, without expectation of other reward, then a little bread, or some such small hire'.[139] Basque-made objects travelled across native trading routes, reaching as far inland as Ontario.[140] French authors, including de Lancre, complained that the natives only communicated with Europeans in a form of pidgin Basque.[141] While this may reflect French impressions of both languages and people as foreign and exotic, linguists have suggested that some modern Amerindian tribal names could have a Basque origin.[142] In 1625, the chronicler Lope de Isasti reported that the Innu of Newfoundland would reply when greeted: *apaisak obeto*, Basque for 'the priests are doing better'.[143] (Isasti was himself a priest.)

While the Atlantic trade was potentially lucrative for all who took part in it, the main financial profits and risks were made by those who owned and equipped the expeditions.[144] Basque merchants drew on complex financial markets in cities as far away as Burgos and Bordeaux to secure funding and mitigate the sizable risks. In 1609, the merchant Adam de Chibau, one of the key figures during the witch-hunt's early stages, lost one of his five ships taking part in the Newfoundland run, while another, one of two that had sailed to Brazil, had been seized by the authorities there.[145] Insurance helps make sense of de Lancre's accusation that a Ciboure merchant used witchcraft to cause the loss of his own vessel – contracts were structured in such a way that from the merchant's perspective, it was better for a ship not to return at all than with a disappointing catch.[146] The costs of provisions also show just how capital-intensive the business was, further pointing to the chasm that separated the rich and the poor. A commercial contract signed between Chibau and Bayonne merchants to supply just two of the ships bound for Terreneuve mentions 270 cuintals of ship's biscuit, 179 barrels of cider, a small quantity of wine, 3,300 *fanegas* (or bushels) of salt (for salting the cod) as well as 1,400 *livres* in money.[147] As we shall see, Chibau's attempts to cement his high social status helped feed the witch-hunt. But the investment risks meant this was also a world where the rich could tumble far – and they could lash out as they fell. Ever riskier loans, dismal returns and low fish prices eventually sank Chibau both financially and socially. In January 1608, even before the loss of two of his vessels, he wrote to his son-in-law and business partner in Bilbao that 'in his life' he never faced such 'misery as now'.[148]

Whilst merchants and financiers were able to manage at least some of their risk, the sailors out at sea could lose their lives. 'The sea,' a contemporary Basque proverb went, 'has no branches which you can grab when you are drowning.'[149] A sailor's life was full of dangers, even leaving aside vengeful whales. Attacks – whether by pirates or by licensed corsairs at times of war – leave the biggest footprint in the archives. French Basque shipping was affected by England's war with Spain (1585–1604), when Lapurdi ships were easily confused with their Spanish Basque cousins. No less a figure than Sir Walter Raleigh captured a Bayonne vessel in 1591, while a vessel belonging to a certain Martin Guerre carrying a staggering 100,000 cod was taken to Bristol in 1593.[150] In 1612, the struggling English Newfoundland colony reported on the 'much cruelty' that the English pirate Peter Easton inflicted on the 'Portingals [and] French where by near all thear fishing voyags wear overthrown [and] maney of them, left thear ships [and] fled into the woods'.[151] The Labourd, it must be said, was home to corsairs as well: if Lapurdi merchants petitioned the English crown, Portuguese, Irish and English ones complained to Paris about French Basques.[152]

The weather could also be dangerously unpredictable. Sea ice often prevented access to the Strait of Belle Isle (which separates Newfoundland from the Canadian mainland) until June. The onset of summer brought icebergs

**Figure 1.2** A Basque sailor at prayer in stormy waters. Painting on wood (late sixteenth century). (Image courtesy of the Itsasmuseum, Bilbao.)

drifting down from the north. More dangerous still were those instances when ice enclosed whaling ships in the harbours on the south coast of Labrador.[153] In the winter of 1576–7, some 300 Basque whalers died when ice imprisoned their ships there.[154] Surviving the encounter with the ice meant confronting the harsh winter that followed. In 1615, three vessels from San Sebastián shipwrecked on the coast of Iceland during a fierce storm, and most of the survivors were killed by the local population (Figure 1.2).[155]

While witches were seemingly never held responsible for icebergs, the raising of storms was part of their métier. In 1609, sixteen-year-old Jeanette d'Abadie from Ciboure testified that Lapurdi witches would gather at sabbats in Newfoundland 'to excite tempests and storms to cause the loss of ships'. According to 28-year-old Marie de la Ralde, witches perched on a ship mast, 'not daring to go down below because the ship had been blessed and that from there they threw powders and infected with poison all [the fish] that the poor sailors had dried ashore'.[156] The Inquisition archives similarly contain a report from solidly inland Zugarramurdi of a cloud of witches raising a storm to sink ships approaching the Saint-Jean-de-Luz and Ciboure harbour.[157] In the famous sabbat engraving that accompanied de Lancre's *Tableau*, it is neither the feasting nor the dancing that first draws the eye but the vast cloud at its centre, an act of weather magic which witches seemed to enjoy as if it were a turbulent rollercoaster ride (the wind suggestively playing with their clothing; Figure 1.3).

Tales of magic and witchcraft permeated sailor lore well beyond the Basque country.[158] Given the many dangers and hardships posed by the sea, we need to take these fears seriously. Their consequences were all too real. Modern ethnographers discovered that some sailors still refused to utter the Basque

**Figure 1.3** A cloud of witches: the central vignette of the 1613 sabbat engraving.

word for witch, *sorgin*, when out at sea.[159] Conversely, rituals – both magical and religious – were performed to protect vessels prior to departure. The Bayonne missal of 1543 includes detailed instructions for the blessing of a ship: the elaborate ceremony held in front of its bow, on its deck and its stern included reciting passages from the gospel of Matthew in which Jesus calmed a storm and walked on water.[160] In nineteenth-century Lekeitio, the sailors received blessed flowers from the local convent which they would burn at the ship's bow to keep witches at bay.[161] Model ships suspended mid-air continue to hang in Lapurdi churches as votive objects to this day, in thanksgiving for graces received.

How did life at sea affect Basque habits and customs more widely? Pierre de Lancre had an almost ready-made answer. The sea was a *chemin sans chemin*, a pathless passage, and sailors were throwing themselves at the mercy of a 'restless element'.[162] The judge believed that this reliance on the tossing and turning of the elements infected the Basques with an inconstancy of their own, which that most fickle of masters, the devil, exploited. Crucially, however, Basque sailors faced all this tossing and turning of the sea together. Where bad weather was concerned, witches could also be perceived as working collectively to harm entire communities, by sinking their ships or destroying their harvests. In practice, witchcraft suspects, as individuals of flesh and blood with relations of their own, just as often divided communities into those who feared them and those who knew and defended them. As we shall see, some evidence for sailors uniting to defend their womenfolk appears to be based more on historians' wishful thinking than reality. And yet, the importance of their collective fateful intervention at the very end of this witch-hunt cannot be overstated.

## Exotic women

Strange, exotic things dwelled at the margins of the known and familiar. The Labourd's position at the edge of the French monarchy aided perceptions of the territory as an essentially female and feminized space, assisted by the absence of the men at sea. Pierre de Lancre was a keen observer of the Labourd's womenfolk. He described their elaborate clothing in fine detail which increased the enchanting effect they had on him. Their time-consuming hair dress caused 'the sun to cast its rays on these tufts of hair as it would on a cloud'. This in turn gave them their bewitching eyes, 'as dangerous in love as in witchcraft'.[163] Their strange dress exoticized the women, and their allure imperilled the distance between the elite Frenchman and those he was sent to judge.

While de Lancre's rhetoric was unusually gendered and imaginative, his was not the only travel account that 'othered' the Basque country by marvelling at its women. While the women's headdress reminded the judge of the well-endowed Greek god Priapus, the chronicler Sébastien Moreau observed in 1530 that the women wore 'a great horn which they have on their head'. What this headdress must have looked like was captured by the German painter Christoph Weiditz who visited the Iberian peninsula in the 1520s (Figures 1.4 and 1.5). Weiditz was as transfixed as de Lancre: he drew more than a dozen images of Basque women climbing mountains, visiting churches, drinking cider and so on. Both

**Figure 1.4** A Basque woman wearing traditional headgear. Christoph Weiditz, *Trachtenbuch* (c. 1530/1540). (Nuremberg, Germanisches Nationalmuseum, MS 22474, fol. 328.)

**Figure 1.5** An unmarried Basque woman. Christoph Weiditz, *Trachtenbuch* (c. 1530/1540). (Nuremberg, Germanisches Nationalmuseum, MS 22474, fol. 332.)

men wondered at the hair of the younger women – or rather, the lack of it. During the 1565 royal visit to Saint-Jean-de-Luz, King Charles IX took great pleasure in watching 'the girls dance *à la mode du Basque*' – their unmarried status was indicated by their shaven heads.[164] Even the fairly balding Montaigne, who will not have met many Basques, was struck that the women considered themselves 'more beautiful with heads shaven'.[135] Nor was it just male travellers who were fascinated. When the novelist Marie Catherine La Mothe visited Bayonne in 1679 she, too, was struck by the bronzed skin, the 'brilliant eyes', and 'lively spirit' of the Basque ladies who came to introduce themselves.[166]

It is not just the appearance of Basque women that exoticized both them and their territory, however. The Labourd's reliance on the sea did so as well, and it did so in a highly gendered way. At the same time as Basque sailors traversed the Atlantic, devils moved in from the New World, taking advantage of the territory's liminality. The success of Catholic missionaries in the New World, Japan and elsewhere allegedly caused the devils to set up shop in the Labourd 'as their principal abode, making themselves little by little absolute masters of the country, having won over the women, children and most of the priests and pastors'. De Lancre claimed that English and Scottish wine merchants travelling to Bordeaux had seen 'great flocks of demons in frightful human form' on their way to France. The Labourd was, in effect, a mini New World, essentially pagan and, thus, a safe space for demons. De Lancre's ethnography implicitly and explicitly compared Basques to Native Americans. Like the Indians of Hispaniola, for instance, who snuffed *cohoba*, a hallucinogenic herb, the Lapurdi smoked tobacco (they were early adopters) which the women grew in their small gardens: 'I do not know if this smoke mentally disturbs them as this other herb disturbs the Indians, but … it gives their breath and body so stinking a smell that no creature unaccustomed to it can stand it.'[167]

'Othering' a foreign people has almost always meant feminizing them, as a way of asserting the observer's (masculine) superiority. What, in de Lancre's mind, eased the path of the devils tremendously was the absence of the men at sea. Only boys and old men guarded the homes in their absence, 'people lacking in proper conduct and judgement, whom the devil handles as he pleases on account of their weakness'. The judge's hostility to the 'inconstant element' plays a role here too. Their time away caused the men to hate their wives and feel suspicious of their children, uncertain whether they were really theirs. Upon their return in winter, 'they spent their whole day stuck at home, drinking and eating everything, leaving no provisions for their families'.[168] Cultural practices which allowed young Basques to 'try out' marriage – heavily resisted by Bishop Echaux and others – further cemented such alleged indifference.[169] When husbands abandoned their roles as providers, women chose 'another father for their children, offering them as a present to Satan'. Indirectly, then, in de Lancre's analysis, it was the sea that caused 'the women to become witches and bedevilled', while the men returned 'to being savages and sailors'.[170] This fascinating presentation of failing patriarchy ties together the Labourd's economy, its household structures and its predilection for witchcraft. In 1619,

Lope de Isasti would push this reading further still, claiming that women joined the devil's service to obtain a form of child support. The devil also acted as a vital communications provider, giving them news about 'their husbands and sons who go to the Indies, and to Terreneuve and Norway'.[171]

De Lancre's fascinating but problematic analysis of failing patriarchy – which made women, as witches, bear the brunt of their husbands' shortcomings – not only gives us an early glimpse of his personality, it also reveals deeper truths about the Labourd and its witch-hunt. Lapurdi women really were strikingly independent, in part because their husbands were away and might not come back. To quote another Basque proverb: 'the sailor's wife is all too often married in the morning and a widow in the evening.'[172] Whatever de Lancre might have thought, Basque women were quite capable of managing their affairs in their husband's absence and without the devil's assistance. Wives did not keep possession of their dowry upon marriage but instead became co-owners of their husband's family estate – if the husband's parents were still alive, the young couple would be known as the 'young lord' and 'young lady' of the house.[173] Husbands could not dispose of marital goods without the consent of their wives, and the same applied for anything she acquired 'through trade or by her industry'.[174]

Basque women who did not aspire to marriage could instead pursue an alternative religious vocation. So-called seroras fulfilled a series of caretaking functions in churches across the Basque country. Depending on their community, they were charged with preparing their church for Mass, decorating it on feast days, ringing the bells, greeting worshippers and so on. Seroras served a role that was at once considered feminine (household tasks) and deeply religious (the handling and cleaning of sacred objects).[175] De Lancre was deeply suspicious of them; he regarded their position as a diabolic invention and accused them of 'corrupting' the priests. The judge's worry that priests and seroras would defile their churches – committing unspeakable acts together during those moments when they were left alone in a sacred space – tells us a great deal about the sexual fantasies that underpinned his gendered imagination. The presence of two seroras (as well as a considerable number of priests) among those on trial demonstrates that his fears and fantasies were also acted upon.[176]

De Lancre's tortured theories also cover a second, more difficult truth that we will unpack later: the witch-hunt of the Pays de Labourd, among many other things, also constituted a breakdown in family structures, in which young people accused their elders of witchcraft. The role played by teenage accusers is the witch-hunt's most perplexing and most unsettling feature. The sources, as we shall see, are exceptionally unhelpful in making sense of their actions. What is clear, however, is that there was ample precedent within the Basque country for witchcraft accusations, especially by children.

## The *sorginak*

The Basques have another saying: 'everything that has a name exists'. They certainly had a word for witches: *sorginak* (singular: *sorgin*).[177] Its etymological origins are murky. The root may have been Latin. *Sors*, the casting of lots, also provides the root for the equivalent French word *sorcier*, and just like the French suffix '-ier', the Basque ending 'gin' or 'egin' refers to the accompanying profession.[178] Both *sorciers* and *sorginak*, then, were literally casters of lots, but they were always much more than that. As witches and evil spirits, the *sorginak* haunted the Basque landscape. They were associated with caves, notably the eerie tourist ones just outside of Zugarramurdi, which were also the site of the witches' gathering in Pío Baroja's novella, *La dama de Urtubi*.[179] Basque witchcraft lore really is exceptionally rich by European standards. Modern folklorists have gathered stories about witches, their secret meetings and (especially) their transformations into animals from across the Basque country.[180]

But this lore is dangerous too. As the literal stuff of legend, it can be repackaged for political purposes as an original, indigenous religion.[181] Even transposing it to the seventeenth century is not without its difficulties. The famous Basque word for the witches' sabbat, the *akelarre*, probably originated during our witch-hunt, as the result of a misapprehension by Spanish inquisitors who, like de Lancre, relied on interpreters. Their misunderstanding transformed a specific gathering place for the Zugarramurdi witches – probably a meadow filled with poisonous flowers, called *alka* or cock's foot – into a generic name for the sabbat, the 'field of the billy-goat [*akerr*]'.[182] Folkloric traditions, although they exemplify the deep roots of witchcraft in Basque culture, can best be understood as the product of centuries of accretions of this sort. Historians can use such later material only with great care. (Pierre de Lancre used the word *akelarre* only once and probably first came across it in a pamphlet from Spain.[183])

While the Pyrenees hosted some of Europe's earliest witchcraft trials, the Basques were particularly precocious.[184] The first definite case of sorcery among Navarre's exceptionally well-preserved trial records involves 'a certain Jewish woman, disreputable on account of her spells and incantations' in the town of Lizarra in the year 1300. Another, somewhat more doubtful case of a woman from Tutera accused of 'giving herbs' goes back even earlier, to 1279. North of the Pyrenees, the earliest known trial for witchcraft, involving four 'herbalists', who 'poisoned the people and committed many witchcrafts', took place in 1328 or 1329 in Saint-Jean-de-Pied-de-Port, the capital of (eventually French) Lower Navarre.[185] What makes these early trials remarkable is that they predated the demonization of witchcraft, a theological idea which only slowly won adherents in learned circles during the fourteenth and, especially, fifteenth centuries.[186] These early accused are not yet called *sorginak*. The first documented use of the word dates back to 1415 when a woman in Pamplona was fined for slandering her neighbour as 'a *sorguina*, herbalist and sorceress', although this suggests that the term was already widely understood as an insult.[187]

Inhabitants of the Iberian peninsula regarded witchcraft as a particularly Basque phenomenon. In the late fifteenth century, the Pamplona canon Martín de Arles discussed the widespread belief in 'these female witches, who mostly thrive in the Basque region in the northern part of the Pyrenees'.[188] In 1494, when witches first came to the attention of the recently founded Inquisition, they were not called *brujas* – the Spanish word – but *sorginak*.[189] The Basques themselves regularly petitioned for royal or inquisitorial support in their witchcraft dealings. As early as 1466, the province of Gipuzkoa complained to King Enrique IV of Castile about 'the many evils and damages [witches] were inflicting on the land'.[190] Their successful petition for local judges to be given the right to sentence suspects without the possibility of appeal anticipates the Labourd's petition to the French king (to another Henry IV!) by some 150 years. The complaint gave rise to a veritable tradition. In 1530, Gipuzkoa resolved to set up a special committee to address witchcraft at its general meeting, and in 1555, several towns in the province petitioned the generally reluctant Inquisition for an investigation into witchcraft.[191]

Beyond attempts at obtaining official sanction or support for anti-witchcraft campaigns, the Spanish Basque country, on at least two occasions, was also swept up by panics from below, conducted by overzealous judges and usually prompted by the testimony of young children. Navarre's deadliest wave was probably the first. A 1525 witch-hunt led to the death of over fifty witches in the valleys of Roncevalles and Salazar. As with the work of the 1609 royal commission almost a century later, the death toll was the work of a (in this case, single) judge sent by the Consejo Real or Royal Council, a secular court based in Pamplona, to investigate the situation locally and without meaningful oversight. Much of what we know about this witch-hunt comes from a legal effort by the judge's heirs to obtain their share of the confiscated goods.[192] The situation was very different in 1575–6, when the Consejo Real kept tighter control over the situation, and eventually the Inquisition stepped in.[193] Here, it was the council's execution of two witches that appeared to give licence to the local communities to start their own hunts and 'to cleanse these mountains of such wicked people'.[194]

Navarre's second major witchcraft panic even spread into France. During the summer and autumn of 1576, Boniface de Lasse, then the Labourd's lieutenant, conducted a witch-hunt riddled with irregularities in which some forty people died. De Lancre, who read the (lost) trial documents and is our only source, disingenuously claimed that those convicted 'through ignorance or simplicity' chose not to appeal their sentences in Bordeaux.[195] De Lasse appears to have been a particularly unsavoury character – in 1572 he was banished from Bayonne for a year and a day after he got a local girl pregnant.[196] To an even greater extent than the 1609 witch-hunt, the events of 1576 survive solely because of de Lancre. They have never before been connected to a wave crossing over from Navarre. The border's greatest magic trick is a disappearing act. Seen from France, Lapurdi witch-hunts seem like novel, demonic intrusions, seemingly coming from nowhere. The border can hide both deep roots and connected tissue from view.

Scraps from French archives show that witchcraft fears persisted north of the Pyrenees. In fact, the witchcraft problem was gaining in urgency in the 1580s, as it was across the weather-beaten continent at the time. In 1582, four mostly coastal villages to the west of Bayonne – Biarritz, Guéthary, Anglet and (probably) Bidart – successfully petitioned King Henry III for a witchcraft commission, after they claimed to have been 'afflicted by an infinite number of male and female witches'.[197] On 17 September 1582, the Bordeaux Parlement sent a single judge, Joseph d'Andrault, to try the accused. What he found is, unfortunately, not recorded. De Lancre, who had joined the court a month earlier, never mentions these trials. A prohibition on torture and the possibility of appeal may well have resulted in a different outcome. The Lapurdi petition was part of a growing pattern. Around 1587, the representatives of the territory of Mixe, in Lower Navarre, petitioned the small kingdom's Estates for help because 'the greater part' of the parish of Amendeuix-Oneix was bewitched.[198] In 1594, several communities, including La Bastide-Clairence which bordered the Labourd, petitioned the same Estates for each to be allowed to elect 'two trustworthy gentlemen' to prosecute and punish suspected witches, and their request was apparently granted by the duke de La Force, the viceroy.[199] As with the 1582 trials, these limited sources do not reveal the outcome of these more informal witchcraft commissions.

We began this chapter with Braudel and geographic determinism. We are ending it with a survey of the deep roots of witchcraft beliefs in the Basque country. Geography offers no good answers for the origins or endurance of those beliefs. They cannot be blamed on the 'thin' mountain air, nor was the Basque country in any sense remote or isolated, cruel or backwards. But geography, and particularly the border, does explain why the witch-hunt of the Pays de Labourd may have seemed *novel*, both to French judges and to many historians. The chapters that follow show how many of the fears and narratives surrounding Basque witchcraft, the sabbat and even the role of children had deep roots which the border helped remove from view. The solution that Labourdi authorities eventually turned to – a witchcraft commission – had clear precedents as well. When witchcraft again seemed a problem in the Pays de Labourd in the early 1600s, officials were treading a well-worn path. The next chapter shows how the social and political conflicts we have been charting grew into a widespread witchcraft panic, which was similarly rooted in geography and which could apparently only be sorted by outside judges with unchecked powers.

# Chapter 2
# Beginnings (1603–1608)

On 17 January 1609, a very official-looking document left Paris for Bordeaux, bearing both the royal signature and the royal seal. It was addressed to two Bordeaux magistrates, Jean d'Espagnet and Pierre de Lancre, and it began by informing them of some terrible news. To the king's great distress, his 'dear and beloved inhabitants of our Pays de Labourd' had for the past four years been afflicted by 'so great a number of male and female witches that they have as it were infected all places.' Indeed, the letter went on, the situation was such 'that the inhabitants will be forced to abandon their homes and lands' if an immediate remedy were not forthcoming. So terrified were the residents that they dared not let their children leave their homes or 'they would immediately be caught by this evil, because these sorts of people are so wicked that they not only exercise their spells and their art on beasts and crops, which they destroy, but even on the people themselves.' Such crimes deserved exemplary punishment. Espagnet and de Lancre were ordered to the Labourd to root out the witchcraft problem.[1]

The lengthy preamble of these letters patent, as they are officially called, is not some artless factual report. The petitioners will have had a substantial hand in their composition, and the two men charged with the commission knew the letter was coming. De Lancre would have seen identical wording already – an earlier version of the commission, dated 10 December 1608, had been addressed to him alone.[2] The paperwork setting up the commission has provided the starting point for many earlier accounts of the Basque witch-hunt. Some blame the witch-hunt on the first Bourbon king – they are keen to topple 'good king' Henry from the pedestal which even the crowds of the French Revolution famously left untouched[3] – or they cast local elites as naive innocents, 'sheep' who accidentally invited in the wicked wolf, Pierre de Lancre.[4] Building on our understanding of the Pays de Labourd as a fractured and factious world, we will begin, not in Paris or Bordeaux, but in the Basque country in order to reconstruct the circumstances that led up to the creation of the 1609 commission.

The edict already provides us with some useful starting points. It traces the beginnings of the witchcraft panic back four years, that is to 1604 or 1605. The explicit mention of children being 'caught by this evil' is striking and important. One of the most conspicuous features of Basque witch-hunting has been the role played by children and teenagers. Absent, however, is any mention of the witches' sabbat, the study of which would become the overriding obsession of Pierre de Lancre's *Tableau*. By contrast, the references to harm to crops, livestock and people point us to some of de Lancre's blind spots. They remind us that this witch-hunt, like many others, was also propelled by the fears and pressures of everyday life.

Sources for the origins of the Basque witch-hunt remain disappointingly scarce, but there is more material than historians could ever have suspected. To begin with, there are two additional witnesses to the witch-hunt who have not yet been heard. Bertrand de Haitze was a young parish priest in Ustaritz when the witch-hunt took place. In 1641, towards the end of his life, he felt compelled to record his version of the events in his village's baptism register.[5] Unlike de Lancre's *Tableau*, which never concerned itself with chronology, this note, not even a page long, offers us a miniature history of the witch-hunt from beginning to end. A second account was left by the friar Mathias de Lissalde, whose convent was founded in 1610 in response to the disorders. Lissalde, whose last name suggests Basque roots, had been one of the first friars to arrive.[6] What makes these reports so valuable is that they appear completely unaware of de Lancre's *Tableau*, or indeed of each other.[7] While they disagree on certain points, they help us escape the judge's perspective. In that sense, they do more than just fill in some of the blank space that remains, they also give a sense as to how the witch-hunt was perceived and experienced in the wider community.

Equally important is another type of source: the account books of the communities of the Pays de Labourd themselves. Judges, jailors, executioners and interpreters all required payment. They are extremely valuable but frustrating sources, offering strange details but often not telling us what we would most like to know. We learn the locations where one of the Bordeaux judges (not Pierre de Lancre) changed horses on his way down to the Basque country,[8] the name of the Bordeaux landlady who housed some of the teenage witnesses[9] and the size of the hams given as presents to the Bordeaux judges.[10] Vital details still elude us. Financial records, by their very nature, do not document the words of accusers and accused, only the sums paid to record or translate them. On many occasions the outcome of the trials is unknown.

There is a philosophical problem here as well as an evidential one. When does a witchcraft prosecution become more than a collection of trials? When does it rise to the level of a full-blown panic? By late 1608 or early 1609, the Basque witch-hunt had 'infected all places' in the Labourd. In fact, it had already spread beyond it and into Spain. In December 1608, a young girl, María de

Ximildegui, had returned from Ciboure to the Spanish village of Zugarramurdi – perhaps her parents wanted to keep her out of harm's way – and she quickly accused other villagers of being members of a secret witches' cult.[11] By that stage, parents across the Labourd had started to sleep in churches with their children, to prevent them from being caught by witches at night and taken to the sabbat.[12] But when did this start? At what stage did witchcraft become a serious enough threat to spark a panic? When did these witchcraft fears spread beyond anyone's control? We need to answer these questions before the witchcraft commissioners arrive.

## Giving hams to judges

Witch-hunting was usually a money-losing business. The suspects themselves were all too often poor and marginalized, their belongings too pitiful to sustain further prosecutions. In the Rhine-Moselle region of Germany – one of the epicentres of the European witch-hunt – the financial costs created a strange 'start-stop' staccato rhythm: the activities of local witch-hunting committees ground to a halt whenever the money ran out, only to resume a decade or so later.[13] In Spain, the Basque witchcraft panic caused severe financial difficulties for the Logroño Inquisition tribunal, as the witches – unlike most other prisoners – were too poor to pay for their sustenance.[14] The high cost of justice was one reason why witch-hunting in France never reached the levels seen elsewhere in Europe. The Parlement of Paris, the most august of France's courts and, as Pierre de Lancre already recognized, the most sceptical in witchcraft matters, instituted obligatory appeals in 1624 for witchcraft cases within its jurisdiction.[15] It made witchcraft persecutions not only expensive but also fruitless. Its Bordeaux counterpart, although occasionally (and, as we shall see, wrongly) praised for its scepticism, had a higher conviction rate but its wheels were equally greasy and slow.[16]

French justice was both complex and costly. At the base stood a myriad of little-studied seigneurial law courts, overseen by whichever local lord (*seigneur*) or entity had jurisdiction.[17] We do not even know how many of these courts there were.[18] They would have numbered into the tens of thousands across the kingdom, and their ability to dispense 'high', 'middle' or 'low' justice differed according to the precise title of their fief or charter.[19] As a noble town, for instance, Saint-Jean-de-Luz possessed its own court, as did Bayonne. At the regional level, the Pays de Labourd possessed a court seated at its capital, the village of Ustaritz.[20] The territory's privileges provided for a *bailli* – the lord of Amou in our period – as the 'ordinary judge' who dealt with 'all matters and actions, both civil and criminal' in the first instance, although in practice, this duty was undertaken by a lieutenant. Punishments, too, reflected local customs: in

Lapurdi, the most severe crimes, including murder, arson, forgery and rape, required death by decapitation – a rather aristocratic method of execution – but there is no indication that any of the territory's witches died that way.[21]

On top of this tapestry of local courts sat an equally convoluted hierarchy of royal courts. Certain crimes, most obviously treason, were automatically beholden to them. Others were heard by them on appeal.[22] In the case of the Labourd, the first court of appeal was the *sénéchaussée* in Bayonne.[23] In 1552, Henry II created an extra layer of appeals courts, the so-called *présidiaux*, partly as a money-spinner for the crown.[24] The nearest of these was in Dax, in the Landes region north of the Adour river. At the pinnacle of French jurisprudence sat the Parlements that acted as the highest courts of appeal in the land.[25] The pretensions of the so-called sovereign courts were grand. One French jurist writing in 1586 likened them to 'places of sanctuary ... to which the children of God can retire when they are being pursued'.[26] The Parlement of Bordeaux was the last place of refuge for the accused witches of the Pays de Labourd.

The complexity of the French legal system, praised by one prominent historian as 'one of the most beautiful showcases of the monarchy', had profound implications for the administration of justice.[27] Any plaintiff had to make a great number of decisions: the choice whether or not to sue (extra- or illegal avenues were, of course, also available), the selection of the right tribunal, the choice of procedure and how far to take the proceedings.[28] Informing all of these decisions was the vexed issue of cost. Royal judges owned their offices (their sale was one easy way by which the crown made money), and the great care and rigour with which they jointly examined cases resulted at least partly from the fact that both sides had to pay so-called *épices* or 'emoluments' for the pleasure, which made up a sizable part of the judges' income.[29] All other court officials, from bailiffs to clerks, also required payment.[30] The Saint-Jean-de-Luz officials supplemented these payments with gifts of ham. There was nothing untoward about such presents. In fact, they were well-chosen – hams were widely seen as a French Basque delicacy, as they still are today.[31]

It is difficult to overstate the impact of court costs on the justice system. It was eminently possible to bankrupt the opposing side through legal pettifogging, miring a case in ever greater complexity through further suits and counter-suits in rival jurisdictions.[32] As far as the judges were concerned, civil suits were more profitable than criminal ones, which was partly why the Parlements operated a rotation system so that magistrates did not have to serve on the *Tournelle*, the criminal chamber, for long.[33] (In 1617, the great systematizer of French legal practice, Bernard de La Roche-Flavin, denied that rotations took place because death sentences changed 'the natural gentleness of the judges, making them rather cruel and inhumane.'[34]) Yet, even in criminal cases, justice did not come cheap. Only in the most severe crimes would royal prosecutors act at the crown's expense, principally when the monarchy itself was the target, or for 'horror crimes' that caused public outrage.[35] In other instances, the victim would have to underwrite the court costs as a *partie civile,* with no way of knowing what the final expense or outcome would be.[36]

The general workings of French justice, therefore, already suggest two reasons why the country witnessed exceptionally low levels of witchcraft prosecutions. On the plus side, the elaborate appeals process brought heightened scrutiny and removed the accused from the locality in which suspicions first arose. More problematically, the legal process also imposed such high costs that it thwarted the pursuit of justice *in general*. For historians, however, these financial underpinnings are a blessing, providing us with an alternative set of sources when the trial records themselves are missing. The few surviving witchcraft-related documents in the local archives are almost all payment receipts from jailors, interpreters and judges for services rendered. Even then, records for the period in question only survive for two Lapurdi communities: Bayonne and Saint-Jean-de-Luz.[37] The latter, fortunately for us, was the witch-hunt's early epicentre.

The account books of Saint-Jean-de-Luz provide glimpses of everyday life: officials busied themselves with repairs to the local church, with the maintenance of the water fountain and with construction work on the new bridge across the river Nivelle.[38] Other entries, however, record a wide range of criminal activity, from misdemeanours to actual riots. In 1604, for instance, the officials paid the town herald to pursue a local man from Guéthary, a village to the north of town, for publicly exposing himself. The same account book also reveals the arrest of a surgeon who had wounded a person and that 'part of the community' subsequently broke him out of prison.[39] These registers hint at communal tensions, but like glow worms at night, to appropriate one of de Lancre's elaborate Baroque metaphors, they shed only a limited amount of light.[40] They list a payment to a notary for an official account of the breaking down of the prison door but that document, like many others, is lost. The exhibitionist from Guéthary will forever remain a single-line entry. If the law caught up with him, we will never know whether he had simply lost his clothes on the beach.

Similar question marks surround the first witchcraft trial that took place in Saint-Jean-de-Luz. On 10 October 1603, a group of officials arrived in Saint-Jean-de-Luz from Ustaritz: the Labourd's most senior law official, Pierre de Chibau, was accompanied by his secretaries and herald.[41] Pierre, the 'Monsieur le Lieutenant de Labourt', was a relative of the financially unlucky merchant Adam de Chibau, whom we met in the previous chapter and will meet again.[42] The town's own legal counsel had come from Bayonne. They had assembled to hear the case against Marie de Haristeguy accused of practising witchcraft 'in broad daylight and in public'. We know nothing more about Marie's crimes, only that the trial lasted four days. Details about her background are scarce. She certainly belonged to the town's elite. Male Haristeguys had been prominent merchants who were often elected to the town's council. A fragmentary baptism register shows that Marie acted as a godparent alongside one alderman and was godmother to the daughter of another.[43] Her tax contributions suggest she may have been a widow of considerable wealth.[44] Her social status and the high costs indicate that the trial was a serious and public affair.

At the end of the trial, the town's *abbé*, Martin de La Masse, escorted Marie – the 'prisoner' – to Bayonne, where the inevitable appeal would have been heard by the *sénéchaussée*. (We know because La Masse had his travel expenses reimbursed.[45]) On 31 October, a herald was paid for escorting witnesses to a judicial confrontation.[46] On 2 March 1604, the town paid its lawyer 'to make some pursuit against a woman accused of being a witch who is in Bayonne', suggesting that Marie was still in prison.[47] Her reappearance in the account books as a taxpayer suggests that she was released at some point in 1605.[48] But that need not be the end. Although she does not appear on the surviving lists of prisoners, Marie could have been ensnared by the 1609 commission's investigations.

There are no further references to witchcraft for the years 1603 and 1604, but the account books hint at other and greater turbulence ahead. The *jurat* or alderman in charge of the town's accounts in 1603, Jean de Goyetche, would become a leading witchcraft suspect.[49] The 1604 accounts are more interesting still because the *jurat* responsible, Martissans de Haurgues, was targeted by unspecified legal proceedings. On 2 June 1604, he paid for a copy of a summons he had received. On 23 July, Haurgues (reimbursing himself) travelled to Bayonne for legal advice as to how he should proceed in this conflict among the officials 'and to avoid the great cost and expense which could occur in the Parlement'. By that time, barely halfway through his term in office, Haurgues had already decided to step down, returning the communal coffer to the new mayor, Jean de Haristeguy.[50] The documents do not tell us whether Jean was related to Marie, still imprisoned in Bayonne, though within the wider web of factionalism we are about to confront, it is a distinct possibility. Jean and Marie may have served as godparents together.[51] In 1605, Guiraud de Sanson, one of Haurgues's opponents and now the town's elected mayor, would appeal to the Bordeaux Parlement for aid in the fight against witchcraft.

# Calling in the commissioners (attempt #1)

Much about the early origins of the witch-hunt remains unclear. We do not know the cause of the conflict among Haurgues and the other officials. It could even have been witchcraft, given the mention of the Parlement. What is certain is that, with Sanson as mayor, the officials of Saint-Jean-de-Luz turned to the Bordeaux Parlement for help in solving their apparent witchcraft problem. One of this first group of Bordeaux judges, Étienne de Cruseau, who travelled to the Labourd observed in his diary that 'the whole business was upon the request and pursuit' of Sanson and his colleagues.[52] Given the size and scope of the Parlement's jurisdiction, such commissions were a standard way to address specific local problems, especially in places far away from the metropole. The procedure had been used ever since the court was created in the mid-fifteenth century.[53] In 1593, for instance, Cruseau had been sent to Bayonne, as fears of a Spanish takeover of the city peaked, to try around twenty suspects for an unspecified crime that may well have been treason. Late in 1598, he agreed to a commission to investigate usury in Bergerac because (as he wrote in his diary) he had personal business to attend to elsewhere in the Dordogne region. He did not record whether similar motives played a role in accepting the commission in 1605, only that on Tuesday, 13 September, he set out for Bayonne with two colleagues.[54] It was Cruseau whose travel expense claim still survives in the archives.[55]

Unfortunately for us, Cruseau did not care to record what happened in the Basque country. His comment that 'several particularities happened without honour, pleasure and profit, all because of the indiscretion of God knows who' offers the most arresting instance in our history of a witness or participant who could have provided us with vital information but instead looked away. All that the judge tells us is that he fell ill. He lamented at length that he was forced to stay behind in backward Bayonne while his colleagues returned home.[56] (In 1608, he would be exempted from further official travel on account of his 'kidney stones and gout'.[57]) Still, Cruseau's explicit mention of Saint-Jean-de-Luz's mayor and aldermen makes it clear that the witch-hunt originated there, and the town's account books provide additional details about what the judges got up to. During the spring and summer, a growing group of witchcraft suspects had been imprisoned, awaiting interrogation by the Bordeaux judges.[58] According to a notary hired by the town – one of many who would later pursue the community for payment for his services – a total of twenty-two people had been arrested, among them Jean de Goyetche, the official who once recorded the costs of Marie de Haristeguy's trial, and three of his sisters.[59] This is a large cluster of suspects, and it stands to reason that when the royal letters patent referenced the origin of the witch-hunt, it was this group and the work of this earlier – non-royal – Parlementary commission that the document had in mind.

Linking these prosecutions to the wider social and political turmoil is difficult. Our financial sources are too fragmentary. One crisis, however, must have been relevant because it was a spiritual one. In late 1604 or early 1605, the bishop of Bayonne, Bertrand d'Echaux, had placed the town of Saint-Jean-de-Luz and its inhabitants under an interdict.[60] Interdicts were serious affairs – they prohibited the saying of Mass and the performance of the sacraments, meaning that Luzians could not be baptized or receive the last rites. They were very much in the air at the time – in April 1606, the papacy placed Venice under one such interdict in a conflict over church property.[61] In response, Saint-Jean-de-Luz paid for masses to be said in neighbouring Ciboure and Urrugne, and it appealed the interdict to the Bordeaux Parlement and the royal council.[62] Echaux's ban was in retaliation for the community's refusal to meet the costs of a recent pastoral visit, as had been customary. Another issue, however, was a prestigious burial spot inside the church of Saint-Jean-de-Luz, which had belonged to the community and which Echaux, perhaps out of spite, had ceded to the merchant Adam de Chibau.[63] Around this time, Chibau also acquired a noble title and began to style himself as 'Sieur de Saint-Julien' in notarial deeds.[64] His attempts to bolster his social status thus sparked a backlash that fed the town's wider conflicts, both spiritual and demonic.

Even against this background, justice would not be rushed. The accused witches remained imprisoned in Bayonne's prison for over a year, while the testimony against them was rigorously examined. Saint-Jean-de-Luz reimbursed several witnesses for the cost of travel to Bayonne but the judges did not simply confine themselves to interrogations.[65] On 9 October 1605, the town's mayor, Guiraud de Sanson recompensed the 'commissioners' for the costs of a visual inspection of the places 'where the witches hold their sabbat or assembly'.[66] In 1609, Jean d'Espagnet and Pierre de Lancre would attempt similar inspections for evidence of the sabbat.[67] What their predecessors found is not recorded. While a sick Cruseau remained in Bayonne to sulk and recover, his colleagues returned home apparently without having sentenced any of the prisoners.[68] The sabbat's early prominence is significant, given the extent to which the nocturnal gatherings would dominate both de Lancre's *Tableau* and the reports of Spanish Inquisition officials later.

On 18 December 1605, two weeks after Cruseau struggled home, one of the aldermen mentioned in his diary, Martin d'Oriotz, set out for Bordeaux to reinforce the community's legal team and 'to pursue those accused of witchcraft', assisted by a notary.[69] The town's judicial infrastructure was costly and impressive and included lawyers on retainer in both Bordeaux and Bayonne. These were put to hard work, but backup was apparently needed in Bordeaux. Oriotz remained in the city until early August 1607, receiving regular payments for looking after 'the affairs of the community'. He would for a time even be joined by a second *jurat*.[70] While the judges in Bordeaux deliberated and were being lobbied, the witch-hunt in the Labourd appeared to be spreading beyond Saint-Jean-de-Luz, with resistance to the trials growing locally among the relatives of the accused as well. In March 1606, two Saint-Jean-de-Luz officials were in Biarritz where they accused a priest by the name of Etchegaray of attempting to suborn the testimony of the witnesses against the accused witches, in particular 'a girl from Saint-Pée' called Marguerite de Hareder.[71] Both the 'young' and the 'old lady of the house of Etchegaray' – a mother and her daughter-in-law – had been among the prisoners, presumably the priest was their relative.[72] Oriotz raised the issue directly with the Bordeaux Parlement, alongside a more obscure attempt to corrupt the testimony of another girl, Marie d'Aguerre.[73]

On 3 October 1606, after nearly a year of deliberation, the Bordeaux Parlement issued a judgement ordering the transport of twelve witches, some of whom had by then been in prison for sixteen months.[74] On 22 November 1606, Bayonne's jailor escorted them to Bordeaux and promptly sued Saint-Jean-de-Luz for lack of payment. With a wife and six children to support, he claimed that the cost of feeding the prisoners had bankrupted him.[75] Six of the accused were housed in the *Conciergerie*, the Parlement's own prison, four in the city's *Maison commune* and a further two in the prison of the province of Guyenne.[76] Among those imprisoned was Françoise de Haristeguy – her name alone is underlined in the record. Better known as 'Hihy', she was presumably a relative of Marie de Haristeguy, the first woman to be accused in 1603.[77] Among those released under caution were Jean de Goyetche, the former alderman, and his three sisters.[78] Their experiences in prison would have been extremely unpleasant. Bayonne's royal prison was not cleaned until 1614 when even the city's officials agreed that it was in a 'bad state'. Others died of hunger and disease there.[79] Those transported to Bordeaux were subjected to physical examinations. Physicians searched their bodies for the devil's mark.[80] Oriotz also paid 25 *livres* for the suspects to be tortured and for three Basque interpreters so that the judges could hear their testimony.[81]

It was not just town officials and the accused who travelled to Bordeaux. The witnesses against them did so as well, again at the community's expense. The widow of a Bordeaux attorney was paid for housing a group of 'girls who had come to testify against some accused of witchcraft from 16 December 1606 to 9 May 1607'.[82] We do not know their names or their number, but we do have those details for a small group of seven witnesses who stayed in Bordeaux for three weeks in December 1606. They included Marguerite Hareder and Marie d'Aguerre, both of whom had already been threatened by witches' relatives, and Catherine de La Masse, who would be similarly targeted later.[83] They were accompanied by Catherine's mother and stepfather. For these young witnesses, the journey to the unfamiliar metropole may well have been the adventure of a lifetime, though their time in Bordeaux itself can hardly have been a positive experience. The city was ravaged by plague in 1607, and several teens fell ill.[84] Oriotz paid Catherine's mother to stay behind to look after them.[85] What the witnesses told the Bordeaux judges is lost to us; the financial documents predictably leave us in the dark. From a later document, we only know that they must have mentioned the witches' sabbat.[86] That is itself already a revelation. Teenagers and the witches' sabbat would go on to dominate de Lancre's *Tableau*. Both were already central to the Basque witch-hunt years before he arrived on the scene.

Of the Saint-Jean-de-Luz accused, only Françoise de Haristeguy was executed at considerable cost to the community.[87] Two further sources indicate that there were additional executions, almost certainly from other Lapurdi communities. One Bordeaux chronicler reported that 'several male and female witches were executed in this year who confessed to things that were horrible to hear'.[88] Another account refers to 'repeated' burnings of Basque witches in the city prior to the 1609 commission.[89] These details fit the fragmentary evidence that witch-hunting was already spreading beyond Saint-Jean-de-Luz and across the Labourd. The remaining Luzian suspects were released in stages from April 1607 onwards, a move that likely was replicated across the board. Although the Parlement apparently ordered the *présiaial* court in Dax to pursue 'further investigation' against some of the prisoners – including Jean de Goyetche – a later document described this ruling as a 'grace' and no further action appears to have been taken.[90] It was around this time that Oriotz gifted three hams to a Bordeaux lawyer who attempted to intercede with the court's first president on the community's behalf.[91] Did the *jurat* feel embittered as he presented the hams? Saint-Jean-de-Luz's officials had thus far little to show for their efforts.

In a certain fashion, the Parlement's pardon anticipates the so-called Edict of Grace that the Inquisitor Alonso de Salazar Frías used to absolve confessed witches after the witchcraft panic crossed the border into Spain.[92] Although the Inquisition, as a religious institution, was principally concerned with the salvation of souls and thus more used to offering absolution in exchange for a confession, both judicial bodies recognized that vast legal bureaucracies could not hope to cope with the problems raised by a witchcraft panic. In the longer term, this realization set the stage for the nimble and deadly 1609 witchcraft commission. In the short term, the release of the accused witches did nothing to resolve the growing communal tensions, especially when witnesses had repeatedly testified against them. The escalation of the crisis during the spring and summer of 1607 exposes the fault lines that ran through Saint-Jean-de-Luz, and indeed, the Labourd more widely, while doubtless also exacerbating them. Pardons are by no means always a panacea.

## Taking a notary to an ambush

With tensions rising during 1607, new sources help us piece together what comes next. These legal depositions are by no means neutral documents. Drawn up by Saint-Jean-de-Luz's mayor and aldermen, they are pervaded by a growing sense of panic, not just about witchcraft but about intimidation and sedition, possibly even the collapse of all authority. The conflict expanded well beyond the town, as those involved increasingly resorted to extra-legal means. The growing use of threats and violence transformed the witch-hunt into a proper panic. Some – notably Tristan d'Urtubie, the Labourd's most discontented nobleman – resorted to physical force because they could; others went to extreme lengths out of desperation. We often imagine the witch as an isolated, often female and elderly figure, who acted as a scapegoat for a community's misfortunes.[93] Accusers might have hoped for a return to normality after the malignant force in their midst had been excised, but they were unlikely to get it. Witchcraft was in the eye of the beholder: witches were, in other words, witches *to other people*.[94] Many were also mothers or fathers, daughters or sons, or as in the case of the Goyetche family, brothers and sisters. Executions, far from offering a cure, left festering wounds: relatives whose reputations were also tarnished and whose anger was unlikely to abate any time soon. In Saint-Jean-de-Luz, the accused's kin were determined to intervene, even if the Bordeaux Parlement had already attempted to draw a line under the entire witchcraft affair. Their actions will reveal some of the kinship networks that sustained the early stages of this witch-hunt.

On 28 May 1607, then, we finally hear from some of the protagonists. Around nine that evening, a resident from Accotz, a village on the outskirts of Saint-Jean-de-Luz but (often unwillingly) part of its jurisdiction, knocked on the door of Guiraud de Sanson, who had the presence of mind to start a record of what transpired.[95] The villager, one Pedro de Caralde, reported that Catherine de La Masse, one of the witnesses against the witches, had returned to her parents' home bloodied and unable to speak. The resident asked the *abbé* to come forthwith but given the lateness of the hour, the mayor demurred and decided to confer with the other officials in the morning.[96]

But Sanson would get little sleep that night. Between four and five in the morning he was woken up by Catherine's stepfather, who reiterated the request and provided more details. He explained that the girl had left for the windmill around five in the afternoon, to grind a bag of wheat. After Catherine, clearly hurt, struggled home later that evening, she had not been able to utter a single word.[97] Marissans de Jalday, the girl's mother, who had accompanied her to Bordeaux, arrived two hours later. She, too, requested the mayor's presence. The confidence with which these parents approached Sanson directly and with such urgency may be because Catherine was a relative, perhaps even the daughter, of Martin de La Masse, a former mayor.[98] Still, as Catherine was unable to speak and thus name her attackers, the officials considered travel to Accotz pointless. They asked the girl's mother to update them on any changes to her condition.

Their inaction does not indicate a lack of interest. In fact, when Sanson started his account, he must have appreciated the opportunity that the news provided. If the Bordeaux court's April ruling had meant to draw a firm line under the proceedings, the assault effectively re-opened them. The document took care to note down the local uproar: 'A good number of the inhabitants and citizens of Saint-Jean-de-Luz' demanded that the attack should neither be covered up nor remain unpunished. While these citizens were pushing against an open door, Sanson and his colleagues would have to wait a full week before the girl had regained the ability to speak and thus denounce her assailants. Marissans explained that her daughter had been ambushed by a group of men, all of them allied to the accused witches. The details she revealed were shocking, and the *abbé* and *jurat*s decided to call a town meeting in response.[99]

On Monday 4 June, the day after Pentecost, the town crier was ordered to call for an immediate meeting, in keeping with the Lapurdi custom that such gatherings could be held whenever urgent business demanded it. Embarrassingly, however, most of the inhabitants could not be found, and the meeting had to be pushed back by a day. Local religious practice meant that 'the greatest part of the inhabitants' had climbed Larrun (or La Rhune), the mountain that towered above the community, 'to pray to God and to celebrate Mass'. Its peak was home to the Chapel of Saint-Esprit, one of many such sanctuaries that dotted the Basque landscape.[100] By the time de Lancre arrived, both the mountain and the chapel had become prominent sabbat sites. Unlike the witches, however, the inhabitants of Saint-Jean-de-Luz could not leap from the mountain in a single jump, and the assembly had to be rescheduled for the next day.[101] It was around ten in the morning on Tuesday, therefore, that the community assembled in church for an extraordinary town meeting. After Mass, the magistrates 'called the said community to conclave in the form to which we have been accustomed' – Saint-Jean-de-Luz at the time lacked a town hall; most Basque communities held such meetings in churches after service had ended or even in the cemeteries outside.[102] The officials described what they had learned from Catherine's mother and requested that the girl be allowed to address the congregation. This was granted. With Catherine still too weak to walk, the community even paid for her to be carried.[103]

On Sunday 10 June, between ten and eleven in the morning, after the divine service had ended, Catherine de La Masse came forward to speak. The deposition does not record whether the magistrates questioned the girl themselves beforehand, but it is almost inconceivable that they would not have. Her speech was dramatic – in no small part because the men she was about to accuse were present in church. It still has a powerful effect on the reader centuries later. The document that contains her testimony, originally begun by Sanson, switches from the third to the first person. Her words must be somewhat fictionalized – at least it is a French translation of a Basque speech.[104]

If Catherine was nervous, she did not show it. Speaking with a 'completely assured countenance', she swore to speak the truth and asked the audience to hear her and dispense justice. She described her trip to the mill with her sack of grain on 28 May. She had stayed out longer than she should have. It was getting dark as she returned home through the forest. It was there that a group of eight men lay in wait, whom she proceeded to name. They included a brother and two brothers-in-law of Jean de Goyetche – their wives presumably were also among the accused – and a member of the house of Etchegaray. That family, as we saw, had already threatened Marguerite de Hareder and had already lost one member, Françoise de Haristeguy, to the flames. Catherine identified one of Jean's brothers-in-law as Sanbat de Chibau, and it is striking that Goyetche himself is described as 'a relative of Adam de Chibau', as if his relationship to this wealthy aristocratic merchant most appropriately defined a person who had once held elected office. The document does not comment on the fact that a teenager who lived outside of Saint-Jean-de-Luz knew these prominent men by sight. As Catherine had known their relatives well enough to accuse them of witchcraft in Bordeaux, perhaps this should not surprise us. In fact, she claimed to recognize one of her assailants from the witches' sabbat itself.[105]

According to Catherine, the men threatened her, telling her that she had two choices: death or retracting her witchcraft accusations. She should admit that 'she had falsely accused Jean de Goyetche, relative of Adam de Chibau, and brother of one of those who was held, as well as his three sisters' and one further person.[106] They had brought a notary with them ready to record that it had instead been her stepfather and the town's officials – Sanson and Oriotz are mentioned by name – who had suborned her testimony. The incident shows how law and violence could be extensions of one another, all part of a single toolkit of conflict resolution. (By the same token, Oriotz, still in Bordeaux, reported the incident to the judges there and sued the assailants.[107]) We have already caught glimpses of factionalism at the top of Saint-Jean-de-Luz society from the financial records: Catherine's deposition in front of the entire community brings this conflict – the town's officials *versus* the equally mercantile Chibau-Goyetche clan – wide out into the open. This does not mean that witchcraft fears were just cynical weapons in a power struggle: it is all too natural to assume the worst of one's enemies.

Catherine's terrifying predicament in the woods continued a little while longer. In the face of such overt aggression, the girl persevered, insisting that her testimony against the witches had been truthful. Dissatisfied, her assailants threw the sack of flour she had been carrying against her stomach which floored her. They held her down so that Jean's younger brother could put a stick in her mouth to keep it open and force her to drink from a vial. He informed Catherine that this was a potion that would prevent her from speaking. Then they just left her there.

Employing a magical potion is an odd and therefore possibly desperate act on the part of the Chibau-Goyetche family. Perhaps they felt that the release of the prisoners would not be the end of the matter. More likely, they were working towards full exoneration. Whatever their motivation, the strategy worked for a short time, as the potion appeared effective for a few days. And yet, Catherine's clear and composed testimony – not in front of the Bordeaux judges who did not speak her language but before a town assembly which did – caused community tensions to spill over, especially given that some of those she mentioned were present. One person in the audience, one Martin de la Sagne, stood up and noted that she had only identified seven of her eight assailants by name, asking her to identify the eighth. She replied: 'The eighth person is you, and you know very well that it is true. You did not touch me. You were a little further near a tree with Rabillagne [another member of the group].' When La Sagne challenged her to describe what he had been wearing, she replied that she could not. It was getting dark. Besides, she had been floored by a sack of grain and had a stick inserted in her throat.[108]

When the officials confronted the assailants with Catherine's allegations at the town meeting, a general ruckus ensued. The men pressed themselves forward, revealing knives and half-swords that they had hidden under their coats. The crowd disarmed them. When shortly after Jean de Goyetche, the former alderman Catherine had accused of witchcraft, arrived carrying a sword, he was prevented from entering the assembly. It is difficult to interpret these communal actions. Sanson's account presented them as a sign of the community's support for its officials and its displeasure with the Chibau-Goyetche clan, their 'audacity and lack of respect' shown towards the people and 'the grace that the Parlement has given you.'[109] As the alleged assailants were allowed to leave unharmed, the response could also more neutrally be interpreted as an attempt to preserve the peace. Whatever Catherine said, did or thought during the disturbance is not recorded. In fact, although we have some indications of her later fate, we shall never hear her voice again.

Catherine's testimony was explosive, and we should examine our own (intellectual and emotional) responses to it before proceeding. If we take it seriously – and the nature of her injuries and the response of those she accused strongly suggests that we should – we should not lose sight of the fact that she had earlier accused prominent members of the community of witchcraft. We may not know the precise details of those allegations, yet their contours are evident. The teenage witnesses who testified in front of de Lancre and Espagnet in 1609 accused witches of taking them to the sabbat against their will. Catherine's references to the witches' sabbat suggest that she and the other witnesses had levelled similar accusations during their 1606–7 stay in Bordeaux. Our own reactions to Catherine's assault – so terrifying, so real – may help us perceive why communities responded in the way they did to accusations of forced abduction. Catherine's accusations also bear a striking resemblance to those of Abigail Williams and Betty Parris during the witch-hunt in Salem, Massachusetts, some eighty years later.[110] Afflicted by spiritual apparitions, these young women also faced down their accusers inside a church. Catherine's testimony had an impact even on those who were not there. Our two additional witnesses – Bertrand de Haitze and Mathias de Lissalde – both located the origins of the witch-hunt, not with the trial of Marie de Haristeguy or with the actions of the 1605 commission, but with Catherine's public denunciation of her assailants.

Writing decades after Catherine's deposition, Bertrand de Haitze, the Ustaritz parish priest, recorded in his baptism register that the witch-hunt had 'its origins in the Accotz quarter of Saint-Jean-de-Luz in the said year, when two peasants of Accotz came into altercation the one with the other. During this altercation one reproached the other of witchcraft, in such a way that not only Saint-Jean-de-Luz but even the rest of the Labourd was thrown into this disaster'.[111] Mathias de Lissalde, the Recollect friar, highlighted other aspects:

> A woman who wanted to avenge herself against one of her neighbours, her enemy, accuses her of being a witch. The credulity of the people of this country had made this condition [*witchcraft*] notorious. The relatives of the accused were offended, everyone took sides and hostilities were sparked on all sides.[112]

We should not expect either witness to corroborate our reconstruction fully. Human memory is flawed, and they wrote years after the fact. Looking back at events in 1641, Haitze placed the altercation in 1608, not 1607. Neither man was present at Catherine de la Masse's testimony or they would have mentioned it. Yet, we can still hear echoes of the original assault in Haitze's account, in terms of the location (Accotz) and date, while Lissalde's includes a telling reference to the offended relatives of witches. Both reports were shaped by knowledge of what came next and both, but especially Lissalde, placed the blame for the witch-hunt not on de Lancre or Henry IV, as we have seen modern historians do, but on one young woman. It may be helpful to think of the two men more as 'emotional' witnesses than historical ones: their evidence pinpoints the true onset of the witchcraft panic. They perceived this event to be the real beginning – reasonably so, given that any executions so far had been in faraway Bordeaux. With allegations now fully in the open, physical violence was about to break out in the Pays de Labourd.

## Maintaining (dis-)order

Towards the end of July 1607, after two months of upheaval, the officials and 'community' of Saint-Jean-de-Luz again pleaded with the Bordeaux Parlement for assistance. The opening lines of their document are striking. As a result of the community's pursuit of Jean de Goyetche, 'relative of Adam de Chibau' and others accused of the crime of witchcraft, 'the said Chibau, merchant of Saint-Jean-de-Luz, has resorted to every method possible to harm not only [the officials] but also the witnesses who deposed against the said Goyetche'.[113] We might read these lines as an implicit rebuke, or at least as a reminder, to the Parlement that its unwillingness to act had led to the present situation. Just as striking, however, is the explicit presentation of Chibau as the evil genius opposing the persecutions of his kin, starting with the attempt to suborn Marguerite Hareder's testimony back in March 1606. The officials' evident fears mean we need to treat their words with care – they were terrified that their opponents were stirring 'the people to sedition to prevent the said pursuit' of witches.[114] Curiously, Chibau is never depicted as a witch, despite his apparently sinister machinations behind the scenes.

As with most, if not all the Saint-Jean-de-Luz officials (and indeed, inhabitants), Chibau's considerable income was derived from the sea. At this precise moment, however, he was entering a period extreme financial stress, so much so that he had to borrow funds from his son-in-law in Bilbao to keep up appearances in the face of his growing losses and debts.[115] His business difficulties – he lost several ships – were compounded by legal troubles in Bordeaux, where Oriotz pursued him for non-payment of debts to the community.[116] Just as important was Chibau's role in the aforementioned interdict, a ban on the sacraments that had placed the souls of the entire community in peril. While the interdict was overturned by the archbishop of Auch by June 1605 at the latest, the magistrates pursued the matter further in both Paris and Bordeaux.[117] The same notary who assisted Oriotz's pursuit of the witches in Bordeaux also travelled to Paris to obtain a direct order from the king to Echaux to officially lift the ban himself and absolve the inhabitants of Saint-Jean-de-Luz, which the bishop did on 31 March 1606.[118] Oriotz meanwhile pursued both the bishop and the merchant in the Bordeaux Parlement regarding Chibau's prestigious burial plot. The officials even appealed to the king to intervene because of the bishop's many connections inside the Parlement.[119] While the outcome of the case is unclear, it unfolded alongside the witchcraft persecutions.[120] The community of Saint-Jean-de-Luz truly kept the bread of the Bordeaux judges well-buttered – and well-stacked with Basque ham.

Chibau's financial difficulties may well nod towards economic factors at play that are lost from view. Witches destroyed livelihoods as well as lives – the 'beasts and crops' mentioned in the royal letters. Unfortunately, the surviving sources are of no help to us here. What they do make clear is the paramount importance of social status in this conflict. There was no greater disgrace than a witchcraft accusation. Witches abandoned their social and religious obligations for a pact with humanity's infernal enemy. If witchcraft persecutions had truly ended after the Parlement's ruling, those damning accusations had not simply vanished. The assault on Catherine de La Masse was an attempt to restore family honour. The struggle over Chibau's future burial place, located inside the same church where the community met for its deliberations, is just as telling. Both conflicts reveal the destabilizing potential of the pursuit of honour and status in a small community beset by internal divisions and threatened by external forces.

Throughout the late spring and early summer of 1607, the town's public celebrations – events that should have fostered community cohesion – descended into chaos and conflict. Following Catherine's denunciation, violence erupted again on 14 June 1607, when the next major event on the church's liturgical calendar – the feast of Corpus Christi – took place. A man called Martin de Barandeguy, a close relative of Chibau, took a halberd (an axe blade mounted on a long shaft) to interrupt the solemn procession as it was leaving the church in pursuit of the Holy Eucharist.[121] His wife Marie had been examined in Bordeaux and his daughters had also been accused of witchcraft.[122] His aim, the officials alleged, was to injure them, and great scandal would have ensued if he had not been disarmed. Barandeguy quickly came back with a spear and a dagger 'to execute his pernicious plan, which he would have done had the people not stopped him'.[123] His swift return and the fact that no further action appears to have been taken against him shows the weakness of the officials' position, while the disturbance also undermined their position at the head of a communal event.

The situation escalated still further when shortly afterwards – a date is not recorded – Tristan d'Urtubie, one of the Labourd's two leading noblemen and a future sponsor of the witchcraft commission, intervened in an argument on behalf of a 'close relative', Adam de Chibau's wife. (Other sources identify her as Urtubie's aunt.[124]) The aristocrat's intervention, involving twelve armed men carrying swords, daggers and guns, is described in some detail. Urtubie ignored both pleas from the town officials 'to not use force, violence, and assault' and their promises that the person involved – the nature of their supposed offense is not mentioned – would be punished if they were guilty.[125] Urtubie had ways of making his own justice, pursuing whichever way was more convenient, whether legal or extra-legal.

The feast day of St John the Baptist, the town's patron saint, on 24 June provided a further opportunity for Chibau and Urtubie to cause not just trouble, but also (in the eyes of the town officials) full-blown 'public sedition'. Armed and masked horsemen hidden in Chibau's (presumably fairly sizable) home galloped through the town 'making a thousand insults and using threats in front of the homes of the mayor, other officers, and all those whom they wish'. The next day, with the feast's celebrations still ongoing, a 'domestic servant' of Urtubie walked through the town with a hunting rifle and a hunting dog, harassing a group of people dancing on the street. When the gun was taken away from him, the servant ran to Chibau's home and returned with a posse of armed men, causing 'a grand sedition' in which several were wounded and one permanently maimed. The town officials protested that there would have been deaths, but for the sudden arrival from Spain of the wife of the French ambassador to Madrid, Guyonne de la Mothe. Their complaint noted that 'the desire to welcome her honourably appeased the tumult', a comment that again underlines the paramount importance of honour and its preservation.[126]

**Figure 2.1** The Chateau d'Urtubie. (Photograph by author, August 2019.)

The last incident that Saint-Jean-de-Luz's officials chose to report occurred on another solemn feast day, that of St James on 25 July, when several of them were meant to travel to the village of Hendaye for the celebration, the prior of its church being their close relation. This would have caused them to pass by the Chateau of Urtubie, the castle through which this noble family traditionally controlled the road to Spain and where the current lord was now said to lay in waiting (Figure 2.1). The officials accused him of assembling 'a large number of Bohemians [cagots, the region's ethnic minority] as well as soldiers from Lower Navarre and Béarn whom he had hidden in his house to kill the said mayor and other inhabitants of the said place of Saint-Jean-de-Luz as they passed by to go to the said place of Hendaye'. Forewarned of the attack, the magistrates decided not to travel. Instead, they drafted their panicked appeal to the Parlement, pleading that 'such excesses which tend towards popular sedition should not remain unpunished', and they called on the judges to intervene.[127]

It is difficult to assess the extent to which the officials' lives were really in danger. The last conspiracy was literally a non-event, which could well have existed entirely in their fevered imagination. The document is perhaps most useful for the insight it gives into the mental state of a group that saw itself as underequipped and under siege. Their plea almost imperceptibly slides away from witchcraft, first to other sources of conflict and from there to allegations of violence inspired purely by hatred. Evidently, the officials' anxieties about their personal safety did not inspire further witchcraft suspicions. However depraved their alleged behaviour, Chibau and Urtubie were *not* cast as witches. Witchcraft was an important part of the tensions and conflicts that engulfed the Pays de Labourd, as well as a vehicle for their expression, but at this stage at least, it was neither the beginning nor the end of the trouble that the territory found itself in.

## When at first you don't succeed

Saint-Jean-de-Luz, like the Labourd or the Basque country as a whole, was no island. Its internal conflicts leaked out, drawing in a girl originally from Saint-Pée, a nobleman based near Urrugne and a parish priest in Hendaye. On one level, witchcraft was just one conflict among many: the tensions between Saint-Jean-de-Luz and Ciboure, two communities that struggled to share one natural harbour; the clashes between the towns and the noblemen over taxation; and lurking behind it all, the Franco-Spanish border and its threat of disorder. But all these conflicts were also tied together. Witchcraft was travelling along these other fault lines, seeping into other conflicts, even though the connection is not always clear and no conflict would ever be completely taken over by it.

While the sources leave even Saint-Jean-de-Luz in almost complete darkness during the remainder of 1607 and the early months of 1608, there are some indications that witchcraft fears and persecutions were spreading outward from Saint-Jean-de-Luz. It was during this time – or perhaps somewhat earlier – that Tristan d'Urtubie, the ally of those accused of witchcraft in Saint-Jean-de-Luz, began rounding up witches himself in Urrugne.[128] One source is inconveniently late. On 1 April 1611, the bishop of Pamplona, Antonio Venegas de Figueroa, sent a lengthy document to the Council of State in Madrid regarding the escalating witchcraft crisis in the Spanish Basque country and pointed to the hunt's French origins. The sceptical bishop had much to say about overeager preachers and local Inquisition officials. Yet, the border also plays an important role in Venegas's account of the witch-hunt's beginnings – in early modern Spain, bad things often came from France.[129] The bishop, a rabid *francophobe*, was thus keen to present the witch-hunt as French rather than Basque in origin. He thus began his submission by pinning the original blame for the witch-hunt on 'the lord of Urtubie, a French nobleman [who] seized on his own authority some old women'.[130] Venegas's report contains multiple demonstrable factual errors, yet from everything we have seen, Urtubie acting 'on his own authority' would certainly have been in character.[131]

The bishop's denunciation of Urtubie receives support from an unlikely source. In 1611, Inesa de Gajén was unfortunate enough to be arrested for witchcraft for a second time. This arrest took place at the Spanish fortress of Hondarribia, just across the Bidasoa river, where the authorities discovered that she was still carrying the papers of her original acquittal in France. Gajén, who apparently had lived in Hondarribia for seven years, readily admitted that she had been prosecuted for witchcraft in Hendaye, a village which traditionally had been an annexe to Urrugne and part of Urtubie's domain.[132] Urtubie had locked her up in a dungeon before she – like the Saint-Jean-de-Luz witches – was shipped to Bordeaux. Her trial ended in the same way as that of Jean de Goyetche above, with her case remitted to the présidial court in Dax where she was released.[133] Gajén's first trial is not dated, but the similarities suggest that it may have moved in tandem with that of the Saint-Jean-de-Luz accused, which would date it to the spring of 1607. Bishop Venegas's testimony presents Urtubie's actions as a preamble to those of the royal commission, suggesting perhaps a somewhat later date. Urtubie would act as one of the sponsors of the witchcraft commission; it seems that these events merged in the bishop's mind.

There are hints in the archives that the commission's other future sponsor, Amou, was also getting into the witch-hunting business around this time. In October 1608, the city council of Bayonne gave permission to a certain Auger de Ségure to use their prison to house five Lapurdi women accused of witchcraft.[134] They referred to Ségure as the 'self-described [*soy disans*] *assesseur criminel* of the territory of the Labourd', as if they were not entirely convinced by his credentials.[135] The position of *assesseur criminel* roughly translates as assistant criminal judge, so his authority ultimately derived from Amou's as the territory's *bailli*. Ségure would later provide some services to Espagnet and de Lancre which place him in Saint-Pée, Amou's principal residence.[136] Almost instantly, Bayonne's aldermen regretted their act of goodwill. Ségure did not remove the prisoners over Christmas as he had promised (when presumably they had hoped to close it for a well-earned break).[137] More importantly, the *assesseur criminel* also failed to provide the funds for the women's sustenance. By March 1609, one had already died 'of misery' while the others were dying of hunger.[138] The Bayonne councillors won the inevitable lawsuit in Bordeaux but were denied any compensation because, as their lawyer put it, they needed to be taught a lesson and 'no longer lend out their prison to anyone'.[139] The four surviving women awaited the arrival of the 1609 witchcraft commission, but their ultimate fate is unknown.[140] The Labourd was also terrorized during the summer of 1608 by a thief who, dressed as the devil, woke up sleeping shepherds and scared them into handing over their best sheep. He used 'certain spells' and 'enchantments' to make sleeping guard dogs lie and was hanged in Bayonne in December 1608.[141]

By late 1608, the witchcraft suspects themselves were on the move, possibly because news of further action against witchcraft was brewing. When María de Ximildegui arrived at the Spanish village of Zugarramurdi in December 1608, she may not have been the first to cross the border. She certainly would not be the last. Witchcraft suspects from both sides would cross the border to escape justice. Pierre de Lancre later likened such refugees to 'bad pieces of furniture for which we need to create no inventory'.[142] Yet, María's travails before her arrival in Spain also indicate how knowledge and thus fear of witchcraft had spread with the witches themselves. She had lived in Ciboure, Saint-Jean-de-Luz's smaller rival across the river Nivelle, and had travelled to a parish priest in Hendaye to obtain absolution – the same priest whom the Saint-Jean-de-Luz officials had hoped to visit during the summer of 1607.[143] The extent to which María de Ximildegui was actually regarded as a witch is debatable. Her age and her later testimony to the Spanish inquisitors make her akin to teenage witnesses such as Catherine de La Masse, Marguerite de Hareder and those later interviewed by de Lancre, victims of witchcraft rather than witches themselves. By the time the commission arrived, there would be many more like her.

Whether they were intending to get María away from witches or from future judges, her parents' decision to send her away was a sensible one, even though it ultimately helped spread fear and misery in Spanish Navarre.[144] By October 1608, with witches imprisoned in Bayonne, further action against witchcraft at the Lapurdi level appeared inevitable. It was around this time that the Biltzar, the assembly of representatives from the Labourd's parishes, charged the territory's two noblemen, Amou and Urtubie, with the task of petitioning the king for a royal commission. This outcome seems logical given the experiences of Saint-Jean-de-Luz so far and harked back to a long Basque tradition of petitioning for such witchcraft missions. Where the 1605 judges engaged in little more than fact finding, the territory was petitioning for the next commission to have 'sovereign' power.[145] As the king's letters patent later made clear, the witchcraft commission was to all intents and purposes a time-limited mini-Parlement of its own.[146] The normal wheels of justice were too cumbersome and unwieldy to cope with the witchcraft problem, and the commission was an attempt to cut through the legal red tape.

The petition for a royal commission, therefore, also reflected the high cost of French justice and the extent to which it had frustrated persecutions so far. When, in February 1609, the French crown insisted that the Bordeaux Parlement register its edict forthwith, it mentioned the costs of the appeals, the transport of prisoners to the metropole 'and the other great ensuing inconveniences and expenses'.[147] This had been the aim from the outset. The Labourd's poorer communities were taking proactive action to manage their liabilities and promote the commission as a cost-effective solution. On 17 November 1608, aldermen from the communities of Urrugne, Hendaye and Ciboure appeared before their big-city counterparts in Bayonne. They explained that the commission was meant 'to avoid the great cost and expense which such a pursuit would have caused if it had been done in the normal way'. The communities successfully asked Bayonne to join the pursuit and use its influence at court. And while they solemnly declared to exempt the city from any of the costs, we have learned to take such promises with a grain of salt.[148] Whether Espagnet and de Lancre proved to be as cost-effective as the communities had hoped is an open question. The only document pertaining to the witch-hunt to survive in the Ciboure archives is a receipt for a negligible sum of money that the community paid out only under protest and at the express command of the two commissioners.[149]

Delegating the petition to Amou, as *bailli* or governor of the territory, made sense. Urtubie's presence, however, may surprise us as he held no official position. Perhaps, the prominence of Hendaye and Urrugne, two villages within his domain, in pushing for the commission played a role. We have, of course, no way of divining Urtubie's thinking. His actions so far – assisting relatives accused of witchcraft while pursuing witches himself – suggest that the factions in this conflict cannot straightforwardly be divided into those of witchcraft sceptics and zealots. A cynical take would be that, as an agent of chaos, Urtubie stood to benefit from the instability regardless of the outcome. His role as one of the commission's 'promoters' also raised his standing within the territory.[150] Urtubie's support for the commission certainly fits with his general approach of combining violence and the law to further his own ends. Married to the daughter of a Bordeaux judge, Urtubie appreciated the possibilities of legal action. In fact, the original decree had tasked only a single Bordeaux judge with sorting out the witchcraft problem, someone related to Urtubie by marriage. His name: Pierre de Lancre.

There are two reasons, then, why we must temporarily leave the Pays de Labourd. We need to turn to Paris and the wider geopolitics of the years 1608 and 1609 if we are to understand why the petition for a royal commission was approved. Given the slow and costly wheels of normal French justice, the witch-hunt of 1609 would not have happened without this royal commission, and it likely would never have been granted to any other territory. Yet, even more urgently, we should head to Bordeaux. We must examine Pierre de Lancre as an important actor and our principal source for what follows, and we need to get the proper measure of his colleagues in the Parlement, who have been held up as his heroic sceptical opponents for far too long.

PART TWO
# Outsiders

# Chapter 3
# Judging the judges

Justice, for Pierre de Lancre, was like a palm tree, which carries its fruit and leaves in the same way, nobly at the top of its stem. Palm trees were also, he wrongly believed, indestructible and almost age-less. Like these trees, 'judges must justly carry the leaves and fruits of their offices; they should be incorruptible, and they should not let their holy desire of dispensing Justice to each in all equity and righteousness grow old'. True justice was a blessing from God, and good judges never forget that they ruled in front of Him, 'this great Judge who sees and hears everything'. As judges, they were almost participating in the divine: 'it is a beautiful thing being a judge and being just, especially to exercise justice justly is a totally divine thing.' Corrupt judges, by contrast, were like birds of prey, soaring high in the sky but with their eyes fixed firmly to the ground below.[1] Was de Lancre a palm tree or a hawk? If the former, did he drop the occasional coconut? We must ask this question before we turn to examine the witchcraft commission, but the answer will take a few chapters to unfold because we also need to get to know his colleagues better.

De Lancre's exalted depiction of early modern French justice was one of the many things he shared with his Bordeaux colleagues. Other magistrates or *robins*, as they were commonly called (after their ostentatious robes), also considered justice a 'Holy thing'.[2] In his standard 1617 work on the Parlements, Bernard de La Roche Flavin likened them to the Roman Senate, describing the courts as 'the soul, reason, and intelligence of the commonwealth'. La Roche Flavin traced their origins to the beginnings of the monarchy, when the first kings 'created assemblies of lords and barons of the kingdom to advise and consult on the affairs of state and justice' and, more indirectly (and implausibly), to a 'council of druids' that existed when Julius Caesar invaded Gaul.[3] Key to the dignity of the Parlements was the fact that, as the highest courts in the land, they were 'sovereign'. The courts reflected, took part in and carried out the royal will – or at least, they claimed to. The faithful exercise of justice was the king's most sacred duty; the biblical image of the king as judge was a recurring theme in France's coronation ceremony.[4] The Parlements accordingly were more than mere courts: they also registered royal edicts and claimed for themselves the right to scrutinize them.[5] The self-regard of the Bordeaux court was so high that one of its magistrates (very improbably) recorded King Henry IV as saying that 'if he had not been king, he would like to have been councillor of the Court of the Parlement of Bordeaux'.[6]

These sovereign judges also insisted on their nobility. It was commonly agreed that the judges were noble by reason of their office – they needed to be in order to judge any noblemen who appeared before them. Yet, they were also noble because the judges had said so themselves; they even extended their *ex officio* nobility to their offspring in their rulings.[7] They were, therefore, much more than mere state employees. The judges owned their offices and could buy or sell them at will, with the cash-strapped crown making a tidy sum by creating and selling new ones. From 1604, a special tax called the *Paulette* even made offices hereditary. Its payment prevented the office from reverting to the crown if the holder died unexpectedly. Its introduction followed stories about unscrupulous heirs keeping judges on their deathbed 'alive' or pickled in salt long enough to rush through any sale or transfer.[8]

Pierre de Lancre was a proud member of this elite legal community, famed especially in Bordeaux's case for its literary pretensions. His colleagues were the intended audience of his *Tableau*, which at times lapsed into dense legalese. Phrases such as 'to instruct a fuller inquiry' (which, in fact, usually meant release without charge) would be immediately obvious to this desired readership, but not to us.[9] De Lancre's description of the Basque country and its people – and the apparent gulf that separates them from him – reflects his high self-worth as a member of this noble tribe of semi-divine office holders. (This exalted status was suitably upheld and confirmed when the devil tried to assault de Lancre in his sleep and failed.) Historians have thus far been keen to present de Lancre as an outlier among his peers. The judges, it was claimed, resisted his appointment because they 'knew better than anyone his fanaticism, his cold cruelty, and utter contempt of the Basques'. One historian even claimed that the witch-hunt was a secret rescue mission devised by the Parlement aimed at transporting most of the accused witches to Bordeaux and out of harm's way. The occasional execution was the necessary price for this humanitarianism (burn 'a few hapless victims at the stake – they would have been burned anyway').[10] None of these arguments are remotely plausible. They stem from a deeply felt need to make sceptical elite heroes out of de Lancre's colleagues. The traditional narrative offers a compelling morality tale which requires responsibility for the witch-hunt to be consolidated in de Lancre's hands. In that reading, the opposition of other elite men is highly desirable. If we ever hope to restore agency to the witches of the Labourd, unshackled from the *Tableau*, then we must go down the opposite path. The chapters that follow instead focus on what de Lancre shared: with his peers in Bordeaux and with his senior colleague, Jean d'Espagnet, who led the mission to the Basque country.

## Sounding like a judge

The pretensions – and claims to real political power – of the Bordeaux Parlement were symbolized by its residence, the medieval Palais de l'Ombrière, from which the English had once ruled the city (see Figure 3.1). Surviving representations show it dominating the Bordeaux skyline just as its magistrates dominated the city's political and intellectual life.[11] While not as ancient or as prestigious as its Paris and Toulouse counterparts, the court's jurisdiction covered most of France's southwest, extending across the Atlantic coast from the Labourd in the south to nearly as far as La Rochelle in the north.[12] The opening of the Parlement every year on 12 November, the day after Saint Martin's Day, was a public occasion, accompanied by a solemn Mass, for which the magistrates donned their most official 'red robes'.[13]

Étienne de Cruseau, the diarist among the judges, faithfully recorded the elaborate opening orations by the court's first president. They give a sense of how the Parlement's legal, intellectual and literary aspirations intersected. In 1606, for instance, President Guillaume Daffis attributed the recent plague and

**Figure 3.1** The Palais de l'Ombrière. Nineteenth-century engraving. (Bordeaux, Bibliothèque municipale, Delpit 23/57.)

harvest failures to 'the lack of justice, which had not been accompanied by charity', and he discoursed marvellously about the shortage of fruit:

> For this reason he discussed the abundance of Egypt caused by the inundation of the Nile and passed on to the oracle to the people of Delos who should double the size of their altar to Apollo. He finally concluded that we too should double the square and cube of the altar of our justice to end the contagious plague and languishing famine.[14]

While the flowery rhetoric, meandering classical borrowings and elaborate metaphors may undercut the sincerity of such moral reflections, they elicited praise from Cruseau and imitation by de Lancre.[15] Our judge would adopt a very similar writing style, and he would incorporate a similarly rambling perambulation by Daffis on the reality of werewolves in his witchcraft *Tableau*.[16]

This type of imaginative writing for its own sake has a long tradition within the august halls of France's Parlements, but it is perhaps most associated with *La Puce de Madame Des-Roches* (The Flea of Madame Des Roches, 1582), the early modern equivalent of a poetry slam that originated when a group of Paris judges were sent to Poitiers in 1579 – 'to banish dreadful evil from Poitou / to dispense justice to all in equal weight', as a sonnet by their leader, Étienne Pasquier, had it. Two local women, Catherine and Madeleine des Roches, ran a highly regarded local literary salon. As he later recounted, the judge was about to be defeated by Catherine, 'one of France's most learned and wisest women', running out of material in a poetic match-up, when 'a flea came to land right in the middle of her bosom'.[17] This mundane event seemingly launched a thousand poems providing endless fodder for Parisian judges to wax lyrical about the flea and its well-chosen environment in French, Latin and Greek (to which Catherine then replied).[18] Much like Daffis's orations, *La Puce* poems show how the consummate mastery of French (and, secondarily, Latin and Greek) defined a robin's nobility and worth. The art of persuasion stood at the heart of the legal metier, while the Parlements were, by their very name, places not just for speaking (*parler*) but conferring together (*parlementer* or *pourparler*).[19] This was especially true in Bordeaux, where the Parlement had established itself as the city's *foyer de culture*, its cultural and intellectual centre, even before the publication of Michel de Montaigne's *Essays* (1580).[20] The Paris printer of *La Puce*, Abel L'Angelier, had his bookshop located within the galleries of the Parlement's palace and published works by the luminaries of all the sovereign courts, including Montaigne.[21] In 1607, Pierre de Lancre, a literary late bloomer in his early fifties, would join their ranks when the printer published his first work, a wordy philosophical treatise which he (unhelpfully for us) also called a *Tableau*.

One genre to which de Lancre's witchcraft *Tableau* belonged was firmly legal in nature: that of the published *arrêts mémorables* or 'notable judgements'.

The first and certainly the most famous – then and now – of these *arrêts* was published in 1561 by Jean de Coras, a councillor of the Toulouse Parlement.[22] That case was one of imposture, with some Basque roots. A pretender – later identified as Arnaud du Tilh – had persuaded the family and wife of Martin Guerre that he was their missing relative who had abruptly left to go to war eight years earlier. He was not successfully unmasked until the sensational return of the 'real' Martin just as the judges were trying to reach their verdict.[23] Historians, following the trailblazing work of Natalie Zemon Davis, have long focused on the agency and perspectives of protagonists such as Martin's wife Bertrande de Rols (who seems to have preferred the imposter over the real version), just as this book attempts to recover those of the inhabitants of the Labourd. Yet, Coras's interest in recounting the tale lies elsewhere. For Coras, the judgement was a 'prodigious history' (*histoire prodigieuse*) – indeed, as he later clarified, it was 'the greatest, most extraordinary, most remarkable' tale of deception 'that one could read in any history, whether Greek or Latin, ancient or modern'.[24] Coras chose to publish the *histoire* for the same reason de Lancre published the *Tableau* fifty years on, because he thought it made for a good story and it allowed him to display his erudition, in the form of 'one hundred beautiful and learned annotations'. While some were relevant – discussing, for instance, why the fake 'Martin' might have lost the ability to speak Basque – others were free-flowing discussions about the nature of friendship or the love that wives should feel for their husbands.[25] Much like de Lancre's *Tableau* before us but on a smaller scale, Coras's *Arrêt mémorable* underlines the importance of studying the judge – and the storyteller – before studying the trial, even when the return of the real Martin Guerre meant that in that case little judging needed to be done.

Coras and de Lancre both wrote to share their remarkable, exciting and entertaining discoveries with their equally erudite readers. In a more haphazard manner than Coras, de Lancre wove official documents – sworn testimony, Daffis's *arrêt* about werewolves, an account of the *auto de fe* in Logroño – into his *Tableau* and used them as a launching pad for digressions that validated his membership of this world of parlementary *belles lettres*. Eloquent pens like de Lancre's are not simply beguiling, they are also dangerous. One modern editor of the *Tableau* was so struck by the 'elegance' of de Lancre's prose that he seemingly lost sight of the fact that this 'work of a lifetime' was built on the deaths of others.[26] The transformation of legal cases into stories recounted *for* pleasure and *as* shows of learning was fundamentally dehumanizing. In the case of Pasquier and the other judges visiting Poitiers, their imagination was more exercised by a single flea than any person who appeared before them.

The high status and even higher self-regard of France's senior magistrates shaped de Lancre's view of the Basque country as an exotic and fundamentally alien space, which was almost as opposed to all that was proper and French as the demonic netherworld itself. The archetype of de Lancre as a cruel, zealous and bigoted witch-hunter obscures an ugly truth: that even the act of recounting his witch-hunt brought de Lancre pleasure. This unpleasant elite mentality presents us with other insights as well. Coras's prejudices, as Natalie Zemon Davis famously showed, caused him to be blind to Bertrande's role feeding her new and improved husband important background information.[27] The *Tableau*, too, often reveals more than the author realized.

Of course, not everyone shared the judges' positive assessment of their Parlements. The crown did not. French kings grew increasingly less tolerant of the Parlements' claim to scrutinize the royal will. They increasingly resorted to expedients to enforce the registration of their edicts, and in 1667, Louis XIV stripped the courts of their 'sovereign' title altogether.[28] As a man of war, Henry IV had little patience for legal niceties and his relationship with his Parlements was often tense.[29] As a former governor of Guyenne, he knew the Bordeaux magistrates particularly well – and he certainly would never have wanted to join their court.[30] In January 1608, after the Parlement had resisted no fewer than twelve direct orders to register an edict that would have increased the court's fees and thus royal revenues, the king pointedly recollected the many slights that the 'wicked Company' had inflicted on him when he was still merely the (Protestant) claimant to the throne. 'All my Parlements are worthless,' Henry told a Bordeaux delegation, 'but you are the worst of all.'

The king's 1608 diatribe accused the judges of unseemly self-enrichment: 'Is there a peasant whose vines do not belong to a president or councillor? One only has to be a councillor to be rich instantly.'[31] This alternate image of justice corrupted by profit-seeking resonated in wider society. It reflected both the negative perceptions of the sale of offices and the high costs of going to court.[32] The Bordeaux poet Eustorg de Beaulieu even penned a satire which presented his own 'diabolical' legal troubles over an inheritance as an encounter with Lucifer, the prince of darkness, himself. Beaulieu's criticisms focused, as the king's did, on costs and delays ('Flee these pleas, for they are an expense / for which grief is the only recompense').[33] Such criticisms reflect a fundamental aspect of elite French justice: official salaries were enhanced by *épices*, charges paid by the litigants directly to the judges, which did nothing to encourage the swift resolution of legal cases.[34] These two factors – the magistrates' right to remonstrate with the king and their investment in their offices – will also be essential to understanding the Parlement's seemingly frosty reception of the royal letters authorizing the witchcraft commission.

# What to do with witches

One straightforward way to separate de Lancre from his Bordeaux colleagues has been to emphasize their supposed witchcraft scepticism. The sceptical attitude of the Paris Parlement is well known – it even annoyed de Lancre in one of his later works – but it was not necessarily shared by its provincial counterparts.[35] The Parlement of Rouen treated witchcraft with particular severity.[36] Unfortunately, where the records of other Parlements have often survived exceptionally well, those of Bordeaux have been substantially lost through fire and negligence.[37] Two arguments, however, have been advanced in favour of the Bordeaux court's supposed scepticism: the absence of evidence and the enduring influence of Michel de Montaigne's mild spirit.[38]

It has been claimed therefore that the Bordeaux court was 'a bastion of parlementary scepticism' because the earliest reference to a conviction dates back to 1594, 'later than any other provincial [P]arlement'.[39] We know of this particular case for the same reason we know of Martin Guerre and the Basque witch-hunt: because it was remarkable and a judge decided to discuss this *histoire prodigieuse* in print.[40] In February that year, the Parlement heard the case of Jeanne Bosdeau from the inland region of Limousin on appeal. What interested Florimond de Raemond – one of the court's many *literati* and, as it happens, de Lancre's brother-in-law – was Bosdeau's elaborate description of the witches' sabbat, which he incorporated in his 1597 *L'Antichrist*, a polemical work about the approaching End Times.[41] Bosdeau's descriptions are nearly as remarkable and fantastic as those encountered by the commissioners in the Labourd fifteen years later, and de Lancre, who had been involved in the case as well, certainly regarded it as a precedent. The trial also impressed Étienne Cruseau, the judge and diarist, who recorded details that the pious Raemond omitted.[42] (Perhaps *déjà vu* explains Cruseau's subsequent lack of interest in Basque witchcraft.)

As a young girl, Bosdeau had been seduced by an Italian magician. He introduced her to the devil who appeared, as he often does in witchcraft trials, as a goat, though in this case, with a burning candle between his horns. Jeanne was among the first to describe the sabbat as a Black Mass, an elaborate inversion of Catholic ritual, as Basque witches later would as well. A person wearing priestly vestments – Bosdeau had accused a local curate, but the devout Raemond omitted that fact – said Mass 'in their fashion, with the back turned towards the altar'. A burnt black root substituted for the white Eucharist, water for communion wine and the devil's urine for holy water. Raemond praised Bosdeau's 'remarkable frankness and innocence ... for a peasant woman, she was articulate, continuously persisting into the fire'.[43] The case made an impact on de Lancre. The 1613 sabbat engraving he commissioned included a depiction of the devil as a goat with a light burning between his horns (Figure 3.2).[44]

The Bosdeau trial was sensational, but it was hardly the first. One local chronicle reported cases of witchcraft as early as 1429, when Bordeaux was still under English rule.[45] The 1582 witchcraft commission to Biarritz offers a more recent precedent, set at a time when witchcraft cases were clearly on

**Figure 3.2** The devil as a goat on a throne, vignette from the 1613 sabbat engraving.

the rise across Europe. Even the famed humanist Michel de Montaigne, whose mildness has often been invoked, toned down his witchcraft scepticism in his *Essays* in the early 1590s.[46] Raemond, who had purchased Montaigne's seat at the Bordeaux court, lamented that the prisons were filled with witches: 'not a day passes that our judgements are not bloody and we return to our houses sad, afraid of the hideous and dreadful things the witches confess.'[47] The judge was exaggerating but not lying. The court heard at least two witchcraft cases in 1593, both on appeal from the Basque country. On 16 January, the court ordered the release of Navarrine de La Borde, originally from Anglet but living in Bayonne, apparently after she maintained her innocence during torture.[48] Two months later, on 14 March, the judges ordered an unnamed female witch from the Basque-speaking province of Soule to be 'hanged and strangled' and her body burnt to ashes.[49]

The demonic did not abate after that. In 1595, the Bordeaux court permitted a tenant to end the lease of a property that was haunted by a spirit in the shape of a small boy.[50] In 1603, the court sentenced a teenager, Jean Grenier, to life imprisonment for lycanthropy – at age thirteen, he was likely the youngest person ever to be convicted as a werewolf.[51] The case fascinated de Lancre, who would interview Grenier upon his return from the Labourd as another curiosity for inclusion in his *Tableau*. When de Lancre was assigned to the Tournelle, the court's criminal chamber, in November 1608, it proved a good preparation for the Basque witch-hunt.[52] The court sentenced two witches that term, both of them male. One of the executions took place only a month before Espagnet and de Lancre departed for the Basque country.[53]

Devil talk even affected the Parlement itself. A chronicle composed by one councillor reported on a golden-tongued lawyer, versed in the black arts, who failed to impress the Bordeaux judges and set himself up as an alchemist instead.[54] Rumours also centred on the physician, a Scotsman named Andrew MacRedor, who had been hired to look after 'sick poor patients' in the Parlement's prison. He was reputed by several to have been a magician, including de Lancre who insinuated that the good doctor used 'the thousand despairs' he found among those imprisoned to encourage 'the making of execrable agreements with Satan'.[55] And while de Lancre believed he had survived the devil's attempts to harm or ensnare him, other judges were not so lucky. When all the members of an investigative commission to the seaside town of Teste-de-Buch died within a year of their return, witches ('of which there are a great many in those parts') were rumoured to have been at work.[56]

The scepticism of the Bordeaux court, then, is vastly overstated, but it is still true that de Lancre tried to push his peers in a more zealous direction. When de Lancre discussed the court's jurisprudence in witchcraft matters, he cited the Bosdeau case and others as precedent, but above all, he advanced his own handiwork: 'so that there will be no more doubts as to whether the Parlements condemn [witches] to death or not, in this year 1609 the court of the Parlement of Bordeaux condemned an infinite number of them.'[57] De Lancre presented the commission's work as judgements by the *entire* Bordeaux Parlement, and as a model for all sovereign courts. It was a daring claim; perhaps only a self-proclaimed palm tree of justice would dream of making it. The high self-regard does not bode well for those who appeared before him.

# Chapter 4
# Throwing roosters at lions

Pierre de Lancre believed in many things. He believed that elephants were smart and that they could even be taught to write in ancient Greek.[1] He also believed that they were afraid of swine and chameleons.[2] When aggravated, these noble animals could be calmed by the sight of a sheep, just as lions were by a flattering, flavoursome monkey.[3] He believed particularly strongly that the rooster's crow caused lions and serpents extreme pain and allowed that they possibly hurt demons as well.[4] In the spring of 1612, a visit to Cardinal de Sourdis unexpectedly provided the opportunity to test one of these natural antipathies. The archbishop of Bordeaux had the Spanish painter Luís Pascual Gaudin working with him at his home. (De Lancre described the little-known Gaudin as 'so excellent … that the wealthiest kings and potentates of the world run after a work from his hands' but he had clearly forgotten his name.) How the subject came up is unclear, but the painter, a devout Carthusian monk, buzzed with excitement when he learned that Bordeaux was home to an actual lion – drawing this noble animal would help him prepare a portrait of St Jerome, the church father who was typically represented with one. De Lancre seized the opportunity, as he proudly reported in his *Tableau*. The lion was summoned and, in front of an audience of over a hundred spectators, a white rooster was repeatedly thrown into its cage. Twice it landed on the lion's head, once between its paws. Yet, the noble animal never moved, however much the distressed rooster cried out in its attempts to escape. Only when it landed between its legs, did the lion deign to give the lucky bird a bit of a push.[5]

With this experiment, the judge took part in a tradition of testing and observing that was by then more than a century old. Naturalists had been subjecting Pliny the Elder's *Natural History*, de Lancre's classical source of knowledge (or credulity) about the animal kingdom, to detailed scrutiny since the 1490s.[6] The publication of this vast compendium of ancient knowledge about the natural world helped revive the tradition of natural history, dedicated to collecting, organizing and observing the physical world in all its diversity. As a scientific tradition, natural history privileged the rare, the monstrous and the prodigious as sources not just (or no longer) of horror but also of wonder, curiosity and delight.[7] The subject inspired vast collections of wonders, both natural and handmade. As a young man, de Lancre visited the two most famous of these during his Grand Tour of Italy: the celebrated cabinets of curiosities of Ulisse Aldrovandi in Bologna and Ferrante Imperato in Naples. He recalled searching them in vain for the dried body of a basilisk, the mythical serpent that kills its prey with a single glance, among 'the hundred thousand other rare things that they put before our eyes'.[8] Given their wider contents – they contained 'dragons' and other wondrous creatures – it was reasonable to assume that the two naturalists would have collected a basilisk if they could.[9]

Unable to properly explain the mysterious powers of serpents, chickens and lions, de Lancre invoked 'some secret antipathy with which Nature herself infused all animate and inanimate objects'.[10] Strange though they might seem, such hidden and occult sympathies and antipathies were a normal part of early modern science.[11] The belief that humans could manipulate such occult forces for themselves sustained a vibrant tradition of natural magic, which was especially associated with the Neapolitan philosopher Giambattista della Porta, whose 1558 *Magia naturalis* was filled with potions and recipes. When a young de Lancre visited Naples, he 'often' sought out Della Porta who 'showed us marvellous things drawn from nature'.[12] The lines between natural history and magic were blurred. Perhaps, the most famous natural historian, Francis Bacon, wrote a treatise on sympathies and antipathies in nature, while his posthumous *Sylva Sylvarum* was an attempt to reclaim natural magic from those who had abused the tradition.[13] Positioning the *Tableau* – and the activities on which it was based – within this context of empirical investigation and the testing of received truths reshapes our view of both the Basque witch-hunt and de Lancre's relationship with his fellow commissioner, Jean d'Espagnet, who rather famously dabbled in alchemy. It also suggests that we should look again at what de Lancre's supposed credulity really means and the emotions that his *Tableau* were meant to evoke.

## From credulity to experimentation

Credulity is a problematic concept. De Lancre's investigations of lions, roosters and basilisks may point to his unusual gullibility, but if it does, he was by no means alone. We should situate his witchcraft investigations in a wider culture of experimentation and observation. Law and science overlapped in the early modern period. As lord chancellor of England, Francis Bacon also held high legal office and the impact of his legal training on his views on the interpretation and 'interrogation' (even torture) of nature is well known.[14] Conversely, lawyers who discussed witchcraft had to establish not only its criminality but also whether it was even possible in *nature*. A surviving 1573 pleading before the Paris Parlement against a popular healer of witchcraft, for instance, cited Pliny's *Natural History* on the medicine and magic supposedly once practiced by French druids.[15]

One obstacle may be the common perception that demonology and natural magic – or witchcraft and science – were two opposing forms of causation as antithetical as roosters and lions. It is true that the boasts of a Renaissance *magus* like Della Porta readily exposed them to the charge of having made a demonic pact. Yet, perhaps paradoxically, demonic magic also required its natural counterpart to function – demonology needed the existence of secret properties hidden within nature because demons used them to work their wonders.[16] Similarly, nothing prevented natural magicians and historians from discussing witches alongside other prodigies and advancing natural explanations for their powers. Giambattista della Porta got into trouble for providing the recipe for a witches' ointment which allegedly caused those who applied it to hallucinate and *think* they had flown to the sabbat.[17] While Bacon attributed much of witches' alleged powers to their diseased faculties, he also suggested that these were due to their 'greedily eat[ing] Mens flesh [which] may send up High and Pleasing Vapours [and] may stirre the imagination'.[18]

While both the *Tableau* and the witchcraft commission were foremost legal in nature, both make a great deal more sense when we also view them through a naturalist lens. For instance, it was in the context of the witches' potion that de Lancre mentioned Della Porta, and he proceeded to investigate its nature, composition and use in detail, just as the Neapolitan magician would have done. While law – like science – is about establishing the truth, the witchcraft commissioners sought out details about the demonic netherworld far in excess of what was required for them to reach a verdict about the witches they interrogated.[19] Upon his return from the Basque country, de Lancre went to interview Jean Grenier, the teen wolf that the Parlement had confined to a Franciscan convent for life, and he examined the young man's body for signs of his werewolf past. These investigations do not make de Lancre a trained naturalist, and the *Tableau* is certainly not structured in the way that natural histories typically were.[20] (It is hardly structured at all.) But de Lancre still approached the world with a naturalist's sensibility and with a fascination for occult properties that never wavered. And if de Lancre did not belong to the inner sanctum of early modern naturalists, his senior colleague Jean d'Espagnet did.

The experiment with the rooster and the lion also points to another crossroads on which we must place Pierre de Lancre's witchcraft investigations: between ancient texts and first-hand observations. This is where the value of the *Tableau* lay. It was a vast storehouse providing (exciting!) new information that could be added to the pool of existing knowledge. In his preface to the reader, de Lancre repeatedly declared himself 'content' to simply make public 'the simple confessions of witches and the depositions of witnesses'. On the question of whether witches travelled bodily to the sabbat or in their imagination, de Lancre claimed he would only add to established knowledge what he had discovered because he did not want to be 'boring' – he did not want to 'cite the same authors and compile full sheets of paper'. He similarly noted an established consensus about the main features of the witches' sabbat, 'which is why I will simply report what we have learned through our procedures and will simply say what several notable witches have deposed before us without changing or altering their deposition so that everyone can take from it what they please'.[21] This offer of adding new data to established knowledge – often introduced or concluded with a simple *voici* or *voilà* – was very much in keeping with the practices of collecting and the 'cult of the fact' that defined natural history.[22]

The relation between established knowledge and new discoveries was not always clear-cut. Novelty – and the excitement that comes with it – justified de Lancre's book project. The preface informed the reader that during the commission, 'an infinity of unknown things, strange and beyond all belief, happened about which the books which have discussed the topic have never spoken'. The witch-hunt uncovered new facts, but de Lancre was loath to abandon established, often classical ideas. The two forms of experiential and textual knowledge could sit next to each other, as inert and impassive as two objects in a cabinet of curiosities. A survey of the rooster in classical sources, for instance, ended with a vaguely dismissive 'but returning to our witches, here is what we have seen and learned ourselves and which we consider to be more certain'.[23] At other times, however, experiential data trumped or at least nuanced the textual record. This testing of new observations against old information produced new entangled, more uncertain forms of knowledge, which preserved the truth of *both* text and observation. De Lancre's discussion of roosters and lions offers a case in point. The judge did not reject Pliny's claims about the lion's vulnerabilities. Possibly, the lion survived because the rooster was making the wrong sounds – not its typical cock-a-doodle-doo but cries of fear. Alternatively, the bird's powers might reside in its 'sunny eyes' rather than its crows, which made it unfortunate that the lion was evidently too bored to open its own.[24] This type of fence sitting was not unusual. Sixteenth- and early-seventeenth-century naturalists, however critical of Pliny's errors, had not given up on the idea of so-called *prisca theologia*, the possible existence of true knowledge hidden in ancient texts that could be unlocked if only the right key was found.[25] De Lancre's reluctance to reject any knowledge as outdated did go further than most of his peers – because for him, it could *all* be true. The devil was slippery. Yet, this dialectic between received wisdom and new knowledge, with the latter nuancing, reshaping and enhancing the meaning of the former, was common to many areas of scientific endeavour from alchemy to mapmaking.[26]

There is a fine line, then, between credulity and curiosity. Our expectations about what a witch-hunter is meant to be like have blinded us to the many emotions at work in the *Tableau*, a text filled with excitement and wonder which exoticized human beings and made them into objects worthy of preservation in a cabinet of curiosities. This means that we need to explore de Lancre's truth criteria further – after all, they were literally a matter of life and death. But we should also note how a focus on de Lancre's credulity, his willingness to believe, cements his traditional position as the central villain by consolidating agency in his hands. Like a good magic trick, asking why his witnesses were *believed* obscures their role and diverts our gaze away from other questions: why were these teenagers testifying at all, and how did their evidence come into being? Those are questions for later. We are not quite done yet with the *Tableau* as a fundamentally emotional text.

## The wondrous world of secrets

Conceiving the *Tableau* as, in part, a work of 'scientific' inquiry helps us interpret the work's rich and diverse register of emotions. Casting de Lancre as a bigoted, credulous witch-hunter requires the *Tableau* to be drenched in a language of piety and horror, which steadfastly expresses the shamefulness of what had been discovered. One can, admittedly, find selected passages to prove that de Lancre 'constantly emphasized the distastefulness of the task in which he was engaged'.[27] He was at times acutely aware that too much interest in the demonic was unseemly, if not problematic. In the preface, he even protested that by reporting his discoveries, he did not want to 'act the witch or magician'. Nor did he want the *Tableau* to be an instruction manual for future witches: he did not want 'under the pretext of recounting simply what I have seen when I researched Satan's ruses to avoid their sinister effects, teach anyone how they are done'.

Highlighting such obligatory protestations rather misses the overall tone of the *Tableau* and the fact that its author secretly also relished both the investigations and the writing up a great deal. Halfway through his discussion of sex with the devil, de Lancre conceded that he feared writing about the topic 'because I will be considered still more shameless than they [the witches] are' – not that this concern stopped him. The need to instil modesty was perhaps the thinnest veneer for the judges' curiosity. Espagnet and de Lancre had their young witnesses re-enact the dances of the sabbat, ostensibly 'to deter them from such filth and to make them recognize how even the most modest movement was filthy, ugly and unbecoming an honest girl'.[28] Perhaps his lurid curiosity was called out. In his 1627 *Du sortilège* (On witchcraft), he included a lengthy discussion on 'whether it was better to hide and cover in silence the abominations and evils of magicians and witches than to discover and publish them', which argued that his discoveries, however shameful and pornographic, were all 'to the glory of God'.[29]

Expressions of horror and disgust, then, were obligatory notes but they are at best a minor key – and they never quite resonate as true. A contemporary description of the *Tableau* as containing 'things so strange and horrible that the hairs on the reader's head stand up straight' suggests that these emotions coexisted with an all-pervasive sense of wonder.[30] If de Lancre possessed a trademark phrase, it would be 'it is a marvel'. It was a 'wonder', for instance, that the devil wanted witches to only attend the sabbat where they lived.[31] De Lancre 'marvelled' [*je esmerveille*] that any woman would be willing to kiss the devil-goat on any part of its body, while it was also 'a wonder' that they enjoyed it.[32]

As an emotion, wonder was not unique to naturalist writing: it underpinned many other early modern genres, including two – ethnography and the *arrêts mémorables* – in which we already situated the *Tableau*. In fact, within early modern science, wonder – with its connotation of passive contemplation of the mysteries of God and the universe – mingled with and later gave way to curiosity, an emotion that the Middle Ages had associated with illicit knowledge (like magic) and regarded as a vice akin to greed.[33] We would expect a work like the *Tableau* to denounce curiosity as a forbidden desire used by the devil to tempt humans and lead them astray, and on occasion it does.[34] The *Tableau* once even – without apparent irony – warned that God would punish the 'pernicious curiosity' of judges who sought to examine the sabbat too closely. And yet, for the most part, the *Tableau* evinces the same type of mixture of wonder-turning-into-curiosity present in early modern scientific discourse. It was 'curiosity', for instance, that sparked the investigation of whether witches greased themselves with a potion to fly to the sabbat.[35]

In 1610, upon his return from the Basque country, he sought out the convicted werewolf Jean Grenier, spurred on by the same insatiable desire to know more.[36] The former teen wolf, now aged twenty or twenty-one, confessed that he missed eating human meat, especially that of young girls because it was 'the most tender'. For de Lancre, Grenier's appearance offered visual confirmation of his testimony. His teeth were longer and wider than normal and stuck out somewhat. The consumption of humans and animals had turned them half backwards. His nails had similarly gone completely black from the root up and had been half worn, 'which demonstrates clearly that he had been a werewolf and that he used his hands both for running and for grabbing children and dogs by their throats'. The reformed werewolf's ability to run on all fours reminded him of one of the Basque teenagers he had interviewed. The boy could have passed as a dog and had taken 'a singular pleasure' in showing off his skills to the judge. De Lancre even took him out to the garden where he jumped over a small ditch so easily that he could have been a greyhound.[37]

The judge's curiosity and his desire to test the marvellous moved beyond witches and werewolves as well. From the sixteenth to the nineteenth century, many visitors to Italy, including Mozart and Mark Twain, added a day excursion from Naples to the so-called Dog's Grotto near Pozzuoli. This cave contained noxious carbon dioxide fumes which made the air close to the floor poisonous. For centuries, locals made a busy trade selling small animals, notably dogs, to tourists interested in watching them asphyxiate.[38] (The animals were meant to be revived in a nearby lake.) For de Lancre, the wonder required testing as well as admiration. He went back a second time. His 'curiosity' about the cave's 'wondrous effect' led him to bring 'a particularly big and vigorous dog in order to avoid all supposition'.[39] The judge approached the Basque country in the same way, determined that it would yield its hidden secrets, the exposition of which was another key part of the language of early modern science.[40] De Lancre declared victory, claiming to have discovered 'the majority of the secrets of witchcraft and the sabbat' that had been hidden until then.[41] In 1630, a much-condensed German translation of the *Tableau* appeared under the telling title, the *Wunderbahrliche Geheimnussen der Zauberey* (The Marvellous Secrets of Witchcraft).[42] De Lancre, then, was a man on a scientific mission, keen to find out as much as possible. His fellow commissioner shared those interests.

# The alchemist's witch-hunt

Situating the *Tableau* within this context of scientific inquiry also helps us make sense of the participation of de Lancre's colleague, the noted alchemist Jean d'Espagnet. For most of the seventeenth and eighteenth centuries, Espagnet – not de Lancre – who would have been the better known of the two judges. His 1623 *Enchiridion physicae restitutae* (Summary of Physics Restored) was very different from natural history. Rather than collecting particulars, the *Enchiridion* was a work of natural philosophy which proceeded from a carefully numbered set of principles, the first of which was God. Written in elegant Latin, it came to strikingly original conclusions. It argued that Earth was just another celestial body like the moon and, as a result, 'what prevents us from believing that the moon has inhabitants of its own?'[43] The *Enchiridion* was accompanied by an alchemical treatise, the *Arcanum*, which promised instructions on how to produce a philosophers' stone, an object used for the transmutation of metals. Translated into English, French and German, Espagnet's works were considerably more successful than de Lancre's *Tableau*. In England, the *Enchiridion*'s imagery may have inspired Milton's *Paradise Lost*, while a young Isaac Newton copied down and decoded some of the *Arcanum*'s alchemical instructions.[44] In the later eighteenth century, Denis Diderot, the famed encyclopaedist, still honoured Espagnet as the 'chemical Cicero'.[45] When, in 1697, the early Enlightenment *philosophe* Pierre Bayle looked back on the seventeenth century, he had reason to praise Espagnet as 'one of the learned men' of that period, who had a taste for 'the new philosophy'. Yet, Bayle, with his trademark irony, could not help but undercut the compliment by adding a reference to the Basque witch-hunt to a footnote.[46]

Witchcraft historians have tended to minimize Espagnet's involvement in the witch-hunt. He is often depicted as a harmless eccentric, *un esprit éclairé* with his head in the clouds who was lost on an otherworldly alchemical quest.[47] A royal order for Espagnet to inspect the Franco-Spanish border, it is argued, must have given his junior colleague free rein. One scholar even speculated that Espagnet, one of the Parlement's presidents, left the Basque country early in order to bring the embarrassing witch-hunt to a premature end.[48] Having rescued their subject from the realm of the occult and repositioned it within the wider history of science, historians of alchemy have been just as happy to disclaim Espagnet's involvement in the witch-hunt.[49] They, too, 'hear [his] bureaucratic footdragging'.[50] They note that the men's careers 'diverged': de Lancre continued to write on witchcraft, 'while [Espagnet] was making friends in the scientific circle where [de] Lancre was spurned' – never mind the fact that the same Paris printer published the works of both men.[51] They also argued that witch-hunting and alchemy were radically distinct activities, and that Espagnet only fully turned to pursue the secrets of nature in retirement.[52] While the latter likely is true (Espagnet says as much in a preface), his interest in alchemy can be traced back to at least the winter of 1594–5.[53] There can be equally no doubt about Espagnet's involvement in the witch-hunt. The archival evidence shows the two commissioners working closely together. The border inspection similarly took no more than a week. Nor is there any evidence of the two men growing apart. As late as 1630, a year before his death, de Lancre named his former colleague as the executor of his will.[54]

Far from disqualifying him as an unworldly eccentric, Espagnet's scientific interests made him ideally suited to act as de Lancre's co-investigator. When we place the commission's activities in the Basque country within this context of experimentation and observation, then the questions the two men asked, the objects they examined and the places they visited all fall into place. Theirs was a quest to expose the wonderful secrets of witches and bring the high mysteries of witchcraft – demonic flight, animal transformations and especially the sabbat – into the open. This was, almost by definition, impossible. Witches and demons met in secret in the dead of night. Barring the occasional outside visitor, the sabbat was off-limits to non-witches. The commissioners, therefore, had to rely on 'an infinity of witches who had left the profession and on children who, like secret spies, attended every sabbat'. Yet, they did not settle for oral testimony alone. They also visited alleged sites of the witches' sabbat, and de Lancre triumphantly reported that they once identified the place where the pot had been kept from the indentation it had supposedly left behind ('the witches had moved it the night before'). They investigated the marks left by the devil on witches' bodies in painstaking and painful detail. To ascertain the ointment used for demonic flight, the judges even asked seventeen-year-old Marie Dindarte to 'leave and go up into the air' in front of them. When the young woman replied that she 'would go very well' if she had the right unguent, she was asked to bring some back from the sabbat the next time she went. (Sadly, the other witches would not give her any.) Although their investigations into the flying ointment were inconclusive, de Lancre claimed more success establishing the ingredients of their poisons ('about which we have discovered a great deal more and have learned their composition').[55]

Much about this exoticizing language of discovery is horrifying. It dehumanizes the victims of the witch-hunt by turning them into curiosities. Indeed, de Lancre commonly referred to his victims as 'our witches', and there is an unmistakable sense that, with the *Tableau*, he claimed them as marvels for his collection.[56] Yet, the same gaze that made the Basques less than human also explains why the commissioners accepted their testimony: because they were deemed incapable of dissembling. Michel de Montaigne, de Lancre's relative by marriage, memorably described a traveller who had returned from the New World as 'a simple, crude fellow – a character fit to bear true witness ... so simple that he has not the stuff to build up false inventions and give them plausibility'.[57] The commission's witnesses were not child-like, they often were children. De Lancre quoted the Roman philosopher Cicero who included 'childhood' among the human states or conditions that induce belief (alongside 'sleep, inadvertence, intoxication, and insanity').[58] For Cicero, small children – literally, *parvi*, 'little ones' – often spoke the truth because of their innocence because, like Montaigne's 'true witness', they did not understand its significance. De Lancre, however, introduced the Roman philosopher's testimony in a chapter which detailed sex with the devil to make a rather different point. What his teenagers testified to was so sordid that it had to be true: 'Although she was rather young, her youth makes her incapable of inventing something so filthy.'[59] The judge went on to discuss anal penetration by the devil next. These last comments also stray away from scientific curiosity. We have discussed what de Lancre may have shared with Espagnet and his fellow Bordeaux judges. But there are clearly depths to de Lancre's interests to which his colleagues did not sink and which we might dread exploring ourselves. His name is a surprisingly good starting point to working out what set him apart.

# Chapter 5
# Between a rock and an anchor

When, in 1607, Pierre de Lancre made his first hesitant entrance as an author, he was already in his fifties and his intellectual hero – his wife's cousin Michel de Montaigne – had been dead for more than a decade. The title of his new book – the *Tableau de l'inconstance et instabilité de toutes choses* (Tableau of the Inconstancy and Instability of All Things) – was inspired by one of Montaigne's famous *Essays*. Indeed, it was probably meant as a tribute. But de Lancre, despite his age and social standing, was worried about revealing his identity. When he later did come forward, he admitted that at first he had been like 'a young maiden who was rather ashamed to come out into the light'.[1] His readers had to settle for an acronym with which he signed the dedicatory epistle. P.D.R.D.L.S.D.L. secretly stood for Pierre de Rosteguy de Lancre, sieur de Loubens.

The first R. was the closest that de Lancre ever came to acknowledging his own Basque roots. Around 1510, his great-grandfather Bertrand de Rosteguy had left Juxue, in Lower Navarre, for Saint-Macaire, a small community on the Garonne river, some thirty miles inland from Bordeaux.[2] It was the new rather than the old name, however, that made its omission from the title page so ironic. As far as names go, there can hardly have been a more appropriate bulwark against inconstancy than 'Pierre de Lancre', a name made out of a rock [*pierre*] and an anchor [*l'ancre*].[3] As Pierre – he was the first with that name in a family of Bernards and Étiennes – was born in 1556, shortly after his lawyer father obtained the noble title of Lancre, the choice of first name was clearly intentional. 'The anchor', as de Lancre later decoded his name, was not only 'the hieroglyph of the constancy of God', it was also associated with the apostle and fisherman St Peter [*Pierre*]. His coat of arms featured three anchors – a number and figure which he claimed represented the Holy Trinity (Figure 5.1).[4] It was prominently included (on the *verso* side of the title page) of the witchcraft *Tableau*. In his encounter with the Basques, de Lancre was a bulwark of constancy, not far behind God. (Unfortunately, no portrait of either de Lancre or Espagnet has survived.)

Figure 5.1 Pierre de Lancre's coat of arms. (Mairie de Bordeaux, Musée d'Aquitaine, 12185.)

Names and titles mattered, especially when they cost so much time, money and labour to acquire. Like other parlementary families, the Rosteguys had worked hard to climb the social ladder and to then erase the traces of mercantile wealth that got them to the top. All that generational grifting made de Lancre understandably hostile to the very common Basque practice of calling themselves 'Lords and Ladies of such and such house, even when it is only a pigsty'.[5] Embodying constancy did not help de Lancre to get his head around the concept, however. He struggled to define it: inconstancy was change, which was bad, unless it was for the better.[6] The philosophical *Tableau*, like its witchcraft successor later, is a meandering muddle. The author was worried that inconstancy might infect him, his name notwithstanding: 'having discussed inconstancy, I could hardly avoid its taint.'[7] He would have similar concerns about what witchcraft would do to him in the Basque country.

De Lancre came still closer to representing constancy in retirement. In 1616, he sold his office and exchanged a career in judging for a life of aristocratic leisure on his country estate, just as Montaigne had done.[8] The chateau of Loubens, at the edge of the village of Sainte-Croix-du-Mont, still exists today albeit in much-modified form offering spectacular views of the Garonne valley below. On a clear day, as de Lancre himself noted, one can still see the Pyrenees in the distance – the Basque witch-hunt was neither out of sight nor out of mind. The hill on which the chateau stood was, to his amazement, made of fossilized oyster shells. There, amidst these other relics of the sea, sat our self-identified symbol of maritime constancy, so very different from the inconstant sea-faring inhabitants of the Labourd. In 1622, when he published his second witchcraft treatise, his *L'incrédulité et mescreance du sortilège plainement convaincue* (Scepticism and Unbelief in Witchcraft Clearly Defeated), he invited the reader to visit him at Loubens, where they 'will certainly find, at the top of my Mountain, an old ANCHOR, which I am myself, ready to receive him'.[9]

Montaigne in the startlingly short preface to his *Essays* insisted that his rambling reflections were ultimately about him: 'I am myself the matter of my book.'[10] The *Tableau* is not a confessional text in the way the *Essays* were, at least not explicitly. De Lancre never admitted, as Montaigne did, to any difficulties urinating in public, nor to any struggles in the bedroom.[11] Yet, his writings, as his musings about his name and his choice of subjects suggest, are still fundamentally about him – and about what fascinated him. This was why the *Tableau* straddled so many ethnographic, legal and scientific genres. Unwittingly, Montaigne had sent de Lancre on a deeply personal quest. De Lancre had known his hero at first hand. The philosopher had even witnessed the marriage contract that Pierre de Lancre and Jehanne de Mons, Montaigne's first cousin, had signed on 21 December 1588.[12] Historians have never wanted de Lancre anywhere near their respectable research topics. When *Montaignistes* warily discuss de Lancre, they point to the philosopher's witchcraft scepticism as the great dividing line between them.[13] The judge spent a few awkward pages explaining away Montaigne's inconvenient scepticism, revealing some striking personal details about his departed hero's background in the process.[14] Comparing or counting quotes and opinions does not begin to measure Montaigne's influence, however. The *Essays* were a famously unstructured text – for Montaigne, to essay meant to attempt – because they offered a wide-ranging exploration of what it is like to think freely, and hence to be human.[15] It was Montaigne's journey, not his destination or conclusions that inspired de Lancre. With inconstancy as his guide, de Lancre embarked on a very similar wandering voyage of exploration but with a very different, very deadly outcome.

## In pursuit of inconstancy

When, in 1612, Pierre de Lancre published his *Tableau de l'inconstance des mauvais anges et démons* (Tableau of the Inconstancy of Evil Angels and Demons), he presented it explicitly as a follow-up to his earlier philosophical *Tableau* on the inconstancy of all things: 'having so far shown France the inconstancy of men … I now present you with subjects of much greater elevation and consideration, namely the inconstancy of evil angels and demons.'[16] It only took him a few pages to concede (almost) how flimsy a vehicle inconstancy really was. He twice admitted that only one of its chapters (*discours*) was really devoted to the inconstancy of demons.[17] He mostly discussed witches. When we press the structure of the 1612 *Tableau* even slightly, it falls apart at the seams. The opening discourse about the inconstancy of demons runs out of steam virtually mid-paragraph: the *Tableau* switches radically from witches already having one foot in hell to their purported takeover of the Pays de Labourd, signposted by no more than a simple 'But'.[18] Already by the book's midway point most of the material about the witch-hunt was exhausted, and de Lancre moved on to other interests: the case of the teen wolf Jean Grenier, for instance, and a pamphlet about the Inquisition's *auto de fe*. This was the great advantage of inconstancy: there was no structuring it.

Obviously, de Lancre cared about the opinions of his readers, particularly his Bordeaux colleagues. He would not have started his literary career hiding in the vestibule like a 'young maiden' if he did not. Yet fundamentally, his writings are foremost motivated by *his* curiosity, a quest for knowledge that was deeply self-indulgent and at times explicitly pornographic. This is the great danger of the *Tableau* as a source – seeing the Basque witch-hunt through de Lancre's eyes means seeing only what caught his interest. His prose generally roamed from anecdote to anecdote, exhausting a topic until with another 'but', 'in truth' or *voicy*, it suddenly turns an unexpected corner, unsettling the reader. There is a wandering sense of movement to de Lancre's imagination and to his writing. With delight as his implicit aim, the judge only paused long enough to relish an appealing story, concept or idea. His excitement is palpable both from the tone of his writings and from the way he flitted in almost butterfly fashion from quotation to anecdote to observation in a highly disorganized fashion, as Montaigne had done in the *Essays*.[19] To the modern reader, almost twenty pages and thirty authorities on roosters and their attributes may appear (to quote one exhausted reader) 'somewhat excessive', but de Lancre was doing more than showing off his classical learning.[20] He was savouring these stories in the act of writing them.

There is consequently little to no theorizing. De Lancre's feet landed too lightly on the ground to explore wider implications or connections. He was well capable of discussing ideas that, if grounded and conceptualized further, would have seriously challenged the intellectual underpinnings of the science of demons. In his 1607 *Tableau*, for instance, he acknowledged 'that there is nothing more certain ... than that the senses can be deceived' and that even the eye, 'the King of our senses', can be misled in a thousand different ways.[21] On the subject of mental illness, he astutely observed that 'someone who does not recognize that they are ill cannot find a physician, nor accept a cure'.[22] These sceptical ideas are explored and appreciated. They set up anecdotes and experiences, but these have no depth. They hold no wider significance. Once used, they are discarded, like the witnesses and witches he would end up questioning in the Pays de Labourd. De Lancre cannot be pinned down. He could express his horror at the sordid dances of the Basques and boast of his own moves on the Bordeaux dance floor as a young man, without any apparent contradiction.[23] We could consequently pick some choice pieties to present him as a 'cleric-magistrate' or 'Catholic Reformation man'.[24] But he does not fit the moulds we have chosen for him that easily. De Lancre can only ever properly be caught in movement. Quoting from his writings does not really capture him at all.

Inconstancy was more than a flimsy organizing principle, however. It also led de Lancre down a dark path. When Montaigne, late in life, added a caveat to his witchcraft scepticism, he excused himself for roaming too freely: 'For in what I say I guarantee no certainty except that it is what I had at the time in my mind, a tumultuous and vacillating mind.' It was, in other words, the very act of free-thinking, the inability to trust even one's own mind, that led Montaigne to his position on witchcraft: 'How much more natural that our understanding should be carried away from its base by the volatility of our untracked mind than that one of us, flesh and bone, should be wafted up a chimney on a broomstick by a strange spirit!'[25] De Lancre wandered in the opposite direction. He instead judged that, especially where the demonic was concerned, virtually everything could be *true*. The devil could take on any appearance, after all. In the *Tableau*, the devil's penis could – and did – come in every size and shape.

By expanding the realm of the possible, the devil's inconstancy enhanced the wondrous strangeness of both the demonic netherworld and the Basque country. Inconstancy also drew a sharp contrast between the elite Bordeaux judge, the very embodiment of steadfastness, and the Basques who had surrendered themselves either to the devil or to that 'inconstant element', the sea. Or at least it was meant to, because de Lancre's own constancy was never secure. What was bad was, in de Lancre's imagination, always exceptionally tempting.

## Bad temptations

Constancy *versus* inconstancy is only one of many untheorized oppositions that sustained de Lancre's wanderings in print and in life. Some are spatial in form. De Lancre's rural retirement idyll, where the aged anchor sat on top of a fossilized sea, was the opposite of the Pays de Labourd. This arcadia is constructed and presented as the inverse of the Labourd: agriculture *versus* fishing, immobility *versus* movement, constancy *versus* inconstancy, even wine *versus* cider.[26] The same dichotomy between true and false, good and bad, is also implicit in de Lancre's portrayal of himself not only as a gentleman farmer, but also as a magistrate, Christian and Frenchman. In all of these, he is the inverse of the Basques he interrogated.

To observe how these oppositions worked in de Lancre's imagination, we could fruitfully turn to his 1617 *Le Livre des princes* (Book of Princes), our author's one attempt to write on something that was not witchcraft after his return from the Basque country. Ostensibly this work was a mirror for princes, a genre of political writing that offered advice to rulers, in this case, the young King Louis XIII. (Espagnet composed one around the same time, published by the same Paris printer.[27]) As a manual, the work was well-timed: France in the mid-1610s was in crisis, as the young king sought to escape the control of his mother Marie de' Medici and her favourites.[28] But any reader, royal or not, would search *Le Livre des princes* in vain for any form of political theory. What it instead offers are stark warnings to the young prince to stay away from false adulators and to embrace true friends. The adulator *versus* friend opposition mirrors the dichotomies that we have already glimpsed. Adulators were flatterers – the 'true Sirens of the world' – who shipwreck princes. Strikingly, comparisons with witches are not far behind: 'adulators, false courtesans, parasites ... and other seducers of the natural goodness of princes ... charm them, enchant them, bewitch them, and blind them, as if they are evil spirits and bad demons.' They were worse than Circe, the archetypal witch of Greek mythology, because while she famously turned Odysseus's men into pigs, flatterers with their 'artificial and wily delights' transform the inner life. The adulator, 'like Satan', works his way 'into the heart of a prince', perverts his reason and steers him away from good thoughts.[29] Adulators were bad but they were ever so tempting – like witches.

These comparisons inevitably lead us towards de Lancre's highly gendered imagination. Gendered metaphors abound in his writings. The scholars of his day were dishevelled halfway men: 'they court no other ladies than the Muses, who only present them with books rather than mirrors to fashion and decorate themselves.'[30] Courtiers, too, were inevitably 'effeminate, loose and degenerate souls' (they were also 'fickle and light', like demons).[31] By contrast, soldiers were motivated to fight more heroically in the presence of their monarch, just 'as lovers at a tournament under the eyes of their ladies'.[32] Perhaps the most elaborate metaphor is reserved for witchcraft sceptics:

> vapid and delicate people, who resemble these dissolute women who, while acting all scornfully and delicately, would rather stop their pleasures being named than the pleasures themselves; who taste the sweet delights which they believe a thing to contain rather than the bitterness and infamy that they attach to the word; who blush simply at its sound but do not mind the effect.

Sceptics, delicate creatures that they were, feigned horror at the mention of witchcraft, but secretly, de Lancre claimed, his moral indignation mingling with envy, 'they did not mind tasting and practising it'.[33] The judge would secretly have liked to observe a sabbat – and he must have regretted sleeping through the one the devil held in his bed chamber.

De Lancre's perception of the opposite as both wrong and highly *seductive* needs to be seen through this gendered lens. The judge had exoticized the Basques but he also found the women highly alluring. With the men away at sea, he explicitly represented the Labourd as a feminine and therefore seductive space. He waxed lyrically about the 'bewitching' eyes, 'beautiful' hair and 'immodest' dress of the Basque women. These enchanting qualities put that important dichotomy between the elite Frenchman and the Basque inhabitants in constant jeopardy. Their allure very likely also had an impact on his jurisprudence. When the 'very beautiful' Marie de la Ralde, aged twenty-eight, told the judges that she had left the 'abomination' of witchcraft five or six years earlier, they believed her.[34] Beauty excused at least past witchcraft.

It is also worth noting that the anchor had not always been constant himself. In October 1595, evidence was born of de Lancre's inconstancy.[35] Pierre Bienassis was only given his father's first name. The mother's identity, unfortunately, is unknown. Nor do we know Jehanne de Mons's response to her husband's infidelity. Her marriage to de Lancre remained childless. Illegitimate children were, however, *de rigueur* among Bordeaux magistrates. Jean d'Espagnet seems to have had several.[36] De Lancre's plans for his son, however, show how he contained multiple competing and contrasting identities with apparent equanimity. In June 1613, after his son had completed his studies in Toulouse, de Lancre wrote to the Jesuit General Claudio Acquaviva in Rome exploring his son's possible entry into the Society of Jesus.[37] The Jesuits, the stormtroopers of the Counter-Reformation, were usually not keen on applicants from ignoble births, but de Lancre had been a noted benefactor.[38] In late January 1614, following in the footsteps of his father's many Grand Tours to Italy, the son arrived in Rome where he gained admission to the Society.[39] In 1629, two years before his death, de Lancre petitioned Acquaviva's successor Mutio Vitelleschi, asking whether his son could be transferred to the Society's Bordeaux province for his 'consolation' but the request was denied.[40]

The past three chapters have shown how de Lancre and his 1612 witchcraft *Tableau* emerged out of the literary and intellectual milieu of the Bordeaux Parlement, a culture that celebrated rhetoric and sensationalist pleadings, and whose witchcraft scepticism has been much overstated. This was a culture in which de Lancre sought to participate, and he fully shared the aristocratic outlook and exalted view of justice of his peers. We have seen the ways in which de Lancre and Espagnet were quite well suited as colleagues who embarked on the study of the marvellous and the hidden as much to satisfy their curiosity as to judge the guilty. We have also explored de Lancre's self-indulgent wanderings and his surprising debts to Montaigne.

These different facets of de Lancre's writings hold important lessons for assessing both the *Tableau* and the commission's activities. They show that the work offers only a very partial view, centred on those aspects that fascinated its author. Curiosity propelled de Lancre and Espagnet to investigate those – bad but seductive – hidden aspects of witchcraft such as the sabbat in fine detail. We have seen several reasons why de Lancre at least would have taken such testimony seriously. The inconstancy of demons and the fickleness of de Lancre's own framework meant that everything they said about this hidden world *could* be true. The distance that separated the judge from his witnesses, as innocent children, as beautiful women and as exotic guileless others, also vouchsafed their truthfulness. Observing the witch-hunt through de Lancre's eyes is to see marvels to be enjoyed rather than humans caught up in a nightmare.

All this makes the appeal of the traditional straitjacket of the credulous, bigoted judge more apparent – the executions of innocent women and men should not delight but expose a judge's inner demons. De Lancre never seemed troubled by those. His evident pleasure at recounting his experiences underlines the urgency for us to escape both our biases and his perspective – and aim to recover the perspective of his victims as much as we can. At the same time, as we have also abundantly seen, it will not do to consolidate blame and agency in his hands alone. His colleagues – both on the commission and in Bordeaux – all played their part, as did the magistrates and inhabitants of the Labourd themselves. Only one mystery remains, then, before we can examine the commission's activities, namely the question as to why King Henry IV chose to authorize it, and how – of all available judges – de Lancre came to be chosen. This also brings us to one last and heavily trailed aspect of his identity, that of local partisan, which still warrants our investigation.

# Chapter 6
# The royal will

Later generations have presented the reign of Henry IV as among the most blessed periods in French history. Enlightenment *philosophes* waxed lyrically. Voltaire declared Henry to be one of their own: 'having been persecuted, he was no persecutor. He was more *philosophe* than he realized amidst the tumult of arms, the factions of the kingdom, the intrigues of the court and the anger of two enemy sects.'[1] When Jean-Jacques Rousseau pitched his plans for a perpetual peace, he presented the first Bourbon king as its originator. It was an absurd plan, he admitted, but if Henry and his right-hand man (the actually rather bellicose) Sully were to return, it would have been a reasonable one.[2] Henry owes his reputation as the one 'good king' – the one statue not toppled by the crowds of the French Revolution – to his role in ending France's vicious cycle of civil wars in the 1590s. The chaos that followed his death – 'Louis XIII', Voltaire opined, 'read nothing, knew nothing and saw nothing' – gave his reign an especially bright sheen.[3] His martyr's death at the hands of a Catholic zealot also helped.[4] The earthy plain-spoken king – honest to the point of cruelty – would have been the first to scoff at such praise and dismiss it for the mirage it was.[5] At the moment of his murder, Henry was days away from personally leading his forces again into battle, intervening militarily in a major international crisis. His legacy may have looked very different had he not died when he did.

Henry's authorization of the witchcraft commission, on 10 December 1608, has been used as a weapon to dispel the mythical aura that still surrounds him.[6] Local historians have ascribed a variety of nefarious cynical motives to Henry, apparently keen to solve a 'Basque problem'.[7] None of these are particularly credible, all of them overlook the fact that the impulse for the commission came from the Basque country itself. Unfortunately, the only contemporary record of the king reflecting on the Pays de Labourd tells us remarkably little, but it shows that the king, from neighbouring Navarre, knew the region well. Early July 1609, an envoy from Bayonne approached the king while he was feeding the carp pieces of bread at the royal palace of Fontainebleau. The city's representative was not able to extract anything from Henry about the tax issue which he had been sent to raise. Instead, he had to settle for a string of acerbic comments about the inhabitants' wealth (they were wearing silk) and language (Antoine de Gramont had taught them to speak French at court).[8]

If any discussion at court about the commission is therefore lost to us, some facts are incontrovertible. The king took an active personal interest in the French-Spanish border and knew a great deal about its people. The decision authorizing the witchcraft commission marked something of a departure, even if his viceroy had supported earlier ones when Henry was still only the king of Navarre fighting for the French throne. Henry felt strongly enough about his decision to insist that the initially reluctant Bordeaux Parlement register the letters patent. Educated guesswork can take us a bit further still. Whether the king's authorization was a closely reasoned one or – more likely, given his personality – governed by instinct, it was a straightforward response considering his wider political concerns at the time.[9] During a turbulent spell in France's usually tense relationship with Spain, the stability of a border territory such as the Pays de Labourd was of paramount importance. The decision to send royal representatives to a territory that the crown struggled to control at the best of times made a great deal of sense.

# Cold war

The 1598 Treaty of Vervins ostensibly marked the beginning of more than thirty years of peace between France and Spain.[10] Spain had been heavily involved in France's religious wars throughout the 1590s, placing Bayonne and the Labourd on the frontlines. The French-Spanish border along the Pyrenees may be one of the world's oldest – it might appear 'natural', even to early seventeenth-century observers – but it certainly had not gone cold.[11] A cold war is the more appropriate and common description of Franco-Spanish relations following Vervins.[12] The treaty allowed France to pursue a more assertive foreign policy after decades of internal turmoil. At the same time, Spain, whose northern possessions and alliances surrounded France, remained deeply suspicious of Henry IV as a former Protestant. In 1604, Henry complained to the sympathetic Landgrave of Hesse-Kassel that 'the Spanish are always plotting and preparing some new enterprises against the towns and places of my kingdom'. In March 1605, the king informed his ambassador in England that he had decided to increase his support for the fledgling Dutch Republic in their fight against the king of Spain, their former overlord, because of the 'conspiracies the Spanish continue to stir up against me'.[13] This attitude is not surprising. Spain had been Henry's foe since birth. His Navarrese ancestors had harboured dreams of retaking Upper Navarre, the southern part of Henry's first kingdom which Spain had captured in 1512, although Henry apparently never did.[14]

There was plenty of contemporary evidence to validate the king's suspicions. Around the time of his letter to England, Henry personally interviewed an informant who alleged a Spanish conspiracy against Bayonne and the cities on the Provence coast.[15] If the king declared this conspiracy unfounded, others had been all too real. In 1604, an aide to Henry's foreign secretary Villeroy was exposed as a Spanish agent and drowned in mysterious circumstances. Particularly shocking was a 1602 plot involving the duke de Biron (a marshal of France, no less), the duke of Savoy and the Spanish governor of Milan which foresaw the carving up of France into smaller territories and the creation of a (weak) elected monarchy along the model of the Holy Roman Empire in Germany. Betrayed by a secretary, the marshal was lured to court, eventually convicted by the Paris Parlement and beheaded for treason.[16]

Part of the Franco-Spanish conflict played out in the open. In addition to its support of the Dutch rebels, the French crown also engaged in vituperative trade disputes with Spain, even forbidding trade for a time altogether (although exempting the Labourd and its fishing trade).[17] But most of the shadow boxing took place in secret. If the Spanish were scheming to capture Bayonne and Marseille, then the duke de La Force, Henry's viceroy in Navarre, took part in murky enterprises against Pamplona and Perpignan.[18] If Spain was stirring up trouble among the French nobility, then Henry was involved in conspiracies involving Spain's minority populations. Both Henry and La Force had entertained and supported representatives of the Morisco community of Aragon, the descendants of Spain's Muslim population.[19] In April 1605, a French agent sent to organize a revolt in Valencia was caught and executed, after he divulged his plans to an English spy in Bayonne.[20] The French king also seems to have turned a blind eye to plots by Portuguese *converso* merchants to debase Spain's money by smuggling fake coinage into the country via Saint-Jean-de-Luz.[21]

Partly because of events such as the Biron conspiracy, partly as a form of uniting France, anti-Spanish sentiment in the country was running at a fairly constant fever pitch during the first decade of the 1600s, at least in elite circles.[22] In January 1609, the retired Paris lawyer Pierre de L'Estoile bought yet another anti-Spanish pamphlet – it was 'pure nonsense', he noted in his diary, 'but because it is against Spain it is good and fashionable in Paris'. The diarist may have feigned ironic distance. When Spain's ambassador left the city a month later, L'Estoile clearly joined the 'majority of the good French' in wishing him good riddance.[23] In early 1608, an anonymous author from the French southwest published a pamphlet urging Henry – 'our French Hercules' – to liberate Upper Navarre, his birth right held captive by perfidious Spain.[24] The preface of Pierre de Lancre's 1607 philosophical *Tableau*, addressed to the French, can be situated within this patriotic discourse. In it, he sought to vindicate both Henry and the French stiff upper lip from accusations of inconstancy.[25]

Although the evidence for the continued simmering French-Spanish conflict seems clear enough, the chronology at first sight does not fit. The authorization of the witchcraft commission came at a time when relations between France and Spain appeared to have thawed. The period between 1606 and 1609 is often seen as one of *détente*.[26] The last evidence of French conspiracies with Spain's Morisco population dates to October 1607 when a Spanish spy warned of a meeting involving not only La Force but also the governor of Bayonne, Gramont.[27] During 1608, Henry successfully pushed his Dutch allies to make, if not peace, then at least a temporary truce with Spain.[28] Rumours about a possible Spanish match for Louis, the *dauphin* – as would eventually happen in 1615 – were also rife, and its possibility explains some of the strong negative reactions to the Spanish ambassador's visit to Paris.[29]

In addition, the two events that would eventually push France again towards war would not happen until March 1609, several months after the witchcraft commission had been authorized. On the international scene, the death of the childless and mad John William, duke of Jülich-Cleves-Berg, sparked a succession crisis in the German territory that both France and Spain sought to exploit.[30] Another event close to the French court itself was still more significant. Historians have struggled to describe it with a straight face because of the light it sheds on the behaviour and character of the middle-aged king.[31] The marriage of the prince de Condé and Charlotte-Marguerite de Montmorency was an arranged affair. Henry had become besotted with the fifteen-year-old girl, and her marriage to the deeply indebted First Prince of the Blood was intended as a way for the king to more easily pursue relations with the young bride at court. The groom, however, proved unwilling to play the role of cuckolded husband. (Contemporary accounts allege that the bride was game.) Tensions escalated in the months that followed until November 1609 when the newlyweds fled to Brussels and into Spanish arms. Faced with the same opponent in both conflicts, the two incidents quickly merged in Henry's imagination, although his murder in May 1610 means that the true extent of his bellicose intentions will never be clear. One nineteenth-century historian lamented that Henry's assassination 'has deprived modern history of a war which would have offered some future Homer the subject of a new Iliad'.[32]

The witchcraft judges, thus, conducted their work in the shadow of escalating international tensions. In early June 1609, weeks before the commissioners left Bordeaux, three hundred Spanish soldiers, armed with muskets, pistols and gardening equipment, crossed the Bidasoa river for islands on the French side of the river to destroy the land the inhabitants of Hendaye had been cultivating there.[33] When on 19 July, the commissioners attempted to climb a rock near Hendaye where the witches' sabbat had allegedly been held, 'they achieved nothing that day other than alarming the people of Hondarribia who saw so many horses and people appearing on the coast'.[34] Although no report about this incident survives in Spanish archives, local military observers sounded the alarm to Madrid about the increased French build-up throughout the second half of the year.[35] On 14 August 1609, the increasingly apprehensive *maestro del campo* of Hondarribia's fortifications wrote to the Council of War about French plans for the construction of two forts: one at Socoa to protect Saint-Jean-de-Luz and Ciboure (Figure 6.1), another at Hendaye, immediately across his own position on the Bidasoa river, 'in the place where the church [now] stands which is of the same height as [our] position'.[36] This apprehension was to some extent premature, as it would take at least another decade for their construction to be completed.[37] Still, six pieces of artillery had already arrived at Hendaye and the *maestro del campo* felt powerless to prevent their assembly 'without money or food [as] our men cannot live on bread alone'.[38] Indeed, the apparent reason why soldiers had resorted to raiding the French islands with gardening equipment was because insufficient weapons were available. An inspection in July painted a disturbing picture about the fortress and its living conditions.[39] The situation continued to worsen. In January 1610, amidst rumours that the French might seize a border town to exchange for the princess de Condé, Spain's ambassador in Paris raised the alarm about Hondarribia. The city was barely guarded and 'some of [the soldiers] on the gate facing France were working, one as a shoemaker among other jobs'.[40] The witch-hunt of the Labourd unfolded in the shadow of seemingly impending war.

## Trouble at the border

When the crown issued its first letters patent for the witchcraft commission on 10 December 1608, however, these international troubles were still in the future. While the continent remained at peace for the moment, the French-Spanish border was already showing signs of trouble that year. As de Lancre noted, Spanish troops had launched a surprise attack on the islands that year as well.[41] A second incident involving grazing rights took place at the border between Lower and Upper Navarre.[42] We know most about a border incursion – and Henry's response to it – in Béarn, further inland. On 12 July 1608, the inhabitants of the Spanish Ansó valley, led by a local law official, crossed into the Aspe valley in a disagreement over pastures. They made off with four prisoners and somewhere between 180 and 420 cattle.[43] In all three cases, local Spanish officials were enforcing long-standing claims that their newly confident French counterparts – including de Lancre – now considered unfair. In the case of the Labourd, a 1509 treaty had ceded all the islands on the Bidasoa river to Spain and reserved to that country alone the right to put seaworthy vessels on the river.[44] In the case of the Aspe valley, the duke de La Force, the governor of Béarn and Navarre, sent a judge to interview witnesses, in the same way as

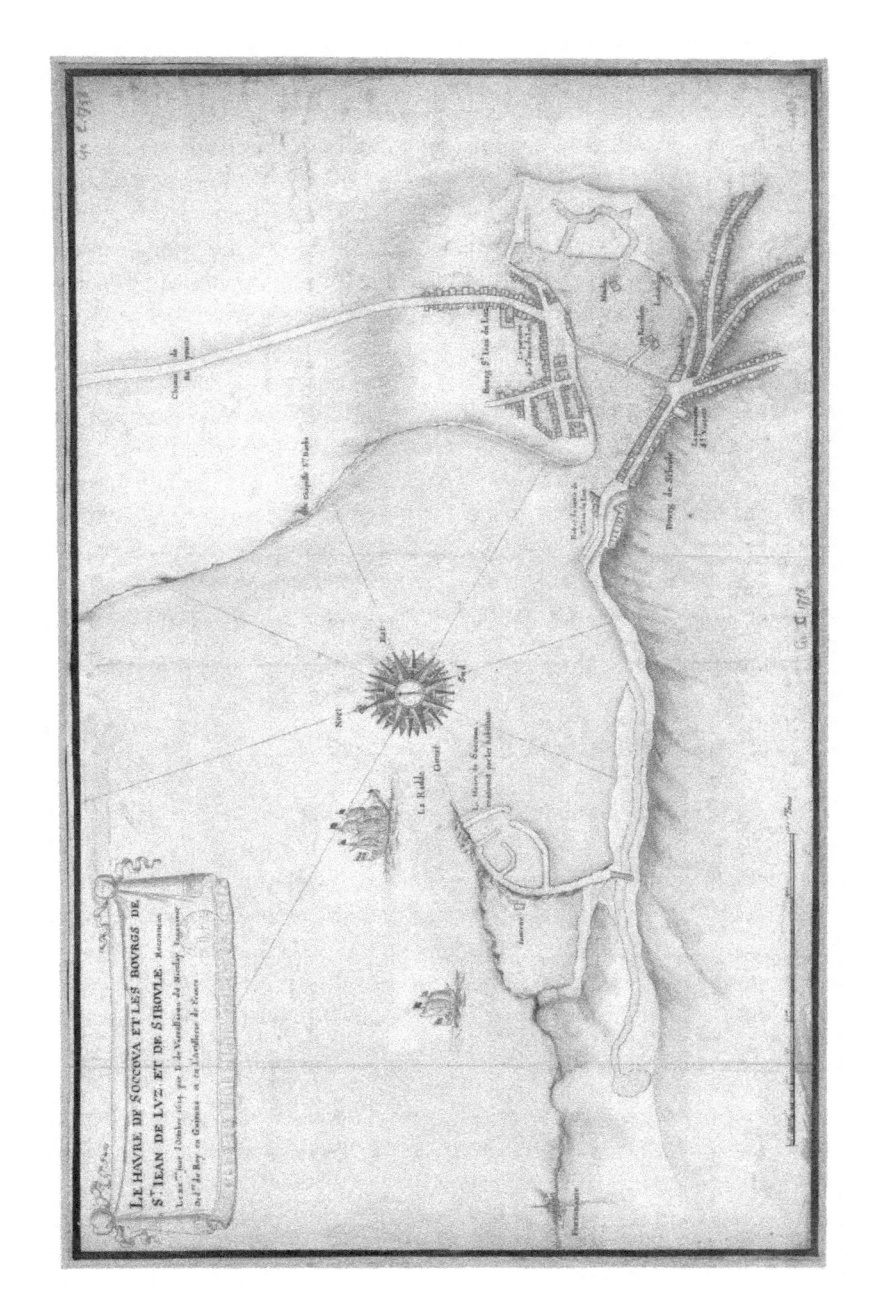

**Figure 6.1** A 1614 map with the new port of Socoa on the left and the towns of Saint-Jean-de-Luz and Ciboure on the right. (BnF, btv1b53027941r.f1.)

Espagnet would in the Labourd a year later.[45] When Spanish reparations were not forthcoming, La Force launched a border raid of his own during which, as he crowed to the king, he captured ten times as much livestock as during the original incursion.[46] Henry's correspondence with La Force – the two were old friends – about the Aspe valley thus lays bare a simple French policy in the Pyrenees: be assertive in the face of traditional Spanish claims, yet avoid war.[47]

Where the Labourd is concerned, Henry's approach towards Spain must have intersected with his suspicions of those immediately on the French side of the border. The king did not require access to Spanish archives, filled with evidence of aristocratic duplicity, to know that the loyalty of the Lapurdi nobles and communities could not be taken for granted. The register of royal patents kept by the Bordeaux Parlement shows that the king was receptive to petitions from the Pays de Labourd in 1608 and 1609 after years of apparent neglect. The register is dominated by Lapurdi interests between April 1608 and July 1609. Saint-Jean-de-Luz, Ciboure, Urrugne and Hendaye all saw their tax exemptions renewed. Tellingly they had long expired, in the case of Saint-Jean-de-Luz as early as 1603, although they may have been continued informally.[48] The reasons given for these 'confirmations of privileges' were partly geographical. The privileges for 'mountainous and infertile' Urrugne referenced the by-now-familiar sterility of the soil.[49] All mentioned the border and the resulting suffering and military service – 'by sea and by land' – in the war against Spain.[50] Yet, the letters patent could also strikingly be upfront that loyalties were being bought: they were issued to fortify communities 'to continue better and better in the obedience they have always shown us', or 'to enhance and augment them in their good will and affection for our service'.[51]

Two edicts, in particular, show a growing preoccupation with order and stability both in the Labourd and in Paris. In February 1609, the king confirmed the rights of Saint-Jean-de-Luz to self-governance, as well as the rights, duties and pay of the town magistrates who saw themselves under siege, not just from witches but also from Tristan d'Urtubie and his allies. In April, the crown modified the regulations concerning the government and policing of Urrugne, Hendaye and Ciboure, although here too it is unclear what changes were made.[52] Privileges were also extended or granted to the local nobility. The crown renewed a fifteenth-century privilege which granted the Urtubie family claims to ship wreckage on the Urrugne and Hendaye coast.[53] Other documents show that Amou, as governor of the Pays de Labourd, was granted a tax on newly built homes in the territory around the same time.[54] The most striking concession, however, was made to Gramont, the military governor and mayor of Bayonne, in March 1609. Hidden in a seemingly insignificant document about merchant fairs is the first royal recognition of the independence of the small town of Bidache – with Gramont as its prince – a status which the principality preserved up to the French Revolution.[55]

Similar significant Easter eggs may well be buried in the other privileges. They are by their very nature difficult to spot. It may be significant, for instance, that Urrugne was deemed particularly deserving of its privileges on account of 'the new quay they have had built for the safety of their ships and other vessels in their port of Socoa'. This project, as we saw, served a military purpose, but it would also provide this community with access to the sea for the first time.[56] In 1610, the Bordeaux merchant Martin Guerre was commissioned to construct it.[57] Urrugne's neighbours, Saint-Jean-de-Luz and Ciboure, did not want the extra competition for their vessels and remained deeply opposed. The port became another source for division and often violent conflict within the territory, with Tristan d'Urtubie as lord of Urrugne predictably taking the lead.[58] During his inspection of the border, local officials asked Jean d'Espagnet to hold a hearing about the Socoa project: it became one more problem, alongside witchcraft and border incursions, for the commissioner to sort out.[59] All of these troubles were linked together by geography and the struggle for resources.

We therefore have two clear reasons why the crown would have supported a witchcraft commission at the border: the growing tensions with Spain and the consequently urgent need to reinforce the loyalty of communities and nobles on the French side. In these circumstances, the presence of royal judges whose judgements were 'with full power' – 'as if they were made by one of our sovereign courts' – must have been quite appealing.[60] Espagnet's inspection of the border further underlined the Labourd's strategic importance and why the witchcraft commission was expedient. As the crown's game of privileges inevitably involved trade-offs – Saint-Jean-de-Luz opposed both Amou's right to taxation and the Socoa harbour – the presence of representatives to enforce the royal will in person was also exceedingly helpful.

When we briefly turn from Paris to Bordeaux, a very similar evidentiary situation confronts us. We know nothing beyond the text of the decrees as they were entered into the Parlement's registers. The gossipy diarist Étienne de Cruseau recorded other conflicts among his fellow judges in 1609 but does not mention the disputed registration of the witchcraft letters.[61] As in other instances, the resulting silence has been filled up with supposition which portray the Bordeaux Parlement as a site of heroic resistance, opposed to de Lancre as an out-and-proud hater of witches or Basques. A survey of the various decrees may already clear things up. The Bordeaux court registered the original letters patent from 10 December 1608 to 4 February 1609, but it added an exception, 'restricting and limiting the power of the said commissioner up to and excluding the death sentence and torture'.[62] By that point, however, new letters patent had already been issued – on 17 January 1609 – to add Espagnet as a second commissioner. This may well have been something of a compromise, especially given his seniority as one of the court's presidents. It is easy to imagine that de

Lancre's colleagues would not have wanted to condone what was, in effect, a one-person Parlement. If it was a concession, however, then it was the only one – and it was rather limited at that because the paperwork kept open the possibility of only one of the judges going. On 18 February, the crown issued so-called *lettres de jussion* rejecting the attempt to restrict the original remit and ordering the Parlement to register the edict 'forthwith and without delay'. This did not happen until 5 June.

This second delay can be explained for practical reasons – which may well have helped rather than hindered the commissioners. The text was very clear that their mission was time-limited to 'six months only, counting from the day of registration'.[63] There would have been no point in registering the edict months before the judges were ready to travel. (They left at the end of June.) We also do not need to look far to explain the court's reluctance. We have already seen how the judges of France's Parlements saw themselves as embodiments of royal and divine justice. The notion of a single sovereign judge, acting with full powers and without oversight, would have drawn opposition. More self-servingly, justice was also the Parlement's bread and butter, and we have already seen the magistrates defend their livelihoods vigorously. Lapurdi officials were desperate for the commission because it would save them money. The *lettres de jussion* were remarkably explicit about this aim. The commission will 'relieve [the inhabitants] from the great costs that have befallen them in the pursuit of appeals, the transfer of prisoners to our Parlement, in addition to the proceedings and other great inconveniences and expenses that follow and which they cannot sustain'. Limiting the commission's powers as the Parlement proposed 'would completely deprive the said territory from all assistance in their extreme situation and destroy the outcome of our good intention'.[64] We do not need to look beyond these two motives – the Bordeaux judges' high regard for their own jurisprudence and their own pockets – to explain their reluctance.

What, then, about the king's choice of de Lancre? It is much more likely that his name was put forth by the petitioners than chosen by the king. Even if the crown possessed a rolodex of Bordeaux judges, de Lancre would have been an illogical choice – in 1606, he had been granted an exemption from a different mission 'not just this time but also for the future' on account of his age and long service.[65] It is significant, then, that one of the commission's sponsors had ties to the Bordeaux Parlement. On 22 April 1598, Tristan d'Urtubie married Catherine Eyquem de Montaigne, the daughter of Geoffrey de Montaigne, an erstwhile councillor at the Parlement.[66] Like de Lancre, Urtubie had married into the Montaigne family. Catherine was a first cousin of Jehanne de Mons, de Lancre's wife.[67] While he acknowledged the role of Urtubie and Amou as 'sponsors of the commission against the witches', de Lancre never divulged this family relationship.[68] In the *Tableau*, his goodwill towards Urtubie occasionally shines true. He praised Urrugne, Urtubie's domain, as 'one of the best parishes of the Labourd'. He abruptly interrupted his analysis of the spread of witchcraft in the territory with praise for the Socoa harbour project, which would principally benefit Urrugne.[69] The omission of this significant personal relationship shows how difficult and treacherous a source the *Tableau* can be. De Lancre's praise for the local nobility 'raised in the French manner' looks rather different when we know that he was, at least to some extent, allied to them.[70] The work's rambling structure and de Lancre's philosophy of inconstancy could cover hidden ulterior motives that we may not always be able to detect, which is why the study of his silences and omissions is so vital.

As often happens in this book, solving one puzzle just reveals another. It is not clear whether de Lancre's colleagues knew of his links to Urtubie, or whether they would have cared if they did. Justice, after all, was also a family business for them. In the Labourd, officials were aware of the many conflicts of interest of the Bordeaux judges. Back in 1605, during its heated conflict with Adam de Chibau and Bishop Echaux over the burial plot, Saint-Jean-de-Luz petitioned the king that the case be moved to Paris. Among the six potentially conflicted judges, the town's officials – or probably more likely, their expensive Bordeaux lawyer – included Geoffrey de Montaigne as Urtubie's father-in-law (and therefore as Chibau's relative by marriage). Yet, the list of biased judges also included 'maistre Pierre de Rosteguy, sieur de Lancre'; not, as we might expect, for his somewhat more distant relationship to Urtubie (of which they may well not have been aware), but because of alleged (and probably unlikely) ties to Bishop Echaux.[71] If only we knew the thoughts of Saint-Jean-de-Luz's mayor and aldermen when one of the judges they once worried about arrived in person armed with vast legal powers. Possibly, Espagnet was added for balance. As one of the Parlement's presidents, he outranked de Lancre. Having previously served on one of the royal councils in Paris, his participation could also have allayed any concerns in Bordeaux or elsewhere.[72] Although the younger man, Espagnet was the commission's senior member. His name appears first on the surviving paperwork.

If the past few chapters have given us a better sense of de Lancre and his colleagues, then they also highlight the importance of geography. The Labourd's position as a border region motivated de Lancre's depiction of the territory as an alien space at the edge of civilization, a mini-New World of sorts. Its position at the edge of France also transformed the commission into a 'scientific' expedition, which examined the Pays de Labourd for signs of something stranger and more hidden still: the witches' sabbat. More prosaically, geography incentivized the French crown to endorse the witchcraft commission, as a way of restoring order at a part of the border that was becoming increasingly unstable and where its authority was weak. Indirectly, the distance between the Labourd and Bordeaux also contributed to a second major factor: the normally high cost of French justice had prevented witchcraft persecutions in the Labourd thus far. This hurdle had now been removed. The *lettres de jussion* warned the Bordeaux Parlement that any attempt to alter the royal letters would 'deprive [the inhabitants] of the great good they are awaiting'.[73] We shall find other words to describe what happened next.

PART THREE

# The Commission (1609)

# Chapter 7
# Into the devil's snare

By the time Pierre de Lancre and Jean d'Espagnet left Bordeaux for the Pays de Labourd on Saturday 27 June 1609, the devil was lying in wait. De Lancre could sense his infernal presence: 'from the outset and as we entered the territory, Satan was watching as if in ambush in order to evade our commission.' Satan, the judge reflected, had virtually the entire territory under his spell. He even made his followers believe that 'he had greater power to burn us and the sponsors of our commission, who were the proper noblemen of the territory, than we had over his followers'.[1] In de Lancre's telling, he was entering enemy territory. In the Labourd, the devil had erected not simply a new religion but a rival political order, defying both God and the king whose authority the two judges embodied.

The devil was not alone in anticipating the commission's arrival. Some suspected witches were awaiting sentencing in Bayonne's prison. A letter on 22 June also forewarned the aldermen of Bayonne to expect the judges on 2 July. The city's lieutenant mayor, Charles de Sorhaindo, on a visit to Bordeaux, asked that the two men were given lodgings. De Lancre and Espagnet wished to be housed separately in two *bourgeois* homes but remain close to one another. They requested two rooms each: a small reception area and 'a room with two beds, one for the said *sieurs*, the other for a manservant, and nothing more'. Sorhaindo had gone to see the bishop of Bayonne, Bertrand d'Echaux, also in Bordeaux at the time, who added his support. The apparent unity must have counted for something – the bishop was perpetually at loggerheads with Sorhaindo's boss, the violent Antoine de Gramont. One of the noblemen besieged by the devil, de Lancre's kinsman Tristan d'Urtubie, would travel to Bayonne to welcome the two judges. The aldermen, Sorhaindo urged, could not reasonably refuse to extend their own hospitality: 'It would cost very little and in time we could profit a lot.'[2] These were ominous words. Bishop Echaux would swiftly regret his early support, while the lieutenant mayor would discover how mistaken his prediction would be, both for him and for his family.

From the judges' arrival in Bayonne on 2 July until 1 November when their work ended, the witchcraft commission was given *carte blanche* to proceed with their investigations as they saw fit. The fragmentary source base and de Lancre's sensationalist retelling of the commission's discoveries have provided plentiful fodder for fantastical reconstructions which bolstered both the size of the carnage inflicted by the commission and the extent of the – human, rather than diabolical – opposition to its work. The impossibly high figure of six hundred executions – nearly five deaths a day for four months – has not gone away.[3] Fanciful tales abound of Basque sailors returning early from their Canadian fishing grounds to rescue their womenfolk.[4] Both strategies solidified the 'four months of terror' into the narrative we have already discussed, that of a gross injustice committed by outsiders on an innocent territory.[5]

As it was with the commission's allegedly late beginning, so it was with its apparently early end. The registration by the Bordeaux Parlement of the royal letters patent on 5 June 1609 started a six-month countdown but the judges spent only four months in the Labourd. Another archival silence has given way to historical make-believe: where the late registration supposedly revealed the Parlement's heroic scepticism, the early end to the witch-hunt has been attributed to one of the two commissioners. Jean d'Espagnet, it is claimed, must have had enough of his junior colleague's antics.[6] The truth could not be more different. Many ties bound the two judges together: Espagnet, a keen investigator of nature's mysteries, shared de Lancre's interest in uncovering a secret world. Most of the surviving archival sources mention the two judges in the same breath; several documents bear both their signatures. Only two 1609 documents, both in the Inquisition archives, refer to only a single French judge – and they mention not de Lancre, but *Espagnet*, his senior colleague. One of these letters, dated to late August, already identified the length of the commission's term as *four* months.[7] It was only during the seven days that Espagnet was away to inspect the border that de Lancre could have acted on his own (and, as we shall see, he probably did).

The commission, then, was always meant to end when it did. Espagnet was due to serve at a special court in the small majority-Protestant town of Nérac, some eighty miles inland from Bordeaux.[8] This so-called *Chambre de l'Édit* had been set up after the Wars of Religion to hear cases involving both Protestants and Catholics. Espagnet had acted as its president before, and his reappointment must have been agreed well in advance.[9] Its annual session opened, like that of the Bordeaux Parlement itself, on 12 November, and a local chronicler recorded Espagnet's arrival two days earlier. Nérac's officials travelled out to meet him and gracefully welcomed back a judge whose 'peaceable disposition, full of prudence and justice in the exercise of your honourable office and otherwise', they had already experienced for themselves.[10] When we add in the travel time, Espagnet would have been left with barely a weekend at home between assignments.

All this is not to say that there was *no* opposition to the commission's work – we shall encounter plenty of instances of that – only that the most basic reconstruction of the commission's activities already exposes the cobwebs of wishful thinking that surround the 1609 witch-hunt. Combining archival evidence with a better understanding of Pierre de Lancre and his elite environment enables us to read the *Tableau* – still our principal source – against the grain. The role played by geography remains paramount throughout. We have already seen how the territory's location fed conflicts over power and resources that tore at its social fabric. The most powerful actor in this witch-hunt, the Franco-Spanish border, is still working its magic on us today: by making the witch-hunt look like, quite literally, a fringe event from a French perspective, it has removed the long and persistent history of Basque witchcraft beliefs from view.

Its role at the time was still more crucial. The possibility of frontier conflict had indirectly led to the commission's creation and would continue to destabilize the Labourd. The territory's privileges allowed its inhabitants to 'be armed at all times' on account of the Labourd's position 'on the extremity of the kingdom'.[11] Yet, if the border caused conflict, it also acted in a different yet related guise: as an agent of justice or, if you prefer, injustice. The border (and the absence or weakness of oversight) emboldened not only noblemen such as Gramont and Urtubie, but even the lowliest of witchcraft suspects because they could flee across it. A great many – 'an infinite number', according to de Lancre – did so, sparking a panic in Spain.[12] They were neither the first nor the last refugees to cross the border, nor would these streams always flow in only one direction.

The link between border and disorder was obvious to contemporaries, for whom it formed the obvious backdrop to the witch-hunt. The friar Mathias de Lissalde, one of the few eyewitnesses to the witch-hunt other than de Lancre, made the connection explicit: 'This territory, on France's border and neighbouring Spain, was in mutiny: everyone was their own master, each person made justice for him or herself.'[13] The possibility of cross-border movement shaped the practice of justice on both sides. According to de Lancre, the commission informed the Spanish Inquisition that the witch refugees were 'bad pieces of furniture' that they did not want back.[14] Similarly, in the wake of the spectacular Logroño *auto de fe* in November 1610, one hardliner at the Inquisition tribunal warned against milder punishment in Spain because it would only encourage foreign witches: they 'will come here from France to seek a place where they are more welcome'.[15]

The early history of the witch-hunt as it unfolded in the years leading up to 1609 also makes clear that de Lancre (and Espagnet) were not responsible for its two principal features: the prominence of the witches' sabbat and the role played by children and teenagers as witnesses. These were already in place before their arrival. The sources for these early stages have been frustrating to work with, tantalizing us with strange details – hams for judges – but staying silent about what we would most like to know. We cannot, therefore, be completely sure whether its main features – young witnesses and the sabbat – were already welded together: that what young witnesses claimed to have witnessed was the witches' sabbat. (If they had not yet been linked, they certainly would be once de Lancre and Espagnet arrived.)

If the early phase of the witch-hunt left much in darkness, then the summer of 1609 feels like staring into the glaring headlights of an approaching car. Suddenly every graphic detail of the sabbat becomes visible – quite literally given the elaborate engraving de Lancre commissioned. The judge's narrative shines so brightly that it takes time for our eyes to adjust, while its light obscures other aspects from view – the loss of life and livestock, for instance, was too mundane to warrant his attention. Still, we are as well placed to tackle the *Tableau* as we can be. We have studied de Lancre's credulous curiosity and its undercurrents: the quest for nature's secrets, the willingness to believe, the professions of disapproval and disdain that barely camouflage desire. If key features of the witch-hunt were already set in place, the curious commissioners and their probing questioning will still have changed its course, while de Lancre as an author will have played up those parts that particularly interested or titillated him.

While the nature of the source material – in particular, the *Tableau* – holds obvious dangers, careful study of de Lancre and his text also offers rewards. The judge's excerpting from the original records – because he thought they would 'please' the reader – mean that the voices even of those he prosecuted are by no means lost.[16] Unstitching the *Tableau* allows us to reconstruct part of the original trial testimony. Read closely, the text discloses voices of scepticism and opposition and reveals relationships between teenage witnesses and accused witches. De Lancre's high tolerance for cognitive dissonance – for inconstancy within his source material – means that the *Tableau* bears witness to opposition to his activities as a judge, much more so than he himself apparently recognizes. While the sabbat – and the possibility of visiting it – clearly mesmerized him, the witches' assembly also emerges as something of a hermeneutical key. For a fantastical and fictional event, it sheds a surprising amount of light on daily life in the Basque country. Unlocking it will open doors to understanding the role and agency of the children and teenagers at the heart of this tragedy. Later chapters will examine these two central characteristics – the sabbat and the role of children – before we turn to the opponents of the witch-hunt. But first, we must reconstruct the commission's whereabouts during its four-month mission. Piecing this together from passing references to dates and places will help establish not only precisely where the judges went, it will also help us work out what happened and who died.

## Mapping a witch-hunt

The *Tableau* was not a travel diary. The judge was too excited to relate his discoveries – the sabbat! – to be delayed by practical preambles, his prose was too elegant and polished to be tarnished by mundanity. These omissions may also have aided de Lancre. It is possible – likely even – that they glossed over irregularities, perhaps even acts of malfeasance. If so, we should try to recover them. To achieve this, we do require the sort of outline that de Lancre was unwilling to provide. When the *Tableau* offered dates, it did so in passing, almost by accident. We can combine these with other sources. We can deduce the commission's whereabouts, in part, from gifts by Bayonne's officials, who offered the judges an entire 'barrel of claret' on a return visit to the city (likely late August/early September) and gave them two pounds of lemon peel to consume 'as a snack' on their onward travels.[17] While the Spanish Inquisition appears to have been oblivious to earlier witch-hunting in the Labourd, the Logroño tribunal monitored the judges' activities closely as it began to investigate the unfolding witchcraft problem on its side of the border.

The commission did not dally in Bayonne. Already on 19 July, they had travelled the full length of the Labourd to the village of Hendaye on the border. There they assembled 'a rather good company' with which to climb a rock on the coast nearby – 'because we wanted to leave no stone unturned' – for evidence of the witches' sabbat. The location was so close to the frontier that the Spanish fortress of Hondarribia across the river raised the alarm.[18] The judges also wasted no time in sending agents into Spain to apprehend suspected witches who had fled. (Despite de Lancre's later public claims, some furniture was apparently worth recovering.) On the same day as the judges ascended to the sabbat, an Inquisition official from the coastal town of Mutriku, some forty miles from the border, reported the arrival of two men with a warrant to take a certain Catalina de Lesalde, who had been living in the town for six months, with them to Saint-Pée.[19] Five days later, another local commissioner sent a more detailed letter to the Logroño tribunal, this time from San Sebastián. The letter claimed that the two Bordeaux judges had already captured 'a great number' of witches, including 'several French priests'. It seems that Lapurdi officials – likely the same two men – came looking for an unnamed wealthy widow from Saint-Pée, described as 'one of the principal' witches, who had bribed her French jailor and fled to Spain.[20]

When Juan Valle de Alvarado, one of the three inquisitors based at the Logroño tribunal, set out mid-August to investigate the developing witchcraft problem first-hand, he came to a very similar conclusion as the local commissioner in San Sebastián, although he curiously overlooked de Lancre's participation. On 20 August 1609, Valle reported from the monastery of Urdax, just across the border from France, about the 'great disquiet' affecting the region:

In France they proceed against [witches] in the places near here where there are many with great rigor and ... they hold the trials with much brevity, although they tell me that the judge proceeds well, as he is a president of the Parlement of Bordeaux and the places where this evil sect exist requested him to.[21]

A list of the locations the commission visited tends to confirm the inquisitor's impression of the speed and efficiency of the French judges, while several sources indicate that Bayonne's public executioner was also kept extraordinarily busy. On 29 September 1609, the nearby town of La Bastide (now La Bastide-Clairence) asked Bayonne's deputy mayor Sorhaindo if they could urgently employ the executioner's services: 'tomorrow, which will be the market day of this town we would desire to have some male and female witches executed who have been condemned to death.'[22] This set of executions did not involve the Bordeaux judges at all, or at least not directly because they were elsewhere at the time. But Espagnet and de Lancre had used the same 'young and well-shaped' executioner at the village of Urrugne in late July – de Lancre was scandalized that one of the convicted women, called Detsail, refused the so-called kiss of pardon, despite the man's handsome features.[23] The same person must similarly have been used for the interrogation, torture and execution of several female suspects that the Bayonne aldermen handed over to Espagnet and de Lancre on 12 October.[24] Group executions also took place in Saint-Pée (from about 21 to 30 September),[25] in Saint-Jean-de-Luz (in the autumn)[26] and in Ustaritz, the village which traditionally served as Labourd's capital and seat of judgement.[27] At least one execution – and probably more – were carried out in Hendaye (mid-July and early August),[28] in Ciboure (mid-September)[29] and Ascain.[30] Others probably took place in Cambo-les-Bains (early October)[31] and Biarritz,[32] both of which the commission certainly visited. De Lancre's comments make additional stops seem unlikely.[33] Officials from Sare escorted more than a dozen 'witnesses' to Saint-Pée for questioning by the commission.[34] Espagnet's inspection of the border did not meaningfully slow down its work. The president's surviving account indicates that he was away only from 21 to 27 September, when de Lancre interrogated at least some suspects on his own.[35]

We can, therefore, reconstruct the commission's route with some precision (Map 7.1), using educated guesswork (in italics) to fill in the gaps between stops that can be more securely dated. The resulting visualization immediately illustrates just how small the affected area was. In fact, most of the Labourd's twenty-seven parishes were never visited.[36] Barely twenty miles separates Hendaye from Saint-Pée. The commission's efforts evidently focused on the parishes that fell under the influence of its two principal sponsors – Hendaye and Urrugne in the case of Urtubie, Saint-Pée in the case of Amou – as well as the witch-hunt's original epicentre, Saint-Jean-de-Luz and its neighbour Ciboure. Many of these

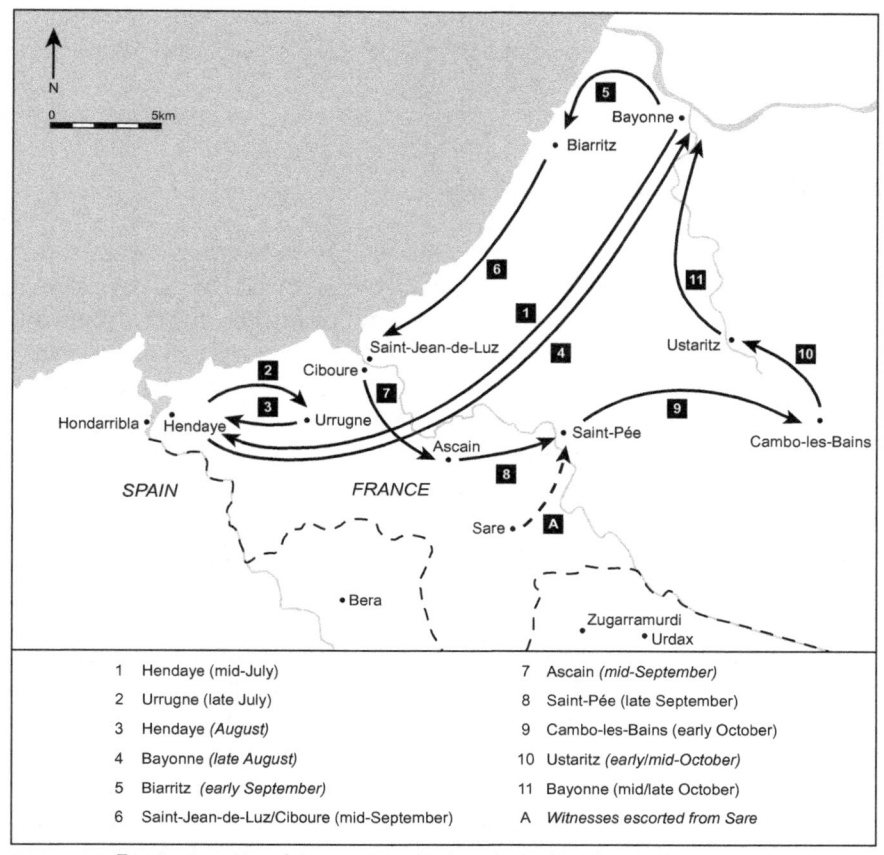

**Map 7.1** Reconstruction of the witchcraft commission's most probable route.

| | |
|---|---|
| 1 Hendaye (mid-July) | 7 Ascain *(mid-September)* |
| 2 Urrugne (late July) | 8 Saint-Pée (late September) |
| 3 Hendaye *(August)* | 9 Cambo-les-Bains (early October) |
| 4 Bayonne *(late August)* | 10 Ustaritz *(early/mid-October)* |
| 5 Biarritz *(early September)* | 11 Bayonne (mid/late October) |
| 6 Saint-Jean-de-Luz/Ciboure (mid-September) | A *Witnesses escorted from Sare* |

communities – along with Bayonne – had pushed for the commission's creation in the autumn of 1608.

If the area affected by the witch-hunt was small, then the prosecutions themselves were intense and, perhaps as a result, it generated a panic that spread well beyond it. Other Lapurdi communities appear to have brought suspected witches to Bayonne for sentencing by the commission.[37] La Bastide, where magistrates seemed to have acted independently, lay outside the Pays de Labourd, in Lower Navarre. After the original witchcraft scare in Zugarramurdi earlier in 1609, the arrival of French witches helped spark a larger panic over the summer which spread across the Spanish Basque provinces of Upper Navarre and Gipuzkoa. Local officials set to work prosecuting the witchcraft refugees, but their enthusiasm posed an evident jurisdictional problem in the eyes of the Spanish inquisitors. Witches may have been the devil's allies, but even these could not be prosecuted in Spain if they had committed no crimes there.[38] The fact that de Lancre and Espagnet banished – rather than executed – some of the accused must have further contributed to the spread of witchcraft fears south of the border.[39]

## Counting casualties

Establishing the route that the judges took makes it easier to assess the estimates of the number of witnesses heard and the witches executed. De Lancre claimed to have heard evidence from sixty to eighty 'famous witches' and five hundred 'witnesses'.[40] The number of witnesses – which included children as young as six years old – varied across the *Tableau* and may just mean 'more than he cared to count'.[41] The judge only gives us the names of about two dozen. This does not include the principal witness in the early witch-hunt, Catherine de La Masse, though she may well have testified. Given the town's role as the witch-hunt's epicentre, Saint-Jean-de-Luz features remarkably little in de Lancre's *Tableau*, and as a result, other early protagonists, such as the merchant Adam de Chibau and mayor Guiraud de Sanson are similarly temporarily absent. We may, however, plausibly identify the other key witness of the early trials, Marguerite de Hareder, as the Marguerite from Saint-Pée, aged sixteen or seventeen, in de Lancre's *Tableau*. Her name, age and origin all fit. Marguerite testified that the witch who used to take her to the sabbat had 'recommended her to another woman' after she was taken to Bordeaux, indicating that she had been involved in the 1605–7 trials.[42] Perhaps unsurprisingly, given de Lancre's interests, the majority of the named witnesses were female. Some were already in their early twenties – ten-year-old Bertrand d'Handuch and eleven-year-old Catherine de Naguille were the only ones who likely had not yet reached puberty.[43] Recognizing that these teens were witnesses rather than witches reveals a disturbing void at the heart of the *Tableau*: witness testimony makes up the bulk of the *Tableau*'s borrowings, we barely hear from the accused witches at all.

If we set aside the implausible figure of six hundred executions, then we are left with the figures de Lancre himself provided: that of sixty to eighty 'famous' witches, several of whom, he later noted, had been banished rather than executed. One further wrinkle is the fact that the sixty to eighty figure refers to famous 'Sorcières', *female* witches (de Lancre thought them worthy of a capital letter).[44] We know that the commission also executed men, including three priests. An often-cited rival figure is offered by Alonso de Salazar Frías. The sceptical Spanish inquisitor put the number of persons 'condemned' by the French commission at 'more than eighty persons' – without, however, specifying a sentence.[45] The difference between the two figures is marginal, and there seems to be no reason to prefer Salazar's over de Lancre's, when the French judge had just as little incentive to overstate the number, as he had to count correctly.

If we included only those instances in the *Tableau* where a victim's name or place of origin, is known, we arrive at a much more modest figure of only eleven executions. This certainly is too low. We cannot overlook oblique references to other deaths, including group executions of an unknown size.[46] We are also all too aware of de Lancre's biases, as a judge and as an author. The fact that almost all those named in the *Tableau* served some crucial role at the witches' sabbat – musicians, 'queens' and priests – highlights the extent to which his interests warp our source base. We should not take the visible tip of this iceberg – the sabbat, the part that fascinated de Lancre and which he considered worth recounting – as the witch-hunt's entire body mass. The geographic imbalance in the *Tableau*'s evidence is just as worrying: Saint-Pée and Sare are particularly well represented, while we know the name of only one of 'those who were condemned to death' at Saint-Jean-de-Luz.[47] The reason is unclear, but it leaves Saint-Jean-de-Luz, the original epicentre, in the dark at a key moment. We do not know whether the commission retried any of the original accused released during the witch-hunt's earlier stages. The archives are also unhelpful. They yield the name of only one additional victim, from Bayonne.[48]

What is indisputable, however, is that the judges relied on local knowledge and support. As we saw, by late July, a Spanish official was able to report the arrest of 'several French priests', which suggests that the commission acted swiftly – and de Lancre himself specified that the priests included 'several called before us' as well as 'several others' whom the judges had found themselves.[49] This allowed them to work quickly and, as we saw, group executions took place in many, if not all of the places the judges visited. We may not know the size of these groups but even a low multiplier of four or five executions per plausible location brings us close to fifty casualties. The *total* figure, including those executed or simply killed before or after the commission, is even more difficult to establish but it likely did not exceed one hundred.

The reasons for widespread panic, then, are quite clear. The death toll, while nowhere near six hundred, was considerable given the confines of time and space. The communities would have witnessed the spectacle of group executions, and we can only hope that the judges employed the so-called *retentum*, by which prisoners were strangled before the fire was lit.[50] Even the prospect of this grisly work generated further lawlessness as possible suspects fled to Spain – or possibly even boarded the fishing vessels setting out for Terreneuve. Some, including a boy from Ustaritz who was only nine years old, travelled as far as Logroño to be absolved by the Spanish Inquisition.[51] The identity of the witches' victims – that is, the children and teenagers who testified against them – must have been another source for panic and distress, especially for their parents.

Even de Lancre recognized the significance of one final panic factor: the identity of some of the suspects. The judge admitted that the execution in Ascain of a seventy-year-old parish priest called Arguibel caused a 'great uproar' in Bayonne and 'terror in the whole of the Pays de Labourd'. In total, the commission arrested eight priests from the territory, all of whom stood accused of holding Black Masses at the witches' sabbat.[52] Another clergyman ultimately executed was the 27-year-old Pierre Bocal from Ciboure, whose entire family was suspected of witchcraft.[53] Writing in 1641, our other eyewitness, the Ustaritz priest Bertrand de Faitze who could not have been much older than Bocal in 1609, reported that some still refused to have their children baptized by priests tarnished by the scandal.[54] As we shall see, the execution of the priests, however, provoked not just 'terror' but also resistance. Before we can turn to the growing opposition, we need to study in greater detail the two main features – the sabbat and the teenagers and children who witnessed it – that endowed this witch-hunt with a cogent structure and terrifying internal logic that ultimately unleashed misery in an area well beyond the small coastal part of the Labourd the judges visited.

# Chapter 8
# Of village musicians and dancing queens

Pierre de Lancre was obsessed with the witches' sabbat. He made every effort to visit sites where these nocturnal gatherings had been held. A first attempt to inspect an outcrop near Hendaye had to be abandoned – the slope was too steep, and de Lancre was no rock climber – but on a return visit, he made out where witches had kept the cooking pot in which they made their potions.[1] The commissioners asked at least one suspected witch to bring back ointment from the sabbat so that she could fly in front of them.[2] De Lancre readily believed that witches congregated even in his bed chamber.[3] His near or second-hand encounters with the sabbat never left him. The subject dominated the *Tableau*, and he commissioned an extravagant engraving for its second edition which has shaped how historians have thought about such gatherings. When he returned to witchcraft again in retirement, he described his new book – the *L'incrédulité* of 1622 – as 'the anti-Sabbat, the great declaration against Satan and his allies'.[4] Jean d'Espagnet's views are more difficult to divine but he composed a poem, written in Latin meter, about the sabbat's more lurid ceremonies for inclusion in his friend's *Tableau*.[5]

As a result of de Lancre's expansive interests, his writings have not only shaped our understanding of Basque witchcraft but that of witches' gatherings across early modern Europe.[6] In reality – or rather, in 'reality' – the sabbat was hardly a uniform, coherent or static concept, even at the level of elite beliefs. As the site where the devil welcomed his new followers, it emerged roughly in tandem with the demonic pact during the later Middle Ages.[7] From its origins as a rather mundane gathering of imaginary heretics, the sabbat evolved over time, sponge-like absorbing more details as they were uncovered and published – as illustrated, for instance, by the 'discovery' of Black Masses at the sabbat in the 1590s. This gradual development explains de Lancre's excitement at hitting the proverbial mother lode – 'an infinity of unknown and strange things, beyond all belief, about which the books on the subject have never spoken' – all in what he saw as a god-forsaken corner of France.[8] The fact that the sabbat was off-limits to non-demon-worshippers further aroused his curiosity. De Lancre was obsessed with what witches did in the shadows, and the sabbat engraving he commissioned made observable what would otherwise be hidden from Christian eyes. Visual illustrations of the sabbat in general followed a similar path of elaboration. Sparse for most of the sixteenth century, these images became ever more Baroque and (quite literally) incredible during the seventeenth.[9] Crucially though, while such sabbat depictions began to circulate within European art and literature, actual witches' gatherings were at most a muted presence in witchcraft confessions across much of the continent.[10] Rather than flying on a broomstick or on 'goat'-back, witches often told their interrogators that they walked home on foot, if they went at all.

Where the sabbat is concerned, the Basque witch-hunt was exceptional. This chapter studies the Basque sabbat – often, but likely erroneously called the *akelarre* – as a key organizing principle of the witch-hunt as it spread across Lapurdi and into Spain. Even more so than in other contexts, de Lancre's role as the 'mythmaker of the sabbat', as my colleague Thibaut Maus de Rolley and I have called him, is as much a hindrance as a help for the historian.[11] The surviving archival material barely offers us a fleeting glimpse of Basque sabbats before 1609, other than indicating their presence. Now de Lancre reveals all. At the same time, his dual position, as both an overtly curious judge and an overly enthused author, complicates the interpretation of this sudden cornucopia. What role did de Lancre play in the creation of all this sabbat testimony? The horrid tales he describes – of cannibalism, vampirism and a great deal of demonic sex – must be rooted in something other than reality, but where did they come from?

## Sources for the sabbat

Historians have rather neglected the witches' sabbat, certainly when set against the vast amount of attention that the wider subject has received. Methodological worries about truth and reality have made the sabbat into a realm where few have dared to tread. As a result, the older nineteenth- and early twentieth-century historiography, which secretly often still shapes the ways witchcraft historians approach things, particularly makes its presence felt here. On the one hand, the so-called rationalist impulse to attribute such lurid stories to the warped imagination of the judges can be hard to resist, both in general, but – inevitably – especially so in de Lancre's case. One witchcraft scholar similarly likened the Inquisition's interrogation methods to 'a form of brainwashing'; leading questions taught the accused the 'kind of *truth*' expected of them.[12] By contrast, the opposite, so-called romantic approach held up sabbat stories as remnants or memories of pre-Christian beliefs, perhaps even a coherent pagan fertility cult. One prominent modern adherent of the romantic view – though admitting that de Lancre's 'eye [was] sharpened by hatred' – nevertheless claimed he 'observed the object of his persecution with a penetration often absent in the more detached observers of the subsequent century'.[13] Not coincidentally, the two opposing – realist *versus* romantic – positions emphasize different sides of de Lancre's role. The first attributes the creation of the testimony to de Lancre's activities as a judge, while the second privileges his role as an observer and author.

The truth behind the sabbat probably lies somewhere in the middle of these extremes, as it so often does. Historians have come to see witchcraft confessions as a form of co-creation between male judges and their (often female) victims, taking seriously 'the creative work which the witch herself carried out, translating her own life experiences into the language of the diabolic, performing her own diabolic theatre'.[14] The sabbat stories collected by de Lancre are expressions of lived experiences – we shall hear echoes of visits to market fairs, of church services and dances at weddings. They also reflect apparently deeply rooted folkloric ideas. These stories did not spring wholesale from de Lancre's imagination. They predated his arrival and trapped him with their unexpected strangeness. But we cannot ignore his potential role in shaping the words of his witnesses, both as a judge in the interrogation chamber and later as an author, when he decided what to play up and what to leave out.

We are fortunate, then, to possess an unexpected set of sources that enables us to get a better measure of de Lancre's dual role as a judge and author. These rival documents also prime us to see what is *not* there in the *Tableau* and reveal the true significance of understated or muted elements in the text. For different reasons, the Spanish Inquisition was nearly as obsessed by the sabbat as de Lancre, treating witchcraft much in the same way as it treated its other religious targets: Jews, Muslims and Protestants. Like them, witches were seen as members of a heretical sect, though a particularly 'diabolical, vain, false and infernal' one.[15] The Inquisition's attention, thus, also centred on the sabbat as a site of idolatrous worship, and Basque sabbats – or *juntas* (gatherings) – had already perplexed inquisitors for generations.[16] The question whether sabbats took place in real life or were demonic illusions (the devil causing witches to *imagine* they attended them) proved especially vexing. In time, the reality of the sabbat would divide the three inquisitors of the Logroño tribunal into two warring factions, pitching the sceptical Salazar against the 'believers' Juan de Valle Alvarado and Alonso Becerra Holguín.[17] The latter two drew up a lengthy manifesto defending the reality of the sabbat as a place where witches really feasted, danced and even got rained on.[18] Although the original depositions no longer survive, a great deal can be reconstructed from this and other Inquisition documents. There are strong reasons to pay attention to such sources: the testimony recorded was filtered through a different legal bureaucracy – it never passed through de Lancre's hands.

Of particular interest is Zugarramurdi, the village just across the border from Lapurdi where this wave of witchcraft fears apparently first made landfall in Spain. In fact, this part of the Inquisition testimony predates the arrival of the French judges by some way. The wheels of Spanish justice simply worked much more slowly than the French commissioners. Their famous *auto de fe* took place only in November 1610 and their bureaucratic infighting lasted much longer still – but the inquisitors had a head start. The ten suspected witches arrived from Zugarramurdi in Logroño, in two groups, in January and February 1609, at a time when the Bordeaux Parlement was still debating the royal letters patent setting up the French commission.[19] Inevitably, the surviving Inquisition sources come with interpretative difficulties of their own, as all confessions to imaginary crimes do. The second group of Zugarramurdi witchcraft suspects travelled to Logroño in February 1609 to prove to the Inquisition tribunal that they were *not* witches – yet after months of confinement they all ultimately confessed.[20] While their confessions are deeply problematic as accounts of what really happened, as narratives they can throw valuable light on the sabbat beliefs as they existed in the Labourd *before* Espagnet's and de Lancre's arrival. The majority of the suspects imprisoned in Logroño had already confessed by the time de Lancre and Espagnet arrived in the Pays de Labourd, and all had done so by September 1609.[21]

The Zugarramurdi testimony also matters because the village was ultimately not very Spanish or even Spanish Basque at all. As Inquisition officials well knew, mountains separated the village and the neighbouring monastery of Urdax from the rest of Spanish Navarre. Unlike the fortress of Hondarribia, which (remade into a luxury hotel) still looks down on France from across the Bidasoa river, these Spanish localities slightly further inland were situated in the same valley as the Labourd.[22] Economically, though not politically, Zugarramurdi and Urdax were part of France. In the early 1590s, when France and Spain were at war, the monks at Urdax were still permitted to export metal from their forges through the port of Saint-Jean-de-Luz, despite warnings that it will be used 'to make ships and weapons against the Christian religion because most of the iron made in this way will be taken by the enemies to England'.[23] When, in 1611, it came to confiscating the witches' meagre belongings, the abbot of Urdax, León de Aranibar, warned the inquisitors that there was only French money and 'not a single *real*' to be found 'in these lands'.[24] The inhabitants, too, had strong ties to their Lapurdi neighbours, speaking the same dialect and intermarrying.[25] It was precisely Urdax's position as a Spanish outpost in France which would make its abbot a valuable source of information (as Aranibar promised he would be, when he applied for a position with the Inquisition in September 1609).[26] Where historians working on the Spanish side of the witch-hunt have used Zugarramurdi as their starting point, we can use the same testimony to look *back* towards France, reflecting sabbat narratives as they had already developed in the Labourd.

The surviving Zugarramurdi testimony is permeated with references to sabbats and witchcraft on the French side of the border. Miguel de Goiburu, the 'king' of the sabbat, led an exchange visit to the Ciboure gathering, reflecting perhaps María de Ximildegui's original testimony.[27] The devil 'señor' of the Zugarramurdi sabbat had similarly been invited to visit Ascain by his counterpart there.[28] French witches attended the Zugarramurdi gathering in return. María de Yriarte was impressed by a French girl who played with large castanets and whose dancing included particularly high jumps.[29] Twenty-year-old Joanes de Sansin, Goiburu's nephew, reported that enterprising sabbat participants sold little candles from Saint-Jean-de-Luz to those who had forgotten to bring offerings to the devil of their own.[30] Goiburu also related the story of a sailor, who promised a barmaid in Ascain the most elegant bodice she could ever wear if she taught him to be a witch.[31] Two of the Zugarramurdi suspects reported on an attempt to sink four ships near Saint-Jean-de-Luz. Conversely, almost nothing in their testimony looks towards Spain. The only exception is a visit by the devil and the witches of Zugarramurdi to pay homage to the 'principal' devil of Pamplona, surely a mocking reference to the church hierarchy – the city was the seat of the local bishop.[32]

The villagers of Zugarramurdi, therefore, must have been well aware of what was happening across the border, even before María de Ximildegui arrived from Ciboure and began to make her accusations in late 1608. The circumstances in which the Inquisition arrested the first witchcraft suspects in the winter of 1608–9, then, may also throw some light on the experiences on the French side. An initial group of four witchcraft suspects was apprehended by a local Inquisition official in January and escorted to Logroño.[33] This group, all women, included 22-year-old María de Jureteguía, the first person María de Ximildegui had accused. In a tense public encounter between the two Marías, Jureteguía felt unwell, emitted 'a very foul-smelling breath' and then confessed.[34] In the month or so that followed, at least ten further suspects, many of them related to Jureteguía, were subjected to intense public pressure and, as a result, also admitted they were witches. Around Christmas time, a ceremony was held in the packed church of Zugarramurdi in which this group publicly asked for and received forgiveness.[35] In the traditional narrative, still hailed by the village's witch museum, this informal reconciliation 'undoubtedly' would have solved the witchcraft matter in an 'admirable manner', if only outsiders – that is, the abbot of Urdax and the Inquisition – had not become involved.[36]

How the original group of four women came to be selected for transport is unclear. Yet, having already publicly acknowledged their guilt back home, they promptly confessed to the Logroño inquisitors upon arrival. By mid-February, this testimony, now lost, was sent to Madrid for scrutiny by the Suprema, the Inquisition's Supreme Council.[37] The little we know about these confessions comes from a set of follow-up questions composed by the Suprema, which were clearly geared towards establishing the reality (or not) of the sabbat.[38] There was, however, also a second group of six self-confessed witches about whom we know much more. This group of three women and three men belonged to one extended family and was likely related to the first.[39] It was led by Graciana de Barrenechea, a matriarch already in her eighties.[40] The inquisitors were visited by royalty; Graciana eventually confessed to being the queen of the sabbat.[41] This second party has often been represented as travelling to Logroño out of their own free will, but this is only technically true. If the public ceremony in which the witches were pardoned is lauded as a noble local initiative that should have ended the matter, then this journey is depicted as a 'valiant and daring' rescue attempt.[42]

This narrative, exalting communal self-reliance and plucky local heroes, does not appear especially plausible, even on its own terms. One does not normally send octogenarians on rescue missions. When we ignore the border and view Zugarramurdi confessions as the product of a witchcraft panic that was in fact well under way, the narrative crumbles altogether. Given the circumstances and the crimes to which the group confessed, the 'admirable' reconciliation ceremony looks rather odd. The surviving material reveals the communal pressure used to extract public admissions of guilt out of these six women and men – among other acts of intimidation, a crowd had forced its way into their homes searching for evidence of toads (the quintessential ingredient of Basque witchcraft).[43] Following the transport of the first four suspects, the pressure on the others to report themselves to the Logroño tribunal must have been immense. Far from being a rescue mission, their journey was an act of desperation.[44] When the six suspects arrived in Logroño, they told the clearly sceptical inquisitors that they 'came in search of the truth' and claimed that their earlier confessions had been forced out of them.[45] The group must have felt that they had no choice. And in truth, they had not. The inquisitors were looking to apprehend four more witchcraft suspects just as they arrived.[46]

The Zugarramurdi material, thus, has real implications for our understanding of the Labourd as a territory that had already descended into chaos and disorder. The acts of popular intimidation fit the description by friar Lissalde, quoted in an earlier chapter: 'everyone was their own master, each person made justice for him or herself.' The actions of the accused witches – travelling to Logroño in a hopeless attempt at exoneration – are on a continuum with the attempts by the relatives of the Saint-Jean-de-Luz suspects who tried to force Catherine de La Masse to retract her accusations. Yet, if Zugarramurdi offers another instance of factionalism – embedded in a distinct set of family relationships and perhaps reflecting other social, economic or political rivalries – the village also suggests that the witch-hunt evolved into a much more popular phenomenon. If Saint-Jean-de-Luz officials and Lapurdi noblemen had led the early charge against witchcraft, then by late 1608, or early 1609 at the very latest, fears had become widespread, and ordinary villagers had taken justice into their own hands. The role played by the local church and its curate – who encouraged the second group of six to travel to Logroño 'and tell the truth and then all would be well' – is also noteworthy, especially given the grim fate that awaited some Lapurdi priests.[47]

What, though, about the sabbat? Any similarities between the *Tableau* and the Zugarramurdi testimony would be all the more striking because the Basque words spoken by the accused were filtered through different languages and legal systems.[48] As de Lancre put it, 'their [Spain's] form of justice is the complete opposite from ours'.[49] Unlike the French judges, the Spanish Inquisition normally refrained from using torture and only seems to have used it slightly later in the cases of two suspected witch-priests.[50] Nevertheless, where the French commissioners did not have the luxury of time, the misery of long confinement in Logroño, during which the devil allegedly visited the Zugarramurdi witches in their cells, must have been a torment in and of itself.[51] The different objectives of the Inquisition as a religious institution are also worth stressing. Its aim was to save the souls of the accused, and as a result, those who confessed and showed themselves penitent would be publicly reconciled with the church – and then they would live. To de Lancre's amazement, it was the *negativos*, those who *refused* to admit their guilt, who would be executed at the *auto de fe*.[52] As they all confessed, the original Zugarramurdi suspects were not among the six witches executed in November 1610. (Half of them, however, passed away during two prison epidemics in late 1609.[53])

We have danced around the subject of the Basque sabbat long enough. It is time to face the witches' gathering and decode its meaning. The Zugarramurdi material offers a rich vein of witchy ore which we can mine and compare to the *Tableau*. The similarities can help us unpack some of the sabbat's origins in folklore and daily life, whereas any differences offer suggestive evidence of de Lancre's role as a judge, author and editor.

# Toads and thrones

The elaborate engraving that de Lancre commissioned for the second 1613 edition of the *Tableau* provides the inevitable framing device for any investigation of the Basque sabbat. We know little about its composition. Its creator, the Polish-born and Paris-based engraver Jan Ziarnko, had evidently done some independent research: two visual elements, a flying witch and a salamander, appear to have been copied from an earlier sabbat engraving by the Dutch artist Jacques de Gheyn II (Figure 8.1–8.4).[54] There is no evidence that Ziarnko had himself visited the Basque country. If he had, his depiction of female witches would have been less generic. None of the women wear the characteristic

**Figure 8.1** A witch on a broomstick, from Jacques de Gheyn II, 'Witches Preparing for Sabbath' (c. 1610). (Metropolitan Museum, 2001.648.)

**Figure 8.2** Ziarnko's copy of de Gheyn's witch, fragment of the 1613 sabbat engraving.

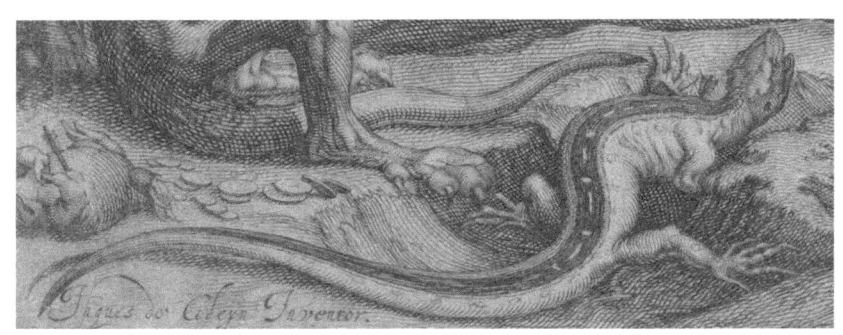

**Figure 8.3** A salamander, from Jacques de Gheyn II, 'Witches Preparing for the Sabbat'.

**Figure 8.4** Ziarnko's copy of de Gheyn's salamander, fragment of the 1613 sabbat engraving.

**Figure 8.5** Scenes A and B from the 1613 sabbat engraving: 'Satan in a golden chair in the form of a goat' and 'the queen of the sabbat crowned to his right' (our left) and 'a less favourited one to the left'.

Basque hairstyle and headdress, for example. That said, the assignment must have come with detailed instructions from de Lancre himself. The engraving is accompanied by a key which describes the various scenes at length.[55]

Let us start, then, as Ziarnko's engraving does, with representations of the devil. In the Spanish sources, the devil was represented mostly as an ugly black man or as a goat, seated on 'a great throne in royal dignity'.[56] He appears in the latter form in the Ziarnko engraving, although that of a 'tall man dressed in black' was another of the devil's preferred options in the *Tableau*.[57] The queen of the sabbat, who is seated beside him, was a striking presence both in Zugarramurdi and in the Labourd (Figure 8.5).[58] While de Lancre did not report the presence of any 'king', he described one of his victims, 73-year-old Petry d'Aguerre, as the sabbat's 'master of ceremonies and governor'.[59] The French judges' questioning seems to have yielded further details about aspects of the devil's appearance, something the Inquisition sources are otherwise silent on, often the product, as we shall see, of the imagination of individual child witnesses.

As the references to queens, kings and governors illustrate, both sets of sources depict a strongly hierarchical sabbat, generally based on seniority, with clear job descriptions. Similar hierarchies also permeate other parts of the Ziarnko engraving.[60] Lurking at the edge we find, rather fittingly, 'several poor witches who were sent to the corners and do not dare to approach the great ceremonies' (Figure 8.6). More prominent are the 'great Lords and Ladies and other rich and powerful folk', who appeared 'hidden' and, in the case of the women, 'masked' so as not to be recognized (Figure 8.7). Older witches,

**Figure 8.6** Scene E from the 1613 sabbat engraving: 'Poor witches reduced to the corners ... who do not dare to approach the great ceremonies.'

**Figure 8.7** Scene L: 'The great lords and ladies and other rich and powerful folk who transact the great affairs of the sabbat'.

explicitly called *maestros* or teachers in the Inquisition material, played a crucial role in bringing and introducing young children to the devil (Figure 8.8). In fact, the Zugarramurdi sources make us aware of the extent to which these teacher-pupil bonds were often blood relations – 'witch dynasties' – an understated presence in de Lancre's *Tableau* that we shall study more closely.[61] On both sides, musicians who performed at the sabbat (and, it seems, also at other venues) were prime targets and they, too, feature in the engraving (Figure 8.9). In Zugarramurdi, Juanes de Goiburu, Miguel's son, and Juanes de Sansín, Miguel's

**Figure 8.8** Scene C: 'A witch who presents a child that she has seduced.'

**Figure 8.9** Scene G: The musicians at the sabbat 'to the song and music of which [the witches] leap and dance'.

nephew, played the drums together.[62] Originally sentenced to life imprisonment, they would be released in the spring of 1613.[63] Espagnet and de Lancre executed a blind drum player called Ansugarlo from Hendaye, and likely several other performers as well.[64]

Closer study reveals further notable similarities even within the details. The devil, for instance, financially rewarded both French and Spanish Basque witches for seducing and offering children to the sabbat.[65] On both sides, the children had to renounce all aspects of the Christian religion and kiss the devil, including under his tail and on 'his shameful parts'.[66] The devil gave the older witch a toad,

**Figure 8.10** Scene M: 'The small children, who away from the ceremonies, [carry] white sticks and rods, each guarding the flock of toads that belong to those who usually take them to the sabbat.'

dressed up in colourful velvet, for the benefit of their new novice, which was to act as their guardian angel.[67] (Miguel de Goiburu's was dressed in yellow.[68]) The children were meant to look after these at the sabbat while the witches were otherwise engaged. This inventive combination of toad- and child-care forms a particularly arresting part in the Ziarnko engraving (Figure 8.10).[69] The scene was probably purposely relegated to a corner to reflect the children's position at the sabbat: despite their renunciation of Christianity, the children and teenagers were very much represented as apprentices and victims. They were kept away from the potion-making and continued to be taken to the sabbat by their 'teachers', which helps to explain why they were foremost seen as witnesses, rather than as witches (Figure 8.11).[70]

One further notable feature of the Zugarramurdi evidence is the devil's vampirism. Although animal familiars were known to draw blood from witches in England, and witches were said to suck blood from their victims (perhaps especially in Spain), the devil is rarely, if ever, depicted as a blood-sucking figure.[71] Yet, the Zugarramurdi witches all confessed that the devil drew blood from them during the ceremony, creating wounds that took a long time to heal.[72] Although certainly preoccupied with the devil's mark, de Lancre did not discuss this aspect of the initiation rite. Yet, vampirism does occur in the *Tableau*. Sixteen-year-old Jeanette d'Abadie, for instance, reported that the devil created a small wound

**Figure 8.11** Scene K: 'Several witches come to the sabbat on broomsticks, others on goats accompanied by the children they have taken and corrupted, whom they come to offer to Satan.'

on the little toe on the left foot 'from which he then sucked blood' so that his witches would never confess.[73] Here, the comparison with Zugarramurdi reveals the significance of aspects of the sabbat that remained mostly submerged in the *Tableau*, perhaps because de Lancre's interest lay elsewhere.

Still more unusual are the versatile roles played by toads in sabbat narratives on both sides of the border. Some were akin to the familiars in English witchcraft trials – they were demons in disguise, though this was rarely, if ever, spelt out. Mature witches thus possessed especially large toads, at times as large as a pigeon or a chicken, with whom they were seen dancing, and which the children were not allowed to approach.[74] Spanish sources are richer here because, unlike de Lancre's *Tableau*, they frequently move beyond the sabbat. They show that witches looked after these toads at home, where they acted as demonic alarm clocks, letting their owners know when the sabbat was due.[75] While these toady familiars provided a liquid (used for demonic flight, among other things), real toads were also unceremoniously used as ingredients during the witches' potion-making (Figure 8.12).[76] The Zugarramurdi sources describe the harvesting of such toads in great detail. The devil here emerges as a strikingly human figure, leading his witches on toad-finding expeditions and praising their domestic potion-making – 'yours is perfect' – as if he were the master chef on a television cooking show.[77] Yet, a passing comment by de Lancre makes it clear

**Figure 8.12** Scene I: 'There is the cauldron on the fire in order to make all sorts of poisons, either to kill and injure men, or to destroy livestock. One [witch] holds the snakes and toads in her hand, the other cuts off their head, flays them and puts them in the cauldron.'

that Lapurdi witches, like their Zugarramurdi cousins, also brewed their potions at home.[78]

The sabbat offered plenty of other amenities besides the potion brewing, the induction of novices and the toad-centred child-care. Witches on both sides attended the sabbat in animal form, notably as dogs, cats and pigs.[79] Both French and Spanish testimony also discussed at great length the sabbat as a site where priests performed Black Masses, including communion and the elevation of a (Black) Host.[80] The 1594 trial of Jeanne Bosdeau back in Bordeaux had already exposed de Lancre to the concept of the Black Mass, but the fact that several priests fled the territory before the commission's arrival indicates that it did not originate with him. On both sides, the devil was also comfortable enough to personally lead services which professed him to be the true god.[81] An unnamed 'very famous' witch similarly told de Lancre that the Black Mass was said 'with more pomp [at the sabbat] than in the true church' and that 'witchcraft was the best religion'.[82] A notable feature of this Eucharistic service, present on both sides of the border, was the collection of 'alms', which witches were expected to offer the devil (and which, in the Labourd, were said to fund a witchcraft legal defence fund).[83]

A Black Mass cross-border comparison reveals one particularly arresting detail about the Eucharist: having abandoned Christ, the Zugarramurdi suspects were no longer able to see the real Host – that is, the communion wafer which Catholics considered to be Christ's real body – during Mass.[84] It was María de Ximildegui's desire to see Him again rather than a 'black cloud' that had brought her to repent her entry into the devil's service.[85] The religious significance of this was not lost

**Figure 8.13** Scene D: 'Behold the banquets of the sabbat, [where] every [witch] has a devil with her and at this feast they serve no other meat than carrion, flesh of the hanged, the hearts of unbaptized children, and other filthy animals, all of which completely outside the customs and practices of Christians, all tasteless and without salt.'

on the inquisitors, yet only traces of these experiences in church remain in de Lancre's sabbat-centred *Tableau*. 'Before she was saved', 28-year-old Marie de la Ralde could only see the Host as 'black even when it was white'. Jeanette d'Abadie still trembled whenever the priest elevated the communion wafer.[86]

The Basque sabbat was not only the inversion of a church service, it was also a feast, though this was very much a potluck affair. Witches not only supplied the grisly meat themselves, they even (according to de Lancre) brought along their own silverware.[87] As 'queen' of the Zugarramurdi sabbat, Graciana de Barrenechea confessed to taking some of the human meat home with her, as a perk of her position, where she and 'friendly witches' consumed it with some bread and wine.[88] Stories of witches devouring dead infants, especially unbaptized ones, were common across Europe – and they prominently featured on the Basque menu as well (Figure 8.13). Yet, evidence from Zugarramurdi also focused on witches digging up the remains of dead *witches* from cemeteries for the living ones to feast upon. The devil even thoughtfully provided additional dental protection so that the older witches could consume these unwholesome bodies.[89] The same point is made in passing by de Lancre, who revealed it as a 'secret' he learned from one of his witnesses.[90] Its full significance would not have been apparent without reference to the testimony from Zugarramurdi.

This insalubrious meal, in turn, set the scene for further merriment, or as the key below the Ziarnko engraving put it, quoting a well-known French proverb, *après la pance vient la danse* – 'after the belly comes the dancing'. From here on, the comparison with Zugarramurdi becomes less rewarding as the Spanish material provides less detail about either the dancing or the demonic sex that followed. De Lancre's interests – in particular, his single-minded preoccupation with the sabbat – thus clearly shaped what part of the testimony survived though, so far at least, mostly through omission. What happened beyond the sabbat interested him little, but we have picked up traces of what he overlooked or ignored. To get a better sense of the more explicit sabbat material and its origins, we should reflect on the significance of the many similarities, great and small, we have identified so far, before we proceed towards the dancefloor and beyond.

## Diabolical theatre

Thus far, our comparison has yielded a set of beliefs, many of them highly specific, that straddled the French-Spanish border. The detailed similarities indicate that they cannot be reduced to projections and preoccupations of two separate groups of interrogators. Several years after the panic had first started in Saint-Jean-de-Luz, sabbat imagery had become highly developed. By late 1608, the villagers and townspeople of Zugarramurdi and the Labourd must already have developed a good sense as to what the sabbat involved. If we approach these interrogations as 'diabolical theatre', then the resulting co-production drew not just on the expectations of the judges but also on the deep wells of folkloric knowledge. Witchcraft was in no sense new to the Basque country, and neither was the sabbat. Many of the ingredients we have uncovered so far reach back to previous witch-hunts. Poisonous toads, for instance, were also a key ingredient of the 1576 witch-trials in the Labourd, and they also featured in at least half of the witchcraft cases that appeared before the royal courts of Pamplona.[91] Specific folkloric beliefs may well have attached to other animals as well, notably roosters (whose crowing was believed to end the sabbat on both sides[92]) and goats. A sabbat queen features in at least one earlier witch-hunt in Spanish Navarre – her role may have been inspired by the figure of the serora, the lay religious women who looked after churches.[93]

The most exceptional features of the Basque sabbat – the devil's vampirism and the consumption of dead witches – must belong to this same category of folkloric knowledge.[94] They obviously do not reflect personal experiences. Yet, while those interrogated were drawing on these wells of shared information, they were also mining their lived experiences for helpful parallels. Marie de la Ralde told the Bordeaux judges that there was 'no harm in going to the sabbat', likening it to attending a wedding, and added that she had 'much more fun and enjoyment [there] than when going to Mass'. Some only went to the sabbat 'to dance', while others compared it to a 'parish fête' or 'famous fair'.[95] In 1613, de Lancre added that 'the sabbat is like a fair' with merchants 'arriving from all over'.[96] Later he recalled a 'famous witch' continuing to visit the sabbat after her arrest 'in order to go dancing; she thought nobody could be offended by that'.[97] In that sense, elements of the sabbat – bringing one's own plates of food to a village feast, contributing alms at the end of Mass, going to a dance – reflected the realities of daily life. It also explains why musicians who played at village events found themselves specifically targeted on both sides.

These two sources – shared folkloric knowledge and personal experiences – did not travel on parallel tracks but combined to generate sabbat testimony. How they came together is perhaps best illustrated by a trope more pervasive than even the ubiquitous toads: the myth of the unwitting intruder. Although such sabbat spectators, almost always male and often clueless husbands following their wives on a suspicious nocturnal adventure, were also reported in other parts of Europe, they formed a particularly prominent part of the Basque source material.[98] Horrified at the sight of the sabbat, the shocked outsider would exclaim the name of Christ or the Virgin, at which point the infernal gathering would instantly disappear, often leaving the hapless spouse stranded far from home. De Lancre reported an 'infinity of examples in our records' of the sabbat vanishing and leaving the intruder 'in a very wild place far from home' – so many that he seems to have become tired of recording them.[99] (Or perhaps he was just envious.)

We already unwittingly encountered several versions of this myth from the Zugarramurdi sources when we surveyed their Lapurdi connections. The French girl with the large castanets leapt so high that one witch accidentally let out an admiring 'Jesus' and the sabbat vanished. (Such leaping also featured in the *Tableau*; de Lancre even mentioned a competition.[100]) The sailor who had attempted to bribe an Ascain barmaid into teaching him witchcraft was so horrified by the devil's ugliness that he did the same.[101] The mariners attacked by witches on board their ships had the good sense of 'invoking the name of Jesus and Holy Mary'.[102] Even the exchange visit to the Ciboure sabbat ended abruptly after an impressed visiting witch inadvertently invoked Christ in admiration.[103] The lost testimony of the first four Zugarramurdi suspects must have featured further versions because the Suprema, intrigued by its implications for the reality of the sabbat, asked about it.[104] These intruder stories come from a rich vein in popular culture; variants also featured in the 1575–6 witch-hunt (on both sides of the border) and modern ethnographers have collected variations on the same theme from the wider Basque region.[105] Yet, the Zugarramurdi witnesses were doing more than just reproducing stories they probably had often heard told: they were also making these stories their own, rooting them in particular places and times and endowing them with striking levels of detail. We are given the name of the Ascain barmaid's employer and the acrobatic French girl's place of origin.[106]

Just as these sabbat narratives were not imposed by elite judges, they were also not ancient and static survivals of pre-Christian beliefs. Rather, they are the moving (in both senses of that word) product of engrained cultural beliefs and shared everyday experiences. This also suggests that they were embellished over time, emerging out of the continued interaction between judges and accused. They must have developed very rapidly since the first hints of the witches' sabbat emerged in the surviving records in 1605 but they likely also contained commonplace elements, like accidental strangers and poisonous toads. With one possible exception (which we shall hold in reserve for the next chapter), we do not really know what the sabbat looked like before 1609. But we can fast forward and examine later Inquisition testimony to make this process of gradual elaboration and embellishment more credible. A brief consideration of additions to the sabbat – elements missing from the Zugarramurdi testimony that emerged during subsequent Inquisition questioning – confirms the impression that, under questioning, the sabbat gradually began to look less 'real'. Over time, it became an event that witches flew rather than walked to, and even attended in spirit rather than in the flesh.

Strikingly, the first ten Zugarramurdi suspects never mention being replaced in their bed by a replica demon. Such replicas were a staple in the demonological literature: they added narrative plausibility (spouses would not become suspicious) and they glossed over inconsistencies (if a witch was discovered to have been in bed when she was meant to be at the sabbat). For the demons, there was the added bonus of more sex: they could have intercourse with unsuspecting husbands and harvest their semen. These demonic bedfellows were simply absent from Zugarramurdi: two of the witches claimed that they successfully fobbed off their innocent husbands when they grew too curious about their absences. (Graciana de Barrenechea said she had been visiting a neighbour who had been unwell, and Estevania de Nabarcorena said that she had gone spinning).[107] The eventual emergence of so-called *succubi* and *incubi* (female and male demonic seducers, respectively) under interrogation, however, was likely only a question of time, for the reasons already given. When the inquisitors Juan de Valle and Alonso Becerra drew up their manuscript, they included a chapter on demonic replacements as another proof of the reality of the sabbat. Tellingly, their earliest evidence of such replacements came from arrests in the autumn of 1609, and their evidence about sex demons was later still.[108]

Despite de Lancre's evident interest in all matters sexual, there are strong grounds for suspecting a similar absence in the Lapurdi material, at least before the commission arrived. Basque *incubi* and *succubi* are virtually absent from the *Tableau*. While he had encountered 'many examples of incubi as well as succubi in the books', the judge was disappointed never to have come across an example of a husband being replaced with an *incubus*. De Lancre did claim, however, 'to have encountered an infinity of experiences' in which the devil acted as a *succubus*, replacing a wife in the marital bed. Despite this, the pages upon pages he produced on the topic still only came from the books he had read.[109]

Even if *succubi* emerged in the Lapurdi confessions, they likely did so only in response to the judges' questioning (and de Lancre's reading). The stories may well have been too boring to be excerpted. Yet, the process of elaboration under questioning was real. The *Tableau* reveals the inevitable emergence of demonic substitute bodies during the confrontations between witches and their young accusers. Demonic replicas explained how children could continue to be taken to the sabbat by witches who were already under lock and key.[110] Similarly, the possibility of demonic offspring logically followed all these questions about sex. We should expect judges to raise it, but it took time for affirmative answers to emerge. Diabolical pregnancies were absent from Zugarramurdi, and try as he might, de Lancre could find no evidence in the Labourd.[111] It took until the spring of 1611 for painful two- or three-month pregnancies to emerge in Spanish Navarre. In two neighbouring villages, witches confessed to giving birth to toads – further evidence in Valle's and Becerra's hands that the sabbat could not have been a diabolical illusion.[112]

The commissioners, supported by local agents, not only built on pre-existing witchcraft suspicions and accusations, but their interrogations were also based on a set of sabbat beliefs that were by then well founded. De Lancre considered many of them so quixotic, so strange that he cannot possibly be said to have invented them himself. (In fact, it was their extraordinary strangeness which made him want to share his findings with the world.) Yet, the Bordeaux judge was also keen to hear more details, especially about dancing and sex, and he possessed a high threshold for cognitive dissonance. His demonological reading prompted at least some of the questioning, even if he evidently did not always receive the answers he was expecting. The commissioners are not the only factor worth considering here, however. Given the role that lived experience and the individual imagination played in these diabolical theatrical productions, we should also expect a measure of diversity across witches and witnesses. The tropes we have charted so far were a common treasure trove used by those questioned for further elaboration, creating not just confessions and accusations but, as we shall see, stories of opposition to the witch-hunt as well. It was not just the French judges' questioning, therefore, but also their willingness to give the imagination of children and teenagers free rein that yielded a much richer and diverse set of highly imaginative depictions of life at the sabbat. Before we turn to their role in the witch-hunt, let us consider some the stories these young people told.

## The devil, a tree trunk

The *Tableau*'s many different and contrasting descriptions of the devil's appearance show the judges tapping into a world of children's fantasies. While de Lancre took the goat or black man form to be the most common – he chose the former for the engraving and discussed them first – he also excerpted other descriptions, often explicitly tied to his teenage witnesses. The devil also appeared, for instance, as 'a big dark tree trunk, without arms and feet, sitting on a chair, having some sort of face like that of a big, terrible man'. Thirteen-year-old Marie d'Aguerre said that the devil looked like a goat but that he popped up out of 'a big jug' placed at the centre of the sabbat. Similarly, fourteen-year-old Janne de Hortilopits denied that she had kissed the devil's backside, saying that it was instead the devil who 'kissed the small children on the behind'. Ten-year-old Bertrand de Handuch told the judges that there was a big devil and a small one. While the boy had kissed the big devil's behind, the small devil had kissed his. Bertrand and Janne both came from the same village of Sare, and he was likely responding to and elaborating on the girl's testimony. (As we shall see, these children were likely interviewed in groups.) We not only get a sense of what was asked, but also how the imagination of these children and teens built on these questions, and on each other's answers in their own ways. De Lancre evidently did not mind such versatility, observing only that the devil, like some sort of investment manager, 'takes pleasure in diversifying all that he does at the sabbat'. Inconstancy, after all, was the devil's defining characteristic: 'The devil', de Lancre noted in the margin of the *Tableau*, 'is as inconstant and invariable in his form as he is in everything else.'[113]

The testimony that de Lancre gathered about sex and dancing at the sabbat needs to be interpreted in the same way – as the interplay between shared cultural tropes, imaginative elaborations of witnesses and the judges' curiosity. De Lancre espoused a set of highly flexible truth criteria, and the youth of his witnesses further assured him they were speaking the truth. He found one sexual comment by Marie de Marigrane – that the devil had sex with pretty witches from the front and ugly ones from behind – so shameful that it had to be true: 'her youth was incapable of so sordid an invention.' Marigrane further claimed that during sex, the devil made his witches cry 'like women in childbirth' and, in an apparent attempt at contraception, that he always withdrew his member. It is all too facile for us to roll our eyes at de Lancre's credulity; yet, a fifteen-year-old could easily have picked up these stories in a world with little privacy. Others drew on the observations of animal sexuality which was similarly a normal part of village life. Johannés d'Aguerre, age unknown, presented the devil as a goat, though with its penis attached to its backside; he added that the devil 'knew the women by moving and pushing it against their front'. A sixteen- or seventeen-year-old witness testified that, though the devil had taken on the form of a goat, he had chosen the penis of a mule because this animal was 'the best endowed'.[114]

It is equally possible that some testimony was based on first-hand experience. Sixteen-year-old Jeannette d'Abadie, de Lancre's star witness, told the judges about 'the tremendous pleasure' she experienced merely describing her own sexual encounters with the devil. Her testimony may well have had some basis in fact: Abadie also confessed to having sex with her cousin at the sabbat. Yet, for de Lancre, this combination of youthful innocence and sexual experience acquired at the sabbat still validated her testimony. She called 'everything by their rightful name more freely and shamelessly than we ever dared to ask her, which wonderfully confirms the reality of the sabbat'. While some elements drew on real-life observations and experiences, other descriptions give us a sense of the fantastical imaginings that could also be at work. The devil's penis, for instance, was variously endowed with scales, made of metal and of horn ('which is why he makes the women scream so much').[115]

The judges' curiosity played its part in stimulating such testimony, especially where sex and dancing were concerned. De Lancre 'often' asked 'the girls and beautiful young women' (and possibly, given the wording and his personality, only *them*) what pleasures they hoped to find at the sabbat, ostensibly because he worried for their well-being, 'very delicate and soft' creatures that they were. Similar motives prompted the commissioners to make their teenage informers, male and female, re-enact the dances that they held at the sabbat, 'to deter them from such filth, making them see how much even the most modest movement is sordid, vile and unbecoming for an honest *girl*'.[116] While the sexually explicit subject matter was too transgressive to be visually represented, the Ziarnko engraving prominently featured two different types of dances. The first, an after-dinner exercise, is also presented as a prelude to the sex that will follow: 'each demon leads the [witch] who was near him at the table underneath this accursed tree. There the first has their face turned towards the middle of the dance circle, the second towards the outside, and the others all follow likewise. They hop, dance, and party, with the most indecent and dirty movements they are capable of' (Figure 8.14). A second group of naked 'women and girls' can be seen dancing all looking outwards (Figure 8.15). It is the latter image that seems to match most closely de Lancre's description of the dances which the teenagers performed for him 'with their hands so much behind their back in this circle dance that they drag their bodies with them' which also caused their bellies to 'stick out' and 'swell' in front of them. De Lancre devoted an entire chapter to mapping out the different types of dances that took place at the sabbat, in which he often linked their sordid nature to their foreign (Spanish or Basque) influence.

**Figure 8.14** Scene F: After dinner, 'each demon leads the woman who was next to him at the table towards this cursed tree; there the first one faces inwards, the second outwards, and the others follow the same pattern'. Then they dance 'with the most indecent and sordid movements they are capable of'.

He also described the so-called Bohemian dance, one of the few glimpses we get of the role that the *cagots*, a persecuted ethnic minority, may have played in this witch-hunt.[117]

Where dancing is concerned, the Inquisition material is much more subdued. The one notable parallel is the prominence of leaping and jumping which featured heavily in both. De Lancre even reported an instance of witches jumping off Larrun, the Labourd's tallest peak. One reason for this difference must be de Lancre himself, who was not only fascinated by these seemingly frenetic and eroticized dances but also fancied himself to be an excellent dancer *à la Françoise*.[118] Yet, the role played by the fertile imagination of children and teenagers in the Lapurdi witch-hunt also helps to explain this discrepancy. They showed themselves capable of imagining the devil as something other, or something more, than a mere goat or a dark man. This is not to say that the children's testimony was not equally as important on

**Figure 8.15** Scene H: 'A group of women and girls, all dancing with their faces turned away from the dance circle.'

the Spanish side – indeed, Lu Ann Homza has shown us as much. Rather, at this early stage, the inquisitors had not yet interviewed the youngsters for themselves.[119] (Their testimony during the 1611 Visitation would confirm, if not prompt, Salazar's scepticism.[120])

The evidence of the first Zugarramurdi suspects offers few explicit details about witches' sexual encounters with the devil; we may suppose that the inquisitors, unlike their French counterparts, did not press the subject too closely. There is one striking difference, however. The devil emerges from de Lancre's *Tableau* as a heterosexual figure, indeed almost aggressively so. The Ziarnko engraving depicts the sabbat as virtually a female- (and demon-)only space. When the devil ordered his witches to couple up in ways that 'nature abhors the most', all the combinations listed – daughter and father, sister and brother – were incestuous but straight.[121] De Lancre's focus, where sex was concerned, was solely centred on the female accused. When witches, 'instead of keeping silent, blushing, and crying', seem to relish describing their sexual encounters with the devil, 'believing the caresses of this sordid demon to be more worthy than any just husband that they could ever encounter', de Lancre claimed to be outraged but he was likely titillated at the same time.[122]

By contrast, male homosexuality forms a notable presence among the early Zugarramurdi evidence. In their report, Valle and Becerra observed that witches not only had intercourse with the devil (he engaged in 'normal and anal intercourse with the women and sodomy with the men') but also with each other, 'male with female and male with male'.[123] De Lancre also recorded the devil as having anal sex with the female witches but is entirely silent on the men.[124] What do we make of the difference? To some extent it may reflect specific personal experiences. Juanes de Sansin and Juanes de

Goiburu, the two musicians at the Zugarramurdi sabbat (and first cousins), confessed not only to sex with the devil but also with each other.[125] Yet, they were not the only male suspects confessing to sex with male devils: Miguel de Goiburu, Juanes's father, made a similar confession, as did a number of later male Zugarramurdi suspects.[126] In this context, a fleeting reference in the *Tableau* to two teenage boys 'sleeping together' may take on new meaning.[127] (As we shall see, the work may also contain an even more ephemeral and uncertain reference to lesbian sex.) If we cannot ground these stories in lived experiences – or at least not all of them – then they could also reflect popular beliefs. Perhaps early modern Basques conceived of the devil as strictly male. As we saw, *succubi* – female demons who have sex with men – were entirely absent from both the Labourd and Zugarramurdi. Either way, these homosexual encounters in the Zugarramurdi source rank among the Basque sabbat's most unusual features. Their (virtual) absence from the Labourd likely owes much to de Lancre's heterosexual imagination, both as an editor and (very likely) as a judge.

Decoding the witches' sabbat, as a site of the collective imagination, will therefore always be challenging. Our knowledge ultimately is finite: one limit is what de Lancre is willing, able and interested in telling us. Yet, we have also seen how unstable and even, often, contradictory the *Tableau* is as a source. No reader could ever regard its portrayal of the sabbat as static, polished or finished. De Lancre's own authorial voice is often lost amongst a cacophony of witches and witnesses, whose words he stitched together. The Zugarramurdi testimony helped us destabilize the *Tableau* still further, bringing the sabbat narratives circulating in the Pays de Labourd more clearly into focus. The comparison throws fresh light on de Lancre as an editor and as a judge, pursuing the sabbat and its most intimate secrets more ardently than any other person before or since. The many similarities across the border reveal de Lancre's value as an observer and show that we should not exaggerate his agency as a judge – the inquisitors, after all, heard the same stories, de Lancre did not invent them. At the same time, the Zugarramurdi sources also disclose the significance of elements – the eating of dead witches, the devil's vampirism, the gay sex – that were muted presences in the *Tableau* because they interested de Lancre less, if at all. The devil was at times literally hiding in the details.

We are not quite done with sabbat narratives, but we have already attained a much better sense as to how they were constructed out of folkloric traditions and lived experience, and how they emerged out of a dialogue, not only between judges and those testifying, but even among the witnesses and witches themselves. The roles played by lived experience and 'diabolical theatre' also suggest some ways in which the sabbats – even as imagined spaces – could act as sites of resistance to the commission's work. Indeed, there is a great deal more to say about the agency of de Lancre's (and Espagnet's) witches and witnesses.

But all these considerations do bring us back to one fundamental question: why were these unfortunate souls testifying at all? To really understand how their testimony came into being, we also need to study the way the commission operated and how it conducted its questioning. This means, above all, paying attention to the children who stood at the witch-hunt's centre.

# Chapter 9
# Child spies

María de Ximildegui encountered the devil during a sleepover. One night before her fateful move to Zugarramurdi, when she was still living with her parents in Ciboure, she had arranged to stay over at a neighbour's, a friend called Catalina.[1] María had done so many times before, but this night was different: Catalina suggested that they secretly go to a party. This promised the sort of youthful impropriety that early modern moralists often warned against, and María was up for it.[2] Between ten and eleven in the night, when the rest of the house had gone to bed, the two girls snuck out 'without having gone to bed or anyone in the house hearing them'. They walked only a few hundred metres to reach a sandy area just out of town where a big gathering was taking place: 'everyone was enjoying themselves and they were dancing as much as they wished' – and the devil was seated on a throne. There was so much noise, so many instruments being played, that María felt overwhelmed. She did not realize that 'those who were there were witches, nor that the host was the devil, nor that [the visit] was a bad thing'. At the end of the party, the two girls walked home, opened and closed the door without making a noise, undressed and shared a bed together.[3]

Like all testimony emerging from the Basque witch-hunt, María's passed through the hands of interpreters and judges before reaching us. What remains of her words has survived because two Spanish inquisitors, the 'believers' Valle and Becerra, used it in their manifesto against the sceptical Salazar. The events described – to the extent that they could have happened – can perhaps be situated in 1607, although María's testimony dates to the early part of 1609.[4] It is somewhat of an outlier, probably because of its early date. The sabbat, as she described it, simply feels more real than some of the other narratives we have encountered – its apparent reality was also why Valle and Becerra used it as proof. They emphasized that she 'always went on foot and she never greased herself' with a potion to fly there.[5] Where María unwittingly walked to the sabbat, almost all the children and teenagers interrogated somewhat later by the Bordeaux judges claimed to have been abducted by adults. They were taken to the witches' gathering against their will. If Ximildegui's testimony supports an earlier argument – that the sabbat as an imaginary space was elaborated over time – then it is still more unique for other reasons. It is the only sabbat narrative from the Pays de Labourd not to have passed through Pierre de Lancre's hands. It is also relatively complete. The sabbat may have fascinated de Lancre, but he rarely excerpted testimony from a single witness at any length.[6] His more thematic survey of the sabbat offered the children's initiation barely a sideways glance.[7]

This chapter is devoted to recovering the agency and (to the extent that we can) the perspective of the children and teenagers caught up in the Basque witch-hunt.[8] Opening it with María de Ximildegui's testimony may help us centre the experiences of young people that have been all too often brushed out of this witch-hunt. We have already studied de Lancre's sense of wonder and his apparently boundless capacity to believe. Historians usually do not move on from there. His credulity acts as a convenient cloak obscuring the agency of his witnesses: 'one marvels at the ease with which an experienced lawyer, already in his fifties, gives credence to the undisciplined imaginings of frustrated children and adolescents.'[9] As innocent victims, these children have received plenty of sympathy from scholars over the years, but they are still to be silenced – their testimony should never have been heard, let alone believed – so that responsibility and blame can be placed squarely on de Lancre.

The roles of children and teenagers are not that easily erased; they stand at the heart of the witch-hunt itself. As we have seen already, notably with the dramatic testimony of Catherine de La Masse in the church of Saint-Jean-de-Luz, adolescents had played a major part in escalating the witchcraft panic from the beginning. Groups had been taken to Bordeaux for questioning. Their parents rightly worried about them. Seemingly snatched away and taken to the witches' sabbat against their will, how could they not? Across early modern Europe, the idea that children were more easily susceptible to spiritual influences, from the devil or from God, was widespread.[10] Basque fears were more specific because parents knew that it had happened before. Children had acted as catalysts for witch-hunting in the Basque country for a century or more. Using evidence for Spanish Navarre, Lu Ann Homza has shown that 'infected children' (as one Inquisition official called them) played a similarly crucial role as the witch-hunt spread into Spain.[11] Their role in the Basque witch-hunt was exceptional by any standard. In the Labourd, the commissioners used them as their 'secret spies'; they observed the sabbat at night and reported back during the day.[12] But children featured in many early modern witch-hunts, and historians have long been aware of this. Denunciations of 'the wanton mischief of undisciplined youngsters' and 'little monsters' go back decades, but there has been surprisingly little analysis, perhaps because the topic has been so difficult.[13]

Calling the young people at the centre of this hunt child-witches may seem a convenient shorthand but it would be fundamentally wrong. Despite their presence and even participation at the sabbat, they were *not* witches – the witch-hunt simply could not have happened if they had been.[14] Child-witches as *witches* deserved death. De Lancre admired the Lorraine judge and author Nicolas Remy for presiding over the execution of 'criminal children', including a boy 'under the age of seven' who had received poison at the witches' sabbat out of the devil's hands. 'We should not spare the life of a child', de Lancre declared, 'so we may protect the many others they will devastate with their wicked ways, through witchcraft, poison, or otherwise.'[15] He disapproved of the leniency his Bordeaux colleagues had shown towards the teenage werewolf Jean Grenier a few years earlier, sentencing the thirteen-year-old to life imprisonment rather than death. 'Feed and tame a wolf,' he warned, 'it will still be a wolf.'[16]

But neither the Lapurdi communities nor the Bordeaux judges saw the teenagers as witches. They were bewitched innocents who needed to be protected and whose word could be trusted. Almost all the bewitched youths who were caught up in the Basque witch-hunt appear to have escaped execution. They were treated as *witnesses*, not witches, even though what they witnessed was the witches' sabbat. Whether they visited the sabbat by accident, as María de Ximildegui claimed she had done, or were taken by force, they were unwilling spectators and participants. In other words, Basque teens existed in a strange, legal Goldilocks zone; they were old enough to testify but young enough to be victims. Their treatment raises important questions about how the early modern period viewed children and adolescents and defined legal responsibility.

We need to find out, therefore, when early modern childhood ended and innocence was lost. We also need to take stock of our own attitudes. Fear and paranoia about widespread child abuse – 'save the children' – have been the building blocks of the most grotesque conspiracy theories of our own age. A famous British study of the so-called satanic scare of the 1980s and early 1990s drew its inspiration from the Basque witch-hunt. Although the study deconstructs and criticizes the image of children as innocent archetypal victims of evil, it nevertheless perpetuates it by attributing – as the traditional narrative did – most of the agency to adults who put words into children's mouths.[17] Recent American scholarship has shown that some of the abuse allegations of the period were credible, and that preoccupation with the 'witch-hunt narrative' caused some cases of child abuse to be unjustly dismissed.[18]

We, as a society, are thus much better placed to understand the panic of parents than we are the perspective of children. Young people are great storytellers, who can keep reality and fantasy apart and tell credible lies based on the world they know. Children today recognize that magic is false, but they readily believe in miracles. One child psychologist predicted that a trip back in time would show that early modern children took witches to be 'an extraordinary but credible part of reality'.[19] We also need to accept that children can be cruel and have a strong sense of in- and out-groups. During the French Wars of

Religion, they were capable of committing violence against those belonging to other faiths.[20] What makes this witch-hunt so unfathomable is that some children seemed to accuse their own relatives of witchcraft. Like others that we have challenged, the presumption of child innocence has turned this witch-hunt into a more comfortable morality tale, with helpless victims, evil judges and us the reader as the arbiter between them. The truth is messier. Even if they escaped execution, de Lancre's witnesses were nevertheless victims not just of witches but also of the legal process – their bodies were prodded for further information about the sabbat. They were victims, but with their words they caused the deaths of others.

The mental world of children is hard enough to access even in the present, and our sources – primarily de Lancre's *Tableau* – adopt a very different vantage point. But it pays to keep an open mind. The testimony of María de Ximildegui, who followed her friend to the sabbat, already directs us towards important factors: the sociability among children and teens, and the possibly subversive role played by youth culture. Young people built this demonic netherworld together in groups. Before we get there, we need to see how children and teens fitted within the commission's day-to-day activities and how de Lancre and Espagnet co-opted them. This chapter's first two sections, then, explore why children were treated the way they were – why they were witnesses, not witches – and how they acted as an informal extension of the commission's personnel. While much remains unknown and unknowable, the crucial aspects of this witch-hunt fall into place once we look at how the children engaged with each other, with their anxious parents and with the persons they accused of witchcraft.

## Witnesses *versus* witches

From the outset, the *Tableau* emphasized a distinction between the witnesses and the accused witches. The preface promised the reader a 'straightforward account of the depositions of the witnesses and the confessions of the accused', reproduced in their original 'naive' form. As we saw, de Lancre offered up the testimony of 'sixty to eighty famous witches and five hundred witnesses'. What set the latter group apart from the former is not immediately made clear because they too 'had received the devil's mark (which wonderfully confirms their testimony)' and therefore they had also entered the dark lord's service. The witnesses, in fact, attended the sabbat on a daily basis: witnesses either 'go to the sabbat every day and make every effort to release themselves' or they 'confess they have been and no longer go, having liberated themselves from the sabbat and the devil'.[21] The inflated figure of six hundred executions – first cited at the very end of the seventeenth century – can be traced back to legitimate bewilderment about the difference between these two categories. The number seems to have been arrived at by adding together the two categories (eighty witches + five hundred witnesses) and then rounding up.[22]

What is not apparent at all from the *Tableau*'s opening pages is the main difference between the witches and the witnesses: age. That these witnesses were children and adolescents becomes apparent only as the book unfolds. De Lancre's silence suggests how legally questionable the issue of trusting this type of testimony – *by* children and *about* the witches' sabbat – might have been. Only in the letter of dedication – to Sillery, the chancellor of France – did he briefly mention children, in their role as the commission's spies. The judges, de Lancre claimed, arranged for the witches to be followed to their nocturnal assemblies, 'by an infinity of witches who had left the profession and by children who, like secret spies, attended every sabbat'. Through them, 'we have discovered [everything] to the smallest detail'.[23] Claims such as these show how symbiotic the relationship between the Bordeaux judges and Basque youths had become – the children were foot soldiers making incursions into the demonic nether realm on the commissioners' behalf. The passage also makes it clear that the witnesses did not only testify about the sabbat but also *against* the witches. And yet, the reference to *former* witches, also apparently left unharmed, shows that the difference between the two categories was decidedly murky. Why would one trust the testimony of a former witch? Why would one believe that they abandoned the devil? How did they leave his service? And why did their past crimes not deserve punishment? These are good questions that de Lancre does not answer.

Still, the larger and crucial point is clear enough: the vast majority of those interrogated about the sabbat, then, were not witches at all – they were witnesses. And as strange as that may seem, de Lancre and Espagnet were following precedent that had already been set. Children and teenagers had already been escorted to Bordeaux during the witch-hunt's earlier stages where they were confronted with the accused witches. From at least 1605, the Basque witch-hunt had been sustained by the testimony of children and teenagers, and in fact, it remained so as it spread into Spain.[24] María de Ximildegui was to all intents and purposes another 'witness', and the two inquisitors who defended the reality of the sabbat against the sceptical Salazar treated her as such, even praising her as a 'girl of good understanding and exemplary life'.[25] In Spain, too, groups of children were not only the victims of witches, they became, as their foremost historian put it, 'relentless accusers and eyewitnesses'.[26]

The sabbat, as we saw in the previous chapter, stood revealed as a highly structured society of evil-doers: the witches were led by kings and, especially, queens. The children were evidently at the bottom of this hierarchy. The younger Zugarramurdi witches confessed to having had a *maestro* or teacher. Twenty-year-old Joanes de Sansinena, for instance, identified his uncle Miguel de Goiburu as the teacher 'who made him a witch and whom he was serving'.[27] Perhaps taking this relationship literally, six children in Urrugne accused their schoolteacher of taking them to the witches' sabbat.[28] While the very youngest were given toads to guard ('the children who guard the toads are only spectators'), it is striking how many witnesses claimed to have been present from an early age. De Lancre estimated that 2,000 children had been dedicated to the devil and possessed the insensible witch's (or devil's) mark to prove it.[29] Teenagers confessed to having had sex at the sabbat, and some seemed to have overindulged in it. The commission's star witness, sixteen-year-old Jeanette d'Abadie, not only had commerce with the devil but a 'hundred times' with other men, yet never outside the sabbat which, for de Lancre, confirmed that the gatherings were real. Both her evident sexual knowledge and her abstinence outside the sabbat (so she must have learned it *there*) 'wonderfully confirm the reality' of these infernal meetings.[30]

The age, innocence and ignorance of the witnesses could excuse demonic deceptions as well as imperfections or inconsistencies in their testimony. De Lancre claimed that 'to better deceive the children and those who start attending these feasts ... the devil wants to make it seem like the [witches] are eating; they chew like cows and move their jaws as if they are really eating'.[31] In the 1613 edition, perhaps in response to criticism from his Bordeaux colleagues, he even excused young women for having sex with the devil because they were 'unaware of the evil they were performing'. For them, demonic intercourse was akin to sex 'with some god, as the virgins in antiquity [who] gladly prostituted themselves for and mixed with their false gods', which had similarly been devils in disguise.[32]

Of all the many activities at the sabbat, potion-making does appear to be the only one from which children and teenagers were actively excluded. It highlights how the witnesses were first and foremost victims – the victims of witches, in fact. This is most evident in the way that they travelled to the sabbat. María de Ximildegui may have attended by accident, but these later witnesses were abducted. Witches stole children straight 'out of the arms of their father and mother'. They could also be given a 'bewitched and poisoned apple' or a piece of bread that would make them not only defenceless but even 'burn with desire' to go to the sabbat.[33] The royal letters patent that set up the witchcraft commission claimed that the petitioners did not dare 'let their children leave their homes without them being immediately caught by this evil' – presumably they referred to this type of sabbat snatching as well.[34]

The clearest evidence for the way the two categories – witnesses and witches – worked comes from the sole example when one accidentally transgressed their assigned role – and paid the ultimate price. Even though she was only seventeen years old, Marie Dindarte from the inland village of Sare was 'one of the most notable *witches*' de Lancre had encountered during his campaign. She made the mistake of confessing that she flew alone to the sabbat when her neighbours had left without her. Worse than that, she had taken three children with her, which together with her flight hours, made her into one of the Labourd's most (in)famous witches, notwithstanding her youth. Very likely, the girl had no idea what boundary she had crossed. Marie had confessed 'continuously without torture'. She had accused other witches who were also sentenced to death, 'partly on her testimony and evidence', until she found herself on the scaffold alongside them. Only then, when it was too late, 'did she deny everything'.[35] By inadvertently and tragically crossing an important yet, for her, invisible line, Marie showed how the normal classifications fuelled this witch-hunt. Two girls of a similar age made the same mistake of taking children to the sabbat 'although they themselves were very often taken by others' – their ultimate fate, as so often in this history, is unknown.[36] The impunity with which witnesses could testify as the victims of witchcraft offers at least a partial explanation for why the witch-hunt took on the dimensions that it did. Their agency as accusers depended on their passivity as victims, but it enabled them to testify and damn others without danger to their own lives.

De Lancre's excitement at discovering Marie's true nature could hardly be contained because *witches* hardly ever confessed willingly: 'a female witch who flies in the air hardly ever confesses because she is one of the famous teachers.' As Marie's accidental transgression shows, de Lancre possessed an almost child-like ability to take testimony literally and at face value, without regard for any wider repercussions. Other witnesses, as we saw, were *former* witches, and this is similarly only reported as fact. As a result, the category of witness thus seems to even encompass the 28-year-old Marie de La Ralde 'who left this abomination five or six years ago'.[37] As this suggests, other factors also underpin this distinction between witches and witnesses. Age and appearance emerge as important but by no means airtight markers. Septua- and octogenarians appear prominently among the Labourd victims, as they do in Zugarramurdi.[38] Many of the young or attractive witnesses did not *look* like witches. When searching for the devil's mark, for instance, the judges permitted the Bayonne surgeon they hired to examine only the bodies of the suspected witches, *not* those of the witnesses. It was 'more reasonable', de Lancre wrote without revealing the surgeon's name,

> to extinguish in him the carnal desires that such visits could inflame (by making him see only living old flesh, so horrible that it is a wonder that even the devil would wish to know them), rather than exciting him by visiting, probing, touching and testing these young little girls, who in this country are much too willing to show their mark in whichever part of the body it may be.[39]

(It is striking how, while imagining these sexual encounters, de Lancre finds it easier to empathize with the devil rather than with the women.)

Some, though by no means all, of the witches fit the stereotype of the witch as a figure who has lost her desirability through old age. One of the most prominent and recurring witches was Necato. (Our judge seems particularly taken with her because her name, in Latin, was associated with death.) The 1613 edition of the *Tableau* added a striking image of her as having so 'effaced' her sex that she could have passed as a man or a hermaphrodite: 'because she entirely had the face, speech and posture of a man, she even [appears] rude, swarthy, and darkened as a forest creature or savage who only frequents the woods and the mountains, bearded like a satyr, with eyes that are small, deep-set, furious and fierce like those of a wild cat.' So frightful was her appearance that the 'young boys and girls who she took to the sabbat' could not bear to look at her when they accused her in front of the judges.[40] Necato's actions possibly also transgressed her gender role. A witness accused her of 'sleeping with a 20- to 25-year-old girl called Sandoteguy'.[41]

This distinction, that the young people de Lancre and Espagnet interviewed were not treated as witches because they did not *look* like them, has considerable mileage. It may also explain the judges' favourable treatment of 28-year-old Marie de la Ralde – we are told that she was 'very beautiful'.[42] We have seen de Lancre describe the girls as 'beautiful' and 'very delicate' on other occasions. Yet, as with all arguments, there are limits to how far age and beauty alone will get us. Neither the witches nor the witnesses were exclusively female. The small group of male witnesses seems to skew younger, perhaps because boys as young as twelve could join the crews setting out for the Canadian fishing grounds as apprentices.[43] Perhaps predictably, de Lancre shows barely any interest in the men's appearance. The female suspects, however, did not always fit the stereotype either, and some even subverted it. Unlike the elderly queens of the Zugarramurdi *akelarre*, the devil chose 'young and beautiful witches' to be at his side in the Labourd. The Bordeaux judge vouchsafed that these queens were 'endowed with a certain beauty that was much more distinctive than the others'. At least one was put to death at Urrugne – we already encountered her refusing the executioner's 'kiss of pardon': 'she did not wish to pollute [her] pretty mouth that used to be stuck to the devil's behind.'[44]

Age may also explain the prominence of teenagers among the witnesses. There are only two prepubescent children among the roughly two dozen witnesses who can be identified by name.[45] Teens appear to have been particularly useful: old enough to bear witness, but, when seen from the right vantage point, still young enough to count as victims. This attitude doubtlessly served its purposes but also reflected the malleability of early modern childhood, when young people were often old enough for one thing but not another. In France, the age of consent even varied by territory according to local custom. In Bayonne, boys could legally make a will from the age of fourteen, girls from the age of thirteen, but they could not sell any property without the consent of a parent, guardian or judge under the age of twenty-five.[46] The rules were different again for the Pays de Labourd, which had its own set of privileges.[47] The onset of puberty – usually defined as twelve years for girls, fourteen for boys – emerges as an important marker of credibility, and de Lancre acknowledged its importance, even though he maintained that the testimony of younger children could be trusted as well. In the *Tableau*'s final section – probably in response to criticism – he defended the use of witnesses as young as six years, assuming they accused those who took them to the sabbat 'staunchly and without ever changing' and possessed the devil's mark.[48] (More on those marks later.) For the most part, however, he peppered his work with testimony of those 'of the right age': that is, older teens and young former witches.[49] The absence of identifiable pre-teens from the *Tableau* thus suggests how controversial their use may have been.

Young children were nevertheless an active part of the witch-hunt and, as part of large anonymous groups, they were part of the fabric of the *Tableau* a well: '200 to 300 children universally' told the commissioners that they were abducted at night 'even though they were in the arms of their parents, brothers or sisters, without waking anyone up'. Elsewhere, de Lancre claimed to have witnessed 'a hundred depositions from many children, aged between six and twelve and older, [who] all made a pact with the devil, renounced God, and received an insensitive seal and mark, like they were his slaves'. Towards the book's close, he claimed to have seen 'more than 500' child witnesses – more than the figure mentioned in the preface – who had been taken to the sabbat and been given a stick with which to guard toads.[50] These allusions raise important questions about the relationships between younger and older witnesses. How teenagers and pre-pubescent children interacted with and viewed each other is one of the witch-hunt's enduring mysteries. De Lancre's omission of almost all pre-pubescent testimony makes an answer impossible.[51]

It may well be that the commission's main innovation was the use of *younger* witnesses. We do not know the age of the witnesses who were taken to Bordeaux for questioning during the earlier stages of the witch-hunt, only that some were described as 'girls'. They could all have reached the age of puberty. Still, even if the commissioners expanded the age range of their witnesses, they still used a great many teenagers. De Lancre claimed that two of the witch-priests had no fewer than forty eye-witnesses 'of the right age' against them – enough to convict them, even though they never confessed.[52] These children and adolescents, then, were in some ways an extension of the commission's workforce, acting as trusted spies at the sabbat and as expert witnesses in the courtroom. For us to make sense of their experiences – and to understand how they came to take on this seminal role – we must first work out how they fitted within the commission's working practices.

## The commission at work

We have little sense of what a typical working day would have looked like for the commissioners as they crisscrossed the Pays de Labourd. Pierre de Lancre did not tell us, just as he did not tell us the route that the commission took. As so often, historians have filled this silence with a great deal of speculation. His colleague Jean d'Espagnet is supposed to have abandoned de Lancre for an investigation of the highly unstable border with Spain. De Lancre's sole assistant, it seems, was his Basque interpreter, who, it was argued, played a crucial role in spreading the witchcraft panic into Spain.[53] Reality was very different. The witch-hunt of the Pays de Labourd was not a one-man mission. The two judges worked side by side, and they were assisted by a coterie of formal and informal support staff, drawn from both Bordeaux and the Basque country. Children, as the commission's spies, were a vital extension of that apparatus, but to truly understand their role and the deadly consequences of their testimony, we must delve more deeply into the commission's daily activities.

A newly discovered manuscript may be of use here. Espagnet's report on the border inspection has laid seemingly undisturbed amidst the vast collections of France's national library in Paris. On one level, it is a frustrating read. It only mentions witchcraft once near the end, when it describes Espagnet's return journey on horseback to the village of Saint-Pée 'to continue work on our commission concerning the crime of witchcraft in the Pays de Labourd'. Yet, for the one week – from 21 to 27 September 1609 – that the two judges were apart, the document kept a meticulous record of Espagnet's movements and the procedures he adopted. It stands to reason that some of these were also followed by the witchcraft commission.

We can assume, for instance, that communities welcomed the commissioners in the same way the officials of Saint-Jean-de-Luz greeted Espagnet. The mayor and aldermen of Saint-Jean-de-Luz promised the president of the Parlement that 'they will not fail to obey the will of His Majesty and our decrees'.[54] Where the witchcraft commission was concerned, the royal letters patent demanded obedience from all officials, including 'mayors and magistrates ... on pain of rebellion'.[55] The arrival of the witchcraft commission may have also been accompanied by a church service. Pierre de Lancre reported attending one at Cambo-les-Bains on 4 October 1609, a Monday.[56] More ominously, churches were also spaces where Basques conducted their public business, but no evidence of the judges addressing local congregations has survived.

After these formal (early afternoon) pleasantries, Espagnet's inspection of the border moved at a brisk pace, with the judge often starting work at 7 in the morning or earlier.[57] The witchcraft commission must have adopted a similar work ethic, if they were to interrogate the many, many witnesses and witches in the limited time available. Espagnet's report also reveals a procedural factor that makes de Lancre's witness figures appear more plausible. When, on 25 September, the president questioned fourteen older male residents on their shared experiences of living across a river from dangerous Spaniards, he interrogated them as a *group*. Espagnet submitted a set of nine articles for their comment. After they conferred amongst themselves (the entire examination lasted from 2 pm to dusk), 'they made us understand via the interpreter' that they had agreed a shared set of responses.[58] The witchcraft commission appears to have adopted a similar approach, interrogating children together, or at least in each other's presence. The judges had witnesses re-enact the dances of the sabbat together, while even some of the individual descriptions of the sabbat read as if they were built on – or bounced off – the words of others. De Lancre's description of the devil's rather varied appearance at the sabbat, studied in the last chapter, ended with the comment that 'all were agreed that there was a big chair which appeared golden and very pompous'.[59]

During his away mission, Espagnet was assisted by at least two members of staff: his personal clerk from Bordeaux, Charles Dubley, responsible for summoning witnesses and keeping the official record, and a certain *Monsieur* de Hyrigoyen (a blank space for his first name was not filled in), 'clerk [*greffier*] of the Pays de Labourd taken by us ... to translate the Basque language'.[60] The support staff for the witchcraft commission was substantially larger (which also makes the barrel of wine sent by the Bayonne aldermen, mentioned in an earlier chapter, a more proportionate gift). The letters patent setting up the commission permitted the two judges to delegate their authority to others who could 'assist you and work either jointly with you or separately in the instruction of proceedings'.[61] This they apparently did with Auger de Ségure, empowering the 'self-styled *assesseur criminel*' of the Pays de Labourd to try the suspects he had rounded up before the commission's arrival.[62]

Three further junior Bordeaux officials pop up in the *Tableau*, all in rather curious circumstances. Two of them, a clerk and a lawyer (*procureur*), overheard a suspected witch in church shout *barrabam, barrabam* ('the devil! the devil!') just as the priest at the altar was raising the Eucharist. Not knowing 'the importance of these words', the two men reported the incident to de Lancre afterwards who was only too delighted to enlighten them.[63] Still stranger was the incident attributed to another Bordeaux lawyer; a certain Laurent de Moisset, who had 'assisted' the commissioners in Bayonne and 'encountered' two women while travelling along the coast towards Hendaye. The purpose of this journey is entirely unclear – perhaps he had been sent to prepare that village for the judges' arrival. The two 'non-witches' (as the *Tableau* calls them) claimed to have overheard a thrashing at a sabbat so savage and loud that they could hear it from far away – they even recognized the usually fearsome Necato from her screams as she was being beaten by a male witch.[64]

Like many others spread across the *Tableau*, these anecdotes are purposely perplexing. They showcase the strange new worlds – a Basque surface world and the demonic one hidden underneath – that the judges were entering. Each also has a separate objective. The first allowed de Lancre to flaunt his demonic expertise to his underlings (and to us!), while the second furnished proof that the sabbat was a real physical space that outsiders could observe, even hear. Our judge's tales of the demonic often raise more questions than we can hope to answer. Yet, when we approach his excitable and at times surreal narrative from an angle, it reveals basic facts and details – such as the presence of support staff – that can help ground the commission's operations in the real world.

For the same reason, it is important to make visible the layer of translation that kept the Bordeaux judges at a remove from the Basque world that surrounded them. Their inability to speak the local language exoticized both the Pays de Labourd and its inhabitants. The need for translation must have made accused witches look more 'other' and perhaps more guilty as well. The language barrier not only fed de Lancre's curiosity, it was also a source of anxiety, making visual confirmation more important. While the judges inspected alleged sabbat locations for proof, the bodies and emotions of witches and witnesses provided a more immediate conduit to the diabolical. De Lancre disagreed with those witchcraft theorists who had claimed that witches could not shed tears because a forty-year-old woman from Biarritz had 'cried so bitterly as I have ever seen a creature cry'. He observed female witches in Bayonne endure torture 'in such a manly fashion and with such joy' that they dozed off – it seems that they passed out.[65] Such claims neatly fit the exoticizing discourse that we are trying to escape. Early modern ethnographers often presented insensitivity to pain as an unnatural attribute of barbarity. The witches' 'manly' fortitude supports de Lancre's othering of the Basques, making them seem less than fully human. He took a particular interest in the devil's marks for the same reason, and famous visitors were even invited to help search for them.

As a result, the *Tableau* conveys some unease about the role and reliability of translation. De Lancre even conceded that 'our ignorance of the Basque language gave our interpreters the freedom to inform themselves properly without us being any the wiser'. Such an admission should worry us – after all, we are equally reliant on the quality of their work – and it might provoke some radical scepticism whether any aspect of the witch-hunt can ever be knowable. Yet, as we have seen in the previous chapter, Basque sabbat testimony remained remarkably consistent, even when it was filtered through two very different – French and Spanish – legal systems and crossed into two different languages. The number of different interpreters used, both in the Basque country and in Bordeaux, provides further assurance. The Parlement used two interpreters simultaneously; the commission also used several, though perhaps not at the same time. De Lancre claimed that 'the witches were also questioned on the witness chair before our colleagues and assistants who almost all understood the Basque language'.[66] Concerns about the reliability of the testimony, then, remain vastly overblown, while the judge's description also illustrates how crowded and semi-public the interrogation chamber must have been.

De Lancre never identified any of the interpreters by name but did reveal the use of a priest who volunteered his services to the commission. That the commissioners decided to employ priests – they also turned to canons of Bayonne cathedral – is surprising for several reasons. Clerics, 'installed by the devil in almost all the most famous parishes', featured prominently among the commission's victims. As we saw, concern about carnal desire had caused the judges to limit the role of the surgeon to inspecting the aged skin of the older witches. Although de Lancre apparently had similar qualms in this instance – it was 'shameful to a priest to hear an infinity of testimony about sex with the devil' – he did not act on them. The priest, he admitted, 'felt greater shame asking our questions' about demonic coupling than the girls had in answering them: 'thirteen- to fourteen-year-old little girls expressed themselves more freely than we dared ask.' They 'express themselves so happily and with such joy about their shameless embraces, and about the length, width and size of the [devil's] natural equipment that these sordid testimonies cannot pass through [the interpreters'] mouths and chaste ears without causing them offence'.[67]

Historians have identified the cleric as Lorenzo de Hualde, the parish priest of Bera, a town in Spanish Navarre. As Bera would rapidly develop into a Spanish hotspot for witchcraft accusations and vigilante justice, this not only turned him into de Lancre's trusty sidekick but also made him a central conduit – alongside María de Ximildegui, Zugarramurdi's first accuser – for the witchcraft panic's spread from France into Spain. During the autumn of 1609, Hualde gathered Bera's bewitched children in his home, which he decorated with blessed herbs, candles and crucifixes to shield them from the devil.[68] (He also allegedly used violence to extract confessions out of them.) When a French official travelled to Logroño to attend the famous *auto de fe* of November 1610, Hualde was the Inquisition employee who acted as his escort.[69] Yet, important though the priest was, it is unlikely that he was de Lancre's interpreter, and he certainly cannot have acted in that role for the full four months. An important biographical detail provided by de Lancre does not match Hualde, nor does the chronology.[70] Bera's priest must have already opened his rescue centre for bewitched children while de Lancre and Espagnet were still out in the field in the Labourd.

But even if Hualde had been involved, he was not some Sancho Panza to de Lancre's Don Quixote, but part of a coterie of lawyers, notaries and interpreters who assisted the two commissioners. The judges drew on the expertise of a surgeon and executioner to help furnish the proof they needed. They even hosted some socially prestigious visitors, given the territory's position on the main route between France and Spain. De Lancre proudly showed one nobleman, the count of Saint-Pol, a magical object – a cloth belt drenched in a witch's blood – that had been confiscated.[71] When France's new ambassador to Madrid, André de Cochefilet, and his wife passed through the region, they were invited to witness the pricking of the witch's mark, with the territory's leading nobleman, Antoine de Gramont, doing the honours (see Figure 9.1). Gramont forced the needle so deeply into the girl's arm that 'the entire company and even he himself felt some concern about it'. The mark being apparently insensible, however, the girl herself 'pushed [the needle] in until the very end without any pain or feeling whatsoever'.[72]

Figure 9.1 Posthumous (?) portrait of Antoine II de Gramont (date unknown). (Musée Basque et de l'histoire de Bayonne, D.2001.1.1.)

Pierre de Lancre described at some length the successful strategy the commission's surgeon developed in searching for the mark, while the suspect was blindfolded. Holding a pin in his left hand and a 'very fine awl' in the right, the surgeon would use the top of the pin to prod the woman's body making her squirm and 'pretend to complain as if she had suffered some great pain', while at the same time piercing her 'to the bone' with the awl, about which 'she did not say a word'. Physiologically this procedure may well have worked, as the skin's more powerful and more rapid pain receptors drown out any deeper underlying pain. Yet, inevitably this approach also created false positives, and it happened 'several times' that the mark proved sensible when the surgeon tried to show it to the judges. To avoid the experience, the witches 'attempted to hide their marks' – de Lancre claimed that the devil taught them how to scratch them off: 'But none of this prevented us from visibly discovering the mark.'[73]

The extensive search for the devil's or witch's mark, painful though it must have been, did not formally count as torture. We know much less about the official use of torture during questioning, for which the commissioners presumably relied on Bayonne's executioner. Judges in Bordeaux but especially in Paris seem to have gradually lost their faith in its reliability during the early seventeenth century.[74] When de Lancre downplayed its use, he may have been responding to these growing hesitations. Torture may also not have been needed. The judge pointed out that several of the commission's witches were sentenced based on the testimony of others, without ever confessing themselves: 'an infinity of other famous female witches, for whom we had certain evidence, who at the point of death could never chase away the devil from their understanding in order to confess their crime, they fell silent and never knew how to say their Lord's Prayer, nor the Ave Maria, nor the Creed.'[75] Unconfessed and therefore unsaved, their very public deaths will have made an indelible impact on all those present.

These executions bring us back, at last, to the judges' most important agents: the 'secret spies', the children and teenagers who had acted as witnesses. It was through them that the commission's tentacles stretched out to the sabbat itself. It may seem perverse to approach them as an extension of the judges' mission rather than as their victims, but the two roles were not mutually exclusive. Some even claimed to possess a level of expertise that de Lancre seems to have coveted. One unnamed girl from Biarritz attempted to show the judges how to recognize witches by a mark – a toad's foot – which the devil had placed in their left eye: 'but we were not able to verify this point.' Jeannette de Belloc, a 24-year-old former witch, claimed to be able to see a devil sitting on the left shoulder of alleged witches. The judges summoned her to test this: 'she made some attempt to see [a devil], but it was impossible for her to show this to us.'[76]

Witch-finders like these played a prominent part in a great many hunts across Europe. Some were or had been witches themselves. In Scotland, Margaret

Aitken, the 'great witch of Balwearie', was a major figure behind the witchcraft panic of 1597 – she similarly claimed to recognize fellow witches by looking them in the eyes.[77] Children were more obvious and more trustworthy expert witnesses than convicted witches: they were innocent victims, rather than co-conspirators. As such, they acted as crucial catalysts in earlier Basque witch-hunts. In 1525, two girls, aged nine and eleven, were pardoned by the Royal Council in Pamplona and used as witch-finders in a hunt that cost over fifty people their lives. In 1595, the village of Araitz, not far from Pamplona, saw a string of accusations, based on the testimony of a twelve-year-old girl who claimed to recognize witches by a toad-shaped mark in their eyes.[78] In the wake of the French witchcraft commission, child witch-finders also crossed into Spain. In late 1610, the sceptical Jesuit Hernando de Solarte encountered a French boy in the Spanish town of Aranatz who claimed to be able to recognize witches 'on sight' – his expertise was based on his possession of a witch's mark which was found to be no more than an old abscess.[79]

Child witch-finders, then, were deeply entrenched in Basque witchcraft history. The main difference between France and Spain was that the inquisitors at the Logroño tribunal acted forcefully against such informal expertise, even at the height of the panic. At their *auto de fe* they also banished a self-appointed witch-finder in his early twenties. (The threat to their authority was obvious; the university student claimed to be an Inquisition employee as well.[80]) By contrast, the French judges relied heavily on precisely this type of expertise, which, in some cases, was provided by local officials. It was the 'mayors of the parishes' who 'provided' a seventeen-year-old girl called Morguy – no last name given – 'to be forever at our side'. 'An evil witch' had taken her to the sabbat for several years but, as with some of the other witnesses, Morguy had escaped the sect: 'it was principally she who would visit the young boys and girls of her kind who she had recognized at the sabbat and who were given to us as witnesses.'[81] The girl was 'famous in the Pays de Labourd for her special knowledge of the mark that the devil leaves on the children and witches who go to the sabbat'.[82] It was, therefore, she rather than the lustful surgeon who was charged with inspecting the bodies of the commission's young witnesses.

The commission folded both children and young former witches into its activities, valuing them as witnesses and victims, and validating their testimony and even, in some cases, their skills. As we shall see, the commission seems to have also housed and fed groups of them, at least for a time. Some sort of hierarchy seems to have existed among the witnesses. Even some with evident expertise still had their bodies examined for an insensitive mark. It was Jeannette de Belloc who claimed to see devils on the shoulders of witches, whose body Gramont had pricked for the mark. The bodies of all, or almost all, witnesses were subjected to prodding and abuse because the devil's mark confirmed their testimony. The world that these witnesses helped build – the accusations that they levelled – also caged them; their past words made for chains that were difficult to escape. When we approach the commission as a communal and collective enterprise, rather than a tale of bad individuals, we have no need for the sort of victim-blaming that caused historians to denounce specific teenagers for their 'psychopathic personality' and 'mythomaniac tendencies'.[83] Having established the role that these children played, we will now dig more deeply into their group dynamics, the relationships between parents and children and between witnesses and accused. The witnesses possessed real agency. If the commission was meant to cynically pursue a carefully predetermined set of suspects, then the children of the Pays de Labourd proved to be a fundamentally flawed targeting mechanism.

## The stuff of nightmares

When called upon to offer his own explanation for the witchcraft outbreak in the Pays de Labourd, Pierre de Lancre pointed first and foremost to the territory's men. They had failed in their role of providers. Their absence, away at sea or in the New World, prompted mothers to offer their children to 'another father', Satan. This created an opening, perhaps even a vacancy, that the devil exploited, gaining admission via 'the women, children and the majority of the clergy and priests, [having] found a way of relegating fathers and husbands to Newfoundland and other places where religion is entirely unknown to more easily set up his reign'. De Lancre offers a fascinating analysis of failing patriarchy, where the absence of the men, transformed into 'savages and sailors' by the inconstant sea, turned the women and children into followers of Satan.[84]

Even though the judge's analysis invokes the devil, it is not without value. Children and teenagers played a crucial role in this witch-hunt. Parents understandably panicked about their progeny's apparent bewitchment. Yet, de Lancre's comments also obscure the full horror of the witch-hunt by inverting the direction of traffic: mothers did not offer their offspring to Satan; children *accused* their parents of witchcraft. Mothers certainly turned to the witchcraft commissioners. When de Lancre and Espagnet arrived in Urrugne, they presented six (probably younger) children to them because they had been taken to the sabbat by an imprisoned witch and beaten so savagely there that they were left bleeding. (When the judges asked to see their buttocks for themselves, the children claimed a 'certain water' had washed off the beating but, interestingly, 'we still found all of them marked'.) These mothers, 'in the company of an infinity of others touched by the same misfortune', saw the judges as an alternative solution when their only remedy so far – 'filling the churches at night to prevent transport to the sabbat' – was failing.[85] At another unnamed village, a group of mothers accused a single female witch of taking their children to the sabbat, 'a dozen children which these poor fathers and mothers carried into our presence every day to get us to pity them'.[86]

The relations between parents and children, as well as those amongst the children themselves, are key to how the witch-hunt unfolded. While travelling through an area of Spanish Navarre known as the Five Towns (*Las Cinco Villas*), the Jesuit Hernando de Solarte gradually discovered that parents were forcing their children to confess to witchcraft. The parish priest of Bera, Lorenzo de Hualde, whom we encountered already, went to extraordinary lengths to make his sixteen-year-old nephew confess after other children had seen him at the sabbat, going so far as 'to tie him to a bed naked and give him so many lashes that he had to be carried out in sheets, struggling to breathe'.[87] Lu Ann Homza, using slander trials from Pamplona's secular courts, has shown that parents (and, indeed, others) likely encouraged children into making specific witchcraft accusations, as children could not be prosecuted for public insults.[88] Another, perhaps, stronger impetus for parents on the Spanish side of the border to force their children to confess was to keep them safe, whether from witches or from judges. A general Edict of Grace absolved those who admitted their guilt: children who confessed received both spiritual and legal protection.

The same factors were probably at work in the Labourd. We saw that relatives of the early Saint-Jean-de-Luz suspects tried but failed to force Catherine de La Masse into admitting that her stepfather was behind her witchcraft accusations. Even without a formal edict, witnesses enjoyed a protected status as the victims of witchcraft. Unfortunately, sources for Lapurdi are more limited than those that survive for Spanish Navarre, leaving much unknown or unknowable. The only contemporary witchcraft slander case does not involve child witnesses. The territory lacked a Solarte or a Salazar, willing to lend a sympathetic ear to a child retracting a witchcraft accusation or describing parental pressures. And yet, in other ways, the *Tableau* provides ample evidence of deep parental concern: witches stole children out of their mothers' arms, and parents slept alongside them in churches sometimes even keeping them awake at night to prevent them from being snatched.[89] Children were made to wear hand-shaped amulets around their neck made of stone, silver or lead to 'chase away the evil spirit'.[90] As we saw, parents pleaded with the commission to stop witches from taking their children. All that makes it likely that concerned parents would confront their offspring about hair-raising sabbat stories. It would be an understandable approach, but one which certainly backfired.

Just as important as the relationship between parents and children were those amongst youngsters because they were generally going to the sabbat *together*. María de Ximildegui went to the sabbat accidentally, not knowing what it was, unlike later accounts of forcible abductions by witches. Yet, her narrative also foreshadows two central themes of the Lapurdi testimony: children and teenagers travelled to the sabbat together at night and they socialized there.

The legal process encouraged these children to stick together, long before they crowded into churches at night for their safety. They were sent to Bordeaux for questioning in groups in late 1606. The commissioners were also working with bands of children. Local officials from Sare, a village the commission never visited, escorted more than a dozen 'witnesses' to Saint-Pée for questioning.[91] They, as well as other witnesses, slept together while in the commission's care. In Urrugne, 'between twenty and twenty-five witnesses' slept in two rooms in the same house in which the witch Necato was also held. In Saint-Pée, a group of witnesses stayed in the same lodgings as de Lancre, 'where they slept out of fear of being taken'.[92]

This did not stop the sabbatical visits. In Saint-Pée, fifteen witnesses were taken to the nocturnal assembly 'by the women who usually took them there', while at Urrugne 'almost all went to the sabbat'.[93] Marie Dindarte, the seventeen-year-old who turned out to be such 'an excellent witch', testified that the devil himself opened the window of the children's bedroom in Saint-Pée (located below de Lancre's own chamber) in order to take the Sare witnesses to the sabbat, 'when we had told these poor people that they would be safer in our lodgings than elsewhere'. These children not only slept but also testified together. The Saint-Pée youngsters 'who went to the sabbat nearly every night' were summoned when a local girl claimed to be attending the sabbat in her birth village of Sare instead: 'they all ingeniously confessed to us that they had never seen her at the sabbat at Saint-Pée.' This world-building was communal and difficult to escape. All the Sare witnesses agreed with Dindarte's description of their night-time excursion, except for one: 'all confessed this to us but one, who by common consent was found not to be seen [at the sabbat], what he also very strongly and firmly denied.'[94] Another murkier incident, reported by de Lancre in the margins of a later work, suggests individual children may have been pressured, perhaps even beaten, by their peers, to conform: 'one girl, aged eighteen, [after being] beaten at the sabbat, she denied at first all that she had confessed, [but] she could in the end not deny it, having been convinced by her companions who went to the sabbat with her every night.'[95]

No wonder, then, that the commissioners woke up to news from the sabbat every morning. They were not judging events after the fact but were co-opted as actors in an active drama that was still unfolding, further deepening their involvement. But this level of complicity was a two-way street. Children will have received inducements for their testimony, whether intentionally or otherwise. Across the border, the Jesuit Solarte on his visit to Bera discussed the ulterior motives of the bewitched children with Hualde's nephew, the unnamed boy ('with the morals of angel') from whom the parish priest had tried but failed to violently extract a confession. The sixteen-year-old told the Jesuit that all the children housed by his uncle 'used to eat millet [*animal fodder*] but now are given very well to eat and drink and say what those who ask the questions want them to say'.[96] However temporary they may have been, the sleeping arrangements in de Labourd indicate something similar was at play there. There was certainly plenty of validation and encouragement. De Lancre was impressed with some witnesses, praising their 'marvellous spirit' and clear testimony.[97] The judges were more than willing to accept their sabbat testimony, and the reality of demonic deceptions and substitute bodies, to square it with the physical imprisonment of both the accusers and the accused.

And yet, we cannot make sense of the true victims of the witch-hunt, those accused and executed as witches, whose words are almost entirely absent from the *Tableau*, without paying attention to the group behaviour of the children themselves. The witch-hunt's most notable targets – priests and parents – were both figures of authority and a threat to group cohesion. With their churches taken over by sleeping children, the territory's clergy were intimately involved in attempts to solve the 'dream epidemic', the nightmarish visits to the sabbat. Priests were the first and most obvious port of call in the spiritual fight against the devil. When they failed to protect children from evil, they fell under suspicion of witchcraft themselves. In the summer of 1608, María de Ximildegui travelled from Ciboure to a 'wise' priest in Hendaye for absolution, 'who supplied her with great spiritual remedies with which to resist the devil'.[98] In February 1609, Jeannette de Belloc, one of the witnesses in the *Tableau*, turned to the same prior, Jean de Harrousteguy, for similar reasons but she also forced him to tell 'his aunt to leave [the girl] in peace and stop taking her to the sabbat'.[99] Evidently, the devil was getting closer, entangling the prior's family, if not yet the priest himself. Priests not only failed to release the children from the witches' clutches, their attempts to do so also posed a threat to the world that the children were building together. Releasing individual children from the devil's snares threatened the group. Ciboure's two priests were executed based on the testimony of dozens of 'witnesses', including sixteen-year-old Jeannette d'Abadie.[100] Accusing priests of holding Black Masses at the sabbat, at times even inside their own churches, effectively aligned failed protectors with the infernal enemy.[101]

Lax clerical standards explained why the Labourd's churches were no longer safe from demonic incursion. De Lancre's imagination was inevitably triggered by seroras, the celibate lay women who looked after churches. To his horror and titillation, seroras would be left alone with the priests 'in the darkness of the morning, during the churches' time of silence at noon, and in the evenings' after dusk. Even the altar, de Lancre implied, was not safe from their lust behind closed doors. Although two seroras were prosecuted, the judges remained focused on the priests, 'the greater part [of whom] are witches'. De Lancre declared, somewhat defensively, that 'so many small innocent children' and other 'impartial' witnesses had 'seen priests at the sabbat' that action needed to be taken against 'some of the most accused'.[102]

Priests, as we already saw, had families as well. The 27-year-old Pierre Bocal had barely said his first mass in Ciboure before being accused of witchcraft. (He had apparently used Black Masses at the sabbat for training exercise.) His entry into the priesthood bolstered his family's social prestige and seems to have provoked envy. Witnesses claimed that he 'amassed an infinity of money' during the offertory in church.[103] Bocal's mother, who 'raised and educated her son badly and perhaps dedicated him to Satan from birth', held a similar collection during her son's first Black Mass at the sabbat.[104] The Bocal family in Ciboure shows how witchcraft suspicions could also attach themselves to families rather than to individual women or men.

The preservation of the group may also provide at least a partial explanation for children who accused their own relatives. That children did not wish to leave this new group is suggested by the fact that new witches took over transport to the sabbat after their predecessors were executed. In Ascain, fourteen- to fifteen-year-old Catherine d'Arreioüaque, who stayed awake in church 'with several other boys and girls', was taken home by her father after the execution of the witch who had abducted her. On her first night home, however, another woman came to take her instead. Parents may well have seemed a threat to group cohesion in the same way that priests did. A second factor, equally unprovable, is that children imbibed witchcraft suspicions that had attached themselves to their family's reputation. Witch dynasties or families are present in the sources. Concerns about lineage were a prominent feature of the Zugarramurdi trials. De Lancre denounced the 'infected bloodline' of a 48-year-old woman from Villefranque who took her child to the sabbat and whose parents were known witches.[105] Perhaps, children were also simply reflecting the wider crisis in authority that was infecting the Labourd; this breakdown in family relationships certainly chimes with the factionalism and the collapse of communal ties that we have seen in many other contexts.

Although we have a precise figure for the number of priests arrested (eight) and executed (three), the number of parents who fell victim to the witch-hunt is impossible to measure. Was it enough to inspire new fears and change parental behaviour? Or were accusations confined to specific long-suspected families only? We do not know. The fact that children levelled accusations against relatives is, however, undeniable and more than just anecdotal. Marie de Marigrane, a fifteen-year-old girl from Biarritz, was often taken to the sabbat by her aunt and grandmother. Marie de la Rat, aged seventeen, testified – in her mother's presence – that the woman had led her to the sabbat. Catharine, aged eleven, and Marie de Naguille, aged sixteen, had been taken by their mother, Saubadine de Subiette. We could also infer that two informers, Marie d'Aguerre, aged thirteen, and Johannés, age unknown, were related to the notorious 'governor of the sabbat', Petry d'Aguerre (aged seventy-three), who was executed along with 'most' of his family.[106] De Lancre, in a revealing 1613 addition to the *Tableau*, observed that the devil liked it when witches dedicated their own children. Unlike 'wise women, nurses, or other witches … fathers and mothers when they give their children, give a part of themselves'. The devil was able to 'have greater domination by right and control over the bodies and souls of these poor children' as a result.[107]

A final, unanswerable question is to what extent the children realized the consequences of their actions. As we saw, one teenager ended up on the scaffold herself because she did not realize that her independent travel to the sabbat made her a witch. A lengthy addition to the preface of the 1613 edition shows the children lamenting their parents' deaths – while attending the sabbat. The judges had 'reduced [Satan] to such extremity that people at the sabbat publicly complained about him'. In particular, 'the boys and girls of the executed female witches and other relatives reproached him that you promised us that our imprisoned mothers would not die, and yet they were burnt and reduced to ashes'.[108] What do we make of de Lancre's apparent triumph over the devil? Is it possible to view the devil as a stand-in for de Lancre? Could it have been the judges, rather than the devil, who broke a promise to the children that no harm would come to the accused?

If so, this does not help us parse the devil's alleged response to these lamentations. He sought to pacify the children by convincing them that their mothers were merely resting 'in a certain place where they were much better at ease than when they were in this world', and he encouraged them to call out their names: 'Then each of these poor mistaken girls cried out the one after the other, as someone who wants to hear an echo. Each called for their mother, asking her if she was dead and where she was currently. Each responded that they were in a much better place and more at peace than before.'[109] It is a disturbing thought: the devil as these children's sole source of solace. Perhaps, the words reflect real world attempts at consolation. Whatever their origins, we can only hope it brought the young witnesses some peace.

# Chapter 10
# Opposition

The last few chapters have grappled with the reliability of our principal source and have attempted to escape its perspective. Pierre de Lancre's fascination seems to infect everything, in much the same way the devil supposedly infected the Pays de Labourd. We have, however, made a great deal of progress. Mentions of dates and places, along with a range of archival sources, made a tentative reconstruction of the witchcraft commission's route possible. A comparison with Inquisition sources not only revealed striking similarities between the French and Spanish sabbat stories but also showed the extent of de Lancre's editing: toad-finding expeditions did not interest him much, nor did the devil's sex with male witches. Reading the *Tableau* against the grain has helped us capture the role of Basque teenagers, and we glimpsed what the witch-hunt may have looked like through their eyes. As the witches' victims and accusers, they were nurtured and supported. They were effectively the judges' allies – used and abused, for sure, but also given a surprising degree of agency.

What, though, about the commission's opponents? What about the accused witches, their relatives and those who believed in their innocence? How can we use a work as slippery and partisan as de Lancre's *Tableau* to do justice to them? Ironically, the *Tableau* has often been read precisely for this purpose, in an oppositional manner, searching for traces of hostility and opposition to the commission's work. Everyone wants a hero, and witchcraft history started as a quest for principled opponents, 'men with courage enough to tear away the mask, men of integrity'.[1] With Salazar, the Inquisition seemingly supplied one for the Spanish Basque country. The situation in the Labourd was different. Yes, elite judges – Espagnet and the Bordeaux Parlement – have been identified and cast as sceptical adversaries. But in reality, the traditional argument about the Lapurdi witch-hunt demands a different, more satisfactory type of opposition. If the witch-hunt really was the work of outsiders inflicted on an innocent territory, as historians once claimed, then *local* resistance was urgently needed.

One particularly striking episode included in the *Tableau* seemed to offer historians just the right sort of home-grown heroes: the sailors who travelled to the fishing grounds off Newfoundland and returned just in time to save their kin. Some local historians have even suggested that they must have been warned and returned early – a logistical impossibility unless they were warned by witches travelling at supersonic speed.[2] Their return to Saint-Jean-de-Luz in the autumn, de Lancre lamented, created 'such disorder and so great a crowd that there was neither order nor safety in these executions'. When one 'famous witch', Marie Bonne, who had 'freely confessed' and accused others, was taken to her place of execution, 'men frequently put a knife to her throat, trying to make her disclaim and discharge the several people she had accused'. As a result, 'the witches … feared another death than the one justice had ordered', the judge claimed, demonstrating a rather implausible concern for their welfare.[3]

We should not see this event, the threatening of witches, as a *collective* expression of hostility to witch-hunting. As we have already seen before, families of suspected witches had no qualms about taking the law into their own hands, forcing their accusers to withdraw their allegations. This seems the more plausible reading of the disorder in Saint-Jean-de-Luz: witch-hunting begot more factionalism, rather than collective resistance. After all, those who accused witches had concerned relatives too. We have seen another eyewitness, the Franciscan friar Mathias de Lissalde, depict a state of lawlessness: 'everyone was their own master, each person made justice for him or herself.'[4] The Marie Bonne affair can also be placed alongside another eventful execution recounted by de Lancre, that of Saubadine de Soubiete, 'put to death a little before our commission'. When a nest of toads appeared from above the witch's head, watchers rushed for sticks and stones to throw at her, so that she ended up 'more stoned than burnt' – one of the toads, a black one and apparently her familiar, disappeared and ominously survived the ordeal.[5] In the next chapter, we shall encounter the lynching of a suspect in one of the Labourd's inland villages after the commission's departure. Despite repeated promises, she would not stop taking children to the sabbat.

The evidence, then, for Basque sailors saving the day – and saving their women – is thin at best. The one time we shall uncontrovertibly see them act collectively, in this book's final chapter, it was emphatically not to rescue an innocent victim from a grave injustice. Instead, it is increasingly clear that witch-hunting only caused further chaos, fear and disorder – ironically, the same concerns that had caused the commission to be sent to the unstable border region to begin with, and which the judges had been meant to address. A witch-hunt imposed from above and the outside may well prompt a coherent hostile response. When the impulse for witch-hunting is generated from within, as a side product of the Labourd's many internal conflicts, then we should expect conflict and fear to fragment the territory still further.

This is not to say that there were no sources of resistance. This chapter will study three of them, beginning – quite crucially – with the witches themselves. If, as we have seen, the children and teenage accusers of the Labourd possessed real agency, then we should also not underestimate the role of the accused witches. No archival documents come to our aid this time, but a close reading of the *Tableau* reveals a surprising level of resistance. The work was, after all, partly patched together from the original trial documents. For all his faults as an observer, de Lancre at times appears too distracted, too excited or just too dense to realize the implications of what he relayed. While some of their relatives may have resorted to threats and violence, the accused themselves sought to shield their loved ones, undermine the reliability of sabbat testimony, and even turn the tables against their accusers – using only their words. As accusations spread and the witch-hunt began to target less obvious suspects, different members of Bayonne's elite stepped in to protect their own. There is no evidence that the witchcraft commission ended earlier than planned, but equally it would have been difficult for the judges to carry on their investigations much longer if they had tried.

# When witches attack

On the night of 24 September, the witches of the Labourd finally had enough – or at least, that is what some later told Pierre de Lancre. They had long complained at the sabbat about the devil's inaction in the face of an escalating number of death sentences. His reassurance that the fires of justice could not hurt them – supposedly he created fake 'cold' fires for them to jump through – was not convincing. Nor were they swayed by a grandiose pledge that he would burn the judges himself.[6] He promised his followers that he would have the lords of Amou and Urtubie, 'the sponsors of our commission', killed, and he created 'an illusion' at the sabbat in which they dangled from a tree – a rather ignoble end for the two noblemen.[7] Unfortunately for Satan, this was not enough. The witches wanted to go on the offensive, and under pressure he had no choice but to lead them, perhaps taking advantage of the fact that de Lancre's colleague, Jean d'Espagnet, was conveniently away at the border. It was around eleven at night when the expedition arrived at de Lancre's lodgings in Saint-Pée, a house called 'Barbare-nena' not too far from the castle grounds. The residents were already soundly asleep.

To better mark his entrance, the devil – what else? – first had sex with one of his favourite witches, the 'pretty enough' lady of Sansinena, coupling with her pressed against the door. (De Lancre had interrogated her on his own earlier that day so he felt well equipped to make that aesthetic judgement.) But then 'Barrabam' (as the witches called the devil) seemed to hesitate: he opened the door to de Lancre's room for his followers but did not enter himself. Three 'notable witches' peeped through de Lancre's bed curtains with the intent of poisoning him but to their intense frustration, they could not. They complained to the devil, still waiting in the doorway, that 'they had no way of harming me'.

With their main aim frustrated, one of the local priests proceeded to hold a Black Mass in de Lancre's room, using the devil's black cloak to transform a table into a make-shift altar. The lady of Sansinena said a second Black Mass in the kitchen, an extraordinarily transgressive act for a woman, even in such a domestic setting. Having properly defiled de Lancre's lodgings, 'this splendid troupe' left around half past one in the morning to try their luck elsewhere. They allegedly spent half an hour at the house of Auger de Ségure, the 'self-styled *assesseur criminel*' of the Labourd, whom the Bordeaux judges had co-opted and who lived in Saint-Pée. Then they moved onto the castle itself, the residence of the lord of Amou, one of the two noblemen who had sponsored the commission. They had more success there; three witches 'accosted' Amou in his bed and put a rope around his neck.

Unfortunately for the witches, 'neither the lord of Amou nor I [de Lancre] ever felt anything'.[8] Instead, the judge, who must have been a very sound sleeper, only discovered what had supposedly happened, as he so often did, when he woke up the next morning. The impromptu sabbat in his quarters was by all accounts a sizable gathering. Among those present were the 'eighteen to twenty boys and girls from all ages, from eight to twenty-two years old' who were then under lock and key in rooms below de Lancre's own.[9] Yet, in the judge's telling, he learned the story from only four of them: two girls took part in these house sabbats, the other two had wisely stayed put and saw the witches enter or leave the house.[10] Given his eagerness to observe and study the sabbat, de Lancre was inevitably thrilled to have slept through one. He was perhaps still more excited to discover that, as a divinely ordained magistrate, he was indeed inviolate and beyond the devil's grasp, as the learned texts suggested he would be.[11]

But if de Lancre's embrace of this fictional story makes sense, what did it mean to those who constructed and first told it? De Lancre himself did not quite know what to do with the two teenagers, seventeen- or eighteen-year-old Margueritte and Lisalde (no last names given), who had fully taken part in the night's activities. Their confession presented a 'novelty'; they were the two girls mentioned in the previous chapter who, like the unfortunate Marie Dindarte, had taken other children to the sabbat. Unlike Marie, de Lancre never explicitly identified the two as witches. Alone among the teenagers, they also confessed to actively taking part in the poisoning of their neighbours, greasing their beds and cursing their doorways with unholy water. Their eventual fate is unknown. Perhaps their original abduction, the result of eating 'a bad piece of black bread' given by an 'evil witch' who captured their will, still excused them.[12] They may also have been different in another way. Their lack of a last name, their lower social status (they had been begging for food) and their peripheral status within Saint-Pée – Margueritte claimed that she had attended the sabbat in another village – suggests that they belonged to the *cagots*, a marginalized ethnic minority. The church of Saint-Pée had a separate entrance for them.[13] Whether because of their background or their suspected witchery, de Lancre clearly set Margueritte and Lisalde apart from the other teenagers: the devil's assault was described by 'two witnesses' – youngsters who had wisely remained downstairs – 'and these two girls'.[14]

If the two teenagers saw themselves as witnesses, then their sabbat narrative may well have underlined the severity of their accusations against the three principal witches whom they accused of attempting to harm de Lancre and Amou. De Lancre's key witness, Jeannette d'Abadie from Ciboure, had similarly named a witch who nibbled the ear of a local law official's dead son. (Witches, she declared, did not eat whole corpses.[15]) On the Spanish side of the border, an entirely unbothered Salazar was told by another verbose teen that he had been burnt in effigy at the sabbat.[16] This type of witness testimony heightened the urgent threat posed by witchcraft in general and perhaps made it more believable as well. If, however, Margueritte and Lisalde knew they were themselves suspected as witches, then these attacks – even though entirely imaginary – could also have been *intended* as a threat. A little before the judges arrived in the Labourd, a sabbat took place 'in the house of a servant of the noblemen of the territory' – presumably Amou or Urtubie, de Lancre's relative – during which 'some child' was killed.[17] Margueritte and Lisalde also claimed that during an earlier sabbat, a witch sucked Amou's blood from his thigh while he lay sleeping.[18]

Unfazed, de Lancre packaged these tales up and put them to work for his own purposes. He presented them as proof of the 'good war' that the judges had been waging on Satan, which had been so successful that the devil had become afraid to show himself to his witches, sending a 'small demon' in his place. Thus emboldened, the judges even sought to provoke the devil further. In Ascain, where the sabbat took place on the village square, they placed the gallows on the site where the dark lord's 'golden chair' was meant to have stood – symbolically seizing territory in the same way witches laid claim to de Lancre's bed chamber.[19] As the judge's invulnerability to nocturnal terrors shows, there was little doubt who would win this battle. Even the most devious of Satan's ruses would come to naught when faced with the fire of French justice. De Lancre's boundless curiosity about the demonic is accompanied and made possible by a breezy confidence that he maintained throughout the *Tableau*, almost until the end, interrupted only fleetingly by the allure of the Basque feminine mystique.

And yet, there are inescapable undercurrents in the *Tableau*, more unsettling and dangerous than even the diabolical but ultimately empty threats uttered against the commissioners and their allies. De Lancre's wrapping cannot hide the simple fact that Amou and Urtubie, the sponsors of his commission, were *seen* at the sabbat, not just by two young *cagot* women but also by unnamed witches from Ascain and (probably) elsewhere. The most straightforward explanation for their presence is not the one offered by de Lancre: it is that the two noblemen themselves were witches, accused and denounced by their confederates. The fact that a witch sucked Amou's blood is equally telling in this regard; as we saw earlier, the Basque devil possessed certain vampiristic traits, drinking his witches' blood. We have noted the widespread and violent factionalism in the Labourd in which the two men were heavily involved. We have also seen how class dynamics permeated sabbat testimony: Ziarnko's sabbat engraving featured both 'great lords and ladies' and 'poor witches' relegated to the margins. It should not be surprising that Amou and Urtubie would find themselves denounced as witches. At the same time, it is difficult to see the judges taking such accusations seriously, especially de Lancre, as Urtubie's relative by marriage. As so often, new questions pop up. If Amou and Urtubie were accused of witchcraft, how do we end up with the 'illusion' of them ignominiously dangling from a tree at the sabbat? Were these accusations transmuted into 'illusions' under hostile questioning? Or did these stories – the noblemen as the devil's allies or his targets – exist alongside each other? The answer is unknowable.

Other echoes of opposition in the witches' testimony are, however, unmistakable. The devil, like a priest, was collecting alms at the sabbat for use in the legal trials that 'the witches have against those who pursue them in order to burn them'. He was absent from the Urrugne sabbat for several days towards the end of July. Upon his return, he claimed to have 'pleaded their case against the Saviour and ... have won his case against Him, and he assured [the witches] that they would not be burnt'.[20] These sabbat stories may well have reflected real-life legal squabbles, notwithstanding the commission's broad remit.

The words of the witches also possessed the power to shape the course of the witch-hunt, even if they carried less of a charge than those of the supposedly innocent witnesses who denounced them. The best way to measure their impact would be to examine a single confession at length, but here the *Tableau* and the archives are sadly wanting. De Lancre vastly preferred the probably more sensational testimony from witnesses and barely cited that of the accused.[21] The only confession excerpted in the *Tableau* at any length dates to 3 September 1610, some ten months after the witchcraft commission ended. This almost two-page excerpt, however, still shows how an accused person, transported to Bordeaux after the commission had concluded its work, could use her words to shape the fate of others and perhaps even sow seeds of doubt. Doing so, however, meant accepting the identity of witch and the grim fate that entailed.

That Catherine de Barrendeguy, aged sixty, ended up confessing to the judges of the *Tournelle*, the Parlement's criminal chamber, is not surprising.

She had been imprisoned for nearly a year, likely in an old castle known for its unhealthy location.[22] She confessed 'under torture', although what that involved is not made clear. The judges also confronted Catherine with her own daughter, seventeen-year-old Marie de la Rat, who had denounced her as a witch. Her daughter's accusations fundamentally shaped Catherine's own testimony. When she confessed to taking her daughter to the sabbat, she effectively sought to save Marie, placing her firmly in the witness camp. To further underscore the girl's innocence, Catherine insisted that 'children do not make poisons and are not initiated into so great a mystery until the age of twenty or twenty-four'. Catherine was already doomed; she was rescuing her daughter by confessing, essentially, to being a bad mother.

Other aspects of Barrendeguy's confession appear as we might expect. Witches, especially those caught in a large hunt, were expected to denounce their accomplices, and Catherine did so. She named the devil's treasurer and cupbearer – to de Lancre's predictable excitement – as well as several priests whom she had seen at the sabbat. And yet, her testimony also destabilized the witch-hunt in ways de Lancre appeared not to notice. The devil was, as every early modern Christian knew, the father of lies, and Barrendeguy pushed his deceptions in a highly subversive direction. She cast doubt on the reliability of the children's testimony. 'The devil,' she claimed, 'induces little children to accuse even those who are not witches in order to destroy them.' Even if the witnesses could be trusted, what they said they saw at the sabbat might not have been real. Witches could conjure up fake versions of people whom they wished to harm: 'the devil makes and creates the said figure in response to the prayers of the said witches to cause them to be accused of witchcraft, but in this case the said figure never moves.' In court, she identified two such sabbat statues who suspiciously 'did not move at all', and on the scaffold, she gave her confessor the name of a third.[23] Perhaps, Catherine had accused these three people earlier on. By making them out to be artificial statues rather than active sabbat participants, she clearly intended to exonerate them.

The most radical witchcraft sceptics of the early modern period spotlighted the ideas implicit in Barrendeguy's testimony: that the witch-hunt itself was a grand demonic illusion, that a creature as deceitful as the devil would want innocent persons to be accused of witchcraft and that as a result – the most ironic of ironies – the witch-hunters were unknowingly doing their infernal enemy's bidding. These implications were lost on de Lancre, otherwise so taken with the devil's extreme inconstancy. For him, the creation of innocent representations at the sabbat was merely another 'very notable point of witchcraft'.[24] For Barrendeguy's strategy to be successful – she was sacrificing herself to save her daughter and some of her co-accused – it did not matter if her judges were (perhaps purposefully) dense. If she sowed shimmers of doubt about witchcraft, she also needed her word to be accepted as true. She needed to be guilty for her daughter and co-accused to go free. And the rescue of some also meant the accusation of others. Some of those Catherine accused as genuine witches – the devil's cup-bearer and treasurer, for instance – may already have perished, but others certainly had not. On the scaffold, she repeated her accusation of another witch-mother, known only as Carvart, who had taken her own children to the sabbat just as Catherine confessed she had done. With her final words, 'on the brink of death', Catherine de Barrendeguy insisted that she had spoken the truth: 'she did not wish to condemn her soul for anyone.'[25] Now that her confessor had absolved her of many dark sins, she would not risk her own salvation to save Carvart from the scaffold. Catherine's final, literally damning words may well have sent her there.

Like the sabbat feasts themselves where the foul food is never filling and the witches leave as hungry as they arrive, every unpleasant scrap of information dragged out of the *Tableau* leaves one wanting more, while making us feel complicit at the same time. The relationship between Catherine and Carvart – whether they met in prison or were long-standing enemies – is lost to us. Barrendeguy may well have felt that she needed to dramatically accuse someone to strengthen her confession and save those whom she had absolved. Possibly Carvart had played some role in Catherine's own journey to the scaffold and this was revenge. We know from witch trials elsewhere that it was not unheard of for confessed witches to seek to drag their accusers down with them, claiming they visited the sabbat like they had. Carvart's fate, however, is not recorded.

With their words, then, witches could accuse or absolve others – hence, for instance, the threats of violence levelled at Marie Bonne at Saint-Jean-de-Luz. Other witches on the scaffold would similarly behold a 'great number of their witch-relatives, friends, and neighbours' in the audience before them, who with gestures, signs and prayers beseeched the condemned to exonerate them.[26] With their testimony, confessed witches helped steer the witch-hunt just as much as the denunciations of witnesses. As a result, the larger German witch-hunts gradually climbed the social ladder in search of further victims – mayor's wives almost inevitably became targets – ultimately causing worried elites to clamp down on them.[27] In different circumstances, accusations against Urtubie and Amou could easily have had a similar result, but they were not the only members of the local elite accused. As we shall see in the remainder of this chapter, some elite actors were getting worried and, by October at the latest, they began to make moves to protect their own.

## A shadow of justice

Only one deposition made in front of the witchcraft commissioners has, through pure happenstance, survived in the archives. It was an authorized copy, complete with Espagnet's and de Lancre's signatures. It remained in Bayonne when the original returned with the commission to Bordeaux, where it was eventually lost to the flames. Dated Monday 26 October, it shows perhaps first and foremost that the commissioners continued their investigations until the very last moment – there was to be no rest for the wicked. The deposition – an 'extract from the procedure against Jehanne de Mondens, accused of witchcraft' – also highlights the extent to which we remain in the dark: Jehanne is never named in de Lancre's *Tableau* and she was almost certainly executed.[28] We shall never know how many more people like her there were.

It was not, however, Jehanne de Mondens who was in danger in late October – likely she was already dead – but her daughter, Marie du Cornau, a tailor's wife of about twenty-one years of age. The mother of a young boy, she was again with child at the time. Du Cornau would have known, as de Lancre certainly did, that witchcraft ran in families. Even if she did not, the judges' opening question would have made plain that her deposition was not without danger: had she known her mother was a witch, by hearsay or 'otherwise'? Marie claimed she never had any idea until her mother's imprisonment and confession a month or so previously. She admitted though that her mother 'had some small reputation and some murmurs had been going around'.[29] She was then asked if she knew of any other witches, either by reputation or, again, 'otherwise'. If these questions were meant to eventually be turned back on Marie, as possible proof of her own witchcraft, then the two judges never got there, because the tailor's wife had indeed had first-hand experience of witchcraft. She had come armed with allegations of her own that proved to be very unwelcome to all the important people who heard them.

Local officials had interrogated du Cornau's mother in prison on 17 September.[30] She must have confessed in short order; or at least she had already done so by the time Marie accompanied her husband and her aunt – the unimaginatively named Jehanette ('little Jehanne') – on a visit a few days later.[31] It was during this meeting that her mother revealed the presence of witchcraft at the heart of the city's elite. Mondens 'first of all' accused 'the mother of the lieutenant mayor', Charles de Sorhaindo – the very same person who in June had encouraged the city council to welcome the commissioners and predicted the 'great profit' Bayonne could reap from working with them. But the list of witches that Jehanne denounced to her family, and which Marie now passed on to the commissioners, was long. It included the mother of an alderman – a woman locally known as 'Big Barbe' [*la Grand[e] Barbe*] – as well as two of his aunts. One, called 'damoiselle de Segure', may well have been married into the family of Auger de Ségure, the local law official whose help the judges had enlisted.[32] Marie's accusations also amounted to a spatial attack on Bayonne. Sorhaindo's (unnamed) mother 'resided at the city's main square'. Another witch was married to one of the city's guards; a third was the sister of the 'guard who holds the *chateau-neuf*, one of its bulwarks. Bayonne was the key to the French kingdom, the main line of defence against Spanish invasion. It was secretly being undermined from within.

If Jehanne and Marie spoke the truth, then the city was in imminent danger, and the commission's war on the devil amply justified. Witches were a fifth column, perilously close to destroying Bayonne's well-built defences from the inside. But this is not the full story, however, as subsequent events show. Confessed witches like Jehanne in Bayonne and Catherine in Bordeaux wielded a strange form of power: they could attempt to drag others down to hell with them. Such accusations could be corrosive, especially when aimed at prominent figures. They cast doubt on the witch-hunt's legitimacy and endangered the support of the local elites. The resulting parallel is odd but striking: if witches were not undermining Bayonne's defences, then Jehanne's words were weakening the witch-hunt from within. This threat was not lost on the commissioners. Although Pierre de Lancre never mentioned either Marie du Cornau or her mother in the *Tableau*, he complained bitterly but obliquely about the devil forcing the judges 'to abandon those accused of witchcraft and try the witnesses' instead.[33] One such witness was du Cornau.

What was going through the mind of the young tailor's wife as she stood in front of a royal commission to accuse her social betters? Were these accusations meant to deflect attention away from her? If so, she had gone for the nuclear option, setting in course a trail of very different events that would ultimately do her little good. Marie had much more to say, while the judges listened in apparent stone-faced silence, not even interrupting her with further questions. Jehanne's denunciations had put Marie in a difficult position. They had been at the very least semi-public. By her own account, the jailor and his wife had also heard them (although they were never interrogated), and early modern prisons were hardly private spaces.[34] News of what had happened quickly spread.

On Tuesday 22 September, only a few days after the unhappy mother-daughter reunion, Marie du Cornau bumped into two of the women – *demoiselle* de Segure and 'Big Barbe' – whom her mother had accused, and they knew it. If Marie's accusations in prison were semi-public, this encounter, in the cloisters of Bayonne cathedral, took place in the open. Witnesses would later testify about it, though they suspiciously overlooked the damning parts of Marie's evidence. As du Cornau was talking – probably very awkwardly – to *demoiselle* de Segure, her sister Big Barbe joined in and laid into her: 'she was astonished that her mother Jehanne de Mondens had accused such women of high reputation.' She suggested that Marie visit the prison again and tell her mother that her accusations must have been false, otherwise 'she would feel unwell and not carry her fruit [*her unborn baby*] safely to term'. As she was saying this, the woman placed her hand ominously on Marie's belly and the young woman instantly began to feel sick. Turning to flattery, Big Barbe intimated that Marie's husband could visit her mother in prison instead. If he was able to get Jehanne to exonerate 'so many honourable women', then an 'infinity of *gens d'honneur*' would be in his debt. Big Barbe herself promised 'a good sum of money' to sweeten the deal. Marie, by now seriously unwell, declined the proposition – her mother had spoken 'to discharge her conscience', she could not interfere – and rushed home.[35]

By the next day, Marie was in terrible pain and the remainder of her deposition described the mysterious illnesses that afflicted her. First, she felt extremely cold and then very hot, which caused her to shout and cry loudly, 'as a person attacked by a form of epilepsy', which lasted a fortnight. Amidst all of this, something – or someone ('she did not know if it was a witch or what') – pinched her in bed at night, causing her three weeks of further pain that still had not vanished. Her young son, who slept near her, appeared to languish from that moment. And 'that', du Cornau's lengthy eighteen-page deposition concluded, 'is all that she said she knew'.[36] If the judges had any comeback, then it is not recorded in this official copy; it merely ends with Espagnet's and de Lancre's signatures (Figure 10.1).

Marie's description of the interpersonal conflict followed by illness and disease will be familiar to those who have studied witchcraft accusations elsewhere in Europe. When loved ones or livestock fell ill, it was all too human to blame those with whom one had recently quarrelled, especially if they fitted the stereotype of the elderly woman, as they do here. It is terrain that this study has thus far traversed very little, namely that of *maleficia*, the everyday harm that witches were meant to have caused. It forms the backdrop to most, if not all witchcraft accusations, but we have seen very little of it so far, probably because such fears were too mundane for de Lancre – they were not the witches' sabbat, after all. Du Cornau's words echo accusations from across Europe in other ways as well. She did not directly accuse the two sisters of bewitching her, leaving this for the judges to work out. Causal links between an unpleasant encounter and the subsequent harm were often left implicit in this way. Do not upset a witch by accusing her directly. If she managed to get released, what then? Marie even looked the part of a typical accuser. Young and expectant mothers often directed witchcraft suspicions towards older, post-menopausal women – who could no longer have children of their own and would be envious of the all-too-fragile good fortune of others.[37]

A careful examination of Marie's deposition, then, suggests a different reading from what we might have expected. She ultimately spoke not as the daughter of a witch, but as a victim of witchcraft. She strongly implied that one of the women her mother had accused of witchcraft had caused her to fall ill. Even her body's response suggests that Marie took Jehanne's accusations at face value. The debilitating nature of her illness and in particular its length – she had still not quite recovered – neatly fit the five-week gap between the events described, both in

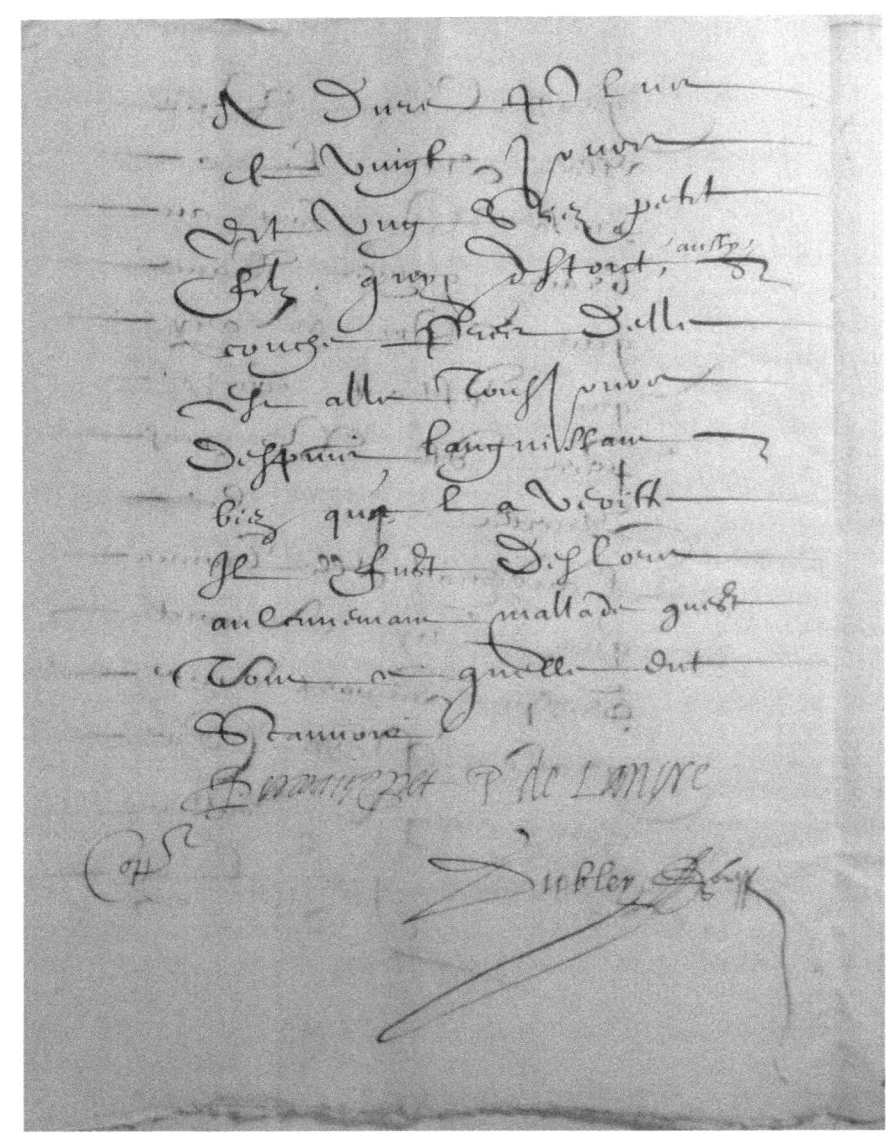

Figure 10.1 Testimony of Marie du Cornau, signed by Jean d'Espagnet and Pierre de Lancre. (Département des Pyrénées-Atlantiques. AD64, AC de Bayonne, FF 58, doc. 84.)

the prison and in the cathedral cloisters, and the moment she appeared in front of the two witchcraft judges. We know nothing about why Marie appeared before them, and why then, weeks after her mother had confessed. She could have been summoned. The judges, as we saw, would have treated her with suspicion, given her tainted family background. But it is also possible that it was du Cornau who turned to the judges for help. Apparently bewitched by the city's leading *femmes d'honneur*, to whom else could she have turned but the two outside judges sent to root out the witchcraft problem?

Whether or not she had been summoned or had testified of her own free will, Marie's deposition ruined her. The judges' response showed that the witchcraft commission offered but a shadow of justice even, or perhaps especially, by its own standards. More remarkable than witches leaping from mountain tops or flying to Canada at supersonic speed is the petition that *demoiselle* de Segure and Big Barbe addressed to the 'lord commissioners deputed by the king for the crime of witchcraft', in which they denounced the witchcraft accusations against them.[38] Marie was even accused of inventing the conversation with her mother in prison, which suggests that Jehanne was no longer alive to repeat her claims.[39] They demanded that Marie 'Souniez' – they evidently did not even know how to spell her last name – should be forced to retract her accusations. If she refused, she should be made to beg for their forgiveness barefoot, be put in the stocks, banished from the city in perpetuity and fined the impossible sum of 500 *livres*.[40] As a result, the pregnant woman ended up in the same prison that once housed her mother.[41]

The audacity of such a petition is breath taking. One wonders how de Lancre and Espagnet would have responded if it had emerged from less privileged and well-connected circles. Perhaps, de Lancre's comment in the preface about trying witnesses rather than witches reflected some handwringing or even guilt on his part. He lamented that 'the officers of justice find themselves quite weak in that place [the Labourd] because of an enemy so subtle and crafty that he very often involves the close relatives of judges in order to implicate them and shut their mouths from the outset'.[42] The judge probably did not have his own relative by marriage in mind – the lord of Urtubie – when he wrote this, though perhaps he should have. More likely he thought of Auger de Ségure, related to one of the two sisters, or perhaps to Bayonne's civic elite more generally. The city's aldermen also sat as the local law court.

After the commission's departure in early November, the sisters sued du Cornau for slander, a crime that fell within the city's own jurisdiction.[43] As historian Lu Ann Homza has shown, slander trials across the border in Spanish Navarre offered accused witches at least a glimmer of justice, although rulings often proved impossible to enforce.[44] Marie cannot have held out much hope for vindication in Bayonne. The Bordeaux judges had left, and the local court was staffed by relatives of those her mother had named. The women's lawyer addressed a lengthy learned petition to the 'lieutenant mayor [Sorhaindo], the aldermen, and council of the present city of Bayonne'.[45] The lawyer had considerable experience with witchcraft. His name features regularly in the account books of Saint-Jean-de-Luz, going as far back as its first witchcraft trial in October 1603.[46] Now the same lawyer, with little irony, argued that calumniators were the 'true serpents and enemies of humankind, sufficient and able to generate every disorder' – Marie, in other words, was the real devil. A copy of Marie's testimony before de Lancre and Espagnet was submitted as evidence (which is how it survived) to prove her 'calumny'. As we saw, witnesses to the incident in the cathedral cloisters conspicuously failed to corroborate her story. Banishment no longer sufficed as a punishment; the gravity of her crime demanded, in the lawyer's view, that she be condemned to be 'hanged and strangled'.[47]

On 16 November, du Cornau was confined to her own home for the duration of her pregnancy, placed under a constant guard to prevent her escape. That sentence was signed by Sorhaindo as lieutenant mayor.[48] His mother had been named as a witch but had (perhaps purposely) not taken part in the slander suit. A final verdict in Marie's case is not recorded and, as so often in this book, her ultimate fate is unknown. Perhaps, confinement was punishment enough and achieved its implicit aim: to stamp out dangerous accusations. As we shall see in the next chapter, the slander trial would by no means stop the witchcraft panic in the Lapurdi towns and villages south of Bayonne. Nor would it halt the prosecution of those Espagnet and de Lancre had transported to Bordeaux when their commission ended. But Marie du Cornau's exemplary fate does appear to mark an end to Bayonne's active participation in the witch-hunt, at least when its own citizens were suspected. As we shall see, foreigners proved to be a different story.

## The bishop and the devil

The final section of the *Tableau* – Book Six – reads differently from those that came before it.[49] De Lancre seems on the back foot, his prose appears even more rambling and contradictory than before: a section defending the use of a priest as the commission's interpreter is followed by another on 'witch-priests' which, according to de Lancre, 'the greater part' of the territory's clergy were. De Lancre's tone lost some of its confidence, almost as if he had lost the upper hand in the war against the devil. At times, he sounded positively apocalyptic. Having already swept across the Labourd and 'violently laying siege' to the citadel of Bayonne, Satan was now planting 'his throne' and holding sabbats across the Parlement's jurisdiction, 'even going so far as to take possession of the square of the ancient Palais Gallienne' – an ancient Roman amphitheatre that is still a Bordeaux landmark – 'which neighbours our walls'.[50] It was the bishop of Bayonne, Bertrand d'Echaux (Figure 10.2), who was responsible for this radical shift in tone.

In Book Six, the judge sounded more like what witchcraft historians have long wanted to hear: defensive and disappointed. It would serve the traditional de-Lancre-as-culprit narrative well if his Bordeaux colleagues turned on him.

**Figure 10.2** Portrait of Bertrand d'Echaux (date unknown). (Diocèse de Bayonne, Maison diocésaine.)

We cannot leave 1609 behind just yet to investigate those claims. But for now, let us note that de Lancre's disappointment, the sole piece of evidence for such claims, is an inadequate foundation for such a morally uplifting ending: the judge's expectations had also been set too high. He had pitched an alternative vision of witchcraft centred on – what else? – the sabbat. De Lancre conjured up the dramatic mental image of sabbats everywhere with Satan pressing against the Parlement's gates to add to the urgency of his call for action. He meant to 'dislodge our scepticism' and have 'all good judges' agree to 'punish by death witches for simply attending the sabbat several times, even though they have not been convicted of any malefice'.[51] This reading would have reshaped the crime of witchcraft. It not only marked a radical departure from the traditional emphasis on the devil's pact and *maleficia*, the death and destruction witches sowed, it even flew into the face of the commission's own jurisprudence, based on the testimony of young witnesses who also 'simply' attended the sabbat without legal consequences. The urgency of de Lancre's plea suggests that his colleagues were unmoved.

For all the doom-laden drama of these final pages, most of Book Six – four of the five sections – is devoted to an altogether different controversy: the role of priests in the witch-hunt. Here too, de Lancre appears to have been commenting on on-going developments in court after 1609. Three priests from Saint-Jean-de-Luz had fled across the border with Spain when they learned that the commission had sent out warrants for their arrest. There they stayed as refugees for nine months, apparently returning only occasionally at night 'dressed as labourers'. They were finally arrested in May 1610, holed up in a house in Bordeaux, where they had come in the hope of overturning the commission's decrees against them. Their trial dragged on until at least January 1611.[52] We shall examine their fate in the next and final part of this book. But for de Lancre, this trial was hugely triggering because it brought him face to face again with a person – an unnamed 'Bayonne official' – who had already become a thorn in his side during the witch-hunt itself.

As the king's almoner and a scion from an old noble family, Bertrand d'Echaux was a figure to be reckoned with, and de Lancre accordingly chose his words carefully. The bishop had supported the Saint-Jean-de-Luz priests (they petitioned the Parlement to be turned over to him for judgement), and he had likely harboured them in Bordeaux. Echaux had once written from Bordeaux urging Bayonne's councillors to support the commission, just as Bayonne's lieutenant mayor had. And just like Sorhaindo, though probably much sooner, he had come to regret that decision. Already within its first month of activities, priests were rounded up across the Labourd, suspected of witchcraft. Others, as we saw, fled. The first execution of a priest nevertheless still came as a shock, as de Lancre himself acknowledged.[53] The parish priest of Ascain, known only as Arguibel, was already in his seventies. He may even have suffered from dementia.[54] He had been interrogated and had confessed in the presence of Echaux's vicar. The bishop himself was away in Bordeaux 'in pursuit', as de Lancre cryptically put it, 'of a matter of importance'. In his absence, the bishop of nearby Dax defrocked the elderly priest ahead of his execution. If Echaux was in Bordeaux to protest the prosecution of his priests, then he was back in Bayonne to personally examine the two Ciboure priests who were next destined for the fire. A native Basque-speaker, the bishop interviewed them personally and publicly defrocked them in Bayonne cathedral. The bishop also interrogated one of the witnesses, nineteen- or twenty-year-old Marie d'Aspilcuete from Hendaye, who described not only the Black Masses but also priests 'deflowering' young women at the sabbat and co-habiting with them in daily life.[55]

Unlike Arguibel and (possibly) Bocal, the other Ciboure priest, the 'sixty-something'-year-old Migalena, never confessed his crime or repented. On the scaffold, Migalena publicly and 'perpetually' prayed the opening lines of the mainstays of Catholic devotion: alternating between the Our Father, the Ave Maria, the Confiteor and the Apostles' Creed. For de Lancre, the priest's inability to finish these in their entirety proved that the devil had clouded his mind, but the display of devotion may well have made a different impression on others. Five further priests were awaiting sentencing in prison. Following the death of the Ciboure priests, they sent a defiant message to the commissioners in which they put their faith in their Lord (which de Lancre inevitably took to mean the devil). The bishop was repeatedly seen crying, and de Lancre struggled to explain away Echaux's tears.[56]

The death of the three priests, de Lancre claimed, pushed Satan into action to save the five others, but Bayonne's bishop was also far from idle. Two of the imprisoned priests had been permitted to pray inside the cathedral one late afternoon and snuck out after a door was suspiciously left unlocked.[57] If their role in the priests' escape is necessarily uncertain, both bishop and devil were, as far as de Lancre was concerned, clearly involved in a legal strategy against the commission's work. The execution of the two Ciboure priests had taken place in Bayonne sometime early to mid-October. The commission was due to end on 1 November. If time was, from de Lancre's perspective, now on the devil's side, then it was the bishop who exploited this. Unfortunately, however, our sole witness to Echaux's legal obstructionism is de Lancre's own defensive account in Book Six. For obvious reasons, the judge was not interested in rehashing his opponent's arguments to an audience of colleagues that may well have been familiar with them already. They seem to centre on the jurisdiction of church courts over priests, as the case of the Saint-Jean-de-Luz clergy would later suggest. This is not a very plausible argument – in France, the royal courts always claimed precedence – but litigation did not need to be successful to run out the clock. After the commissioners themselves declared the argument without merit, the unnamed lawyer for the witch-priests submitted a motion that they recuse themselves, which de Lancre declared 'frivolous'. The lawyer then appealed to the *présidial* court in Dax, the devil providing horses so swift that the commission's representative could not keep up. When that strategy failed, the lawyer also recused the Dax judges and took his motion to a third court, the *sénéchaussée* at Saint-Severs, some sixty miles from Bayonne. This time 'Our Lord who moves more swiftly than Satan when it pleases Him carried the person who defended His cause to Saint-Severs with greater speed than his enemy [Satan] the [lawyer] of the witches'.[58] There, too, the lawyer's petition failed.

This was not, however, the end of the bishop's legal manoeuvring, and it may well have been a distraction from proceedings taking place in Bordeaux. When the witchcraft commissioners moved to sentence the imprisoned priests, they were 'astonished' when the 'official' presented them with a temporary injunction issued by the Parlement's *chambre des vacations*, the chamber which met while the court was not in session. The judgement was a clever ploy to circumvent the commission's autonomy. Even the Parlement as a whole, de Lancre complained, 'could not receive an appeal from our procedures because the king had given our commission full sovereignty and the court itself had verified that'. But the injunction was not addressed to the commissioners but 'to all judges in general'. We are never told what 'all judges' were temporarily prohibited from doing (prosecuting priests? prosecuting witches?), but its implications seemed to go beyond the imprisoned clergy. De Lancre foresaw that if the injunction was held to be legitimate, any future witchcraft convictions by the commission could be appealed in Bordeaux.[59]

Unsurprisingly, then, the commissioners did not accept it: 'we ordered that the parties present themselves before the king, as the arbiter of judges.'[60] But this was merely a face-saving measure. Time was up and Paris faraway. The imprisoned priests were not among those transported to Bordeaux when the commission ended, and they would, to de Lancre's dismay, ultimately all be released. The fact that two of them could have escaped 'in broad daylight' could be taken as a further sign that Bayonne, or its officials, had had enough of witch-hunting, at least where its own citizens were concerned. In 1610, a lawyer acting on behalf of Saint-Jean-de-Luz against its own witch-priests argued that 'all of Bayonne officialdom is suspect and untrustworthy'.[61] As that comment suggests, other communities were not yet done with their witches.

PART FOUR

# Aftermath (1610–1619)

# Chapter 11
# Too many witches

On 4 October 1610, León de Araníbar reached for his pen on a matter of extreme urgency. The abbot of Urdax had been an Inquisition commissioner for just over a year. It had been a highly desirable and prestigious side job, and the abbot had lobbied hard to get it when one of the inquisitors, Juan de Valle Alvarado, visited his monastery in August 1609.[1] But now, he was having second thoughts. The witchcraft situation at the border had continued to deteriorate, even after Pierre de Lancre and Jean d'Espagnet had returned to Bordeaux. The abbot was at a complete loss as to what to do – except to write to his new superiors pleading for help. Araníbar had been appointed principally to watch over the border with France, barely two miles away from the walls of his monastery. His powers as commissioner were limited: he could interrogate suspects but not sentence them or even send them to Logroño without the tribunal's permission. The letter he composed could not sound more desperate. Only the inquisitors could save the situation now: 'These great lamentable misfortunes, which keep growing every day in this land, force me to be importunate and bother your lordships and beg for relief of so many evils.'[2]

There simply were too many witches: 'The evil has reached such an extent that we no longer pay attention to the fact that there are witches (although a multitude of them have been discovered) so long as they refrain from bewitching and infecting others, especially children.' He was crying 'tears of blood' watching parents despair over their offspring, 'their voices calling out to heaven for a remedy'. Witches who confessed their sins almost instantly relapsed, returning to the witches' sabbat with children in their trail. The situation was so desperate that a few days earlier in France – 'two *leguas* [about eight miles] from this house' – villagers had taken justice into their own hands:

> There was an old woman who confessed to being a witch and taking children to the sabbats. Indeed, she persisted in taking them so that there was no curing her, despite her being told many times that if she kept taking the

children, they would stab her. Finally, she replied that she could not stop taking them, that it was not in her hand to do anything else. And with that, they burnt her.[3]

The abbot's horror cannot have been directed at the woman's death, or at least not just. Six convicted witches would face the same grim fate at the hands of the Logroño tribunal at the November *auto de fe*, which the inquisitors were already busy preparing. (They even hoped King Philip III might grace them with a visit.[4]) It was the spectre of vigilantism, and what that might mean for local officials like himself, that especially disturbed Araníbar. As so often, what happened in France – in this case, the village was either Saint-Pée or Sare – was held up to Spanish authorities as a foreboding omen: lynchings would happen unless the inquisitors intervened. They did not.

Lu Ann Homza has shown what came next for Spanish Navarre. Without the aid and support of their superiors, Araníbar and other low-level officials yielded to local pressure, giving permission – which was not theirs to give – to village constables to mimic Inquisition procedures.[5] As in France, the normal wheels of justice simply could not cope with the scale of the panic. The story of the witch-hunt as it spread across the Spanish Basque country is worth pursuing further – Homza has already told it brilliantly. But Araníbar's report has also much to teach us about the Pays de Labourd. It shows how witchcraft fears persisted in the territory and the Spanish villages immediately adjacent to it. The panic's two focal points – children and the sabbat – had not changed. And yet, historians have taken no notice. Like journalists visiting the site of a natural disaster, they left the Labourd once the main crisis appeared to be over. For France at least, the 1610s were meant to be a mere epilogue. Some scholars left to pursue the panic as it crossed the border into Spain,[6] but most followed the judges back to Bordeaux. After the commission's term expired, an unknown number of witchcraft suspects had been transported there, awaiting sentencing by the Parlement. In Pierre de Lancre's absence, and without the testimony collected in his *Tableau*, the Labourd is again left in darkness.

As it was in the beginning, so it is at the (apparent) end. Sources and suppositions conspire to fashion a seemingly convincing narrative, which even provided de Lancre with a comeuppance or repudiation of sorts, however unsatisfactory it may seem in the greater scheme of things. If the *Tableau* created the image of a nefarious witch-hunter imposing his will on a defenceless territory, the book's very existence has dictated the witch-hunt's apparent outcome. It is commonly alleged that de Lancre's Bordeaux colleagues did not share his fascination with the demonic and 'released many prisoners whom he had arrested'.[7] While de Lancre was destined for a long and seemingly happy retirement among his vineyards overlooking the Garonne river, he was at least implicitly censured and disavowed by his fellow judges. (De Lancre passed away on 9 February 1631 at the ripe age of seventy-four or seventy-five.[8]) Paradoxically, the principal (perhaps only) proof for such censure was the *Tableau* itself which, in this view, de Lancre can only have written in order to refute his colleagues' scepticism.[9] This reading is not entirely without merit: as we saw, the sixth and final section of the *Tableau* took on a more defensive tone. But the two claims – the release of the witches and de Lancre's reason for writing – sustain each other in a rather troubling circular and self-referential way: witches must have been released *because* de Lancre was defending himself; the judge must have been writing *because* witches were released. Neither claim is completely false, but they have been taken too far. When they are taken together, they also conspire to remove the Labourd once more from view because they present witchcraft primarily as a legal rather than a social problem. The panic must have subsided once the lawyers packed their bags and left – as if by magic.

Aranîbar's letter shows us otherwise. Far from resolving the witchcraft problem, de Lancre and Espagnet had made it worse, with the territory descending into further factionalism. If villagers resorted to violence, witchcraft trials continued as well, at least for some time. Legal efforts again centred on Saint-Jean-de-Luz, but these were probably part of a larger Lapurdi-wide pattern now lost to us. On 2 July 1610, the Labourd's lieutenant, Pierre de Chibau, pleaded with Bayonne's officials from Ustaritz, the village that acted as the territory's traditional seat of justice. After an epidemic had carried off several prisoners, the lieutenant asked whether the city was willing to receive 'Jehanette de Bardos ... whom we shortly hope to try although she is accused of the crime of witchcraft'.[10] Other references to witchcraft are more elusive, mere glimpses of a wider and ongoing problem. From its council minutes, for instance, we know that Bayonne expelled five girls accused of witchcraft in September 1613.[11] The account books of Saint-Jean-de-Luz point to similar fears, as we shall see. Both these sources also reveal the sizable impact of two events that took place far away from the Labourd and which further fed the territory's social and political crises. The expulsion of the Moriscos, descendants of Iberia's Muslim population, from Spain from September 1609 onwards sent new waves of refugees across the border – this time in the direction of the Labourd. Both Bayonne and Saint-Jean-de-Luz officials were desperate to rid themselves of these new arrivals as swiftly as possible. A second event proved still more consequential. The murder of King Henry IV in Paris by a Catholic zealot on 14 May 1610 plunged the whole of France into turmoil but caused even greater instability at the border. Both crises shaped the course of the Basque witch-hunt in unpredictable ways.

Witchcraft fears did not just cross the border at Zugarramurdi and Urdax, they spilt over in other directions as well. On 10 January 1610, the community of Capbreton, a small village just to the north of Bayonne and the Basque country, asked to borrow the city's executioner for the public whipping of a convicted female witch, whose sentence was confirmed by the Bordeaux Parlement.[12]

(What we should make of this unusually light sentence is unclear; it could be a precursor to her banishment.) To the east of Bayonne, in the village of La Bastide-Clairence in Lower Navarre, a male witch was executed in 1610. He confessed to collecting fines for non-attendance at the witches' sabbat.[13] A resident of the village of Arraute, in the same territory, complained in a notarial document about the length of his detention after a 'witchcraft accusation against him by his own daughter' had 'ruined' him.[14] Both Lower Navarre and Béarn also banished witchcraft suspects, with some ending up in Bayonne.

By the spring of 1611 at the latest, witchcraft reached the impressive fortifications of Hondarribia. As elsewhere in the Basque country, the panic had its roots in the testimony of a group of children and teenagers. When thirteen-year-old Isabel García went out to wash some socks in the communal fountain, an older woman by the name of María de Illarra offered her money to attend a 'meeting' later that day. Much to the girl's surprise, this gathering turned out to be a witches' sabbat held near a remote hermitage in the mountains. Her description of the gathering will by now look exceedingly familiar: the devil, for instance, was again seated on a golden chair. The supposed location showed that witches continued to target and pollute sacred spaces. A second girl, María Alzueta, also thirteen years of age, was lured to a sabbat at another hermitage with the promise of firewood. Her testimony includes further instantly recognizable tropes: the devil rewarded Alzueta's 'teacher', a Frenchwoman called María de Echagaray, with money, while the girl herself could only see the Eucharist as 'black' until she confessed her sins to a local vicar, who 'gave her a relic and the gospels'. She stopped going to the sabbat after her confession, when the Holy Sacrament became white again.[15]

The girls' description of the sabbat speaks to the communal ties that transcended the French-Spanish border. Isabel García testified that the devil spoke Basque with witches from Irún and Hendaye but 'Gascon' – a French dialect – with the witches from San Sebastián and Pasaia, the two principal Spanish ports nearby (which were also home to foreign merchants). The trials in Hondarribia reveal how even local witchcraft suspects could be made foreign by the border: the three named suspects were all identified as French, and they all had married into another group of outsiders, the poorly paid Spanish soldiers based at the local fortress. But their Frenchness was often much overstated. Two had been living in Spain for many decades; only one, Inesa de Gajén, originally from Hendaye, had been swept up by Tristan d'Urtubie's earlier activities. The border through the Basque country, then, also helped to make outsiders out of near neighbours, whose foreignness made them suspect and possibly easier targets as well. On the French side of the border too, witchcraft would become increasingly linked to undesirable strangers. In Hondarribia, the women's prosecutions collapsed when Alonso de Salazar Frías, the famously sceptical inquisitor who was then making his visitation of the Spanish Basque country, refused to take them forward. Even so, the women, as 'foreigners', were still separated from their husbands and banished.[16]

It was not just fears that spread outward from the Labourd, witchcraft refugees continued to stream into Spain as well. In July 1611, one particularly odd assortment of refugees even travelled as far as Logroño, much to the bemusement of the inquisitors. This group from Ustaritz (probably a family unit) consisted of three suspected witches and their nine-year-old accuser. The boy told the two remaining inquisitors (as Salazar was already in the field) that his travel companions, which included his uncle, continued to take him to the sabbat. The adults, in turn, testified that they had fled because of 'the very rigorous justice against witches in the said place [in which] many people were killed' – in their quest for redemption they had decided to take their accuser with them.[17] Valle and Becerra were outraged that 'these strangers have come to this city and exercise their evil deeds in the presence of this tribunal', blaming their appearance on the devil.[18] The arrival of these and other refugees reflected the continued fear of local justice and popular violence in the Labourd, but they also demonstrate something else: the unexpected and certainly unintentional appeal of the Spanish Inquisition to French witchcraft suspects: the Ustaritz group arrived in search of absolution.

In the spring of 1611, the Suprema, the Inquisition's general council in Madrid, had decided to issue an Edict of Grace, which, for a limited period, absolved all those who confessed to being witches and reconciled themselves with the Catholic Church. The fateful decision was a crucial moment for the witchcraft panic as it moved through the Spanish Basque country: there were just too many witches. In the face of the growing panic and escalating legal costs, a spiritual or pastoral approach was perhaps the only possible way forward. It also made sense for a fundamentally devout institution such as the Inquisition to put its faith in the sacrament of confession and the saving power of God's grace. But the result was paradoxical. The offer of effectively free forgiveness encouraged hundreds of confessions, with parents (as we saw already) nudging or even forcing their children to come forward. An edict designed to bring the panic to a close thus ended up further fanning the flames – by making the full extent of the alleged diabolical conspiracy clear. Salazar, whose task it was to administer the edict across Gipuzkoa and (Spanish) Navarre, reconciled more than 1,500 witches during a visitation that was to last almost eight months. (The experience turned him into a sceptic.) This sizable group of self-confessed former witches included, at Hondarribia and possibly elsewhere, an unidentified number of 'important people from the kingdom of France' who sought to be reconciled 'very secretly'.[19] That such absolutions carried no legal weight across the border seemed to take nothing away from their appeal, and these border crossings tell us something of the desperation of suspects as they struggled to leave witchcraft behind them.

The kingdom of France, of course, possessed no inquisition but that did not prevent its officials from looking to Spain for possible spiritual solutions. As we shall see later on, France would pursue similar pastoral rather than legal paths, approaching Lapurdi witches with forgiveness rather than fire. The results were at best mixed and probably even counterproductive, just as they (frankly) had been in Spain. New targets, as this book's final chapter will show, appeared to offer a much less edifying resolution to widespread popular anger and fear. But these developments in the later 1610s are still in the future. For now, let us focus on the continuing efforts to bring the many Basque witches to justice both in the Labourd and in Bordeaux. Alongside the efforts of local officials, this task also fell to yet another outsider: Marc-Antoine de Gourgue was sent not from Bordeaux but from Paris, as the personal envoy of the queen regent of France, Marie de' Medici. Faced not just with witches but also with religious refugees, independent noblemen and an increasingly volatile border, his to-do list proved to be even more daunting than anything his predecessors had been forced to confront.

# To Bordeaux and back

We do not know how many prisoners were taken to Bordeaux when the commission's term ended. De Lancre only commented that the Parlement's prisons were so full that the accused had to be accommodated in one of the city's smaller castles, the Chateau du Ha (the remnants of which now house the main training school for French judges and magistrates).[20] This tells us less than we might think, as even in 1606, the twelve Saint-Jean-de-Luz accused had to be spread across three prisons. Intended only to house defendants awaiting trial, early modern prisons were usually small affairs, so they would easily have overflowed in these specific circumstances. The prisoners, who still could easily have numbered two or three dozen, spent up to three years in Bordeaux in conditions that were likely as bad as those in Bayonne and Ustaritz, and possibly worse.[21] Built on marshes along the now long-buried Peugue river, the Chateau du Ha had a reputation for pestilence, 'stagnant waters [sleeping] eternally at the feet of its walls' (Figure 11.1).[22] From the *Tableau*, we learn that at least four suspects, all women, died in prison in Bordeaux.[23] De Lancre also reports on the executions of three, possibly four, Basque witches in 1610. The first, of an unnamed female witch from Macaye, took place on 12 July. The second execution, of sixty-year-old Catherine de Barrendeguy from Halsou (already discussed), followed in September. Also known as Cathalin de Bardos, Catherine may have been related to the suspect imprisoned in Ustaritz.[24] Neither Macaye nor Halsou, two small villages further inland near Cambo-les-Bains, feature anywhere else in de Lancre's account. Most likely, village officials brought them to Bayonne in the commission's final weeks, and they were transported

**Figure 11.1** The Chateau du Ha, Bordeaux, by Hermann Van der Hem (1638). (BnF, btv1b7741916z.f1.)

to Bordeaux after that. An addition to the second 1613 edition of the *Tableau* reveals the execution of a third suspect: Catherine d'Abaustena. She confessed that she attended the sabbat one last time in between her interrogations, so she could bid the devil *adieu* and show him the 'fig sign' – the premodern equivalent to the middle finger – which she then proceeded to show to de Lancre.[25] Catherine may have been the unnamed witch from Saint-Jean-de-Luz – 'one of the most cunning' – mentioned in de Lancre's second witchcraft book. Catherine – or possibly a fourth accused – confessed that she only went to the sabbat 'to go dancing'. She 'escaped our hands but came to die at those of the Bordeaux Parlement'.[26]

The account books of Saint-Jean-de-Luz shed some additional light on the identities of some of the imprisoned. They allow us to identify four female prisoners by name, in addition to the town's priests who were uncovered in Bordeaux and would join them inside.[27] One was banished by the Parlement, the others disappear from the financial records.[28] They may well have been released. As before, the town officials spared no effort and expense to pursue these cases. They reverted to the approach they had adopted before the commission: they again sent one of their own to oversee the proceedings. In April 1610, they dispatched Joannes de Sanson to Bordeaux 'for the pursuit of the trial against those accused of witchcraft'.[29] Joannes was doubtlessly a relative (and probably the son) of Guiraud de Sanson, who as mayor had called in the Parlement for the first time in 1605 and who left us the vivid account of the attack on Catherine de La Masse the year after. Joannes kept a separate account book listing the expenses he incurred on his mission to the Parlement, just as his predecessor had done in 1606–7. They show that Saint-Jean-de-Luz was not quite done with identifying new witches: two more were sent first to Bayonne, and then to Bordeaux; one would be banished by the Parlement.[30]

Yet, as far as sources go, these ledgers remain intensely frustrating historical documents: as before, they tantalize us with fascinating details that only hint at what we really would like to know. Seven mules and three men, for instance, were hired to send the first witnesses to Bordeaux, but the size and composition of this group – let alone the nature of their testimony – are unknown.[31] At least, we know the size of later ones: twenty-three witnesses were sent in August 1610, other groups consisted of sixteen and nineteen each.[32] As their testimony was linked to particular trials (one confronted the witch priests), none stayed particularly long. From their communal living conditions, we might infer that they were again mostly teenagers: the group of sixteen stayed for thirty days, together with two escorts, in a house especially rented for that purpose.[33] If there was any overlap between the groups, then the witnesses must have been shuttling back and forth between Saint-Jean-de-Luz and Bordeaux with considerable frequency. We do not know what other communities did with their suspected witches. Their records have not survived.

It seems that much of the Bordeaux court's attention centred on the fate of the Saint-Jean-de-Luz clergy. As we saw, three had sensibly absented themselves before the commission could have them arrested.[34] In May 1610, with the support of Bishop Bertrand d'Echaux, they were in Bordeaux hoping to overturn the commission's judgement against them. Instead, they found themselves imprisoned. Saint-Jean-de-Luz's officials certainly had not mellowed: nineteen witnesses were sent to confront them.[35] Sanson's accounts include a payment for seventeen manuscript copies of the town's pleading against the three priests to be disseminated amongst the Parlement's many judges. While none of these copies survive, de Lancre – who had his own reasons to be interested – included long excerpts in his *Tableau*.[36] From this we learn that the priests petitioned to have their case transferred to the church courts (and thus to Echaux's jurisdiction, who would surely have released them). De Lancre presented the failure of this request as a vindication, but in France, the Parlements typically claimed precedence.[37] Saint-Jean-de-Luz also pursued a fourth priest, Martin de Haraneder, who was transported to Bordeaux alongside the two female witches mentioned above.[38] His release is explicitly mentioned: the town had to pay for his return to Saint-Jean-de-Luz.[39] Yet, his colleagues were very likely freed as well. One of Sanson's final payments was for a petition to prevent the release of one priest.[40] At least one other, Jean de Lasson, returned to his position at

Saint-Jean-de-Luz. In 1619, he would play a small but significant role in the witch-hunt's grim conclusion.

The town ledgers kept during 1610 and 1611 show that officials, of course, also spent funds on other matters. Even amidst a witchcraft panic, life muddled on: the streets needed to be cleaned and the town's fountain continued to be a perennial problem, someone was even sent from San Sebastián to fix it.[41] But the town's legal affairs, and particularly its involvement in the witch-hunt, swallowed up most of its expenditure. Between April 1610 and September 1611, Sanson travelled back and forth between Saint-Jean-de-Luz five times, spending nearly 3,200 *livres* on the community's legal affairs, most of it witchcraft related.[42] An interim balance sheet, dated February 1611, puts the sum given to Sansson 'for the pursuit of the trial both against the bishop of Bayonne and the priests accused of witchcraft' at 426 *livres*, and a separate sum 'to pursue the accused of witchcraft' at 1,468 *livres*.[43] These expenses included the inevitable purchase of twelve hams, presumably as gifts for the judges as before.[44]

This sizable investment of official time and money again raises the spectre of the sort of factionalism that we saw dominate Saint-Jean-de-Luz during the witch-hunt's earliest stages. In fact, some of the figures we met then stage a comeback. Catherine de La Masse, one of the early teenage accusers, now found herself imprisoned in Bordeaux.[45] Had she been accused of witchcraft herself? Or was she accused of bearing false witness? Did Pierre de Lancre – who had suspiciously little to say about Saint-Jean-de-Luz in the *Tableau* – play a role in her imprisonment? We simply do not know. What is clear is that the same Saint-Jean-de-Luz officials who zealously captured and prosecuted the town's witches also worked hard to obtain Catherine's release. On 17 September, Sanson made two payments: one 'for putting Catherine de la Masse outside of prison' and another 'for the departure [*sortie*] of Catherine de la Masse', presumably from Bordeaux, after which she disappears from the sources.[46]

Part of the legal end to the witch-hunt, therefore, may well have been the fall from power of the Sanson family. The town's mayor and aldermen were elected for two-year terms through a form of direct democracy which the French crown did not water down until 1654. The year 1612 saw the election of Jean de Haraneder as mayor. Like Chibau and probably Sanson, he was a newcomer who had amassed substantial wealth from the town's fishing industry.[47] (We met him briefly already, when he already had sufficient clout to pursue an English corsair for damages in London and Paris.) He was likely related to Martin de Haraneder, one of the accused witch-priests, and he certainly was married to a Chibau.[48] The Haraneder family would go on to dominate the town's government until the early eighteenth century. A local historian described them as the 'most illustrious' among the town's patrician families, a list that also included the Chibau clan, but not the Sanson.[49] It would be Guiraud de Sanson, rather than any witchcraft suspects, whom the town would subsequently go on to pursue in court.[50]

If suspects were released from Bordeaux's prisons, then part of the impulse may have come from a changing of the guard in Saint-Jean-de-Luz. This did not mean that witchcraft fears had evaporated. The town's ledgers for 1612, for instance, still included a payment to a cartwright for the transport of 'some lewd women and girls' away from the territory, which may well be linked to the crime of witchcraft.[51] Still, the expensive witchcraft prosecutions before the Bordeaux Parlement were abandoned. But what about the Parlement? Can we conclude anything about its jurisprudence? Do the recorded punishments – at least three executions and two banishments – justify a reputation for scepticism? In a second, contemporary witchcraft trial, the Parlement had seen little reason for leniency. In March 1610, the court ordered four Spaniards, travelling magicians (possibly healers), to be 'burnt alive their bodies being turned into ashes, together with their books, characters, costly parchments, charms and other magical objects'.[52] The Parlement also did not keep de Lancre away from further witchcraft trials. In 1613, he was involved in a witchcraft trial that implicated four women and one man in Amou, a small village to the north-east of Bayonne that belonged to one of the 1609 witchcraft commission's sponsors.[53] As the trial's *rapporteur*, it fell to de Lancre to summarize the original depositions for his Bordeaux colleagues. The outcome of this second trial also frustrated him. We again do not know what it was: some may have been banished or simply released. (However harsh the verdict, de Lancre would always have been disappointed.) Yet, his lament may offer the starting point for a realistic assessment of the Bordeaux court's witchcraft jurisprudence: 'The Parlement, although it knows the evils brought by witchcraft across its jurisdiction much better than its ancestors, gets weary and starts to have second thoughts about exposing so many to the gallows.'[54] It was not scepticism that mattered but size. There were too many witches. The Parlement would carry out occasional executions for witchcraft throughout the 1610s, but the ordinary French wheels of justice were simply too bureaucratic, too cumbersome and too costly to deal with a problem as great as the Basque witch-hunt.[55] Perhaps, it was the same insight that led the next senior official, Marc-Antoine de Gourgue, to search for other ways to address the witchcraft panic. The commissions sent from Bordeaux in 1605 and 1609, after all, had achieved little. Gourgue seems to have found his inspiration in Spain.

# Third time a charm?

The inquisitors of the Logroño tribunal would, of course, have been happier had King Philip III graced their spectacular *auto de fe* with his presence, but they more than settled for the presence of Marc-Antoine de Gourgue whom, they believed, had been ordered to attend the *auto* in secret by the queen of France.[56] Months of planning had gone into the two-day event, held in the city of Logroño on Sunday 7 and Monday 8 November 1610.[57] The opening procession alone, set for the day before, involved hundreds of participants, if not more. First came the many lowly officials of the Holy Office: its familiars, commissioners and notaries, 'wearing golden pendants and crosses on their chest'. Many must have come from afar, according to the two surviving pamphlets there were either 900 or 'up to 1,000' of them.[58] Lorenzo de Hualde, the priest from Bera, could have been among them – he had escorted Gourgue all the way from the French border. Perhaps, Abbot Aranibar also took part.[59] The Inquisition's ground staff was followed by a 'great multitude' of monks and friars from 'all' the religious orders from Logroño and beyond: Dominicans, Franciscans, Jesuits and others, they all 'had come to be part of the most famous and pious procession that they had ever seen'.[60] Connecting these first two groups was the guardian of the local Franciscan convent, who was also an adviser to the Inquisition. To him fell the great honour of carrying the banner of the Green Cross, the coat of arms of the Holy Office.[61] The religious were followed by choristers, though what precisely they sang neither pamphlet recorded. The rear was made up of two priests of Logroño's main church and the tribunal's constable who escorted a large cross to a platform, eighty-four feet wide and just as deep, that had been constructed on the city's main square for the occasion.[62] Fires were lit and a vigil was kept all night to protect the venue. As this opening procession already made clear, *autos de fe* were meant to inspire, though what precisely – fear, awe, devotion – depended on the beholder.[63]

The three inquisitors had selected fifty-three women and men from their prison to take part in the event. Historical attention has focused on the twenty-nine witches, five of whom had passed away in prison and were present in effigy.[64] They were doubtlessly the main reason – indeed, the main attraction – for the estimated 20,000 to 30,000 visitors who had come from as far away as France to witness the event.[65] (Gourgue was not the only Frenchman present.) But those sentenced also included a rich assortment of heretics, Judaizers, blasphemers and bigamists.[66] All were forced to play a role in the proceedings that began with a procession led by the three inquisitors early on the Sunday morning. The prisoners were given special garbs, so-called *sambenitos*. Their dress distinguished the penitent from the unrepentant and marked the punishments they would receive: those to be whipped, for instance, wore ropes around their neck. Special caps covered with figures of devils and flames identified those sentenced to death, all six of them witches.[67] They were *negativos*; they had 'denied', as one pamphlet put it, 'the truth that had been so well proven'.[68] Unlike the other participants, they had been informed of their fate the night before in the hope that they would confess, but to no avail. At the end of the first day, they were released to the secular authorities and executed. Five others who had passed away in prison were represented by wax statues, accompanied by coffins of their bones – these would join the living on the pyre. Reading the sentences that detailed their horrifying crimes took nearly until nightfall.[69]

The Monday intentionally ended on a more uplifting note. With the *negativos* literally out of the way, the second day was a display of mercy for those who had confessed and who would receive lighter punishments in return. The sentences of the 'confessing' witches came last. They were once more so grim and so long – filled with 'things so horrendous and dreadful that had never been seen before' – that daylight was again running out and the inquisitors ordered that the final ones be shortened.[70] As the ceremony came to an end, the most senior inquisitor Alonso Becerra approached one of the penitent witches, María de Jureteguía. She had been the first to be accused in Zugarramurdi but had been an exemplary prisoner: she had helped discover other witches and had heroically resisted the devil's attempts to lure her back. (A published ballad about the *auto de fe* would sing at length about María's sensational testimony.[71]) Becerra now declared her to be a model for others and ordered her to remove her cap and her *sambenito*, her symbols of shame. This unexpected show of mercy elicited admiring cries – 'Long live the Holy Office!' – from the crowd.[72] Finally, a procession chanting the *Te Deum laudamus*, an ancient Christian hymn, returned the Holy Cross from the stage to the church and the doubtlessly relieved penitents to the Inquisition offices. The crowd disbanded, their ears still ringing with two-days' worth of wickedness. They returned home, 'crossing ourselves', as one pamphlet had it, 'all the while'.[73]

We do not know what the many French witnesses to the *auto de fe* made of it all, or whether they too kept crossing themselves on their long journey home. As we already saw, Pierre de Lancre was much impressed from afar, and much despite himself. The event, mentioned prominently on the cover of the *Tableau*, probably spurred the writing of his book; it certainly fuelled his desire to prove the superiority of French justice. Gourgue's private views, by contrast, are lost. Possibly the Jesuit orator, who spoke at his funeral years later, was right when he claimed that the Spanish were unable to corrupt the well-travelled judge 'with their haughtiness' – just as the Dutch could not contaminate him with their heresies, the English with their easy living and the Italians with their luxuries.[74] But Gourgue may also have been sincere when he showered the inquisitors with praise. All three of them were beyond excited to learn of his presence after the event. Half of their self-congratulatory three-page report to the Suprema was devoted to Gourgue, 'a leading and rich gentleman and judge of the Parlement of Paris who the queen had commissioned in the matter of the Portuguese Judaizers and to give passage to the Moriscos coming from these kingdoms'. His escort, Lorenzo de Hualde, had told them that the French judge had attended both days 'with great attention … and much modesty'. The day following the *auto*, Gourgue sent an aide to the tribunal to 'offer his person in service to the Holy Inquisition' and to express 'his admiration for the great diligence and care of the Holy Office'. He particularly praised – and this may well be significant for us – the Inquisition's 'great mercy'. Although greatly taken in by all this praise from an unexpected French corner, the inquisitors still could not give Gourgue, whom they described as 'a very Catholic man, with a zeal for God's honour', a copy of the sentences but they promised him a summary.[75]

We can justly describe Gourgue's as the third commission to be sent to sort out the problems of the Pays de Labourd, after the commissions of 1605 and 1609. The witchcraft panic, as we have seen throughout, had always been only a part of the territory's problems. It had been generated by other conflicts, both within the territory and at the border, but it had also reflected them. De Lancre had described them in the *Tableau* as opportunities for the devil to exploit and create further disorder; Espagnet had officially been sent to investigate one source of instability – the border – and became involved in settling another – the construction of a new port. Gourgue's own thoughts have been preserved in official correspondence, at times even written in code. None of his letters, unfortunately, record how he saw witchcraft fit into his larger mission, but by November 1610, he must have concluded that it did.

As the inquisitors already noted in their letter to the Suprema, Gourgue's main task was to regulate the flow of Morisco refugees streaming into France. It is much less clear whether he also concerned himself with the other issue they mentioned: the growing population of 'Portuguese' in the Pays de Labourd. This community of Iberian merchants, of Jewish rather than Muslim descent, had found a home in Saint-Jean-de-Luz and Bayonne. Their numbers were steadily growing during the 1600s and 1610s. Like the Moriscos, this second group of New Christians (or *conversos*) were another problem of Spain's own making: official paranoia about their religious sincerity was the predictable result of the forced conversion of their ancestors. Despite some connections between them, the two groups need to be discussed separately.[76] There is little to substantiate Pierre de Lancre's hostile complaint that the Jews had 'mixed themselves' with the train of Moriscos leaving Spain. (He also insinuated that Jews had 'in great hordes' moved to Constantinople where they went on 'to mix with the Turks' – a reference he can only have meant sexually.[77])

Whether Gourgue also had the Portuguese (as the *conversos* were officially called in French sources) in his sight is an open question. Only Spanish sources indicate his hostility, and they had eagerly pinned their hopes on Gourgue tackling this source of possible religious subversion on their proverbial doorstep. In 1612, a Spanish spy, in a report to the Spanish Council of State, claimed that Gourgue, who had become his 'very big friend', had concluded that the Portuguese of Saint-Jean-de-Luz were 'all Jewish dogs' and had decided to discuss their punishment and the confiscation of their goods with the queen in Paris.[78] Nothing of the sort happened. As with the praise he apparently lavished on Logroño's inquisitors, the spy's report points to a problem with the sources that we have not yet encountered. Where de Lancre revealed much about himself in print – more than he himself realized – his successor remains a cipher who, like the Basque witches, is mostly seen through the eyes of others. The closest we come to learning anything remotely revealing about Gourgue personally is an anecdote by his former teacher at Leiden University. To later students, Joseph Scaliger mockingly described Gourgue's visit to a cabinet of curiosities. There the young man was shown a full-sized Egyptian mummy and was tricked into believing that it belonged to a Pharaoh. The famous Protestant scholar derided the popish credulity of his Catholic student.[79]

Although Gourgue's private views are lost from view, his background resembled that of the other Bordeaux judges we have met, differing only in that his family's rise through the social ranks of sixteenth-century France had been even more meteoric. Like Pierre de Lancre's Basque Rosteguy ancestors, Marc-Antoine's father Ogier had been a provincial merchant who left his native Landes region for the Guyenne metropole, where he converted a first mercantile fortune into still greater wealth and status in service of the French monarchy. From the 1560s onwards, he became one of the financiers who kept the French state afloat during the religious wars – in the case of Ogier, who provided a loan of 250,000 *livres* to equip the French Navy, quite literally so.[80] By the time of his death, in 1594, he had accumulated a series of offices as well as a noble title that would be passed on to his eldest son, Marc-Antoine. The snobbish Etienne de Cruseau still could not help but emphasize the father's 'very low background' when he recorded his death in his diary.[81] The stellar rise shows how social advancement had been briefly possible in sixteenth-century France as the state expanded. Yet, the same family also shows how this new social elite, centred on the Parlements, France's citadels of justice, would close the doors behind itself and grow rich in government service. Unlike the ultimately childless Rosteguys, the Gourgue continued to supply not simply councillors but also presidents to the Bordeaux Parlement well into the eighteenth century.[82]

The first of these was Marc-Antoine (see Figure 11.2). He purchased the office of councillor at the Bordeaux Parlement in 1596, becoming one of the court's presidents in 1613 and then, in 1616, its first president, no doubt in part in recognition for the services he rendered the crown in the Basque country. Yet, during his mission in the Labourd, between 1610 and 1612, Gourgue was not, in fact, based in Bordeaux but in Paris. In 1604, he had purchased the expensive office of master of requests of the royal household.[83] The duties of these masters – partly legal, partly political – were byzantine and arcane in their complexity even by the standards of the Old Regime. Although masters of requests were technically members of the Paris Parlement (the inquisitors in their letter were not wrong there), their standing and prestige flowed from their proximity to the monarchy. Every Sunday, two of them would accompany

**Figure 11.2** Engraving of Marc-Antoine de Gourgue (1628?). (Bordeaux, Bibliothèque municipale, Delpit 81/27.)

the king to Mass to receive and pass on petitions. One small part of their role was the supervision of justice in the provinces, but the crown could also turn to them for special missions.[84] Gourgue may well have been chosen because of his connections to the south-west, but his authority did not come from the Bordeaux Parlement, but rather from his connection to the royal council and his standing as a personal envoy of the queen regent, Marie de' Medici.

This mattered: Gourgue's commission was not a judicial investigation, as de Lancre's and Espagnet's had been, but a political mission. The archives in Bayonne identify Gourgue's position and purpose quite clearly: he was 'a commissioner deputed by His Majesty [the under-age king Louis XIII] for the passage of the Moriscos'.[85] The Spanish crown had long searched for a 'final solution' to its Morisco problem. In 1587, a Spanish bishop put forth one particularly grim proposal, possibly inspired by Basque fishing expeditions to Newfoundland 'and the Coast of Cod': the cleric advocated castrating or sterilizing the Moriscos and transporting them to these 'quite uninhabited' lands.[86] Less drastic proposals continued to be mooted during the 1600s but only in the autumn of 1609, after a series of humiliating military disasters, was the first in a series of expulsions finally ordered.[87] By 1611, nearly 250,000 people had left the Iberian Peninsula. Most had done so by boat, leaving directly for Islamic lands across the Mediterranean, but as many as 50,000 had streamed into France.[88] Initial attempts to close the border had to be abandoned, given the size of the inflow and the determination of the refugees.[89] In the Labourd, Antoine de Gramont, the governor of Bayonne (who never passed up on an opportunity to make money from the vulnerable), charged 15 *reales* for passage across the border, 'the strong paying for the weak'.[90] Some deemed to be good Christians – in Bordeaux, the archbishop made them eat pork to test their faith – were allowed to settle safely away from the Spanish border, while many more made their way to French ports for onwards journeys to the Levant and elsewhere.[91]

We do not know when Gourgue took up his role in regulating the passage of the Moriscos. We first encounter him at the border further inland, in Béarn, in late August and early September 1610, where he managed to upset the duke de la Force, the local governor who had already been dealing with the situation.[92] In the Labourd, officials were desperate for Gourgue to complete his mission. Bayonne, for instance, petitioned him in October 1611 to request the removal of 'the Moriscos so that they do not infect this land with the Mohammedan law nor carry out any prejudice or damage to this border, in accordance with the king's will'.[93] As so often in this book, the border emerges as an active agent exacerbating foreign dangers. Gourgue promised Bayonne's representative 'that he would remove all the Moriscos from the border as quickly as possible'.[94] But it is not clear at all what, if anything, the royal agent was able to achieve. Bayonne also acted on its own accord and made several attempts to 'empty the Moriscos from the city' – its decrees even attributed 'several major diseases' to their presence.[95] In 1614, Saint-Jean-de-Luz officials similarly paid more than 3 *livres* 'to send the Moriscos away from this place', without specifying how.[96] While the stream of refugees must have worsened wider existing social and political conflicts in the Labourd, it also directly contributed to its witchcraft fears. De Lancre reported the arrival in September 1610 of a certain Don Pedro who set himself up as a witch-finder. The Bordeaux judge did not know whether Don Pedro was of Moorish descent himself or simply belonged 'to the Great Morisco, Satan'. He apparently vanished as soon as he was uncovered, either following the Morisco caravans or returning to Spain to tell others like him that 'there was no welcome for them in France'.[97]

Unlike the Portuguese, few Moriscos appear to have settled in the Labourd. They vanish from Bayonne's council minutes and Saint-Jean-de-Luz's ledgers after 1614, although there is anecdotal evidence for a small, continued presence in some communities, notably Biarritz and Ciboure.[98] Both Gourgue's role and his views throughout this crisis remain something of a mystery. Where others used the crisis to contrast Spanish cruelty with French humanity – Cardinal Richelieu later claimed it showed that France was 'known across the world as a refuge for the suffering' – Gourgue may well have taken a more critical stance.[99] We can ignore the delight of the Jesuit orator at Gourgue's funeral that the Moriscos were unable to touch his Christian piety.[100] Yet, the recollections of one Morisco witness also suggest a devout sensibility on Gourgue's part, in keeping perhaps with his admiration for the Inquisition and the Jesuits. Although originally from Spain, Ahmad Ibn Qasim Al-Ḥajarī (c. 1569/70–after 1640) was not a refugee but an envoy sent to France by the sultan of Marrakesh. After Al-Ḥajarī finally tracked down 'the judge of the Andalusians' in Saint-Jean-de-Luz, he recalled that Gourgue repeatedly told him to return to Christianity: 'You there, I find that you should reconvert to Christianity!'[101] As an out and proud Muslim, Al-Ḥajarī was not convinced.[102] In May 1612, the judge invited the envoy to a dinner at his Paris home, where Al-Ḥajarī worked in vain to persuade his French hosts of the evils of wine and tried to convert his host's mother-in-law to Islam (she later gave him 'a lot of gold coins').[103] The French judge remains difficult to read. Perhaps, the anecdote reveals a level of open-mindedness, but Al-Ḥajarī may also have been amusing dinner conversation, as exotic and oriental a curiosity as the Egyptian mummy of Gourgue's youth.[104]

At first glance, the passage of the Moriscos through the Labourd may appear only tangentially relevant. As we have seen again and again – and as Gourgue seems to have intuited – witchcraft fears and suspicions cannot be separated from the real world, and from the wider social and political problems facing the Labourd. The situation in the early 1610s may well give us a sense of *déjà vu*. Different problems may have emerged, but the solution remained the same as it had been when the witchcraft commission had been set up: weakened by Henry IV's sudden death, the crown was unable to directly impose its authority on a border territory and sent a representative instead. And just as before, conflict also meant opportunities, especially for the local nobility, who knew how to exploit them. The most prominent nobleman, the governor and mayor of Bayonne, Antoine de Gramont, never let a good crisis go to waste. We saw him charge Morisco refugees a toll for border passage; the Portuguese similarly paid him protection money. This was also the moment when he attempted to impose new taxes on the Labourd for his own benefit.[105] He even antagonized neighbouring governors, including the duke de La Force, the Protestant governor of Béarn and Navarre who in time would become a full-fledged rebel.[106]

The Labourd was a long way from Paris but it was of systemic importance. During his final months, Henry IV had pursued a more aggressive policy towards Spain, but the regency led by Marie de' Medici had fewer resources at its disposal and adopted a more diplomatic course which ultimately led to a marriage alliance between the two countries. The exchange of the princesses, immortalized by a Rubens painting, took place on the Bidasoa river on 9 November 1615.[107] (Basque witches put in an attendance by raising a storm at Pasaia which prevented King Philip III from inspecting the port.[108]) Gramont, who was among the noblemen present, had organized an armed escort of 1,000 to 1,200 'well-behaved' Basques who accompanied Anne of Austria, Louis XIII's new bride, to Saint-Jean-de-Luz, where she would spend her first night on French soil without her husband.[109] The situation near the border had been deemed too dangerous for Louis, who waited for his bride in Bordeaux.

From the outset, Gourgue's task at the border was also a peace mission: it was one of people and personnel management, aimed at mending relationships that mattered to the crown and to ensure the long-term stability of the border region, although Gramont ultimately proved impossible to control. As part of its new diplomatic approach, the crown dispatched Bishop Bertrand d'Echaux of Bayonne, the scion of a noble family from Navarre, to negotiate a peaceful solution to a long-standing border dispute in his homeland.[110] Gourgue was therefore tasked with patching up the differences between Echaux and Gramont, but only with limited success. On 2 August 1611, he reported from Bordeaux that the bishop and the governor were again 'in great commotion' and that 'the old quarrels' between them had revived.[111] More serious still was a conflict between Gramont and Antoine de Roquelaure, his father-in-law and the *de facto* governor of Guyenne, the rich and powerful province of which Bordeaux was part. In vain, Gourgue attempted to intercede in a conflict which eerily recalls the witchcraft commission's handiwork.

In March 1610, Gramont had returned early from hunting to discover his wife Louise in the arms of her lover, his bastard half-uncle Marsilien, who did not survive the encounter. Antoine had hardly been an example of marital fidelity himself. At court in 1608, he had started an affair which Henry IV, an expert in adultery if ever there was one, had mockingly described as a 'maritime alliance: the brill and the red mullet' in reference to the girl's voluptuosity and the count's famously red face.[112] Louise managed to escape to a nearby convent, but her husband tracked her down and imprisoned her. On 21 June 1610, her father Antoine de Roquelaure petitioned the Bordeaux Parlement to ensure the safety of his daughter. Cruseau – as riveted by this conflict, as Basque witches had once bored him – noted in his diary that the royal lieutenant feared for his daughter's life.[113] The problem, however, was one of jurisdiction and of power.

The crown had recognized Gramont as the independent prince of Bidache. Although the town was only the size of the proverbial postage stamp, within its boundaries, Gramont could do what he liked. He assembled a local court which duly sentenced Louise to death for her adultery.[114] Gramont had attended de Lancre's and Espagnet's interrogations; it is not difficult to see where the idea for a sovereign court, outside the jurisdiction of the Parlement, came from.

On 25 September, after other attempts at mediation failed, Queen Marie de' Medici instructed Gourgue to visit Bidache and ask Gramont to share with him 'all the procedures, interrogatories, recollections, confrontations, and other acts which have been produced in this affair'.[115] According to a later account, when Gourgue arrived at the bridge that marked the town entrance, he was told that he was only permitted to enter as 'a friend of the family'. If he planned to invoke any kind of jurisdiction, he should turn back – the sovereign of Bidache recognized no other authority than his own.[116] For a time, Gourgue's mediation seemed successful. On 9 October, writing from Saint-Jean-de-Luz, he forwarded a (now lost) account to Paris of his visit 'completely written in my own hand ... for the honour and contentment of both families and their friends'. The envoy also enclosed a letter by Gramont to the queen, in which he promised 'perfect obedience': 'your commands, Madame, have on me such an absolute power that I will never desire anything so passionately than to testify to you through all my actions that no one can rival my affection for your service.' He acknowledged the queen's interest in Louise's well-being, even though she was 'the most unworthy creature who lives under the sky'. And yet, despite the protestations of loyalty and devotion, Gramont declined the queen's request to return to court, claiming that his absence from the frontier would cause disorder.[117] The border again cast its spell, empowering those in its proximity. The prince of Bidache knew he could face down a monarch in his stronghold but would risk arrest if he showed his face in Paris.

Soon after, the border again rendered its warped version of frontier justice. Gramont took advantage in early November of Gourgue's absence in Logroño. Despite his professed concerns about border security, the nobleman left Bidache for a suspiciously timed visit to his sister and brother-in-law in Lauzun to the east of Bordeaux. The aim was to create distance between himself and the act for which he was most certainly responsible. On Tuesday 9 November, at three in the afternoon, with both her husband and the queen's envoy safely away from the scene, Louise de Roquelaure died in murky circumstances. Not long after, Gramont proceeded to court, where confronted with a *fait accompli*, the young king signed letters that absolved him 'of all crimes of which he could have been accused in whatever sort and matter they may have been committed'.[118] As we have seen many times before, early modern justice was a much diminished substance from how we might conceive of it, reduced by political calculations and financial concerns and reshaped by the pull of the border. While various fig leaves were devised to placate Antoine de Roquelaure, Louise's father failed to get any justice for his daughter.[119] Antoine II de Gramont passed away only in 1644, leaving his family firmly in control of Bayonne, Bidache and much of the south-west until the French Revolution. The memoirs of his son and successor, Antoine III de Gramont, do not mention his mother at all.[120]

Marc-Antoine de Gourgue was (thankfully) not a second Pierre de Lancre. But it would have been helpful to know his reaction to the news of Louise's death when he returned from the Logroño *auto de fe*, or indeed to know how he saw his mission's outcome. From our perspective, his efforts to pacify the border may appear none too successful, at least thus far. Both the expulsion of the Moriscos and the death of Henry IV brought further disorder to the Pays de Labourd, and it is difficult to see how witchcraft fears could have evaporated in those circumstances. Where de Lancre saw the connections between the witchcraft panic and the territory's geography – even if only dimly and demonically inspired – we do not know where Basque witches ranked on Gourgue's list of priorities. But deeds speak louder than words, and in Gourgue's case, these do form a pattern: his actions were those of a peace maker. The devout envoy may well have been inspired by the Inquisition's 'great mercy' which he had seen at first hand and praised in Logroño. The abbot of Urdax, who had pushed for a harsher approach, observed the sudden about-turn in France with dismay. On 29 January 1611, Aranibar reported to Logroño that 'this year's judges of the Bordeaux Parlement … proceeded extremely differently from last year's judges … they set free many of those who had previously been imprisoned'. This, he ominously predicted, 'will cause much evil in the French territory'.[121] The abbot's gloomy comments are difficult to parse, or to fact-check. Unlike those of his predecessors, Gourgue's mission had never been a judicial one, nor was it tied to the Bordeaux Parlement. Yet, Aranibar was right to detect a change of course. As we shall see in the next chapter, new spiritual solutions sought to stem the tide of witchcraft, and these were likely inspired by Spain. As in his dealings with Gramont and Echaux, Gourgue would also play the peacemaker between Lapurdi communities, even founding a convent with peace in its name. Sadly, it would not work.

# Chapter 12
# Spiritual solutions

At times it must have felt as if the Basque witchcraft problem might never end. On 23 April 1619, more than a decade after the Biltzar, the Labourd's assembly had petitioned the French crown for a witchcraft commission, its Gipuzkoan counterpart turned to Spain's Grand Inquisitor, Luis de Aliaga Martínez, for a witchcraft 'remedy'. The Basque province, home to the fortress of Hondarribia and the ports of Pasaia and San Sebastián, complained about the – by now very familiar – danger that witches posed to 'children of a young age'.[1] Whether the letter really reflected genuine widespread concern is unclear. Its main purpose was to endorse a petition drawn up by a single local priest. We have encountered him before: Lope Martínez de Isasti would later gain considerable renown as one of the Basque country's first historians.[2] The priest pleaded on behalf of the 'common God-fearing people' of Gipuzkoa that the Inquisition cleanse their province of the 'apostates who have caused so much damage', particularly the 'foreigners from France and Navarre'.[3] Paradoxically, it is Isasti's meandering petition which provides some of the clearest evidence that the panic may, in fact, already have been subsiding. Although he did not realize it, Isasti was already writing history.

In January 1615, the new bishop of Pamplona, Prudencio de Sandoval, had visited the town of Errenteria, some seven miles from Irun and the Bidasoa river, and gave its parish priest – Isasti – a special licence to hear the confessions of witches and absolve them. Errenteria had been one of the witch-hunt's epicentres, and Isasti claimed to have given the assignment his all: he heard confessions, he preached in Basque and he 'exhorted [witches] to return to the Catholic faith'. Yet, the assignment also sent the scholar back to his books, to the infamous *Malleus maleficarum* (Hammer of the Witches) and its more modern successor, the *Disquisitiones magicae* (Investigations into Magic) of the Spanish-Flemish Jesuit Martin Delrio, among other recent works of demonology.[4] Most of the witchcraft he encountered was firmly rooted in the past: anecdotes from his reading and popular rumours he picked up along the way.

Even his few in-person encounters with witchcraft were dated. The priest reported on the fate of a foreign witch, an 'old Frenchwoman called Marichuloco', who lived in Pasaia. Upon her release from prison some three years ago, the authorities expelled her. Boys chased her out of town with stones 'because she had taken children to the devil's sabbat'. She returned to France and died in Saint-Jean-de-Luz – of what causes, whether natural or human, Isasti does not say. Interested in learning more about the demonic, the priest discovered that the three children she allegedly abducted – now ten or eleven years old – were not overly keen to talk. One of the two boys vomited and 'became faint with great anguish' at the prospect. He had to be comforted with 'holy and loving words'. The stories that the priest finally managed to coax out of these children are instantly familiar: they were made to guard toads, the devil took the form of a black goat and so on. What is most striking is that all three of Marichuloco's alleged victims, as well as two or three older children that Isasti also interviewed, were adamant that their witchcraft days were over. The most talkative boy had been rescued by a 'beautiful woman' – she was, in fact, the Virgin Mary – who appeared, in rather Mary Poppins style, at the sabbat to take the children home: 'as the said Marichuloco died soon after, he remained free from this evil.' For the second boy, the accused witch's banishment had sufficed, while the girl told Isasti that she had not been 'in a long time'. In 1609, at the height of the panic, other witches would have instantly taken Marichuloco's place after her death or banishment. Only in the case of one fourteen-year-old boy, converted by a young female witch from Navarre (who seduced him with four apples), was his salvation not quite assured: 'the boy has been given an *agnus dei* [*a blessed object*] and relics, he has confessed well, and there is hope that he will remain cured.'[5] For the most part, then, these children placed the witch-hunt in the past, despite Isasti's enthusiastic attempt at a revival.

Working out the end of a witch-hunt is hard. If witchcraft panics were not (or not only) legal problems, but also social and spiritual ones, then when and how do they conclude? The children's testimonies collected by Isasti suggest that witchcraft fears were abating, or perhaps they were simply returning to 'normal' levels. Witchcraft beliefs were endemic in the Basque country, and they remained so. The stories that we have encountered in the footsteps of de Lancre, Isasti and others had deep folkloric roots. Salazar, the sceptical inquisitor, was factually quite wrong when he quipped that 'there were neither witches nor bewitched until they were talked and written about', although as we shall see, he did have a point.[6] Isasti's petition shows that tales of witchcraft were not going away. Within the area affected by the Great Basque witch-hunt – Lapurdi, eastern Gipuzkoa, northern Navarre – we have some evidence for later witch-hunting. Hondarribia saw another witchcraft trial in 1636, with further cases stretching well into the Age of (supposed) Enlightenment.[7] The region's possibly last 'real' witch trial, in San Sebastián in 1818, still resulted in the accused's banishment.[8]

Perhaps, one way by which witch-hunts ended was when elites, whether out of weariness or out of pragmatism, no longer got involved, when they no longer gave popular fears further oxygen. By 1619, the inquisitors at the Logroño tribunal must have been exceptionally weary, caught up as they were in a diabolical game of whack-a-mole: as one witchcraft panic subsided, another popped up elsewhere in the Basque country. In the autumn of 1615, reports reached them from Bilbao, the capital of Bizkaia, the most western province, that another panic was brewing there: two ten-year-olds claimed to have been taken to the 'meetings of witches'.[9] The allegations sparked another witch-hunt (led by another witchcraft commissioner) that lasted until at least 1617.[10] In 1621, another witch-hunt popped up, this time in Azkoitia in western Gipuzkoa. The town sent an envoy in person to Logroño to plead with the inquisitors to visit and 'to extirpate so pernicious a plague and so many offenses to God, who has miraculously helped us with the discovery of two very famous witches'.[11] Unlike before, nothing much appears to have happened in response to the 1619 and 1621 petitions. It seems that Logroño's inquisitors finally re-learned a lesson their predecessors had already grasped in 1595, when they wrote to the Suprema refusing to get involved in a secular witchcraft trial: 'these witchcraft investigations usually cost a lot of work, trouble, and tears, and they yield little fruit, as experience has shown and [your] Council's letters and decrees imply.'[12]

While more work on these later Basque witch-hunts, and the Inquisition's role in them, is urgently needed, their main lesson is clear and directly relevant: witchcraft persisted and could flare up at times of crisis. But if it was not vanquished in the courtroom, what about other ways of addressing it? This chapter explores two different spiritual attempts at combatting the Lapurdi witchcraft problem, led by Franciscan friars and Jesuit missionaries and sponsored by more outsiders. But could the spiritual approach – of absolving rather than condemning suspected witches – be keeping witchcraft fears alive? Could all the witchcraft talk still be fanning the flames, even if the emphasis is on repentance rather than wrath? The evidence, mostly produced by the friars and missionaries themselves, of course, is not completely clear-cut but it does point in that direction. The Jesuit reports indirectly provide some of the clearest proof that spiritual combat might well have been a losing battle. And the Jesuits certainly gave up. That said, as the next and final chapter shows, the witch-hunt of the Pays de Labourd would not be smothered by elite silence. It was a cataclysmic yet cathartic act of popular violence that brought it to a close.

# Our Lady of the Peace

Nothing ever came easy in the Pays de Labourd or happened without conflict, even the foundation of a convent with peace in its name. Its founding goes back to deliberations by the officials and inhabitants of Saint-Jean-de-Luz in November 1610. The date may well not be coincidental. The discussions took place in the presence of Marc-Antoine de Gourgue, who had freshly returned from the Logroño *auto de fe*. The idea that the people of Saint-Jean-de-Luz might benefit from being 'instructed' by a group of friars, 'edified by their exemplary life, and helped and relieved by their fervent prayer and sacrifice' may well have come from the royal official and, through him, from Spain.[13] The Inquisition's eventual Edict of Grace, issued in the spring of 1611, would likewise foresee the creation of two new convents on the Spanish side of the border.[14] The convent's chronicler, Mathias de Lissalde, credited Gourgue for recognizing that the disorders afflicting the territory were 'the effect of the inhabitants' ignorance and superstition' and that establishing 'zealous religious capable of instructing them' was the right way to 'stifle their divisions'.[15] The convent would offer a spiritual armoury in a territory generally devoid of monastic foundations.[16] With its priests executed (in Ciboure's case) or imprisoned in Bordeaux (in the case of Saint-Jean-de-Luz), both coastal communities really could do with such protection. A surviving partial inscription on the convent's walls from 1645 still acknowledges the community's prayers 'for the inhabitants and sailors of Saint-Jean-de-Luz and Ciboure'.[17]

Among the religious options available, the Recollects were in many respects an apt choice, although they are virtually unknown today. (Understandably enough because they no longer exist.) Recollects were part of the Franciscans, a fractious religious order which spawned movements of reform and renewal at a frightening pace. One seventeenth-century inventory of Catholicism's many religious orders simply gave up on the attempt to describe its many offshoots: 'a large book would not be enough to describe all the reforms, splits, unions, suits, disputes, and changes in dress and rule that have taken place within this great Order.'[18] The Recollects were the exciting new flavour of the day during the early 1600s, especially in France. They had only founded their first community in Guyenne in 1594, but they rapidly expanded after that, taking over one of the Franciscan convents in Bordeaux in 1602.[19] For the most part, however, they kept to smaller towns, making them a good fit for Saint-Jean-de-Luz. Unlike their reforming rivals, such as the Italian *riformati* and the (more aggressive, and ultimately more successful) Capuchins, the Recollects were also seen as essentially French.[20] If the idea for a convent had roots in Spain, then the order called in was homegrown. This was a matter of some importance close to the border.[21]

The foundation received the backing of both Bishop Echaux and Antoine de Gramont, the governor of Bayonne – no small feat given their many and escalating conflicts. Not everyone was on board, however. When the first five or six Recollect friars arrived in September 1612, they were dissatisfied with the site allocated to them.[22] Their eye had fallen on an island between Saint-Jean-de-Luz and Ciboure which was conveniently crossed by the bridge that connected the two quarrelling communities. Claims that the original location was too 'hot' and 'stormy' may only have been excuses; their new site can hardly have been less windy, it was a serious flood risk and lacked access to fresh water.[23] It would, however, place them (as the foundation document put it) 'in sight of all those who travelled across this border from France into Spain, of the public spaces and most of the houses of Saint-Jean-de-Luz and Ciboure, and moreover be very convenient to access' for those living in the wider area.[24] The eventual convent of Our Lady of the Peace would dominate the local landscape. The chapel, erected in 1613, was larger than the parish churches of either community, and the resulting site impressed the many travellers crossing the nearby bridge. One diarist noted in 1670 that Saint-Jean-de-Luz and Ciboure 'often came to blows but since the two parties very willingly recognized these religious as their referees, they live together peaceably and pass as friends'.[25]

Likely the friars realized that the island location would be ideal for keeping the two feuding towns apart. Lissalde, the chronicler amongst them, observed that 'the smallest occasion lit up their reciprocal hatred'. Predictably then, Saint-Jean-de-Luz handing over the island to the friars caused a riot because the inhabitants of Ciboure and Urrugne (and standing behind the latter, Tristan d'Urtubie) felt that it was not theirs to give away. Like the islands on the Bidasoa river, which were claimed by both France and Spain, those on the river Nivelle were disputed by the neighbouring communities. Ciboure objected to Saint-Jean-de-Luz officials erecting a cross at the projected site without them: the inhabitants, Lissalde wrote, 'thought it wrong that the cross was planted without their participation'.[26] According to Gourgue's contemporary account, after the Luzians left, their rivals 'went to the place in great number and, with great contempt for the cross and with public scandal, they tore it down and carried it with them to Ciboure'.[27] If Gourgue and others had not intervened, Saint-Jean-de-Luz residents would have rushed after them. Instead, the royal envoy persuaded the communities of Ciboure and Urrugne to follow Saint-Jean-de-Luz in ceding their claims and agree to the convent, which would be built using charitable donations (and therefore not belong to any town in particular). Gourgue then organized a second planting of the cross with representatives of all the communities present. Saint-Jean-de-Luz would gift him a 'barrel of wine' in thanks.[28]

The founding of Our Lady of the Peace thus brought turbulence in its wake. It is possible that the friars with their prayers alleviated the spiritual anxieties of the residents, long deprived of pastoral support. Their strategic, literally intermediary position may well have thwarted some further violence. Yet, the communities nevertheless remained at odds over the new port at Socoa for most of the 1610s and early 1620s, with Tristan d'Urtubie, for instance, again taking up arms.[29] In 1615, Saint-Jean-de-Luz provocatively offered to absorb its smaller neighbour, claiming that its name 'is known everywhere, whereas that of Ciboure is hardly known to anyone'.[30] The friars' contribution to ending the witchcraft panic may similarly have been, at least in part, counterproductive.

Their chronicler, Lissalde, discussed how the intervention of one preacher, a certain Martin Habas, had backfired. An unnamed woman, who had falsely slandered her neighbour as a witch, was touched by Habas's fiery sermons. If she was real, we could perhaps identify her as Catherine de La Masse, whose denunciations in church marked the proper beginning of the witch-hunt. As we saw, she had been imprisoned in Bordeaux around this time. Her conscience stirred, the slanderer 'not only confessed to being guilty of all the evils which have desolated this territory but believing that she could remedy this by a public confession, she permitted [Habas] to name and accuse her publicly'. Witch-hunts need culprits. In Lissalde's account, it was a penitent woman rather than a wicked judge who took the blame. Unfortunately, the priest's accusations misfired spectacularly: 'The cure was worse than the disease or only increased it. People believed it to be a pretence of devotion. The wickedness begot new sorcerers every day. The entirety of the Pays de Labourd was infected by this contagion.'[31]

The preacher's intervention failed miserably. Lissalde may well have presented Habas as a foreigner, an 'old Spaniard', for that reason, as he was certainly a Saint-Jean-de-Luz native.[32] Lissalde also omits that Habas had, in fact, been the convent's first leader and guardian.[33] This is a striking reworking of the community's early history: its founder's efforts had backfired so spectacularly that its chronicler posthumously transformed him into an outsider. Perhaps, the Recollects discovered that the ready availability of spiritual remedies would also bring the ills they were intended to cure into focus. That would be a lesson that their rival missionaries, the Jesuits, would never learn. Their efforts fell to internal divisions first.

## Jesuits to the rescue

Jesuits were not a common sight in the French Basque country. Their attempts to found a college in Bayonne had consistently failed. French opponents of the Society of Jesus – of which there were many – commonly depicted it as a Spanish order and therefore as a foreign threat.[34] One roughly contemporary pamphlet pushing for a college in Bayonne was forced to refute suggestions that 'the Jesuits are dangerous' and should not be permitted to reside in a 'border city'.[35] The founder of the order, Ignatius of Loyola, as this *Briefve refutation* pointed out, was no Spaniard but a Basque from (Spanish-occupied) Navarre, born a mere 'sixteen leagues' from the city, while the Society itself had its origins in Paris, where Ignatius and the other first companions met while studying at the Sorbonne.[36]

Despite these failed efforts, the occasional Jesuit did pass through, and one of our rare eyewitnesses praised them for bringing the witch-hunt to an end. Whereas Lissalde, the Recollect friar, assigned a seminal role in the decline of the witch-hunt to his own convent (minus its leader), Bertrand de Haitze, in his note in Ustaritz's baptism register, paid tribute to the Jesuits for successfully 'abasing the pride and freedom of the people'.[37] These activities had humble beginnings. In 1610, an unnamed Jesuit from Bordeaux heard confessions in Bayonne. Whether this included any witches is unclear, the semi-public document which recounted the event only singled out one unnamed individual who had secretly committed 'the gravest crime of all' which they had hoped to expiate through acts of penance and charity.[38] A year later, another unnamed Jesuit arrived to preach and explain the Christian catechism. Many of the stories recounted will look instantly familiar to us. One youngster had been flown to the sabbat, but the boy's anxious experience ended, not by his invoking Christ's name, as it usually did, but by making the sign of the cross. He confessed his sins to the Jesuit because he wanted to experience the Eucharist again, a desire that we have seen other repentant witches express as well.[39] The Jesuit's catechism classes, meanwhile, were attended not only by 'a multitude of children but also by serious and leading men'. (The missionary was struck by the beauty of children's native hymns, the teenagers enchanting him as they had de Lancre and the devil before him.) How much his audience took away from his preaching remains an open question, as the Jesuit evidently only spoke French. He composed a catechism 'against magicians and witches' which he arranged to have translated into Basque. This was freely distributed among the people at the expense of a benevolent merchant. What prompted this enterprising initiative was the observation that the Basque were 'remarkably addicted to the magical arts and witchcraft'.[40] The Jesuit was not wrong.

Catechisms, precisely because they ended up in the hands of the faithful rather than the libraries of the learned, were perishable documents, and no copy is known to have survived. Yet, this lost Jesuit attempt very likely inspired a 1617 catechism by the Franciscan (not Recollect) friar Esteve Materra.[41] A native French speaker, Materra apologized for the imperfections in his Basque text. This catechism also targeted witchcraft, acknowledging that witches were worse than pagans and heretics: 'They have renounced all that is true in order to serve their false idol. [They] do everything for him and out of their own free will and indulge in the pleasures of the flesh. They are therefore the most evil on earth and deserve to be cleansed from it.'[42] While therefore acknowledging the reality of witchcraft, the text's principal aim was to refocus Basque spirituality away from the devil and towards God and the saints. In a second edition, Materra even provided suggested prayers for 'when a storm is raised at sea', a situation pervaded by fears of demonic agency. Sailors should go on their knees and collectively pray the *Ave Maria* or, if the storm was particularly strong, the *Salve Regina* or failing that, 'anything that comforts you'.[43] These spiritual solutions, then, did not refute the existence of witchcraft but sought to equip the pious reader with an arsenal of prayer with which to ward off evil. The Jesuit's catechism must have looked very similar.

The visits of 1610 and 1611, written up in polished Latin and sent to Rome, set the stage for a more formal intervention: the creation of an official 'Cantabrian mission', after the ancient Roman name for the region. Plans first appear in the Jesuit archives in the spring of 1613. From the outset, the mission is presented as an initiative of the queen mother, Marie de' Medici herself. The crown was sponsoring similar Jesuit preaching campaigns in neighbouring Béarn and Navarre, where the target was Protestantism rather than witchcraft. On 2 July 1613, Pierre Coton, the queen's Jesuit confessor, sent a (lost) proposal to Claudio Acquaviva, the Society's superior general in Rome.[44] A letter from Bordeaux (also lost) had already made the Jesuit general aware of the project: the provincial of Aquitaine apparently worried that the necessary Basque-speakers might not be found.[45]

The royal patronage suggests that the momentum for the Jesuit mission came from outside the Society. Marc-Antoine de Gourgue, as an intimate of the queen mother, remains the more likely of the two possible sponsors. The judge had been particularly close to the Jesuits: they marked his death in 1628 with a series of elaborate funeral eulogies and interred his heart in one of the Society's houses (as Henry IV's had also been).[46] Given his ties to both the Jesuits and the crown, Gourgue could easily have recommended the project to Coton and the queen mother.

There is a second, unexpected and perhaps unlikely candidate who at least deserves a mention, given his own close ties to the Jesuits: Pierre de Lancre. Throughout 1613, the Bordeaux judge was in touch directly with the Jesuit general in Rome about his illegitimate son's admission to the Society, which the younger Pierre eventually achieved in January 1614.[47] Unfortunately, only the general's side of this correspondence has been preserved, but from it we know the judge also raised other matters relating to the Bordeaux college.[48] In 1615, as de Lancre was contemplating retirement from the Parlement, he even expressed a wish to follow his son and enter the Society of Jesus himself at an unusually advanced age, the most startling attempt at a career change in a life devoted to inconstancy. Both the local provincial and the general in Rome wisely decided de Lancre's 'health and complexion' would not be 'sufficient for the weight of the religious life'.[49]

There is no evidence of either Gourgue or de Lancre advocating for the mission, but we know that the latter was among the first to learn of it. The second, 1613 edition of the *Tableau* includes an entirely new letter of dedication. De Lancre still insisted on the superiority of 'exemplary punishment' over 'impunity'. Nevertheless, he added, 'I believe that good and learned preachers would achieve more than the most severe judges of the world'. After all, it was as difficult to 'exterminate completely the witches from our border in the Labourd' by legal means as it was 'to measure the air and wind that transports them to the sabbat or make the mountains where they live fly'. He celebrated the 'holy decision' of 'our prudent and magnanimous queen' to send the Jesuit mission: 'the inspiration is not only royal but completely divine.' De Lancre's inconstancy has no limits: he remained thankful for the opportunity 'to discover and eradicate this evil race of apostatized Christians, witches, magicians, and diviners'.[50] Exodus 22.18 – 'Thou shalt not suffer a witch to live' – still featured on the *Tableau*'s cover. But, his closeness to the Jesuits, his devotion to the crown and his evident foreknowledge of the mission mean that the possibility that he played some role in its origins cannot entirely be discounted.

By 1613 at the latest, then, Basque witches occupied the minds of leaders in Bordeaux, Paris and Rome. Both General Acquaviva and Coton, the queen's confessor, spent considerable time and energy identifying candidates with the right linguistic skills not only in France but oddly also in Spain, although foreign Jesuits were not normally permitted to operate in the kingdom.[51] Jesuits excelled at cataloguing and keeping track of their members. Using these records, Acquaviva wrote to Jesuit provincials in Barcelona and Toulouse in September 1613. Pedro Juste, the Catalan provincial, was informed that 'the queen of France has asked that we embark on a mission to some villages in the diocese of Bayonne much in need of doctrine'.[52] The general had requested a certain Hernando Juan Socarro, based at the college of Calatayud, only to be told that his Basque was not up to the task. Acquaviva did not approach the Castilian province, even though the Spanish Basque country fell under its jurisdiction. Perhaps, the superior general was weary of the witchcraft scepticism professed by some Basque-speaking Jesuits. Their ringleader, Hernando de Solarte, had even voiced his opposition to the witch-hunt in a letter to Rome.[53] From Acquaviva's perspective, Solarte would have been the wrong kind of Jesuit to send.

Given all these constraints, the mission to the French Basque country as it was assembled ahead of the summer of 1614 was a rather barebones affair, consisting of no more than two Jesuits who, moreover, were forced to work together as a team. It was led by an experienced missionary, Jean Boucher, then in his late forties, who had joined the Society as far back as 1587.[54] Boucher possessed none of the relevant languages but was never hindered by his lack of linguistic ability. When he passed away in 1620, his fellow Jesuits praised his obedience: 'although he was ignorant of the language of the Béarnais, he still never refused to go to their peasant villages, helping them with the piety and zeal that was in him, for he often held two or three sermons a day for the people.'[55] What these villagers made of the spectacle we shall never know. Fortunately for Boucher, in the Basque country he was supported by a young Jesuit novice,

Bernard d'Arain, who was found teaching grammar in the small town of Mauriac in central France.[56] Arain would act as Boucher's interpreter.

For three years, these two Jesuits returned to the Labourd every summer. In Bayonne, they were warmly welcomed by Bishop Echaux. In Saint-Jean-de-Luz, they preached not just to the people but even to the priests against every form of commerce with the devil, an argument which – understandably enough given their experiences – 'the preachers beforehand had altogether feared to touch upon'. Travelling inland, they heard familiar tales of witchcraft: reports of priests who celebrated Black Masses at the sabbat using 'some pitch-black dark round object instead of the celestial Host'. At the sabbat, children still looked after toads. 'Numerous crowds of children from the age of six to seventeen' flocked to the Jesuits with tales of abduction by evil witches to 'the nocturnal *Orgia* of the magicians', where they were forced into demonic pacts, or as their highly polished report put it, 'the profession of the sacred Stygians', after the river Styx in the pagan underworld.[57]

Little, then, appears to have changed since de Lancre and Espagnet left the region. Apparently undaunted, the two Jesuits set to work, hearing confessions and absolving the sins of the young and old. Basques 'flew' to the self-satisfied Jesuits – a rather unfortunate turn of phrase where witchcraft is concerned. Forgoing both church and food, the Jesuits worked all day, drawing crowds from across the border, as far as Pamplona. As with the Edict of Grace earlier, the prospect of absolution exerted an extraordinary pull. Boucher was later reported as saying he had no sweat left. During their 1614 visit, they had restored six hundred 'natives' to Christ. Satisfied with a job well done, they crossed into Spain and visited the shrine devoted to Ignatius in his Basque birthplace of Loyola. On their journey back to Bordeaux, through Lower Navarre, they came across another familiar scene: a witch-finder, in this case a 21-year-old woman with the ability to discern a toad's foot in a witch's left eye.[58]

Jesuits often styled themselves in their accounts in the way Boucher and Arain had – as following in the footsteps of the original apostles, triumphant because God was on their side. Even though the reports were highly stylized, many aspects do ring true, precisely because we have heard them before. The triumphalism likely also reflected a sense of optimism that spiritual means were more effective than judicial ones. As the Jesuits themselves put it, 'experience appears to have taught the prudent that so widespread a fire, greatly strengthened by time, cannot be extinguished through the severity of judges. Their flames will only be hidden for a time, and it will strengthen in the shadows, and after that it will proceed even more violently'.[59] This had been the conclusion to which the Inquisition had come in Spain, following Salazar's advice. The French Jesuits soon discovered, however, that the spiritual route was hardly a miracle cure.

The reports that the Bordeaux Jesuits filed for the 'Cantabrian mission' for 1615 and 1616 were markedly shorter than their initial bravado account. The descriptions still made good use of the same elaborate metaphors, classical allusions and biblical imagery. The mission still bore great fruit, 'the kingdom of Satan' was still being weakened 'every day'. Yet, the two later accounts – each less than half a page long – could not hide that the two Jesuits were as busy as before and that the problem was not going away. In 1615, 'many mortals were released from the power of the devil to whom they had dedicated themselves, using the remedies described by us the previous year'. Toads were still mentioned in 1616 – this time joined by other small animals – and children kept on being taken to the sabbat. There was even another report of a person rescued from the clutches of witches by making the sign of the cross.[60]

Did the Jesuit mission achieve anything? As we saw, Haitze, the parish priest of Ustaritz, believed that it did. There are, however, good reasons to be sceptical, as talk of witches only begot more witches. The Jesuits may well have been fanning flames in summer that had died down during their absence. Their reports provide little evidence of progress; they rather resembled Groundhog Day. One Jesuit eventually had enough. In August 1616, the provincial of Aquitaine Jacques de Moussy reported to Mutio Vitelleschi, Acquaviva's successor in Rome, that the Cantabrian mission had to be suspended unless a new Basque-speaker could be found, perhaps, with the king's blessing, in Spain. Arain, the young Basque novice, had left the mission, apparently of his own volition, forcing Boucher to retreat to Béarn where he inflicted his missionary zeal on another territory whose language he did not speak.[61] We do not know why Arain left. When the Jesuits composed Boucher's obituary, they obliquely referred to him overcoming the betrayal of a 'false brother' whose insults he had to endure.[62] Had Arain grown sceptical of witchcraft, as Solarte had? His departure may well have been the result of a spiritual crisis. He not only abandoned the Basque mission but gave up on his religious vocation as well: the Jesuit catalogue for 1618 lists Arain as having left the Society altogether.[63] There is not a trace of what happened to him after that.

Arain's departure did not quite mark the end of the Jesuits' involvement in the Basque witch-hunt. The hierarchy made a surprisingly substantial effort to find a replacement and continue the effort. In November 1616, Moussy reported to Vitelleschi that he had 'often' written to Coton, the royal confessor, about the need for a Basque-speaker from Spain and – while he was at it – for financial support for the mission as well, but he heard only silence, 'for when he replies to me on other matters, there is not even a single word on this one'.[64] As late as January 1617, Vitelleschi reached out to the Castilian provincial Juan de Monte Mayor to see if two Jesuits who spoke Basque could be sent to the Aquitaine province.[65] After that the trail goes cold.

# Chapter 13
# New witch bottles

On 6 April 1615, the council minutes of Bayonne recorded the escape of two witches, at least one of whom was foreign to the city (she had come from nearby Béarn). The councillors resolved to formally banish them and prohibit their return.[1] The decision was part of a wider pattern. A month earlier, the council minutes had noted 'the great number of poor people' in their city. It was more reasonable, their minutes calmly recorded, to support residents than 'the poor strangers who are pouring in from all directions'. They too would be expelled as soon as the rains had ended; the officials optimistically expected the 'good weather' to return after the expulsion.

If this expectation seems like magical thinking, it worked in part because witchcraft was increasingly being tied to foreignness. On 4 May, the councillors ordered the expulsion of 'the vagabond women and girls ... banished from Béarn and Lower Navarre on account of witchcraft'. They had found work, and a temporary home, with the winegrowers and farmers on the outskirts of the city but now had to uproot themselves again. Their 'licentiousness' and their witchcraft – they were accused of giving people 'epilepsy' – had caused offence to both the public and to God.[2] The pattern in the council's decisions is difficult to miss that spring and evidently reflected concerns for the city's well-being. On 18 May, the councillors went further and decided that a plan was needed to excite the community's devotion and to appease God's anger, again in strikingly unemotional language. Prayers would relieve widespread disease and turn away the storms 'which we see most often occur during this season' when witches attacked crops and vines just as they were about to ripen. The council resolved once more to promptly 'empty' the city of all 'foreign vagabonds'. Their deliberations would be circulated among the city's preachers 'in order to dispose the city's inhabitants towards their devotions and prayers'.[3] Spring, it seems, was an especially perilous time because the season offered both hope and renewal. The worsening climate during the 1610s must have put councillors ill at ease as to what might come next.

Bayonne's decisions in 1615 were part of a worrying, decade-long trend which we have already observed in passing in the previous two chapters: witchcraft was increasingly associated with foreigners. To some extent, this reflected the realities of earlier witch-hunting which had pushed the accused across borders, whether in search of safety or as a result of banishment. The border thus created 'foreign' witches, even inside the Basque country. But witchcraft was almost always tied to otherness. Suspected witches were often those who did not belong, living at the margins of their communities: they were the ultimate outsiders set apart by difference. Witches thus enabled communal bonding; their alleged evil intent allowed communities to unite against them. If witchcraft fears and anxieties finally died down during the later 1610s, then this was also due to a process of transference. Enemies had become easier to find. They were no longer lurking within communities but had come in from the outside. Witches had gradually become more foreign, and the growing number of foreigners had become more threatening. In this final chapter, we shall see how a gradual process of transference – old witchcraft fears in new bottles – found another target.

Orson Welles memorably quipped that happy endings depend on where the author decides to stop their story. Witch-hunts, too, are stories. They were real, of course, but only in the same way witches were real. Nobody was born a witch; humans were made into them. Witches were forged out of the human emotions – grief, anger, fear – of their neighbours. Witch-hunts are similar attempts, but writ large, to give a series of unfortunate, perhaps even traumatic, events narrative coherence, including a beginning and an end. Historians in their attempts to reconstruct what really happened have generally followed in the footsteps of the original story tellers, Pierre de Lancre, chief among them. His *Tableau* unwittingly transformed him into a pantomime villain. The witch-hunt of the Pays de Labourd, however, was not the work of one man, nor even only that of 'elites'. Rather, as we have seen, it was also the product of geography, of life at the border; it emerged out of a constellation of local and international conflicts; it starred a 'cast' of hundreds and all of them, even the children, helped shape its deadly outcome.

So what about the end? Witch-hunts are meant to be the nightmares from which we wake up. We want the skies to clear, for reason to triumph over superstition. That did not happen, at least, not here. The judges' departure did not end the hunt. The missionaries who followed in their wake might have provided an alternative happy ending: one in which other well-meaning elite outsiders brought enlightenment to the stricken territory, but of the spiritual rather than the rational kind. But these religious men, too, laboured in vain. Their continued witchcraft talk may well have prolonged the panic. Would silence have been better? This witch-hunt certainly did not end with a whimper. Witchcraft fears were gradually transmuted and applied to fresh outsiders. Our different approach, decentring de Lancre and focusing on the Labourd, brings other developments into focus, in particular, the growth of a refugee population and the brutal killing of one elderly Portuguese woman in March 1619. If we are to end the witch-hunt anywhere, it really must be there: with a gruesome act of collective violence, a gross injustice which nevertheless served as a communal act of expiation.

## Spying on the Portuguese

The inquisitors of the Logroño tribunal had always been more worried about the threat posed by the Portuguese than they were about witches. On 26 July 1609, the inquisitors took time out from the interrogation of their initial witchcraft suspects to remind the Suprema of the 'many times', since at least 1601, that they 'have given account of the great number of Portuguese who gather in Saint-Jean-de-Luz in France to hold their meetings and ceremonies according to the Mosaic Law'.[4] Watching Portuguese merchants and merchandise cross the border helped the abbot of Urdax, León de Aranibar, to secure his Inquisition job at least as much as his reports on witchcraft.[5] Around the same time as they hired Aranibar and were questioning their first witches, the inquisitors also enlisted the help of a San Sebastián native, a certain Marcos de Ylumbe (or Ylunbe), who endeavoured to infiltrate the Portuguese community in Saint-Jean-de-Luz. The inquisitors wanted him to work out 'where the said Portuguese hold their meetings, who are the leaders and masters among them', what number of them practised 'the ceremonies of the Jews', what their names and aliases were and so on.[6] The spy's first report from Saint-Jean-de-Luz, written on 15 July 1609, was promisingly disturbing but actually contained very little: the pride of the Portuguese when an old pious man sought to refute them, the possession of two vernacular bibles.[7] Perhaps not surprisingly given his heated language, Ylumbe soon gave himself away. We can only imagine the glee with which he was denounced to Gramont, Bayonne's governor, as a foreign spy.[8] By the autumn of 1609, the city of San Sebastián and the province of Gipuzkoa were petitioning authorities in Bayonne for his release from prison.[9] It took Ylumbe six months to smuggle out a letter in which he lamented his harsh treatment – he had been denied firewood in the midst of winter. (His cell, he later noted, was opposite one that housed two accused witches.[10]) His letter continued to press the Portuguese danger and elicit the inquisitors' support. There were plans afoot, he warned, to found both a synagogue in Saint-Jean-de-Luz and 'a university of Jewish heresies with great damage and danger to Spain'.[11] It took at least a year and 'much work' to secure his release.[12] (Presumably, given Gramont's general attitude towards life, money exchanged hands.)

Ylumbe's amateurish spying points to the difficulties of studying this Portuguese community: it is difficult to escape the inquisitorial gaze. As a name, Portuguese is both a reasonably accurate descriptor and a euphemism. In France, it was a catch-all heading for Iberian merchant communities who had been granted important trading privileges by King Henry II in 1550.[13] Their official identity, then, was first and foremost an economic one. Yet, many of those who settled in trading entrepôts like Bordeaux and Bayonne, were of a *converso* background, the descendants of Iberian Jews who had been forcefully converted to Christianity in earlier centuries – indeed, the privileges were especially designed to attract them. (Some persistent myths about Jewish economic roles emerged from the French south-west within a generation of the events described in this chapter.[14]) While France had expelled its Jews long before Spain had, the kingdom lacked an inquisition and therefore promised these migrants less official scrutiny. The sources for Spanish paranoia are, therefore, evident: the community was beyond the reach of the Holy Office of the Inquisition, but these merchants nevertheless continued to travel to and trade with the Iberian Peninsula and remained in contact with other New Christians. This meant that they could spread dangerous heretical or Judaizing ideas and provide escape routes to those looking to leave. The paranoia, in other words, was the result of official intolerance which pushed subversive practices into hiding and made everyone suspect. In 1622, one perceptive Portuguese New Christian urged the Spanish Crown to establish Jewish ghettos, not only to lure back economically successful Jews but also to separate them from sincere New Christians.[15] The idea, inevitably, was not taken up.

Just because the Spanish Inquisition considered the Portuguese of Saint-Jean-de-Luz to be Jews, however, did not mean that they were. Older historiography simply assumed that Iberian *conversos* were 'Crypto-Jews' who continued to practise their ancestral faith in secret.[16] More recent historians have come to regard them as 'cultural commuters' who could glide between different cultures.[17] A range of identities was open to members of France's Portuguese community – several hundred even returned to Iberia and Catholicism and testified against their erstwhile brethren.[18] Only in the later seventeenth century did the communities in south-west France embrace normative rabbinic Judaism as practised elsewhere in Europe, under the influence of (self-styled) missionaries from Amsterdam and other hubs within the wider Sephardic diaspora. In Bayonne, the Portuguese did not stop baptizing their children until the 1660s, a move which coincided with the arrival of one such religious leader.[19] Not long after, the visiting novelist Marie-Catherine d'Aulnoy was shown Bayonne's synagogue. She found it 'nothing remarkable', but it was a sign that the community was now openly Jewish.[20] Bidache, which as an independent principality did not have to indulge in euphemisms, substituted the word 'Jewish' for the word 'Portuguese' in its trading ordinances in the late 1660s.[21]

The evidence for the start of the century, however, still points to a range of religious identities. From the relative comfort of Venice, a contemporary rabbi rejected the possibility of Judaism in France as a 'diabolical illusion', bought at the price of occasional participation in Christian ritual.[22] Yet, this was certainly part of what happened. A defamation case in 1630 Bayonne includes testimony from Basque servants working in New Christian households puzzled by certain cultural practices – the lighting of candles, rest on the sabbat, the abstention from pork and other dietary restrictions. The extent to which such practices, handed down by previous generations, constituted proof of normative Judaism is an open question. (Even willing 'Judaizing' arrivals in Amsterdam had to overcome considerable ignorance about traditional Jewish life.[23]) The fact that the lawsuit started because one member of the Portuguese community publicly 'libelled' another as a Jew also suggests a range of religious attitudes and practices.[24]

The evidence for Saint-Jean-de-Luz points in a similarly conflicted direction. In 1612, the Logroño tribunal drew up a list of twenty Portuguese women and men in Saint-Jean-de-Luz, who had been accused by the 'Judaizing Jews' they had themselves interrogated.[25] The list was headed by Manuel Díaz, a shoemaker by profession, who allegedly had been circumcised in Pisa and changed his name to Jacob. Others were merchants who continued to trade with and travel to Spain, as well as their wives. (One Graciosa Ferrol was said to have taught her husband 'in the things of the law of Moses' because 'he knew very little when he married her'.[26]) A famous Inquisition trial in Mexico City (to which we will return) revealed that Saint-Jean-de-Luz itself could also be a site of conversion. In 1634, Antonio Fernández Cardado confessed that he had apostatized and embraced 'with all his heart' the law of Moses in the Basque town around 1611. Before leaving for the Americas in 1613, he was part of a community that observed a range of Jewish rituals which included fasting 'during the big day around the month of September' (Yom Kippur) and ritual bathing in the sea (an unusual form of mikvah, inspired perhaps by Basque surroundings).[27] Others, however, were not interested. A rare surviving series of letters sent around 1612 show a new convert to Judaism in Venice, the physician Elijah Montalto, struggle in vain to encourage his Luzian brother-in-law to follow his lead. The increasingly desperate tone – 'May the Lord pity your soul and separate you from blind idolatry' – suggests that Montalto's pleas fell on deaf ears.[28] While some therefore rediscovered their roots, others were practising or just lukewarm Catholics. The Portuguese community in Saint-Jean-de-Luz relied on its own priests, at least in part for linguistic reasons. While the town's parish priests were suspicious of their foreign counterparts, they still supported one Manuel Santus 'who lives very religiously and with every decency, even though he converses with the other Portuguese among whom he is not especially welcome'.[29]

The Portuguese of Saint-Jean-de-Luz, then, were a diverse group but any nuance was lost on outsiders. Even the least biased of our Basque witnesses used the general reputation of the Portuguese to bestow praise on rare pious exceptions. Ylumbe estimated that only five out of more than two hundred

Portuguese families in the town were Catholics – the rest were Jews.[30] When, a decade after their expulsion in 1619, a Spanish Inquisition official visited Saint-Jean-de-Luz and questioned Martin Habas about the Portuguese, the Franciscan friar put their number at three hundred families but he praised the handful of 'good and devout Catholics' among them.[31] That was all the nuance that locals could muster. Other moments of crisis – for instance, when Spanish invasion appeared imminent – had coincided with calls for the expulsion of the Portuguese (and, in 1591, the *cagots*), but none were carried out.[32] Instead, the community continued to grow, and so did the hostility towards them. In 1615, a group of New Christians of unknown size travelled from Saint-Jean-de-Luz to the Baltic.[33] Two years later, some seventy left for Amsterdam, in both cases presumably to avoid persecution.[34] The town's account books reveal at least one disturbing incident for that year. A group of Portuguese girls were convicted of theft and executed, and 'delegates of the Portuguese' were made to pay the full legal costs.[35]

These increasing levels of hostility may reflect the darkening political mood across France during the 1610s. The government of Marie de' Medici, the foreign queen mother, grew increasingly reliant on two equally foreign favourites: the Italian adventurer Concino Concini, appointed marshal of France in 1613, and his wife Leonora Dori Galigai, the queen's oldest friend and her lady-in-waiting. As young girls, the two women had played together in the gardens of the Palazzo Pitti in Florence.[36] As the queen's favourites, the foreign power couple became the subjects of numerous venomous pamphlets.[37] The controversial appointment of a Jewish court physician Elijah Montalto added anti-Semitism to this already heady mix of misogyny and xenophobia. (We already met Montalto excoriating his Luzian brother-in-law's blindness from Venice.) The physician, who predictably made it clear that 'he neither intended to hide or fake his religion', became France's first 'official' Jewish resident since 1394.[38] While notionally serving as the queen's physician, Montalto's primary responsibility was to look after Galigai, whose fragile mental health fuelled narratives (of demonic possession and hysteria) which legitimated her downfall and have blackened her posthumous reputation to this day.[39]

None of this ended well. On 23 April 1615, partly to deflect from a series of court scandals (and from Montalto's presence), Louis XIII issued a declaration expelling all Jews who 'disguised themselves in several places in our kingdom' from France.[40] Two years later, on 24 April 1617, the young and increasingly restless king led a coup against his mother's government. Concini was assassinated in the courtyard of the Louvre. (The slowness of French justice had allegedly caused the king to decide against simply ordering the marshal's arrest.[41]) Leonora was imprisoned in the Bastille, accused not only of 'introducing Jews' into the kingdom but also of bewitching the king's mother, a charge that usefully discredited both women. The Paris Parlement, famously sceptical in all other witchcraft matters, sentenced Leonora to be beheaded as a witch on 8 July 1617.[42] Marie de' Medici was swiftly banished – perhaps the nadir but certainly not the final act in a tumultuous and fascinating life.[43]

How much did the residents of Saint-Jean-de-Luz know about the events unfolding in the distant capital? Snippets of news must have filtered through. The town would have received the 1615 declaration, even if the expulsion order remained a dead letter in the Labourd, as it did elsewhere. Basque sailors probably did not know that an angry mob had dug up Concini's body and paraded the hated favourite through the streets of the capital.[44] Even so, much of this heavy Parisian blend of xenophobia, misogyny, witchcraft and anti-Judaism feels eerily familiar. And while it may have inspired or legitimated the horrifying events to come, the connection is probably stronger in the opposite direction. The same metropolitan audiences who once ignored the witch-hunt of 1609 were able to mentally place the lynching of Catarina Fernandes in 1619. Her death found a ready audience who were primed to read it in providential terms. Pierre de Lancre was among them; the event inspired him to devote an entire chapter to 'Jews, Apostates and Atheists' in his second 1622 witchcraft treatise.[45] But this time he was not alone. We know much more about 1619 than we do about 1609, though still not nearly enough.

## Christ's body in a handkerchief

When Catarina Fernandes first appears in the sources, she was already a widow of perhaps sixty years of age. We know that she was originally from Trancoso, a small town in north-eastern Portugal and had only recently arrived in Saint-Jean-de-Luz, but nothing more.[46] Our ignorance of her life before her death is distressing, and it heightens the strange yet unmistakable symbolism of her killing in the run up to Easter. At a time when Christians mark their saviour's death and resurrection, Catarina emerges in the written record only to die for the sins of others. The potential symbolism was certainly not lost on those who killed her, though they drew a different moral lesson: they believed that her death – like Christ's – redeemed the Pays de Labourd and restored the territory's fortunes. News of her killing, unlike those of the Basque witches that came before it, spread far and wide and resonated with anti-Jewish audiences across France and Iberia. The full title of a Paris news pamphlet – 'A Horrible Judgement by God of a Jewish Woman' – shows how the killing of Catarina Fernandes could even be justified as a form of divine rather than human justice.[47]

The chain of events that ended with Catarina's death on Tuesday, 19 March 1619, began with a seemingly simple request the Sunday before. The priest who presided over Mass that day had exhorted all his congregants to seek confession – long considered an Easter duty for Catholics – and to ensure that all those in their care did so as well. Given the wider social tensions we have charted, the request may not have been as innocuous as it appears, but at least one member of the congregation, the lady of Chabadincorenea, took it to heart.[48] Two Portuguese women – a mother and daughter whose names are never recorded – had lodged with her for some time, but they had been joined three or four weeks earlier by Catarina, the mother's half-sister. The two older women had not seen each other in forty years, and Catarina's stay was meant to be temporary. Despite the language barrier, the landlady's daughter 'made' the three women 'understand' the priest's request.[49]

Our closest eye witness, the vicar general of the diocese of Bayonne, Michel Doihadard, left two complementary accounts of what came next: a longer official deposition, signed on 30 March (the day before Easter Sunday) which still survives in the archives, and a shorter letter that he wrote on 22 March to his former master, Bertrand d'Echaux.[50] (Echaux had been promoted to the archbishopric of Tours in 1617, his years of suffering at Gramont's hands coming to an end.) We owe the survival of the letter to Pierre de Lancre who reproduced it in his 1622 *L'Incredulité*, probably from a lost pamphlet.[51] The two documents line up well. Other accounts, composed either later or from a distance, will nuance the vicar's version and reveal some telling omissions. Taken together, they tell a distressing tale of popular violence.

On the fateful morning of Monday 18 March, the day after the priest's request, the three Portuguese women set out to fulfil their Easter obligation, heading for church together where they were joined by about half a dozen others. The priest who heard their confession, Antonio Faria, was himself from Portugal. Although not one of the curates of Saint-Jean-de-Luz's church, he had been a resident of the town for a long time. In his letter to Echaux, the vicar claimed that until that day, Faria 'had not been charged with anything worthy of reproach'.[52] Yet, Doihadard knew that was not true. A few days earlier, two Saint-Jean-de-Luz priests had travelled to Bayonne with the aforementioned Manuel Santus, who had been required to produce his license to celebrate Mass. Pierre de Lissardi and Jean de Lasson much preferred Santus to the two other unemployed foreign priests residing in the town.[53] (Lasson, but apparently not Lissardi, had been among the priests once imprisoned for witchcraft in Bordeaux.[54]) The two were especially suspicious of Faria precisely because of his standing among the Portuguese, most of whom, or so they claimed, abstained from working on Saturdays, did not observe feast days and only rarely attended Mass. And yet, he was 'greatly cherished and loved by them; even those who wish to make their devotions addressed no other priest than him'.[55]

When Catarina and her relatives arrived at church, Faria was not the only one hearing confession. From his confessional, Lissardi kept a close eye on the Portuguese group, perhaps paying only half attention to the local woman confessing her sins to him. Lissardi could see the group lined up along a table ready to receive communion. One by one, the women lifted their hands towards their mouths, but his line of sight and their dress meant that the suspicious priest could not be certain that they had consumed the wafer. When interrogated by Doihadard and other officials later, Lissardi claimed that the last of the group, Catarina, behaved especially suspiciously, winking at him several times. Rushing out of his confessional, the Basque priest grabbed the Portuguese woman by the arm. He had seen her lift her arm to her mouth and from there to her side, and now in her hand, he found the host in the woman's handkerchief.

Uproar ensued. Faria's assistant, a Portuguese student called either Enrique Fernandez or Hernando Enríquez, pleaded with Lissardi in Spanish to not say anything: 'this is a small thing; please do not say anything so there is no scandal.'[56] This achieved exactly the opposite effect. 'What do you mean calling this just a small thing?' the Basque priest roared, 'I have just caught her hiding the Holy Sacrament in a handkerchief.'[57] We have seen how other moments of high drama that fed into the witch-hunt fell on important dates: Pentecost, Corpus Christi and the feast day of the town's patron saint, Saint John the Baptist. The timing of Catarina's attempted 'theft' occurred at a similarly ominous and emotionally charged moment. Jews had been habitually accused of killing young Christians at Eastertide, supposedly in commemoration of Christ's death. This blood libel is often associated with the later Middle Ages but still found adherents in the early modern period, including Pierre de Lancre who claimed that on Good Friday, Jews 'ordinarily crucified some Christian boy'.[58] Local conditions made Catarina's plight even less auspicious. It was only late March, and the sailors had not yet left for the New World. Catarina's actions would play into their fears about that perilous journey as well.

Lissardi did not spell out the perceived harm of stealing the Eucharist but, like the inauspicious symbolic timing, the object had both a specific local significance and a wider Christian one. Catarina later told Doihadard that she only planned to save it for when she got home, where she would have the wafer 'with a little bit of water' – an explanation which rings true precisely because it is so disarmingly naive.[59] The Eucharist was not an afternoon snack. Those present believed that Catarina secretly intended to harm the real body of Christ. Late medieval texts, including the infamous *Malleus maleficarum*, peddled stories of both Jews and witches desecrating hosts which bled as a result, tales that confirmed the miracle of transubstantiation and with it, the truth of the Catholic religion.[60] We have also seen, however, how central the Eucharist was to the Basque witch-hunt. Confessed witches had told stories of forsaking the devil's service because they desired to see and experience the body of Christ again. At the sabbat, witch priests elevated black hosts in mockery of the Mass. Catarina's attempted 'theft' was no small thing but (as the crowd later protested) 'an outrage done to the precious body of Jesus Christ'. Bystanders began to insult her and even Faria whether out of a sense of self-preservation or 'completely moved', as he later testified, 'by the wickedness of the said Portuguese woman', joined in the chorus, calling her 'Jew', 'Enemy of God' and 'Dishonour to [her] Nation'. The priest would have hit her too, he declared, if a group of Basque women had not interjected themselves for the sole purpose of making their own threats. The other Portuguese fled the church. Catarina would have followed them had the local women not restrained her. When her relatives returned home, their landlady asked where Catarina had gone. The two women lied and said that they had lost her.[61]

Local officials instantly realized that the situation was a tinderbox which would set the mixture of local grievances, conspiratorial thinking and growing anti-foreign sentiment aflame. That same day, the rector of the church wrote to Doihadard requesting the vicar's immediate presence, while the town's aldermen urgently sent for Labourd's officials in Ustaritz.[62] Another source, the San Sebastián merchant Martin de Aguirre, claimed that members of the Portuguese community requested the aid of Bayonne's officials (who, given their ties to Gramont, might have been more favourable to them), but the vicar makes clear it was he who notified them.[63] (Aguirre passed on news of the incident in a business letter to an associate, dated 29 March – there is no indication he witnessed what happened himself.) The vicar, thus accompanied by a group of legal officials, set off early the next morning. While *en route* to Saint-Jean-de-Luz, they received news that 'a great group of mutinying people' had assembled on the main square and were 'allied together against the said Portuguese woman and making preparations for burning her'. The town's mayor was able to pacify them temporarily with promises of swift justice. Meanwhile, Doihadard and his colleagues arrived between eleven and midday, almost within twenty-four hours after Lissardi's eagle-eyed intervention. (In his letter to Echaux, the vicar arrives at eleven and heads straight for the church; in the official deposition, he arrives around noon and goes to his lodgings first.[64]) The vicar, for understandable reasons, also glosses over the inevitable jurisdictional ruckus, reported by Aguirre, between Lapurdi and Bayonne legal officials.[65] They ultimately seemed to have acted together.

Accompanied by the rector and a full complement of Saint-Jean-de-Luz, Labourd and Bayonne officials, the vicar first inspects the communion wafer, broken in half, with no 'mixture of saliva' and still contained in the offending handkerchief. They all judged it to be 'a little host which after having been wetted a bit was wrapped in a cloth'. It was while exiting the church that the vicar himself was confronted by the tumultuous multitude near the town's cemetery – a traditional site of unrest. Earlier reports of possible violence had been wrapped up in spiritual anxiety, fears that 'God would punish them if she escaped from their hands'. Now the crowd reflected on a justice system that had not delivered for them in the past. Witches haunted these fears. The crowd believed that the prisoner would save herself through favour and corruption, 'and through the length and formalities of justice' – 'even murderers and other criminals' had been placed 'into the hands of justice' and escaped unpunished.[66] According to Aguirre, the crowd later justified Catarina's death because the Portuguese had 'bought' justice in Bayonne.[67]

The frontier nearby also looms particularly large. Catarina could escape to Spain, as many witchcraft suspects had. For the last time in this book, the border rears its head as perhaps the territory's most formidable agent. Where in other instances, it enabled witchcraft suspects to evade justice, here it acted as a catalyst for the inhabitants to make their own. She should not be allowed to flee. Catarina's crime was so great that 'not a single formality of justice' was needed and all that remained was 'the execution on the field'.[68] The Paris pamphlet, the *Horrible iugement*, added a rather implausibly well-reasoned scene in which the multitude 'speak[ing] amongst themselves in their Basque language' offered other justifications, including a strange frontier rivalry: 'with what face or countenance will we dare to show ourselves in Spain when they know of our lack of zeal?'[69] As best as he could, the vicar attempted to reassure the 'great troupe of men' that justice would be done but that that the means of justice that God had ordained must be followed. Mollified by assurances from the vicar and another Bayonne official, the dignitaries were again on their way.

At their lodgings they interrogated the witnesses, whose testimony in condensed form we already discussed. Around four in the afternoon, they returned to the church and we finally hear from Catarina herself. The officials had chosen to interview her in the sacristy, rather than in the small prison nearby 'to better avoid the rage and tumult of the people'.[70] She admitted that it was the devil, whom she called in Spanish 'the sin' (*el peccado*), who forced her to take the host. (A decade earlier, de Lancre had discovered witches in Biarritz who similarly referred to the devil as 'the sin', or 'Lou Peccat' in the Gascon dialect.[71]) As we saw, Catarina had no sinister plans for the wafer; she was just saving it for later. Everything points towards the actions of a confused older woman rather than a sinister conspiracy. Yet, the opposite reading appeared inevitable. The discovery of Christ's body in a handkerchief crystallized two decades of communal fears about secret foes into a single moment, when one of them was apparently caught in the act and their ploys were brought into the open.

The church of Saint-Jean-de-Luz was no stranger to public disturbances or demonic incursions, and the crowd had no problem violating its sacred space. What seemed to have sparked their intrusion was the arrival of Gramont's deputy, who asked to speak with one of the Bayonne officials. The governor had been the protector of the New Christians in Bayonne and the Labourd, a privilege for which they had been made to pay handsomely and often.[72] The crowd, already angry that the prisoner had been moved, was smelling a stitch-up and, as dusk was approaching, entered the church itself. To confront the commotion, one of the priests attempted to address the crowd in French but was met with hostility: 'We are all Basques, and we have the right to understand what you are saying.' It was not just anger at injustice and the nobility that found its expression here but also fears about lives and livelihoods. It is impossible to distinguish individual voices in this crowd, but the role of sailors in this collective act of violence is hard to miss. Some declared that 'they would never have the courage to again implore God's aid amidst the dangers of the sea to which they were exposed daily if this detestable woman who wished to commit some dishonour to the Holy Sacrament remained unpunished'.[73] As the officials retreated for safety behind the altar, they saw the crowd rushing towards the sacristy door and grab Catarina.

In his letter to Echaux, Doihadard claimed that at first he believed that the crowd would simply return her to the prison so that she could not escape at night.[74] Perhaps this (self-)deception alleviated his conscience for not intervening. More likely, he knew better. He later testified that 'the whole populace rushed towards her, shouting at the top of their voice: "Here she is! Here she is!"'[75] In neither account does he mention that the officials were accompanied by some thirty soldiers from Bayonne.[76] If the vicar really had been under any illusions as to what would have happened next, the ringing of the church bells must have shattered them. Catarina was taken to the middle of the town square and placed in a tar barrel. And then she was burnt alive. Doihadard witnessed the scene, probably from some distance, as he and the other officials returned to their lodgings: 'a great fire surrounded by a multitude of people.'[77] 'Everyone was carrying straw, pitch, and wood from everywhere.'[78] People were running around 'as if it was a bonfire'.[79] According to Aguirre, no other sound was heard than Catarina's screams: 'no other thing than *ay ay ay*.'[80] The vicar only noted that the fire burnt 'a long time'. By morning, nothing was left of Catarina 'but ashes and two rings from her fingers'.[81]

# After the fire

The Basque witch-hunt ended in a bonfire of violence and with the death of an old Portuguese woman. Catarina Fernandes died that Eastertide for the sins, crimes and fears of others. Afterwards, residents justified the lynching as the inevitable result of years of growing suspicions: New Christians were 'Jews and living according to the Mosaic law'. They had been caught before, making unleavened bread for their Passover and even once (or so the vicar was told) holding a night-time ceremony 'with lamps and lit torches' in which 'they whipped the crucifix' – 'and for all these evil deeds they had never been punished'. Being both more visible and more tangible than witches, the New Christian refugees, protected by Gramont, were an alternative outlet for the territory's fears and anxieties. Doihadard himself reflected that the sailors 'about to set out for

Newfoundland' were afraid to leave while the crime remained unpunished.[82] (The *Horrible iugement* vividly described the fear that 'God will sink us all when we go out to sea'.[83])

The potential repercussions of this act of popular violence were severe, and the mayor and aldermen of Saint-Jean-de-Luz acted promptly. There was, first of all, the question of the town's remaining New Christians. At their village meeting, on the morning of the 20th – as usual in church – the town officials, with Gramont's representative by their side, exhorted the people to allow the Portuguese two weeks' grace to leave the town. In his letter to Echaux, Doiharard reported that one 'heard nothing from the mouth of the people than these words: "*ez, ez, ez, oray oray oray berehala*".' Neither the vicar nor de Lancre bothered to translate the phrase, but one does not need to be a Basque-speaker (as Bishop Echaux was) to divine the meaning: 'no, no, no, now, now, now, immediately.'[84] Catarina's landlady had already evicted the unfortunate woman's relatives, and Antonio Faria, the priest, was nowhere to be found.[85] The inhabitants claimed that the departure of the Portuguese was a spiritual necessity – and the echoes of witchcraft are unmistakable: 'these people were the cause of bad weather and since they have been here, those of this land have prospered little.' As if to illustrate that point, two ships nearly sank in the harbour amidst very bad weather that same morning but by evening the wind calmed down and they were saved. In the end, the New Christians were given three days to leave.[86]

The same town officials also acted to avoid any repercussions or punishment for this act of popular violence. The Bordeaux Parlement launched an investigation into the officials' actions (or rather, their inaction), as well as those of 'the rest of the inhabitants'. The *Horrible iugement* claimed that 'several people' were sympathetic to a town moved by 'an excess of zeal for the love of God' but that 'others' considered it a great wrong, both as an infringement of royal authority and because it prevented the discovery of 'important matters … concerning the Judaism practiced' among the Portuguese. Earlier on, the pamphlet insinuated that 'the entire multitude of other Jews who had found refuge in this place' had, in fact, incited the lynching, 'to make the people believe that they were not Jews but good Christians', and to prevent Catarina from confessing their 'daily evils, impieties, and blasphemies' under torture.[87] De Lancre was sympathetic to the view that divine justice 'does not permit such crimes to be buried in the length and formalities of a Parlement', although the former judge in his typical meandering way ultimately did not condone it.[88] Saint-Jean-de-Luz officials worked hard to placate the Bordeaux court. Doihadard's affidavit was clearly meant to exonerate them: it emphasized their attempts to appease the crowds and glossed over the presence of soldiers. The vicar was paid handsomely for it. The town once more invested in hams as gifts to the lawyers and judges in Bordeaux and, in possible poor taste, they even bought some empty barrels which they planned to fill with cider. One of the aldermen travelled to Bidache to mollify Gramont.[89] There is no evidence that the town was ever punished.

As the Portuguese left Saint-Jean-de-Luz in search of new homes, officials elsewhere acted swiftly to keep them out. Many found a temporary refuge in Biarritz, further north on the coast. On 8 April, the councillors of nearby Bayonne decided that they 'could not suffer [the Portuguese] presence so close to this city' and attempted to pressure their counterparts to expel them. The minutes of their meeting with two Biarritz aldermen two days later crossed out the word 'Portuguese' and substituted in the margin 'foreign persons called Portuguese who are nevertheless reputed to be true and natural Jews'.[90] Although initially resistant to outside pressure, it appears that Biarritz soon proved inhospitable as well. According to a later witness, this new expulsion came about after a Basque servant girl had accused her Portuguese mistress of witchcraft. She had been made to throw 'certain things' into the sea, which made the ocean very rough and caused the loss of several vessels. In this case, the sailors were less worried about leaving: they declared instead that any Portuguese still present upon their return would be thrown into the water.[91] On 7 May, José de Elizondo, who as the new abbot of Urdax had taken over the duty of zealously watching the border, warned the Logroño tribunal that the Portuguese were again on the move: 'it will be a matter of great importance that none be allowed to enter Spain from France because since they have been expelled from Saint-Jean-de-Luz they have been displaced and some have come over here. ... The Viceroy has given orders that if any should enter [Spanish] Navarre they should be arrested.'[92] For good measure, the abbot wrote to King Philip III as well.[93]

Despite Bayonne's hostility, many Portuguese settled not far away in a quarter called Saint-Esprit across the Ladour river (and therefore, technically, also outside the Basque country). Beyond the city's jurisdiction and under the protection of the Gramont family, Saint-Esprit would develop into a centre for Jewish life in the French south-west, alongside Bidache, the independent principality held by the Gramont family.[94] Others must have left for further afield, to the Dutch Republic and elsewhere.[95] Certainly, the story of what had happened in Saint-Jean-de-Luz in 1619 spread far and wide, not only in print but also across informal news networks. It resurfaced in 1634 in Mexico City in a sensational Inquisition trial. Although Antonio Fernández Cardado had left Saint-Jean-de-Luz several years before Catarina Fernandes's arrival, a witness nevertheless outed him (rightly or wrongly) as her relative. Details of the event had shifted in the retelling. It had no longer happened in Saint-Jean-de-Luz but in Bayonne. Catarina was witnessed spitting the host into her veil rather than slipping it into a handkerchief. But most interesting is the change in witness: it was now a 'boy' (a *muchacho*) who told a priest. It is a telling addition: Christian boys, as the alleged victims of Jewish atrocities, stood at the centre of the late medieval blood libel.[96] Other versions of the story added different anti-Jewish embellishments. The *Mercure françois*, the newspaper that had ignored the Basque witch-hunt a decade earlier, specified that Catarina's rings, found in the ashes, were 'of great value because she had been very rich'. It also claimed that the Portuguese were 'discovered to be holding meetings and synagogues in the caves' – much as the witches had.[97] The Mexican version, however, points us to a significant absence in our sources, which we already noted ourselves in the last chapter: there were no more children. For them, the Basque witch-hunt had seemingly already ended by 1619.

What about the adults? Prosperity returned to Saint-Jean-de-Luz after the expulsion, or at least, that is what the population itself seems to have believed. When a Spanish Inquisition official visited the town in 1632 to investigate the Portuguese problem, Martin Habas, the Franciscan friar and guardian of Our Lady of the Peace, who had once attempted to resolve the witchcraft panic, testified that there were none left. Habas claimed that the town had prospered since the departure of the Portuguese and that the sailors were again 'happily' making their journeys to the Newfoundland fisheries.[98] Four years later, disaster returned when the Spanish invaded and destroyed much of the town.[99] But that really is a different story for another time.

# Epilogue
# Acts of remembrance

Witchcraft is still with us. For years, historians protested, probably too loudly, that witches had been banished to the past. They embedded the witch 'craze' in the myths that made us modern, providing stories which presented us as more rational, enlightened or humane because we do not hunt witches like our ancestors did. These narratives have been wearing thin. Most of us no longer breathe modernity's breezy optimism about the future. We are no longer convinced that the witch-hunt is completely behind us.[1] Women, we are reminded, are still on trial.[2] We notice the victims of our supposed march of progress and the toll it has taken on our environment. Our conspiracy theories show that reason has never been much of a disinfectant; our politics reveal that grievance, whether real or imagined, is the most powerful human emotion. While some of us have outright embraced the label of witch, everyone, or so it seems, wants to be the victim of a witch-hunt. The magical mantle of victimhood exposes the cruelty, bigotry and irrationality of the other side – our opponents are a bunch of de Lancres.

Perhaps because the subject continues to haunt us, we also live in an age of witchcraft pardons, apologies and memorials. As self-evident past injustices, we continue to imbue early modern witch-hunts with moral meanings, however shaky our own claims to the moral high ground might have become. The recent monuments for the Basque witch-hunt, for instance, are deeply moving. The village of Saint-Pée has cast its deadly flames into durable metal, never to be forgotten. Logroño's circle of trees, one for every victim burnt at the *auto de fe*, not only harks back to sabbat imagery (witches dancing around trees), it is also life affirming.

Pardons, apologies and memorials seek to fix the past in both senses of the word: by correcting it and by pinning it down. As a balm for victims or as an atonement for injustice they can do real good. But they can also be uncomfortable or problematic, or become so over time. Certain ancient monuments – those celebrating empire or defending racial injustice, for instance – have become wounds themselves, the past visibly oppressing the present from beyond the grave. But even in the here-and-now, the human grappling with the immorality of the past is at odds with the open-ended messiness of the historian's job, where we constantly revise and refute the work of our predecessors, knowing that one day we will be revised and refuted in turn.

The Saint-Pée memorial is accompanied by a display which pins the blame for the witch-hunt almost exclusively on de Lancre. It reveals the 'true motives' behind his actions: it was an attack on the Labourd's 'democratic' institutions, on its independent women and – perhaps most tenuously – on the Basque monopoly on trade with Canada's First Nations. Qualifying or disagreeing with these claims in no way downplays the horrors that we have charted throughout this book. Like many others of its kind across Europe, the Saint-Pée notice board simply gives voice to the deep human desire to attribute blame. The victims of the European witch-hunt are immediately visible; we want the villains to be just as obvious. A proper reckoning with witchcraft must contend with questions of culpability, but it needs to begin by recognizing that responsibility was much more diffuse than we would like. We focus on judges and princes and overlook the world around them, just so we can consolidate responsibility into the hands of a select few. We transform witch-hunters into supervillains, just as witchcraft suspects once were. Because we *know* the witch-hunt was a mirage, we discount the genuine fears of those who believed witches were real. We conjure up suitably villainous ulterior motives. Humanity is infinitely more complex than the simple stories we would like to be true.

History is about empathy. It is often said that it is not the historian's task to judge their subjects, only to understand them. All of them. This book moved beyond Pierre de Lancre's perspective – without denying or excusing his importance – and studied all the actors in this tragedy. The French crown, Bordeaux judges, Lapurdi noblemen, Basque children, even the accused witches themselves – they all had compelling motives to behave as they did, without the need for conspiratorial or wishful thinking. Often, it is difficult to imagine them acting other than how they did. There were, in any case, also larger forces at play: the capricious border, the unforgiving sea and, during the 1610s at least, the worsening climate. All of these were beyond anyone's control. The witch-hunt, as a result, did not end after the commission's departure. There is no uplifting final note. There was no justice for the witches and certainly no comeuppance for de Lancre. Witchcraft fears lingered until other targets were found.

This is not the story or the ending any of us would have wanted. It might, however, be the one we need. The witch-hunt charted in this book seems to reflect the darker realities of our own world. Perhaps an age that lost its certainties understands the early modern period better. The moral lesson, therefore, must be a historical one: we should try to meet the past on its own terms. When we encounter supposed witches and their accusers as they really were, as we have done throughout this book, then we also recognize part of ourselves. They were human like us. There is a potential witch and a potential accuser – someone willing to think the worst of an enemy – inside every one of us. The struggle against witchcraft will continue after all the apologies, memorials and pardons are done. After all, the witch is nothing other than a crystallization of humanity's worst emotions, an expression of our worst impulses. Until we recognize the dark side within ourselves, we will never leave her behind. But if we acknowledge our shared humanity and learn to see the world through other people's eyes, then perhaps one day, we can let her fly away.

# Acknowledgements

There is no way this is going to be either short or complete. The road has been so long and so winding that the starting point has disappeared from view. It was around 2009 when a constellation of events first began to transform an itch into a writing project: Luc Foisneau invited me to contribute an entry on Pierre de Lancre to a forthcoming biographical dictionary, and the retirement of my doctoral supervisor, Robin Briggs, encouraged me to produce something 'French' for a special issue in his honour. A holiday to the Basque country with David Lowe in 2012 showed me that the Pays de Labourd, with its beautiful coastline and welcoming people, was well worth revisiting. A temporary teaching post, filling in for the irreplaceable David Parrott at Oxford, gradually helped alleviate my feelings of impostorism as a French historian. Unearthing hitherto unknown documents in the Jesuit archives in Rome made me realize that I genuinely had something new to say. More discoveries soon followed.

If these beginnings seem auspicious, reaching the destination was never inevitable. Even in the rear-view mirror, some roadblocks still look insurmountable. The project would never have succeeded if at key moments institutions, colleagues, friends and family had not stepped in to help. The project – with its many names, dates and places – could first of all never have been completed without research leave. I am especially grateful to the Leverhulme Trust and the Alexander von Humboldt Foundation for saying yes, after the Arts and Humanities Research Council said no. I owe so much to Gerd Schwerhoff for sponsoring my Humboldt application and for hosting me at the TU Dresden. March 2020 proved an ominous time to start a fellowship abroad. It was an unsettling experience, drafting a chapter about the start of a witchcraft panic just as the world appeared to be ending, but I could not have wished for a more supportive and understanding host. A year of study leave from Cardiff University allowed me to finish the inevitably delayed book.

Historians owe some of their greatest debts to their predecessors. Even when we inevitably disagree with them and plot our own journeys, they have mapped out the terrain for us and made us aware of what there is to see. Two neglected earlier studies of the witch-hunt deserve flagging. Francisque Habasque's 1912 article first drew attention to the surviving sources in local Lapurdi archives.

François Bordes's 1977 École nationale des chartes dissertation (published in a much-shortened form only in 1999) demonstrated the value of the territory's financial records and offers transcriptions of some key documents. My book, and especially Chapter 2, could not have been written without their earlier work paving the way.

Just as important are the archives themselves, many of which went beyond the normal call of duty to accommodate or assist me. I am particularly grateful to Nathalie Rebena and to Juan Carlos Mora Afán at the Archives départementales at Bayonne and at the Artxibo historikoa of Hondarribia for their welcome and for replying to the long lists of follow-up queries afterwards. Special thanks are also due to Agnès Vatican and her team at the Archives départementales de la Gironde in Bordeaux for their help in tracking down sources. Many French, Spanish and Italian archives made heroic efforts to stay open during the Covid pandemic. The staff at the Archivo Histórico Nacional in Madrid even supplied me with a certificate that allowed me to cross the city's *cierre perimetral* during one Covid wave. The Archivio di stato in Venice found a last-minute slot for me in similarly difficult circumstances. Pedro Perez-Seoane Garau of the Museo Naval of Madrid kindly photographed a letter at short notice.

Pre-Covid, Yves-Marie Bercé provided me with a reference without which I would never have been able to visit the rarefied but extremely friendly (especially by Parisian standards) library of the Institut de France. (I'm also indebted to Joseph Bergin and Mark Greengrass for forging that introduction.) I also need to thank Ana Amigo López and her colleagues at the Archivo General de Simancas. I would never have found my way to that impressive archive-castle without Glyn Redworth as my guide. Philippe Beitia and Peio Monteano Sorbet answered my queries about the collections in their archives, the diocesan archives of Bayonne and the Archivo General de Navarra, respectively. Elizabeth Garver and Aaron Pratt of the Harry Ransom Center at the University of Texas at Austin were exceptionally helpful in digitizing some of its precious holdings. I owe a special debt to César Manrique Figueroa who consulted the Archivo General de la Nación in Mexico City on my behalf.

I am also grateful for the many opportunities to speak about this project and for the many helpful questions and comments I received. Three locations hold a special place in my heart. In Munich, Hester Schadee and Arndt Brendecke tolerated my first attempt at a lecture back in 2014. Melbourne's early modern community (in particular, Charles Zika, Jenny Spinks and Miles Pattenden) heroically put up with me on three different occasions (in 2016, 2019 and 2022). Sara Miglietti's invitation to give an online talk at the Warburg Institute in 2021 was an intimidating but invaluable opportunity that kept me going in lockdown. I owe similar debts to some exceptionally supportive reading groups. The London workshop organized by Kat Hill, Hannah Murphy, Allison Stielau and Roísín Watson read through a ponderous first draft of the introduction pre-pandemic.

# Acknowledgements

During the first Covid wave, the weekly online Princeton 'Happy Hour' organized by Anthony Grafton and Jennifer Rampling helped keep me sane. I remain grateful to all the participants, in particular, Richard Calis, Mateusz Falkowski, Madeleine McMahon, Aaron Stamper and Spencer Weinreich for their comments on an early Pierre de Lancre chapter. Also mid-pandemic, the Dresdner Hexenküche brought together British and German witchcraft and crime historians online, just as Gerd Schwerhoff and I had originally hoped to do in person. I would like to thank the other participants – Ruth Atherton, Tom Hamilton, Alexander Kästner, Sarah Masiak, Benjamin Seebröker, Andrew Wells and Abaigéal Warfield – for their contributions and feedback. The French crime reading group, organized by Briony Neilson, Claire Eldridge and Tom Hamilton, provided invaluable feedback on the childhood chapter. Warwick's Montaigne reading group livened up my Wednesday late afternoons for more than a year. I would like to thank all the participants, and particularly the hard core – Mathilde Alain, Stephen Bates, Iván Parga Ornelas and Penny Roberts – for their thoughts on the Montaigne chapter.

I have also incurred many other debts along the way. Joëlle Miège, whom I met virtually on a local genealogy forum, introduced me to one of the Basque witch-hunt's other eyewitness accounts, the Ustaritz priest Bertrand de Haitze. Arnaud de Sèze and his family, the current owners of Chateau Loubens, very kindly welcomed me into their home, de Lancre's retreat in retirement, and introduced me to their amazing wine. Amandine Guindet of the Syndicat de la Baie de Saint-Jean-de-Luz et Ciboure showed me around the then ongoing, now completed redevelopment of the Couvent des Récollets into an exciting new cultural space. Many colleagues and contacts helped with specific queries or provided valuable bibliographic suggestions, including Sara Beam, Joseph Bergin, Didier Kahn, Gunnar Knutsen, Chris Langley, Sir Noel Malcolm, Lorenzo Mancini, Földváry Miklós István, Hannah Murphy, Nathalie Rillot, José Alberto Rodrigues da Silva Tavim, Gerhild Scholz Williams, María Tausiet, Ann Taylor, Elizabeth Tingle, Michaela Valente, David van der Linden, Peter Wilson, Amanda Wunder and Beñat Zintzo-Garmendia. I wish I had kept a record of these debts as I incurred them and can only ask for forgiveness for the inevitable omissions.

Many colleagues also commented on draft chapters and lent me their expertise on one of the many fields and areas skirted by this project. The late Natalie Zemon Davis commented on a draft section and shared with me her impressions of Pierre de Lancre. I will always cherish those exchanges. Amanda Scott was a beacon of advice about Basque history and archives and made me see the city of Pamplona through very different eyes. Michael Barkham's knowledge of Basque maritime history is unrivalled and his hospitality in Hondarribia enlivened many of my research visits. Profound thanks are also due to Stuart Clark, Anthony Grafton, Vincent Hiribarren, Adam Horsley, Virginia Krause, Ian Maclean, Madeleine McMahon, Anthony Ossa-Richardson, Lyndal Roper, Margaret Schotte, François Soyer and Joshua Teplitsky for their support and suggestions on draft sections or chapters, which infinitely improved the end result. A simple list does not do justice to their helpfulness – I wish I could thank each individually at greater length.

Closer to home, I would be amiss if I did not thank my colleagues within Cardiff University's School of History, Archaeology and Religion for putting up with me and with my absences, in particular, my medieval and early modern colleagues: Jenny Benham, Lloyd Bowen, Emily Cock, Rachel Herrmann, Bronach Kane, Jasmine Kilburn-Toppin, Marion Löffler, Ashley Walsh, Paul Webster, Mark Williams and Garthine Walker. Lisa Tallis in Cardiff's Special Collections has been my partner in demonology for the better part of a decade. My students, both at the undergraduate and graduate levels, have also had to endure seminars and lectures on Basque witchcraft for many years. Special thanks are due to Alexander Bumstead Díaz for reading an early modern Basque catechism (funded by a Cardiff University grant), to Lívia Guimarães Torquetti dos Santos for her comments on the witches' sabbat chapter (her own work on sabbat narratives is amazing), to Théo Rivière for reading through a nearly full draft manuscript and to Christopher Parry for always asking difficult questions.

Throughout this project, I have been supported by four friends and colleagues – my four musketeers – without whom this book would never have safely come into port. All four have read full drafts of this book, often more than once. Robin Briggs has been generous both with his deep knowledge of French and witchcraft history and with his time. His help with French palaeography was indispensable, especially at the outset of my project, just as his close reading has been at the end. I am so grateful that I continue to be able to rely on the wisdom and advice of my doctoral supervisor long after my thesis was deposited in the library.

Lu Ann Homza has been an unsurpassed source of advice on the Spanish Inquisition and its archives. She has helped me navigate the Salazar papers and alerted me to helpful documents in Pamplona, which she consulted on my behalf. It has been wonderful exchanging ideas and material with her. Historians are not scientists. We do not possess laboratories to repeat and test others' experiments. But many of Lu Ann's astute observations about the role of bewitched children and popular violence in Navarre match my conclusions for Lapurdi. Her 2022 *Village Infernos and Witches' Advocates* is a must-read for anyone interested in the Basque witch-hunt after it spread into Spain.

I would never have gotten the right measure of Pierre de Lancre had it not been for my many conversations with Thibaut Maus de Rolley. Even though the Arts and Humanities Research Council said no to our project, I am so glad that he and I were able to collaborate on a book chapter about him. Thibaut has helped me appreciate de Lancre's *Tableau* as a literary text, rich in allusions, metaphors and wordplay. His research on the trial of Louis Gaufridi in Aix-en-Provence shows the continued significance of witchcraft beliefs in elite French culture during the 1610s.

Tom Hamilton has similarly reshaped my perspective. Tom made me see that witchcraft history can only ever be part of the wider history of crime, and that the study of that subject demands that historians learn to think like early modern lawyers. His knowledge of that historiography is unrivalled. His advice about France's legal archives and about early modern French criminal procedures has been indispensable, helping me to frame my book, unpack de Lancre's legalese and interpret his silences.

At Bloomsbury Academic, I owe a great debt to Rhodri Mogford who saw the potential of this project when literary agents and commissioning editors elsewhere did not. I am grateful for the confidence, professionalism and good cheer with which he shepherded the book through the peer-review process. I am also thankful for the comments and support of the five anonymous reviewers, many of whom went through the text with great care. Aaron Larsen, Clare Copeland and Nina Lamal read the final draft with great care and saved me from many errors. (Any mistakes remaining are obviously my responsibility, as are any new ones that may have crept in since.) Kirsty Harding produced the maps for this volume. Staff at the Musée Basque in Bayonne, the Musée d'Aquitaine and Bibliothèque municipale in Bordeaux, the Special Collections at Glasgow University (in particular, Niki Russell), and the Germanisches Nationalmuseum in Nuremberg helped sort out the image rights.

Finally, the greatest debts are the one's closest to home. I am thankful for the many friends who have enriched my life. Space means I can only really mention the new ones, who helped me and this book through the trying times we all faced. I am ever so grateful for my Dresden friends: Leo Heymann, Sofiya Rachkevych, Oscar Reinecke and Max Rose. I would not have weathered the Covid pandemic without them, without walks along the Elbe or without Catan. Marie and Barbara Findeisen offered a welcome refuge in Bamberg in-between Covid waves. Other new friends – Nina Lamal, Michelle Pfeffer and Karie Schultz – kept me sane from afar with new projects. Suzie Sheehy is not a new friend, but she is an inspiration. For a while our book projects ran parallel to each other, and I treasure our shared writing retreats, digital and in-person. I also owe much to my parents – not only the usual debts, but also for putting up with me during part of the first wave when I temporarily had nowhere else to go. My mum tolerated my attempts at cooking risotto, my dad kindly gave up his home study for me so I could attempt to work. My brother Bart is my rock; my young nephews, Jelle and Lars, are at the moment of writing still totally angelic.

This book, then, owes so much to so many. It is, however, dedicated to only one person: Richard Emms wandered into my life unexpectedly one summer day in Newport, Wales. This book would have been completed much sooner without him, but the last three years would not have been nearly as much fun.

# Notes

## Introduction

1. *Tableau*, 43. Laborde, *Histoire du tourisme*, 15, applies this passage on 'la coste d'Anglet' to Biarritz. Space constraints necessitated the extensive use of abbreviations in the notes. All references to *Tableau* are to the 1612 *Tableau de l'inconstance des mauvais anges et démons*, unless otherwise indicated.
2. *Tableau*, 45, 46.
3. *Tableau*, 96, 30.
4. These figures will be discussed in Chapter 7.
5. Mornay, *Mémoires et correspondance*, 10:428.
6. *L'Incrédulité*, 10 (Advertissemens, paginated separately).
7. See L'Estoile, *Mémoires-journaux*, vol. 10 (November starts on 69); McGowan, 'Pierre de Lancre's *Tableau*', 182, opens with an anecdote from this diarist. For L'Estoile, see Hamilton, *Pierre de L'Estoile*.
8. *Mercure françois*, vol. 1, fols 342v–5r.
9. Only a single copy of the *Discours tres-veritable* survives, printed according to 'la coppie imprimée à Bayonne et à Troyes chez Jean Oudot'.
10. *Mercure françois*, vol. 1, sig. ã2r.
11. Mornay, *Mémoires et correspondance*, 10:428.
12. Davis, 'The Silences of the Archives'; Davis, *Trickster Travels*.
13. Henningsen, *The Witches' Advocate*, chapter 9.
14. Venice, Archivio di Stato, Senato, Dispacci, Spagna 42, dated 6 June 1611.
15. Valencia, *Discurso acerca de los cuentos de brujas*, 235.
16. *Tableau*, sig. ãããã2r.
17. *Tableau*, sig. ã4v.
18. For example, for Caro Baroja, 'Witchcraft and Catholic Theology', 40, de Lancre represents 'an ultimate degree of "sophistication"' where witchcraft belief is concerned.
19. Briggs, *Witches and Neighbours*, 26.
20. Busson, 'Montaigne et son cousin', 484; McGowan, 'Pierre de Lancre's *Tableau*', 183.
21. See the contract in Delpit, 'Pierre de L'Ancre et la sorcellerie', 81–9. This contract was voided but its description matches the contents of the *Du Sortilège*. Its rarity suggests that de Lancre continued with this personal project with another, anonymous printer.
22. Houdard, *Les sciences du diable*, 163.
23. *L'Incrédulité*, 7.
24. Le Mao, *Parlement et parlementaires*, 32–3.

25. For a study of the nineteenth-century 'rationalist' paradigm and its long shadow on later historical research, see Machielsen, *The War on Witchcraft*.
26. See Trevor-Roper, *The European Witch-Craze*, 67, who, however, concedes on pages 79–80 that de Lancre was 'an enchanting writer'; Dravasa, 'Problèmes de sorcellerie', 428.
27. Pearl, *The Crime of Crimes*, 127; Zintzo-Garmendia, *Histoire de la sorcellerie*, 174.
28. See Henningsen, *The Witches' Advocate*, 393; Homza, *Village Infernos*.
29. Michelet, *La sorcière*, 215.
30. For example, Egaña, 'Las brujas vascas y Lancre', 8.
31. Zintzo-Garmendia, *Histoire de la sorcellerie*, 21.
32. For the pilgrim's route through Lapurdi, see Beguerie, *Le Pays basque*, 95.
33. See for example, Jean Muret's account of his 1666 visit: *Je vous écris de Saint-Jean-de-Luz*, 24–5.
34. Thou, *Histoire universelle*, 1:67.
35. Charpentier, *Le Mystère basque*; Arnold, *Le Mystère basque dévoilé*.
36. The viscount of the Labourd sold his remaining rights to the king of England in 1193: Lamant-Duhart, *Saint-Jean-de-Luz*, 27.
37. Veyrin, *Les Basques*, 122.
38. Lancre, *Du sortilège*, 280. For a study of this exceptionally rare text, see Dardano Basso, *Il diavolo e il magistrato*.
39. Veyrin, *Les Basques*, 134–5.
40. On the border, see Dravasa, 'Problèmes de sorcellerie'; Scholz Williams, *Defining Dominion*, 90.
41. *Je vous écris de Saint-Jean-de-Luz*, 7.
42. One author, for instance, suggests that lessons learnt about the end of the witch-hunt could be used to pacify the Basque country in the present: 'Azurmendi disecciona el caso de las brujas de Zugarramurdi'.
43. *Tableau*, 30.
44. Zintzo-Garmendia, *Histoire de la sorcellerie*, 22; 'Azurmendi disecciona el caso de las brujas de Zugarramurdi'.
45. Ospital, *La chasse*, 8; Egaña, 'Las brujas vascas y Lancre', 11.
46. Egaña, 'Las brujas vascas y Lancre', 11.
47. See for example, Lamant-Duhart, *Saint-Jean-de-Luz*, 67–8.
48. Baroja, *La Dama de Urtubi*, 8.
49. For the former, see Soman, 'Witch Lynching at Juniville'; Soman, 'Les procès de sorcellerie', 810–11. Without evidence, Monter has described the Languedoc witch-hunt 'as the largest witch-hunt in French history': Monter, 'Witchcraft Trials in Continental Europe', 3.

# Chapter 1

1. Braudel, *The Mediterranean*, 1:21, 38, 33.
2. Trevor-Roper, *The European Witch-Craze*, 29.
3. Dillinger, 'Germany', 96.
4. *Tableau*, 84; on Larrun, see also Larsen, 'Darkest Forests and Highest Mountains'.
5. *Tableau*, 30.
6. For this plausible population estimate, see *Tableau*, 40.
7. *Tableau*, 31.

8 *Tableau*, 43.
9 *Codex Calixtinus*, bk. 5, chap. 7.
10 Navagero, *Il viaggio fatto in Spagna*, fol. 44v; García Mercadal, *Viajes de extranjeros*, 46, 245.
11 *Tableau*, 31.
12 *Tableau*, 32.
13 Sahlins, *Boundaries*; Nordman, *Frontières de France*. The French distinction between *frontières* and *limites* is particularly helpful. For religious geography, see Brunet, *Les prêtres des montagnes.*
14 See the letters collected in AMH, A-13-II-2-1.
15 AMH, E-7-II-4-21.
16 One notable example, the Bera priest Lorenzo de Hualde, will be discussed below. For further examples of distant Lapurdi relatives, see AHN, Inq., Lib. 795, fols 174r, fol. 258r. Logroño, 17 July 1611 and 11 May 1612.
17 Garibay, *Compendio historial*, 3:556: Lamant-Duhart, *Saint-Jean-de-Luz*, 42–3.
18 Goyhenetche, *Histoire générale du Pays Basque*, 3:203.
19 Hourmat, *Histoire de Bayonne*, 196. In September 1591, a Spanish invasion appeared inevitable: Dop, *Les Seigneurs de Saint-Pée*, 87.
20 Sahlins, *Boundaries*.
21 For the city's official title, see AMH, A-1-25 and 26. For the contrast in attitude between 'villa' and 'lugar', see E-6-VI-6-16, fol. 3r.
22 As de Lancre notes, the dispute goes back to a 1509 treaty: *Tableau*, 34.
23 See for example, the 1599 mission to Pamplona: AMH, E-6-VI-6-20, and the Lapurdi documents collected in BnF, Dupuy 42. For an example of Spanish compromise, see AGG-GAO, JD IM1/13/9, fol. 3r.
24 Chavarría Múgica, 'Justicia y estrategia'.
25 AGN, 029603, especially the argument of Bera's alcalde on fol. 1r–v.
26 Davies, *Renaissance Ethnography*.
27 AHN, Inq., Lib. 795, fol. 85v. Bayonne, 13 April 1610.
28 Kurlansky, *The Basque History of the World*, 19.
29 Monteano Sorbet, *El iceberg navarro*, 75–80.
30 *Scaligerana*, 2:219.
31 Koch, 'Is Basque an Indo-European Language?'
32 Larramendi, *Diccionario trilingue*, sig. ¶3r.
33 Brunel, *Voyage d'Espagne,* 4, 6.
34 *Je vous écris de Saint-Jean-de-Luz*. 24.
35 *Tableau*, 30.
36 BnF, Dupuy 219, fol. 89r. On the linguistic complexity of Biarritz, see Iglesias, 'Recherche sur la situation linguistique de Biarritz'.
37 KBr, MS 21678, fol. 193r. This travel account (1601–14) by one Henningus Frommeling has been partially published: Frommeling, *Les mémoires*.
38 On an attempt to capture three seminary priests, see *Calendar of the Manuscripts of the Most Hon. the Marquis of Salisbury*, 24:178 (item 452). Thomas Marchant to the Earl of Salisbury, *c.* October 1609. For reports on armadas, see BL, Cotton MS Caligula E XI, fols 81–2. Thomas Wilson to Robert Cecil. Bayonne, 18 February 1603; NA, SP 94/9, fol. 51. 'News from Bayonne'. Dated 1/11 August 1603.
39 For the figure of 'trecientas familias', see Ortiz, 'El proceso inquisitorial', 569; for the figure of 'plus de deux mille', see *L'Incrédulité*, 497. For figures elsewhere in France, see Szajkowski, 'Population Problems'.

40 Hawkins, '"Chimeras that Degrade Humanity"', 5.
41 Ricau, *Histoire des Cagots*, 23–7, 61–9.
42 Tuke, 'The Cagots'; Roussel, 'Cagots et lépreux.'
43 Cursente, *Les Cagots*.
44 *L'Église de Saint-Pée-Sur-Nivelle*, 6.
45 Azurmendi, *Las brujas de Zugarramundi*, 40–2.
46 *Tableau*, 208.
47 *Tableau*, 37.
48 Dop, *Les Seigneurs de Saint-Pée*, 85–6; Orpustan, 'Correspondance basque', 11.
49 Knecht, *Francis I*, 359.
50 For a Spanish-language notarial contract, see for example, AD-64, Saint-Jean-de-Luz, III E 9745, fol. 439.
51 NA, SP 78/51, fol. 364r–v, addressed to the French crown but held by the UK National Archives. Undated.
52 *Tableau* (1613), 347–9.
53 See Cohen, 'Torture and Translation', which discusses de Lancre on 911–12.
54 Montaigne, *The Complete Works*, 282 (hereafter, F282).
55 *Tableau*, 408.
56 Arzadún, 'Las brujas de Fuenterrabía', 175.
57 *Tableau*, 39, 29.
58 Dravasa, 'Les privilèges des Basques', 40.
59 Lamant-Duhart, *Saint-Jean-de-Luz*, 164–6.
60 ARSI, Gal. 71, fol. 50v.
61 *Les coustumes generalles*, 37.
62 Dravasa, 'Les privilèges des Basques', 51–62, 30.
63 Nogaret, *Saint-Jean-de-Luz*, 19.
64 *Les coustumes generalles*, 38.
65 Lamant-Duhart, *Saint-Jean-de-Luz*, 166–7, 162, 164.
66 Yturbide, 'Le Bilçar d'Ustaritz', 79. The exception was the territory's *bailli*, a nobleman who presided over the meeting as a royal official.
67 Rillot, 'La noblesse labourdine', 221, although I take issue with her claims about the nobility's fidelity.
68 Lamant-Duhart, *Urrugne*, 81–2.
69 Cotgrave, *A Dictionarie of the French and English Tongues*, 90 (s.v. 'bailli').
70 Bayonne learned of the murder of Henry IV in Paris on 19 May 1610, five days after it happened, which must be the fastest news could travel: AD-64, BB 18, fol. 116. Ordinary travel took much longer. In 1594, it took Marie de Gournay two weeks to travel from Paris to Michel de Montaigne's chateau near Bordeaux (Fogel, *Marie de Gournay*, 125); it took a Bordeaux judge five days to travel to the Labourd: AD-64, Saint-Jean-de-Luz FF 12, Liasse 2/2. A 1606 contract, arranging travel from Paris to Saint-Jean-de-Luz, spelt out the arduous route involved: AN, MC/ET/CV/297 (only the part between Orléans and Tours was by boat).
71 See the list compiled in Goyhenetche, *Histoire générale du Pays Basque*, 2:285.
72 The nobility's position improved after 1630 as a result: Rillot, 'La noblesse labourdine'.
73 AGS, Est., Leg. 363, doc. 26.
74 Gardère, *Les Seigneurs de Bonnut et Arsague*, 31; Dop, *Les Seigneurs de Saint-Pée*, 80–1.

75 AGS, Est., Leg. 363, doc. 26.
76 Dravasa, 'Les privilèges des Basques', 75.
77 *Tableau*, 141.
78 Chesnaye-Desbois, *Dictionnaire de la noblesse*, 12:715, describes Tristan as possessing the honorific titles of 'gentilhomme ordinaire de la Chambre du Roi' and 'bailli d'épée'.
79 Orpustan, 'Correspondance basque'; Satrústegui, 'Relectura de los textos'. On Velázquez, see Hugon, *Au service du Roi catholique*, 644–5.
80 Orpustan, 'Correspondance basque', 152.
81 Baroja, *La Dama de Urtubi*, 13–14.
82 Rillot, 'La noblesse labourdine', 212; Lamant-Duhart, *Saint-Jean-de-Luz*, 110; Nogaret, *Saint-Jean-de-Luz*, 161.
83 Nogaret, *Saint-Jean-de-Luz*, 162–3, does not provide a source or date.
84 Rillot, 'Portrait d'un noble labourdin', 75–6.
85 Pontet, 'Le gouverneur et l'évêque'; Pontet, 'Le choix de Gramont'.
86 Jaurgain, *La maison de Gramont*, 1:354–6.
87 AGS, Est. 363, doc. 42.
88 Hugon, *Au service du Roi catholique*, 85n125.
89 AGS, Est. K 1608, doc. 72.
90 Pontet suggests that Echaux successfully opposed Gramont's appointment as commander of Bayonne's second castle, the *chateau-neuf*: Pontet, 'Le gouverneur et l'évêque', 196. On Echaux, see also Bergin, *The Making of the French Episcopate*, 606.
91 Pontet, 'Le gouverneur et l'évêque', 197; Échaux, *Trois lettres inédites*, 19–21.
92 Bibliothèque de l'Institut de France, MS Godefroy 266, fols 175–6, at 176r. s.l., 15 December 1611.
93 Schalk, *From Valor to Pedigree*, 124–7.
94 Roberts, 'Review of "Blood and Violence"', quoting the medieval historian Chris Wickham. On feuding within the aristocracy, see Carroll, *Blood and Violence*.
95 Beik, 'The Violence of the French Crowd'; Roberts, 'French Historians and Collective Violence'.
96 Beik, 'The Absolutism of Louis XIV'.
97 BnF, Clairambault 362, fol. 309r. Arnéguy, 19 May 1613.
98 Nogaret, *Saint-Jean-de-Luz*, 48.
99 One local account suggests that he held an (informal?) position as Amou's deputy: Lamant-Duhart, *Urrugne*, 81.
100 Nogaret, *Saint-Jean-de-Luz*, 161.
101 Goyhenetche, *Histoire générale du Pays basque*, 3:115.
102 Orpustan, *Nouvelle toponymie basque*, 34–5.
103 Haristoy, 'Fondation de la paroisse', 184; Lamant-Duhart, *Ciboure*, 135–41, 204–7.
104 Haristoy, 'Fondation de la paroisse', 190–1.
105 *Tableau*, 33.
106 Nogaret, *Saint-Jean-de-Luz*, 19–20.
107 Lamant-Duhart, *Saint-Jean-de-Luz*, 48.
108 *Tableau*, 68, 99, 141, 455.
109 Huxley Barkham, 'Los vascos y las pesquerias transatlanticas', 47.
110 Navagero, *Il viaggio fatto in Spagna*, fols 46v–7r.
111 Oihénart, *Notitia utriusque Vasconiae*, 401.

112  BnF, Dupuy 219, fol. 89r.
113  Barkham, 'La industria pesquera', 34–5.
114  Estimates for France put the number of 'gens de mer' during the early seventeenth century at around 350,000, although only a third of these would be fishermen: Le Bouëdec, *Activités maritimes*, 257.
115  Habasque, 'Les traités de bonne correspondance', 565.
116  Goyhenetche, *Histoire générale du Pays Basque*, 3:150–1. For deforestation in the Spanish Basque country, see Wing, *Roots of Empire*, esp. 64, 68.
117  Habasque, 'Les traités de bonne correspondance', 565.
118  Barkham, 'French Basque "New Found Land" Entrepreneurs', 3–4.
119  Barkham, 'La industria pesquera', 71.
120  A full-size reconstruction of a three-master whaling ship (possibly the San Juan which sank at Red Bay in 1565) is currently underway at Albaola near Pasaia and gives a very good idea of the awe-inspiring size these ships could reach: http://www.albaola.com/en/site/building-process. Last accessed on 29 April 2024.
121  Goyhenetche, *Histoire générale du Pays Basque*, 3:145.
122  *Je vous écris de Saint-Jean-de-Luz*, 11.
123  *Recueil des choses notables*, fol. 50r.
124  Bendall, *Shaping Femininity*, 104.
125  Duplá, *Presencia vasca en América*, 29.
126  Huxley Barkham, 'Documentary Evidence', 55; Loewen and Chapdelaine, *Contact in the 16th Century*. Particularly famous is the whaling station at Red Bay, Labrador, a UNESCO world heritage site.
127  Huxley Barkham, *The Basque Coast of Newfoundland*, 6.
128  Hoyarzabal, *Les voyages aventureux*, 3. On this book, see Barkham, 'New Documents'.
129  Hoyarzabal, *Les voyages aventureux*, 2.
130  Goyhenetche, *Histoire générale du Pays Basque*, 3:164. For the latter claim, see *Je vous écris de Saint-Jean-de-Luz*, 27–8.
131  Richards, *The Unending Frontier*, 588.
132  Martijn et al., 'Basques?', 195.
133  Bélanger, *Les Basques*, 113–14.
134  Kurlansky, *Cod*, 21–6.
135  Huxley Barkham, 'Los vascos y las pesquerias transatlanticas', 28; Huxley Barkham, 'Documentary Evidence', 54.
136  See the 1571 account by Garibay and 1625 account by Isasti: Huxley Barkham, 'Los vascos y las pesquerias transatlanticas', 39–40.
137  Bélanger, *Les Basques*, 29.
138  Barkham, *Aspects of Life*, 6, 19–21.
139  Cell, *Newfoundland Discovered*, 117.
140  Loewen and Chapdelaine, *Contact in the 16th Century*.
141  *Tableau*, 30; Douglass and Bilbao, *Amerikanuak*, 55.
142  Bakker, 'Amerindian Tribal Names'.
143  Bélanger, *Les Basques*, 86.
144  Even the 'humblest apprentice' could earn two or three valuable barrels of oil: Richards, *The Unending Frontier*, 588.
145  Barkham, 'French Basque "New Found Land" Entrepreneurs', 18, 19.
146  *Tableau*, 95.
147  AD-64, Saint-Jean-de-Luz, III E 9745, fol. 6r.

148 ARCHV, pleitos civiles, Alonso Rodríguez (dep.), 241–1, part 4, fol. 95.
149 Oihénart, *Les proverbes basques*, 64.
150 Bélanger, *Les Basques*, 146.
151 Barakat, 'The Willoughby Papers', 55. Richard Holworthy to John Slany, 18 August 1612. For accounts of piracy, see Barkham, 'La industria pesquera', 68–9.
152 Valois, *Inventaire des arrêts*, 2:216, 250, 377 (arrêt nos. 8885, 9367, 11061); Rectoran, *Corsaires basques*.
153 Huxley Barkham, 'Los vascos y las pesquerias transatlanticas', 60, 101.
154 Duplá, *Presencia vasca en América*, 28.
155 Einarsson, 'La trágica muerte de Martín de Villafranca'.
156 *Tableau*, 94.
157 AHN, Inq., Lib. 835, fol. 391r.
158 For an unscientific survey, see Rappoport, *Superstitions of Sailors*.
159 Barandiarán, *Brujería y brujas*, 33, 61–2; Sainz Varela and Navajas Twose, *¡Brujas!*, 21.
160 *Missale ad usum ecclesie cathedralis Baiocensis*, fol. 10r–v.
161 Ugartechea y Salinas, 'La pesca tradicional en Lequeitio', 12.
162 *Tableau*, 32, 31.
163 *Tableau*, 42.
164 *Je vous écris de Saint-Jean-de-Luz*, 9, 12.
165 F432.
166 Aulnoy, *Relation du voyage d'Espagne*, 13.
167 *Tableau*, 39, 39–40, 38. On the early adoption of tobacco, see Veyrin, *Les Basques*, 178.
168 *Tableau*, 37–8.
169 On these practices, see Veyrin, *Les Basques*, 261–2.
170 *Tableau*, 38.
171 Caro Baroja, 'Cuatro relaciones', 139.
172 Oihénart, *Les proverbes basques*, 64.
173 Veyrin, *Les Basques*, 256.
174 *Les coustumes generalles*, 17.
175 Scott, *The Basque Seroras*.
176 *Tableau*, 59, 60.
177 Sainz Varela and Navajas Twose, *¡Brujas!*, 21. A Basque friend reported a perhaps still more apt version of this saying: 'everything that has a name is *here*'.
178 Caro Baroja, 'Witchcraft and Catholic Theology', 19–20.
179 For a list of witchcraft sites in Alava, see Sainz Varela and Navajas Twose, *¡Brujas!*, 26–9.
180 Patlapin, *Sorginak*; Barandiarán, *Brujería y brujas*.
181 For example, Lamant-Duhart, *Saint-Jean-de-Luz*, 65.
182 Henningsen, 'El invento de la palabra aquelarre'.
183 *Tableau*, 69, 390.
184 For Catalan witchcraft, see Castell Granados, 'Sortilegas, divinatrices'.
185 Idoate, *La Brujería en Navarra*, 15, 246.
186 Boureau, *Satan the Heretic*.
187 Idoate, *La Brujería en Navarra*, 18. For witchcraft in Navarrese slander trials, see Tabernero and Usunáriz, 'Bruja, brujo, hechicera, hechicero, sorgin como insultos'.
188 Arles, *Tractatus de superstitionibus*, 8.
189 Monter, *Frontiers of Heresy*, 257.

190 Gorosábel, *Noticia de las cosas memorables*, 1:353.
191 Caro Baroja, *The World of the Witches*, 152; Monter, *Frontiers of Heresy*, 263.
192 Rojas, 'Bad Christians and Hanging Toads', 71–2.
193 Monter, *Frontiers of Heresy*, 268–9; Idoate, *La Brujería en Navarra*, 118–21.
194 Idoate, *La Brujería en Navarra*, 103; Rojas, 'Bad Christians and Hanging Toads', 86.
195 *Tableau*, 108.
196 Lamant-Duhart, *Saint-Jean-de-Luz*, 69.
197 AD-33, 1 B 485, fol. 373r.
198 AD-64 (Pau), C 1542, fol. 73. See Veyrin, *Les Basques*, 248.
199 AD-64 (Pau), C 1543, fol. 81. Desplat, 'D'un bucher à l'autre', 123, claims that the request was ultimately denied by Henry IV, but on what basis is unclear.

# Chapter 2

1 AD-33, 1 B 19, fols 123v–4v; reproduced in Villeneuve, *Le fléau des sorciers*, 221–2.
2 Its contents can be deduced from the *jussion* sent by Henry IV on 18 February 1609: AD-33, 1 B 19, fols 124v–5v; transcribed in Bordes, 'Recherches sur la sorcellerie', 216-20 (appendix IX).
3 For example, Dusseau, *Le juge et la sorcière*, 7, 16–18, and the 'avant-propos' of Villeneuve, *Le fléau des sorciers*, 9–11.
4 For the metaphor, see Charpentier, *La sorcellerie en Pays basque*, 30.
5 AD-64, Ustaritz GG 2–9, fols 125–6.
6 Reproduced in Delorme, 'Les Récollets de l'Immaculée-Conception'.
7 A third, late-seventeenth-century chronicle draws on Lissalde's narrative and de Lancre's *Tableau*: Veillet, *Recherches*, 191–2.
8 AD-64, Saint-Jean-de-Luz, FF 12, Liasse 2/2.
9 AD-64, Saint-Jean-de-Luz, FF 12, Liasse 2/16. Her name was Blanche d'Avril.
10 AD-64, Saint-Jean-de-Luz, CC 2, Liasse 1/4, fol. 1r.
11 AHN, Inq., Lib. 835, fol. 340r–v; transcribed in Henningsen, *The Salazar Documents*, 107 (hereafter, *Salazar Documents*).
12 For example, *Tableau*, 41, 98, 208.
13 Briggs, 'Witchcraft and the Local Communities', 204–7.
14 Monter, *Frontiers of Heresy*, 273.
15 *L'Incrédulité*, 798; Soman, 'The Parlement of Paris', 33.
16 Monter, 'Witchcraft Trials in France', 230.
17 Piant, *Une justice ordinaire*, 10, estimates that there are millions of minor civil and criminal trials yet to look at.
18 Hamscher, *The Royal Financial Administration*, 11.
19 Carroll, *Blood and Violence*, 186, puts the number of courts between 60,000 and 70,000.
20 Goyhenetche, *Histoire générale du Pays Basque*, 3:190.
21 *Les coustumes generailes*, 3, 36–7.
22 Hamscher, *The Royal Financial Administration*, 7–8.
23 *Les coustumes generailes*, 3.
24 Ruff, *Crime, Justice and Public Order in Old Regime France*.
25 Champeaud, *Le Parlement de Bordeaux*, 106–7.

26 Louis Servin cited in Soman, 'La justice criminelle, vitrine de la monarchie française', 294.
27 Soman, 'La justice criminelle, vitrine de la monarchie française', 304.
28 Piant, *Une justice ordinaire*, 14.
29 Le Mao, *Parlement et parlementaires*, 248–69.
30 Hamscher, *The Royal Financial Administration*, 12–13.
31 A witness in 1672 observed that the second-best hams in the kingdom came from inland Soule but were known as 'jambon de Bayonne': Goyhenetche, *Histoire générale du Pays Basque*, 2:207.
32 Carroll, *Blood and Violence*, 186–91; Soman, 'La justice criminelle aux XVI[e]–XVII[e] siècles', 20.
33 For the Tournelle of Bordeaux, see Champeaud, *Le Parlement de Bordeaux*, 101.
34 Roche-Flavin, *Treize livres des parlements de France*, 25.
35 Soman, 'Deviance and Criminal Justice', 9–10, suggests that witchcraft was one of these crimes but only offers evidence from the independent duchy of Lorraine in support of that claim.
36 Hamscher, *The Royal Financial Administration*, 17.
37 On the different survival rates of documents from the various communes, see Rillot, 'La noblesse labourdine', 208.
38 For church repairs, see for example, AD-64, Saint-Jean-de-Luz CC 2, Liasse 1/5, fols 1v, 3r; for the fountain, see AD-64, Saint-Jean-de-Luz CC 2, Liasse 1/7, fol. 10v.
39 AD-64, Saint-Jean-de-Luz CC 2, Liasse 1/5, fols 4r, 2r.
40 AD-64, Saint-Jean-de-Luz CC 2, Liasse 1/8, fol. 10v.
41 AD-64, Saint-Jean-de-Luz CC 2, Liasse 1/7, fol. 9r.
42 For the identification of Pierre de Chibau, see Lamant-Duhart, *Saint-Jean-de-Luz*, 180, who dates Pierre de Chibau's appointment 'vers 1600' but does not cite a source.
43 AD-64, Saint-Jean-de-Luz GG 3, fols 27, 67.
44 AD-64, Saint-Jean-de-Luz CC 2, Liasse 1/8, fol. 10v; the list of payments on fol. 43v shows that 'Marie de Haristeguy' was one of the town's principal taxpayers and one of the few female ones.
45 AD-64, Saint-Jean-de-Luz CC 2, Liasse 1/7, fol. 9r. For the identity of the town's *abbé*, see the opening preamble on fol. 1r.
46 AD-64, Saint-Jean-de-Luz CC 2, Liasse 1/7, fol. 9v.
47 AD-64, Saint-Jean-de-Luz CC 2, Liasse 1/5, fol. 2v.
48 The first payment for 'droict de vin' is dated 4 May 1605: AD-64, Saint-Jean-de-Luz CC 2, Liasse 1/8, fol. 10v.
49 AD-64, Saint-Jean-de-Luz CC 2, Liasse 1/7, fol. 1r.
50 AD-64, Saint-Jean-de-Luz CC 2, Liasse 1/5, fol. 6v, 7v; there are various further entries in which Haurgues returns sums of money.
51 AD-64, Saint-Jean-de-Luz GG 3, fol. 33. Jean's name is spelled slightly differently.
52 Cruseau, *Chronique*, 2:3.
53 Prétou, *Justice et société en Gascogne*, 229.
54 Cruseau, *Chronique*, 1:80, 202–3, 2:3.
55 AD-64, Saint-Jean-de-Luz FF 12, Liasse 2/2. He stayed at Lipoustey the first night, Lespéron on the second, Ondres on the third. See also Habasque, 'Épisodes d'un procès de sorcellerie', 54.
56 Cruseau, *Chronique*, 2:3, 4.

57 AD-33, 1 B 19, fol. 74v.
58 AD-64, Saint-Jean-de-Luz CC 2, Liasse 1/9, fol. 12v, for payments for July, August and September. The earlier arrival of some prisoners can be worked out by the different lengths of stay outlined in the jailor's deposition: Saint-Jean-de-Luz FF 12, Liasse 2/8.
59 AD-64, Saint-Jean-de-Luz CC 7, Liasse 3/1, fol. 3v.
60 The contents can be deduced from Échaux's revocation: Haristoy, 'Les paroisses du Pays basque', 29. A precise date is unknown. AD-64, Saint-Jean-de-Luz CC 2, Liasse 1/9, fol. 8r, lists a payment by Sanson for two copies of the text, dated 19 January 1605.
61 See especially Vivo, *Information and Communication in Venice*, 157–99.
62 AD-64, Saint-Jean-de-Luz CC 2, Liasse 1/9, fols 8v, 12v; Liasse 1/10, fol. 25v.
63 Haristoy, 'Les paroisses du Pays basque', 28.
64 See for example, AD-64, Saint-Jean-de-Luz III E 9744, fol. 38.
65 AD-64, Saint-Jean-de-Luz CC 2, Liasse 1/10, fol. 23r. It s difficult to assess how generous these travel expenses were.
66 AD-64, Saint-Jean-de-Luz CC 2, Liasse 1/9, fol. 12v.
67 *Tableau*, 139.
68 A series of payments in Bayonne to the various members of the commission is recorded for 28 October: AD-64, Saint-Jean-de-Luz CC 2, Liasse 1/10, fol. 26v.
69 For the date of departure, see Bayonne, AD-64, Saint-Jean-de-Luz CC 2, Liasse 1/10, fol. 13v; see also Sanson's payment: CC 2, Liasse 1/9, fol. 13v; for the notary, CC7, Liasse 3/1, fols 1v–2r; Cruseau arrived home on 4 December 1605: Cruseau, *Chronique*, 2:4.
70 AD-64, Saint-Jean-de-Luz CC 2, Liasse 1/9, fol. 17v. The last payment that explicitly places Oriotz in Bordeaux is dated 6 August 1607.
71 AD-64, Saint-Jean-de-Luz CC 2, Liasse 1/9, fol. 14v.
72 See the list of names in AD-64, Saint-Jean-de-Luz FF 12, Liasse 2/17, fol. 1r.
73 AD-64, Saint-Jean-de-Luz CC 2, Liasse 1/10, fol. 28r, see also fol. 30v.
74 AD-64, Saint-Jean-de-Luz FF 12, Liasse 2/8.
75 This lawsuit is summarized in Habasque, 'Épisodes d'un procès de sorcellerie', 55. A considerable number of documents in Saint-Jean-de-Luz FF 12, Liasse 2 relate to the jailor's lawsuit.
76 The names are given in AD-64, Saint-Jean-de-Luz FF 12, Liasse 2/3–5.
77 AD-64, Saint-Jean-de-Luz FF 12, Liasse 2/3.
78 AD-64, Saint-Jean-de-Luz FF 12, Liasse 2/8. The jailor's deposition lists the prisoners and puts their total at seventeen, but I would not discount the possibility of another five accused being imprisoned elsewhere. The names of the Goyetche are given in Saint-Jean-de-Luz FF 12, Liasse 2/17.
79 AD-64, Bayonne, BB 18, fol. 524.
80 AD-64, Saint-Jean-de-Luz CC 2, Liasse 1/10, fol. 30v.
81 AD-64, Saint-Jean-de-Luz CC 2, Liasse 1/10, fol. 30r; AD-64, Saint-Jean-de-Luz FF 12, Liasse 2/6. The translator's name is Derhaut; the receipt is dated 3 January 1607.
82 AD-64, Saint-Jean-de-Luz FF 12, Liasse 2/16.
83 AD-64, Saint-Jean-de-Luz CC 7, Liasse 2/1-2, fol. 2r.
84 Bordeaux, Archives de Bordeaux Métropole, 2 S 160, fol. 28r.
85 AD-64, Saint-Jean-de-Luz CC 2, Liasse 2/10, fol. 31v.

86  This can be inferred from Catherine de La Masse's denunciation of her assailants below: AD-64, Saint-Jean-de-Luz FF 12, Liasse 2/14, fol. 6v.
87  AD-64, Saint-Jean-de-Luz CC 2, Liasse 2/10, fols 32v–33r; the community paid for soldiers to keep order, two men to guard the prisoner, two trumpeters and so on. See also Bordes, 'Recherches sur la sorcellerie', 80.
88  Gaufretau, *Chronique bordeloise*, 2:121–2. The 'cette année' given is 1623 but the chronicle's dates are almost always inaccurate. The context makes it abundantly clear that these executions predate (indeed, allegedly inspire) de Lancre's commission.
89  *Annuae litterae*, 519.
90  AD-64, Saint-Jean-de-Luz FF 12, liasse 2/17, fol. 1r; Saint-Jean-de-Luz FF 12, liasse 2/14, fol. 8r.
91  AD-64, Saint-Jean-de-Luz CC 2, Liasse 2/10, fol. 35r.
92  On Salazar, see Homza, 'An Expert Lawyer'.
93  Roper, *Witch Craze*; Rowlands, 'Witchcraft and Old Women'.
94  The claim paraphrases Pierre Delooz's famous observation that 'one is never a saint except for other people': Delooz, 'Towards a Sociological Study of Canonized Sainthood', 194.
95  AD-64, Saint-Jean-de-Luz, FF 12, Liasse 2/14. The document appears to have been compiled in stages, with corrections throughout. It quickly ceases to be a record by Sanson only: the document is signed and witnessed by seventeen officials and 'inhabitants', including curiously, Jean de Haristeguy, whose signature is amongst the smallest and near the bottom. Inevitably, the incident would be raised with the Bordeaux Parlement: Saint-Jean-de-Luz CC 7, Liasse 3/1, fol. 3v.
96  AD-64, Saint-Jean-de-Luz, FF 12, Liasse 2/14, fol. 1r.
97  AD-64, Saint-Jean-de-Luz, FF 12, Liasse 2/14, fols 1v–2r.
98  AD-64, Saint-Jean-de-Luz CC 2, Liasse 1/12 is a *compte* by Martin de La Masse, which was settled on 12 October 1605.
99  AD-64, Saint-Jean-de-Luz, FF 12, Liasse 2/14, fols 2v–3r, 3v–4r.
100  Remnants can still be seen from the modern viewing platform today: Bost et al., *La Rhune*, 16.
101  *Tableau*, 39, 84.
102  AD-64, Saint-Jean-de-Luz, FF 12, Liasse 2/14, fol. 4v; Veyrin, *Les Basques*, 155.
103  AD-64, Saint-Jean-de-Luz, FF 12, Liasse 2/14, fol. 5r.
104  AD-64, Saint-Jean-de-Luz FF 12, Liasse 2/14, fol. 5v.
105  AD-64, Saint-Jean-de-Luz FF 12, Liasse 2/14, fol. 6r–v.
106  AD-64, Saint-Jean-de-Luz FF 12, Liasse 2/14, fol. 6v.
107  AD-64, Saint-Jean-de-Luz CC 7, Liasse 3/1, fol. 3v.
108  AD-64, Saint-Jean-de-Luz FF 12, Liasse 2/14, fol. 7v.
109  AD-64, Saint-Jean-de-Luz FF 12, Liasse 2/14, fol. 8r.
110  For example, Schiff, *The Witches*, 82–7.
111  AD-64, Ustaritz GG 2–9, fols 125–6.
112  Delorme, 'Les Récollets de l'Immaculée-Conception', 651.
113  AD-64, Saint-Jean-de-Luz, FF 12, liasse 2/19; transcribed Bordes, 'Recherches sur la sorcellerie', 212–15 (appendix VIII). The appeal is not dated but was probably sent immediately after the last event recorded took place on 25 July 1607.
114  Bordes, 'Recherches sur la sorcellerie', 212.
115  Barkham, 'French Basque "New Found Land" Entrepreneurs', 15.

116 AD-64, Saint-Jean-de-Luz CC 2, Liasse 1/10, fol. 34r.
117 AD-64, Saint-Jean-de-Luz CC 2, Liasse 1/10, fol. 25v.
118 AD-64, Saint-Jean-de-Luz CC 7, Liasse 3/1, fol. 3r–v.
119 AD-64, Saint-Jean-de-Luz FF 4, Liasse 2.
120 Saint-Jean-de-Luz CC 2, Liasse 1/10, fol. 38v; see also the March 1608 testimony collected in Saint-Jean-de-Luz GG 2, Liasse 5/2.
121 Bordes, 'Recherches sur la sorcellerie', 212. This incident is also recorded in the earlier deposition: Saint-Jean-de-Luz FF 12, Liasse 2/14, fol. 8rv–9r. The latter document identifies Barrendeguy as 'frère d'ung nommé Chibau'. Oriotz's account suggests that proceedings would also be undertaken against the aggrieved husband: Saint-Jean-de-Luz CC 2, Liasse 1/10, fol. 38r.
122 AD-64, Saint-Jean-de-Luz FF 12, Liasse 2/3. Marie had been imprisoned in Bordeaux's *Maison commune*.
123 Bordes, 'Recherches sur la sorcellerie', 213.
124 AD-64, Saint-Jean-de-Luz FF 4, Liasse 1, fol. 1v.
125 Bordes, 'Recherches sur la sorcellerie', 213.
126 Bordes, 'Recherches sur la sorcellerie', 213, 214. The manuscript identifies the ambassador's wife as 'la dame de Barrault'. For her full name, see Viton de Saint-Allais, *Nobiliaire universel de France*, 17:409.
127 Bordes, 'Recherches sur la sorcellerie', 214, 215.
128 Henningsen, *The Witches' Advocate*, 130–1; Zintzo-Garmendia, *Histoire de la sorcellerie*, 724.
129 On the Inquisition's Francophobia, see Monter, *Frontiers of Heresy*, 108, 150, 236.
130 *Salazar Documents*, 203.
131 The bishop mentions the Parlement of Paris rather than Bordeaux, and the presence of only a single judge.
132 Arzadún, 'Las brujas de Fuenterrabía', 360.
133 AMH, B-1-I-5-2, fol. 2r. For a summary of the 1611 trials, see Arzadún, 'Las brujas de Fuenterrabía'.
134 An approximate date of their arrival can be inferred from AD-64, Bayonne BB 18, fol. 21; Bordes, 'Recherches sur la sorcellerie', 87.
135 AD-64, Bayonne BB 18, fol. 9.
136 *Tableau*, 69, 142.
137 AD-64, Bayonne BB 18, fol. 9.
138 AD-64, Bayonne BB 18, fol. 21.
139 AD-64, Bayonne FF 563, doc. 80. Bordeaux, 31 October 1609.
140 De Lancre implies that Ségure was ordered to make 'une plus ample inquisition contre certaines Sorcieres en vertu d'un arrest de la Cour de Parlement de Bourdeaux': *Tableau*, 69. On 142, he suggested that the group Ségure was pursuing had 'eschappees du Parlement de Bourdeaux', possibly the Bayonne magistrates had released them.
141 *Discours tres-veritable*, 4, 5.
142 *Tableau*, 41.
143 *Salazar Documents*, 109.
144 The documents only mention her father, Adame: *Salazar Documents*, 107.
145 AD-64, Bayonne BB 17, fol. 737 (17 November 1608). This is the earliest reference to 'le Pais de Labourt a depputé Messieurs d'Amou et d'Urthubie pour aller supplier le Roy'.

146 AD-33, 1 B 19, fol. 124r; Bordes, 'Recherches sur la sorcellerie', 217 (appendix IX). It is also included in Communay, *Le conseiller Pierre de Lancre*, 52–3 (appendix III), and Villeneuve, *Le fléau des sorciers*, 221–2 (appendix I).
147 AD-33, 1 B 19, fol. 125r (dated 18 February 1609); transcribed in Communay, *Le conseiller Pierre de Lancre*, 54–5 (appendix IV).
148 AD-64, Bayonne, BB 17, fol. 737; see also the notarial document, signed by Urrugne and Hendaye officials on 19 November and by those of Ciboure the next day: AD-64, 1J 160/39, fols 137–8.
149 AD-64, Ciboure, FF 2. The 'quittance' for 36 *livres* is dated 18 November 1609. The documents are not numbered.
150 The judge made their role more specific in the second edition: *Tableau* (1613), sig. õ1r.

# Chapter 3

1 *Tableau* (1607), 807, 813, 793, 796.
2 Chancellor Bellièvre cited in Greengrass, *France in the Age of Henri IV*, 182. For the image of the 'juge-prêtre', see also Le Mao, *Parlement et parlementaires*, 271.
3 Roche-Flavin, *Treize livres des parlements de France*, 1–2, 5; Delprat, 'Savoirs et déboires'.
4 Soman, 'La justice criminelle, vitrine de la monarchie française', 291–2.
5 Parker, *The Making of French Absolutism*, 24.
6 Gaufretau, *Chronique bordeloise*, 1:321.
7 Descimon, 'The Birth of the Nobility of the Robe', 99, 104.
8 Greengrass, *France in the Age of Henri IV*, 204–5.
9 *Tableau*, 142.
10 Villeneuve, *Le fléau des sorciers*, 67; Charpentier, *La sorcellerie en Pays basque*, 31; Soman, 'Decriminalizing Witchcraft', 15; Boscheron des Portes, *Histoire du Parlement de Bordeaux*, 373.
11 Champeaud, *Le Parlement de Bordeaux*, 133–5; Le Mao, *Parlement et parlementaires*, 29–35.
12 Mousnier, *Les institutions de la France*, 254; Boutruche, *Bordeaux de 1453 à 1715*, 81–3 and the source documents included in Métivier, *Chronique du Parlement de Bordeaux*.
13 Cruseau, *Chronique*, 2:50–1. On the elaborate wardrobes of officeholders, see Hamilton, *Pierre de L'Estoile*, 32–7. See also Houllemare, *Politiques de la parole*, 120–1, for the Paris 'séance d'ouverture'.
14 Cruseau, *Chronique*, 2:15–16.
15 Plutarch, *De Genio Socratis* 579B–D. The purpose of the oracle, as Plato explained to the Delians, was to encourage the study of geometry.
16 *Tableau*, 264–311. Daffis's verdict, possibly its autograph, has survived as Austin, TX, Harry Ransom Center, Medieval and Early Modern MS 230 ('Sobre la Licantropía').
17 *La puce de Madame Des-Roches*, sig. â5v, â4r.
18 On the composition's origin, see Jones, 'Contentious Readings'; Larsen, 'On Reading "La Puce"'; Kenny, *Born to Write*, 113–20.
19 Houllemare, *Politiques de la parole*, 35.
20 Boutruche, *Bordeaux de 1453 à 1715*, 198–9; Desan, *Montaigne*, 66–7.

21 Balsamo and Simonin, *Abel L'Angelier*, entries 76 (*La puce*), 204 (Montaigne's *Essais*), 453 (de Lancre). For L'Angelier's prominence as a bookseller, see also Hamilton, *Pierre de L'Estoile*, 48–9.
22 Poumarède, 'De l'*Arrêt mémorable*', 504; Houllemare, *Politiques de la parole*, 327.
23 Finlay, 'The Refashioning of Martin Guerre'; Davis, 'On the Lame'.
24 Coras, *Arrest memorable*, title page, 9.
25 For discussions of the Basque language, see Coras, *Arrest memorable*, 44, 61. A 'table alphabetique des plus notables dictions et sentences' precedes the work. For Coras's life, see Davis, *The Return of Martin Guerre*, 95–103.
26 *Tableau*, ed. Céard, 9, 11. The introduction never mentions the witches who perished.
27 Davis, *The Return of Martin Guerre*, 109, 103.
28 Mousnier, *Les institutions de la France*, 2:251; Mettam, 'France'.
29 See for example, the readmission of the Jesuits and the registration of the Edict of Nantes: Nelson, *The Jesuits and the Monarchy*, chap. 2; Greengrass, *France in the Age of Henri IV*, 106–8.
30 Champeaud, *Le Parlement de Bordeaux*, 308–19.
31 Boscheron Des Portes, *Histoire du Parlement de Bordeaux*, 352.
32 For the sixteenth century, see Boutruche, *Bordeaux de 1453 à 1715*, 204. For later depictions, see Le Mao, *Parlement et parlementaires*, 275–7.
33 Harvitt, 'Gestes des solliciteurs', 319.
34 For the earlier sixteenth century, see Powis, 'The Magistrates of the Parlement of Bordeaux', 87; for the later period, see Le Mao, *Parlement et parlementaires*, 258–63.
35 Soman, 'The Parlement of Paris'; for de Lancre's annoyance, see *L'incrédulité*, 798.
36 Monter, 'Toads and Eucharists'.
37 Le Mao, *Parlement et parlementaires*, 33.
38 For the Parlement's 'reputation for mildness', see Pearl, *The Crime of Crimes*, 139; Monter, 'Witchcraft Trials in France', 223–4.
39 Monter, 'Witchcraft Trials in France', 223.
40 Raemond, *L'Antichrist*, 103.
41 Stuart Clark, *Thinking with Demons*, 351–3; Tinsley, *History and Polemics*, 79–92.
42 Cruseau, *Chronique*, 1:85–6.
43 Raemond, *L'Antichrist*, 103–5.
44 *Tableau*, 104–5. Admittedly, *Tableau*, 72, also mentions the burning light in passing but does not attribute it to a specific Basque witness.
45 Gaufretau, *Chronique bordelcise*, 1:9–10.
46 See the C addition on F962.
47 Raemond, *L'Antichrist*, 103, 105.
48 AD-64, Bayonne, FF 3, fols 565–7.
49 Automne, *La Conférence*, 458–9.
50 Callard, *Le temps des fantômes*, 87–91.
51 Machielsen, 'The Making of a Teen Wolf'.
52 Cruseau, *Chronique*, 2:53.
53 This was the case of the 25-year-old Protestant manservant Isaac de Queyran: *Tableau*, 105, 145–53; the other case was that of Léger Rivasseau: *Tableau*, 125–6, 175.
54 Gaufretau, *Chronique bordelcise*, 1:320–1.

55 *Tableau*, 174; see also Gaufretau, *Chronique bordeloise*, 1:243–4. For MacRedor's employment, see Gaullieur, *Histoire du Collége de Guyenne,* 351.
56 Gaufretau, *Chronique bordeloise*, 2:75.
57 *Tableau*, 105.

# Chapter 4

1 *Le livre des princes*, 623. See Pliny, *Natural History* 8.3.
2 For swine and chameleons, see *Tableau* (1610), fol. 118r (and compare Pliny, *Natural History* 8.9; 8.41).
3 *Le livre des princes*, 623. For elephants and sheep, see Pliny, *Natural History* 8.7; for lions and monkeys, see Pliny, *Natural History* 8.19.
4 *Tableau* (1610), fol. 118r. On the antipathy between roosters and demons, see *Tableau*, 155–6.
5 De Lancre recounts the story twice: *Tableau* (1613), 171; *L'Incrédulité*, 97.
6 Findlen, 'Natural History', 439–42; for a contrasting view, see Ogilvie, *The Science of Describing*, 5.
7 Daston and Park, *Wonders and the Order of Nature*, esp. chaps 5 and 6.
8 *L'Incrédulité*, 96.
9 Findlen, *Possessing Nature*, 17–23.
10 *Tableau* (1610), fol. 118v.
11 Clark, *Thinking with Demons*, 219–31; Daston, 'The Nature of Nature'.
12 *Tableau*, 117.
13 Serjeantson, 'Francis Bacon', 690–1.
14 Serjeantson, 'Francis Bacon'; Merchant, '"The Violence of Impediments"'; Martin, *Francis Bacon*, 72–104.
15 Houllemare, *Politiques de la parole*, 590–1 (appendix V).
16 Clark, *Thinking with Demons*, 235.
17 Ostling, 'Babyfat and Belladonna', 30–72; Eamon, *Science and the Secrets of Nature*, 202–3.
18 Bacon, *Sylva Sylvarum*, 229.
19 Maclean, *Interpretation and Meaning in the Renaissance*, 76.
20 Findlen, 'Natural History', 435; Ogilvie, *The Science of Describing*, 209–64.
21 *Tableau*, sig. ẽ3r, 79, 125.
22 Ogilvie, *The Science of Describing*, 12–13; for examples of 'voilà' and 'voici', see *Tableau*, 174, 177.
23 *Tableau*, sig. ẽ1r, 165.
24 *Tableau*, 171.
25 Mulsow, 'Ambiguities of the Prisca Sapientia'.
26 Davies, *Renaissance Ethnography*, 13; Rampling, *The Experimental Fire*, 340, 354–5.
27 Pearl, *The Crime of Crimes*, 143.
28 *Tableau*, sig. ẽ3v, ẽ4r, 217, 207–8.
29 *Du sortilège*, 3, 4.
30 Perrault, *L'anti-démon de Mascon*, 51.
31 For example, *Tableau*, 30, 91, 95, 500.
32 *Tableau*, 206.
33 Daston and Park, *Wonders and the Order of Nature*, chap. 8; Harrison, 'Curiosity'.

34  For example, *Tableau*, 47, 499.
35  *Tableau*, 86, 111, 254, 314–15.
36  Machielsen, 'The Making of a Teen Wolf'.
37  *Tableau*, 317, 315, 316.
38  Rowland, *From Pompeii*, 103–4.
39  *Tableau*, 327. On Mozart's and Twain's visits, see Rowland, *From Pompeii*, 103–7.
40  Eamon, *Science and the Secrets of Nature*, esp. chap. 8.
41  *Tableau*, sig. ã4r; for de Lancre's light-darkness metaphors, see Jacques-Chaquin, 'Nocturnes sorciers'.
42  De Lancre, *Wunderbahrliche Geheimnussen der Zauberey*.
43  Espagnet, *La Philosophie naturelle rétablie*, 116 (canon 242).
44  Linden, '"By Gradual Scale Sublim'd"'; Newman, *Newton*, 185, 192–5.
45  Kahn, *Alchimie et Paracelsisme*, 529.
46  Bayle, *Dictionnaire historique et critique*, 1:1095.
47  Charpentier, *La sorcellerie en Pays basque*, 32; Villeneuve, *Le fléau des sorciers*, 67; *Tableau*, ed. Jacques-Lefèvre, 11; Ospital, *La chasse*, 19; Zintzo-Garmendia, *Histoire de la sorcellerie*, 154. Less forgiving is Boscheron des Portes, *Histoire du Parlement de Bordeaux*, 373–4.
48  Charpentier, *La sorcellerie en Pays basque*, 140.
49  Newman, *Promethean Ambitions*, 54. For a more measured view, see Kahn, *Alchimie et paracelsisme*, 8–9.
50  Espagnet, *The Summary of Physics Restored*, xvii; more careful is Espagnet, *La Philosophie naturelle rétablie*, ed. Kahn, xii.
51  Espagnet, *The Summary of Physics Restored*, xxi–xxii.
52  Ribard, 'Sur plusieurs frontières'.
53  Marie de Gournay, Montaigne's 'fille d'alliance' accompanied Espagnet and his new wife on a journey from Paris to Guyenne and the two bonded over a shared interest in alchemy: Fogel, *Marie de Gournay*, 125.
54  Communay, *Le conseiller Pierre de Lancre*, 65 (appendix VIII, dated 24 September 1630).
55  *Tableau*, sig. ã4v, 139, 97, 112.
56  For example, *Tableau*, 38, 165. As one editor observed, 'le *je* de l'auteur est omniprésent': *Tableau*, ed. Jacques-Lefèvre, 16.
57  F184.
58  *Tableau*, 217; compare Cicero, *Topica* 75.
59  *Tableau*, 217.

# Chapter 5

1  *Tableau* (1610), sig. a2r.
2  Communay, *Le Conseiller Pierre de Lancre*,
3  This alternative spelling was used on the title page of his 1622 *L'Incrédulité*.
4  *Tableau* (1610), fol. 492v.
5  *Tableau*, 45.
6  Machielsen, 'Lancre, Pierre de.'
7  *Tableau* (1610), sig. a2v.
8  Communay, *Le Conseiller Pierre de Lancre*, 29.

9 *L'Incrédulité*, 41. The capital letters are De Lancre's. For these ideas, see also Maus de Rolley, 'Of Oysters, Witches, Birds, and Anchors'.
10 F2. See also F331; F337–38.
11 F13, F8, F87, F380.
12 Communay, *Le Conseiller Pierre de Lancre*, 47–50, at 50 (appendix I).
13 Boutcher, *The School of Montaigne*, 1:171; Dardano Basso, *L'ancora e gli specchi*, 42; or more obliquely, McGowan, 'Pierre de Lancre's *Tableau*', 183.
14 Machielsen, 'Thinking with Montaigne'.
15 Bakewell, *How to Live*. On the meaning of 'essayer', see Maclean, *Montaigne philosophe*, 10.
16 *Tableau*, sig. ã2v–ã3r.
17 *Tableau*, sig. ĩ1r–v, ĩ2r.
18 *Tableau*, 29.
19 For example, F164.
20 McGowan, 'Pierre de Lancre's *Tableau*', 186.
21 *Tableau* (1610), fol. 141v.
22 *Tableau* (1610), fol. 149v.
23 *Tableau*, 204–5.
24 Pearl, *The Crime of Crimes*, 149, 129.
25 F962, F961.
26 Maus de Rolley, 'Of Oysters, Witches, Birds, and Anchors'.
27 Espagnet, *Le rozier des guerres*.
28 Sawyer, *Printed Poison*; Dubost, *Marie de Médicis*, chaps 23–4; Kettering, *Power and Reputation*, chap. 3.
29 *Le livre des princes*, sig. a2v, b3r–v.
30 *Tableau* (1610), fol. 214r.
31 *Le livre des princes*, 34–5.
32 *Tableau* (1610), fol. 391r.
33 *L'Incrédulité*, 840.
34 *Tableau*, 37, 42, 75, 93–4, 126–7.
35 ARSI, Lugd. 18-II, fol. 383v.
36 Bibliothèque de l'Institut de France, MS Godefroid 273, fol. 20. Bordeaux, 20 June 1643.
37 ARSI, Gal. 46-I, fol. 6r. The contents of de Lancre's letter has to be deduced from Acquaviva's reply. Rome, 13 August 1613.
38 See for example, the offer to trade land discussed in ARSI, Aquit. 2-I, fol. 12v. Rome, 23 April 1613.
39 ARSI, Roma 172, fol. 168v.
40 ARSI, Gal. 46-I, fol. 125v. Rome, 31 August 1630.

# Chapter 6

1 Voltaire, 'Petit commentaire de l'ignorant', 118.
2 Rousseau, 'Jugement sur la paix perpétuelle', 47, 52.
3 Voltaire, 'Petit commentaire de l'ignorant', 118; Babelon, *Henri IV*, 7.
4 Mousnier, *L'Assassinat d'Henri IV*, 261–72; Greengrass, *France in the Age of Henri IV*, 254–9; Pitts, *Henri IV of France*, 331.

5. See for example, Henry's treatment of his son Louis: Pitts, *Henri IV of France*, 319.
6. The date of these first letters patent can be deduced from Communay, *Le Conseiller Pierre de Lancre*, 54 (appendix IV). For recent versions of the myth, see for example, Saint Bris, *Henri IV et la France réconciliée*.
7. For example, Labat, *Sorcellerie?*, 29.
8. AD-64, Bayonne FF 563, doc. 53. Paris, 14 July 1609.
9. On Henri's 'tempérament vif-argent': Babelon, *Henri IV*, 914.
10. Labourdette et al., *Le traité de Vervins*.
11. On France's 'natural borders', see Nordman, *Frontières de France*, 60–6, 88–105. On the construction of national identities in the (eastern) Pyrenees, see Sahlins, *Boundaries*.
12. The 'cold war' expression is omnipresent: Babelon, *Henri IV*, 932; Belin, 'Conclusion', 561; Beiderbeck, *Zwischen Religionskrieg, Reichskrise und europäischem Hegemoniekampf*, 303.
13. Berger de Xivrey, *Recueil des lettres missives*, 6:324 (dated 3 November 1604); 6:360 (6 March 1605).
14. Pitts, *Henri IV of France*, 289. Desplat, 'Henri IV et La Navarre française', 65.
15. See Béthune, *Mémoires*, 2:487–8.
16. Hugon, *Au service du Roi Catholique*, 175, 310–17; La Force, *Le maréchal de La Force*, 1:125–37.
17. Babelon, *Henri IV*, 935; Pitts, *Henri IV of France*, 280. For the exemption, see Valois, *Inventaire des arrêts*, 2:186 (arrêt 8449).
18. La Force, *Le maréchal de La Force*, 1:144–5.
19. For the Morisco perspective, see Green-Mercado, *Visions of Deliverance*, chap. 6.
20. Hugon, *Au service du Roi Catholique*, 589; Babelon, *Henri IV*, 936. On the arrest of the French agent: La Grange, *Mémoires de … duc de La Force*, 1:406. Bertrand de Saulguis to La Force. Saint-Palais, 4 August 1605.
21. Berger de Xivrey, *Recueil des lettres missives*, 7:464 (dated only 1607). Another 'portugues Judio' with contacts in Saint-Jean-de-Luz was arrested with fake coinage and Jewish books in Valladolid in 1609: AGS, Est., L. 215, no pagination. Valladolid, 18 November 1609.
22. Babelon, *Henri IV*, 932–6.
23. L'Estoile, *Mémoires-journaux*, 9:210; 9:226.
24. *Le soldat navarrois*, 34, 226. The publication date can be inferred from L'Estoile's diary: Desplat, 'Henri IV et la Navarre française', 85.
25. *Tableau* (1607), sig. ã8v.
26. Babelon, *Henri IV*, 936.
27. AGS, Est. K 1608, doc. 7. 'Relaçíon que hace Martin de Bustamante.' [Pau], 30 October 1607.
28. Babelon, *Henri IV*, 928; Pitts, *Henri IV of France*, 298–302; Greengrass, *France in the Age of Henri IV*, 245–6.
29. Babelon, *Henri IV*, 916–18; Pitts, *Henri IV of France*, 299.
30. Beiderbeck, *Zwischen Religionskrieg, Reichskrise und europäischem Hegemoniekampf*, 361–448.
31. Pitts, *Henri IV of France*, 307. As Pitts put it, '[e]ven Cervantes would have had difficulty improving on the comedy that followed'.
32. Henrard, *Henri IV et la princesse de Condé*, 8.
33. BnF, Dupuy 42, fol. 66v; the episode is virtually overlooked in Legrand, *Essai sur les différends de Fontarabie avec le Labourd*, 32.

# Notes

34 *Tableau*, 139.
35 AGS, Guerra y Mar, Leg. 721 and 725 contain several letters from Hondarribia, San Sebastián and Pamplona. (Note, for instance, the lengthy letter sent by the 'muy noble y leal villa de Fuenterravia [=Hondarribia]' on 1 August 1609 in Leg. 725.)
36 Simancas, Guerra y Mar, Leg. 725, no pagination. Gonzalo de Luna y Mora to the Consejo de Guerra, Hondarribia, 14 August 1609.
37 Money was being raised for the construction at Socoa in July 1609: AD-33, C 3814, fols 108v–9v, but construction is still debated in 1618: Blaÿ de Gaïx, *Histoire militaire de Bayonne*, 32–3. A small early modern fort remains at Socoa. Its information board claims that work began only in 1627. See also Lamant-Duhart, *Ciboure*, 118–19.
38 AGS, Guerra y Mar, Leg. 725, no pagination. Gonzalo de Luna y Mora to the Consejo de Guerra, Hondarribia, 14 August 1609.
39 AGS, Guerra y Mar, Leg. 725. Thomas Calderon, San Sebastián, 30 July 1609. It reported there was not even a physician to tend to the many sick.
40 AGS, Estado, K 1462, doc. 5. Íñigo de Cárdenas to Consejo de Estado. Paris, 27 January 1610. On 18 March 1610, Cárdenas reported that Henry might want to seize 'alguna placa de las fronteras de España o de Flandes' to exchange for the prince and princess of Condé: Simancas, Estado, K 1462, doc. 60. See also Hugon, *Au service du Roi Catholique*, 180–1eorc.
41 *Tableau*, 35.
42 La Grange, *Mémoires de ... Duc de La Force*, 1:212–13.
43 The initial complaint to the viceroy of Aragon puts the number of livestock at 420: BnF, MS Français 16,138, fol. 2r, but witnesses later put it at 180 (fol. 17v). For the role played by Pedro Romes, the local 'justiciar', see fol. 14r.
44 See Dupuy 42, fol. 5r–v; *Tableau*, 34.
45 BnF, MS Français 16,138, fols 7r and following; *Tableau*, 35.
46 La Grange, *Mémoires de ... duc de La Force*, 2:228–9. La Force to the king. Pau, 23 July 1609. See also Brunet's reconstruction of the impact of these geopolitical tensions on the Val d'Aran: Brunet, *Les prêtres des montagnes*, 128–32.
47 The king told La Force that inhabitants of the Aspe valley were not allowed to negotiate for peace until they had been recompensed, he warned his viceroy for Spanish ploys, and yet also told him that he did not want war: La Grange, *Mémoires de ... duc de La Force*, 2:225–6 (Fontainebleau, 26 June 1609), 2:236 (Monceaux, 27 August 1609), 2:237–8 (Paris, 9 September 1609).
48 AD-33, 1 B 19, fol. 85v (April 1608) implies that the inhabitants of Saint-Jean-de-Luz had received 'lettres de continuation'; those of Urrugne and Hendaye had expired in 1605: AD-33, 1 B 19, fol. 155r (July 1608).
49 AD-33, 1 B 19, fols 150r (April 1609), 155r.
50 For example, AD-33, 1 B 19, fols 85v, 155r.
51 For example, AD-33, 1 B 19, fols 150v, fol. 85v.
52 AD-33, 1 B 19, fol. 139v (February 1609), 150v.
53 AD-33, 1 B 19, fols 123–4. The renewal of this decree from 1475 is not dated.
54 AD-33, C 3813, fols 104r–5r (May 1608).
55 Jaurgain, *La maison de Gramont*, 1:528–9 (appendix XVII).
56 AD-33, 1 B 19, fol. 155v.
57 Bordeaux, C 3977 (loose papers).
58 Rillot, 'La noblesse labourdine, 1610–1630', 212.
59 BnF, Dupuy 42, fols 55–6, 75.

60 Bordes, 'Recherches sur la sorcellerie', 217.
61 See for example, the lengthy discussion of a March 1609 conflict about which chamber of the court a new member should be assigned to: Cruseau, *Chronique*, 2:58–60.
62 AD-33, 1 B 19, fols 123v–4v. The text of the original letters patent has not survived because it was revoked and never registered. Its contents and the Parlement's actions are described in the *lettres de jussion*.
63 AD-33, 1 B 19, fol. 125v.
64 AD-33, 1 B 19, fol. 125r.
65 This was to serve on the bi-confessional *Chambre de l'Édit* in Nérac, considerably closer to Bordeaux than the Basque country: Communay, *Le Conseiller Pierre de Lancre*, 15.
66 Chesnaye-Desbois, *Dictionnaire de la noblesse*, 12:715; Malvezin, *Michel de Montaigne*, 84–5; Cruseau reports that Geoffrey resigned his office in favour of his son in 1595: Cruseau, *Chronique*, 1:120.
67 Malvezin does not list Catherine among Geoffrey's children, but Jeanne's marriage to de Lancre is mentioned: Malvezin, *Michel de Montaigne*, 82–3.
68 *Tableau*, 141; *Tableau* (1613), sig. õ1r; *L'Incrédulité*, 10 (*Advertissements*).
69 *Tableau*, 33, 35–6.
70 *Tableau*, 37.
71 AD-64, Saint-Jean-de-Luz FF 4 contains two folders. Liasse 1 is an undated and unsigned memorandum for the benefit of the mayor and *jurats* of Saint-Jean-de-Luz, listing various conflicts (but not de Lancre); liasse 2 contains the petition to the king and royal council, see fol. 1v and 2r for the references to Pierre de Lancre and Geoffrey de Montaigne, respectively.
72 Ribard, 'Sur plusieurs frontières'.
73 AD-33, 1 B 19, fol. 125r.

# Chapter 7

1 *Tableau* (1613), sig. ī3v.
2 AD-64, Bayonne FF 563, doc. 44 (draft) and 45. Bordeaux, 22 June 1609; excerpted in Communay, *Le Conseiller Pierre de Lancre*, 56–7 (appendix V).
3 Egaña, 'Las brujas vascas y Lancre', 11.
4 For example, Labat, *Sorcellerie?*, 35–6; Zintzo-Garmendia, *Histoire de la sorcellerie*, 234.
5 Labat, *Sorcellerie?*, 31.
6 Charpentier, *La sorcellerie en Pays basque*, 140; Espagnet, *The Summary of Physics Restored*, xvii–xviii.
7 AHN, Inq. Leg. 794, ff. 433v (Logroño, 26 September 1609) and 459v (Urdax, 20 [August] 1609). Two further but later Inquisition sources, dated 1 April 1611 and 24 March 1612, also mention a single judge: *Salazar Documents*, 203, 345. The first of these, a letter by the bishop of Pamplona, may have conflated the commission's work with Urtubie's independent witch-hunting (see Chapter 2).
8 *Tableau*, sig. ē1r, 451; *L'Incrédulité*, 10 (*Advertissements*).
9 De Lancre reported that the commission had been 'verifiee sans aucune modification *autre que du temps*': *Tableau*, 466, suggesting that the four-month term was already set prior to the commission's departure.

10 Pérès, *Chronique*, 240–1.
11 *Les coustumes generalles*, 37.
12 *Tableau*, 382.
13 Delorme, 'Les Récollets de l'Immaculée-Conception', 651.
14 *Tableau*, 41.
15 AHN, Inq., Lib. 835, fol. 355r.
16 *Tableau*, sig. ẽ2v.
17 AD-64, Bayonne CC 306, item 48; transcribed in Communay, *Le Conseiller Pierre de Lancre*, 57 (appendix VI).
18 *Tableau*, 139.
19 AHN, Inq., Lib. 794, fol. 457r. Mutriku, 19 July 1609.
20 AHN, Inq., Lib. 794, fol. 458r. San Sebastian, 24 July 1609.
21 AHN, Inq., Lib. 794, fol. 459v. Urdax, 20 [August] 1609.
22 AD-64, Bayonne FF 563, doc. 70. La Bastide-Clairence falls outside the Labourd. While the commission's authority extended to 'pays circonvoisins', it seems doubtful that it would have included Navarre, not only outside the normal jurisdiction of the Parlement but even outside of France: Communay, *Le Conseiller Pierre de Lancre*, 53 (appendix III); *Tableau*, sig. a4v.
23 *Tableau*, 223. That the commission was at Urrugne in late July can be inferred from *Tableau*, 70–1. The name of the other known Urrugne victim was Marissans de Tartas: *Tableau*, 71.
24 AD-64, Bayonne BB 18, fol. 74.
25 The *Tableau* does not mention executions but the alleged threats on de Lancre's and Amou's life make them very likely.
26 *Tableau*, 117. De Lancre reports on a disturbance caused by the return of the sailors from the New World, which places the execution of 'les sorcieres' later in the autumn.
27 *Tableau*, 125. This relates to the execution of the D'Aguere family.
28 After a failed attempt to visit the sabbat on 19 July, the judges returned a second time: *Tableau*, 139. For early August as the date of the likely second visit, see *Tableau*, 114. A tambourine player from Hendaye was among those executed: *Tableau*, 131.
29 The testimony of Jeannette d'Abadie, de Lancre's star witness, places the commission in Ciboure on 16 September: *Tableau*, 132. The two known executions associated with Ciboure of two priests may have been carried out in Bayonne where they were defrocked: *Tableau*, 447.
30 *Tableau*, 419. The principal victim was an elderly priest called Arguibel, executed in Ascain 'pour servir d'exemple'. De Lancre inspected the priest's home: *Tableau*, 455. References to teenage witnesses interrogated at Ascain suggest the execution of at least one female witch: *Tableau*, 96, 100.
31 BnF, Dupuy 42, fol. 63r–v places the commissioners in Cambo-les-Bains on 4 October. The same date is also given in *Tableau*, 461. A Bayonne document concerning the reimbursement of the cost of wine and fish sent to Cambo is dated 5 October 1609: AD-64, Bayonne, CC 306, fol. 49. The document suggests that the commission's travels were carefully planned.
32 The commission heard from Marie de Marigrane from Biarritz, a girl who testified that all witches from Biarritz had a devil's mark in their eye, and a woman 'pleurant aussi amerement que ie vi iamais creature': *Tableau*, 139, 217, 184, 92. On the devil's mark, see also *L'Incrédulité*, 37.

33 De Lancre later declares to have heard testimony from witches 'en dix diverses Parroisses de Labour': *L'Incrédulité*, 50. This reconstruction fits other lists of places visited in de Lancre's writings: *L'Incrédulité*, 36; *Tableau*, 456.
34 *Tableau*, 76. That they were brought to Saint-Pée is an educated guess based on the testimony provided.
35 BnF, Dupuy 42, fol. 63r.
36 For the figure of twenty-seven parishes: *Tableau*, 30. The precise number changed over time. See the useful maps in Goyhenetche, *Histoire générale du Pays Basque*, 2:161–2.
37 De Lancre referred to a witch brought to Bayonne: *L'Incrédulité*, 125. This may be how de Lancre came to interrogate and execute an unnamed 48-year-old female witch from the village of Villefranque, whose mother remained imprisoned in Bordeaux: *Tableau*, 96–7.
38 The point about jurisdiction is made in a letter to the Suprema: AHN, Inq., Lib. 794, fol. 461r. Logroño, 25 August 1609.
39 *Tableau*, 382.
40 *Tableau*, sig. ẽ3r.
41 *Tableau*, 115, 96.
42 *Tableau*, 95, 140.
43 For Catherine de Naguille from Ustaritz, see *Tableau*, 66.
44 *Tableau*, 382, sig. ẽ3r.
45 See the 'Second Report of Salazar to the Inquisitor General', dated Logroño, 24 March 1612. *Salazar Documents*, 345. The printing privilege for the *Tableau* is dated 13 May 1612: *Tableau*, sig. ã2v.
46 Different historians have arrived at different counts, without providing a breakdown: for example, Bordes, 'Recherches sur la sorcellerie', 108–10, concludes that there were only few, but high-profile executions. I have compared my list with that compiled by Zintzo-Garmendia, *Histoire de la sorcellerie*, 753–6. I include the execution of Marissans de Tartas (*Tableau*, 71) and omit that of Catherine de Moleres, as she was executed in Bordeaux. My list also contains the wife of Petry d'Aguerre; according to de Lancre, 'Petry d'Aguerre, sa femme et toute sa famille, la plus part desquels ont esté depuis executez à mort pour sorcellerie': *Tableau*, 108.
47 The only named witch from Saint-Jean-de-Luz, Marie Borne, freely confessed and accused others: *Tableau*, 117. The 1613 edition identifies two further Saint-Jean-de-Luz witches as Marie Martin and Graci Doihaugaray: *Tableau* (1613), 347–8. Martin is recorded as imprisoned in Bayonne, but her ultimate fate is not recorded.
48 The case of Jeanne Mondens which will be discussed further below.
49 AHN, Inq., Lib. 794, fol. 458r. San Sebastian, 24 July 1609; *Tableau*, 456.
50 The practice had become standard in the Parlement of Paris, where it was used to preserve decorum and the criminal's soul: Soman, 'La justice criminelle aux XVIe–XVIIe siècles', 30.
51 Three teenagers (one aged twelve, two aged thirteen) arrived in Logroño from Saint-Pée, as well as two adults from Ustaritz, in August 1610: AHN, Inq., Lib. 835, fol. 443r. On the boy from Ustaritz, see AHN, Inq., L. 1679, exp. 2, image 213.
52 *Tableau*, 419, gives a total figure of seven, but the math suggests three executions and five further arrests.
53 *Tableau*, 420, 423. The fate of his mother and sisters is not recorded.
54 AD-64, Ustaritz GG 2–9, fols 125–6.

# Chapter 8

1. *Tableau*, 139.
2. *Tableau*, 97.
3. *Tableau*, 141–2.
4. *L'Incrédulité*, 9 (*Advertissements*).
5. A French version of the poem, retitled 'le sabbat', was included in *L'Incrédulité*, 44–51 (*Advertissements*).
6. Blécourt, 'Sabbath Stories', 85, uses the engraving as its starting point to make this point.
7. Bailey, trans., *Origins of the Witches' Sabbath*; Ostorero, *Le diable au sabbat*; Boureau, *Satan the Heretic*.
8. *Tableau*, sig. ẽ1r.
9. Zika, 'The Transformation of Sabbath Rituals'.
10. For example, Briggs, *The Witches of Lorraine*, 137.
11. Machielsen and Maus de Rolley, 'The Mythmaker of the Sabbat'.
12. Henningsen, *The Witches' Advocate*, 62, 67.
13. Ginzburg, *Ecstasies*, 137.
14. Roper, *Oedipus and the Devil*, 20.
15. AHN, Inq., Lib. 835, fol. 386r.
16. Homza, 'Deliberations on the Reality and Heresy of Witchcraft'.
17. Henningsen, *The Witches' Advocate*.
18. Published as Idoate, *Un documento*.
19. The first group of four women had been taken to Logroño by unidentified Inquisition officials and was imprisoned on 27 January 1609, the second group of three women and three men arrived in Logroño around 6 February: Henningsen, *The Witches' Advocate*, 52, 55.
20. AHN, Inq., Lib. 835, fol. 388r; Inq., Lib. 832, fol. 170r.
21. For these dates, see Henningsen, *The Witches' Advocate*, 61–5, 69.
22. The point about geography was well made by Valle in his letter of 20 August 1609: AHN, Lib. 794, fol. 459r.
23. Tolosa, AGG-GAO, JD IM 2/21/16, fol. 3.
24. AHN, Inq., L. 1679, exp. 2., image 1.
25. On the dialect, see Azurmendi, *Las brujas de Zugarramundi*, 13.
26. AHN, Inq., Lib. 794, fol. 434r. Urdax, 8 September 1609.
27. Idoate, *Un documento*, 85. Also reported in AHN, Inq., Lib. 835, fol. 391r.
28. AHN, Inq., Lib. 835, fol. 397v.
29. AHN, Inq., Lib. 835, fol. 388v; and again with slightly different details on fol. 391r.
30. Idoate, *Un documento*, 165.
31. Idoate, *Un documento*, 85; also reported in AHN, Inq., Lib. 835, fol. 391r.
32. AHN, Inq., Lib. 835, fols 391r, 397v.
33. Azurmendi, *Las brujas de Zugarramundi*, 37–8.
34. *Salazar Documents*, 109, 111.
35. Idoate, *Un documento*, 149, suggests that there were more than fifty people present.
36. See also Henningsen, *The Witches' Advocate*, 32–6.
37. On the 'quatro processos de Brujas' sent to Madrid, see the letter from Becerra and Valle to the Suprema, Logroño, 22 May 1609: AHN, Inq., L. 1679, exp. 2,

image 179; these confessions accompanied a letter dated Logroño, 13 February 1609: AHN, Inq., L. 1679, exp. 2, images 219–20.
38  The list of fourteen questions was sent on 11 March 1609: AHN, Inq., L. 1679, exp. 2, image 115 (for the accompanying letter) and 117–19 (for the questions). Regarding the possible reality of the sabbat, see for example, question 5 asking where they left their clothes if they went to the sabbat naked. Question 12 – 'si tenian por cierto que van corporalmente a las d[ic]has juntas' – makes the *Suprema*'s preoccupation with the reality of the sabbat crystal clear.
39  On these familial links, see Azurmendi, *Las brujas de Zugarramundi*, 69. One Logroño pamphlet described the Zugarramurdi prisoners as one large family: 'madres y hijas, y muy emparentados unos con otros': Fonseca, *Relacion*, 4.
40  Although elsewhere listed as a neat eighty years of age, Graciana herself testified that she was 'muy vieja, y que tenia mas de ochenta años': AHN, Inq., Lib. 835, fol. 389r.
41  Henningsen, *The Witches' Advocate*, 55.
42  Azurmendi, *Las brujas de Zugarramundi*, 40.
43  They, at first, told the inquisitors that they made their public confessions: 'por miedo y temor': AHN, Inq., Lib. 835, fol. 388r. For the arrival of a vigilante group of twelve people, see AHN, Inq., Lib. 832, fol. 172r.
44  We can still hear echoes of their original deliberations in Idoate, *Un documento*, 68.
45  AHN, Inq., L. 1679, exp. 2, image 220.
46  AHN, Inq., L. 1679, exp. 2, image 179. Dated 22 May 1609.
47  Idoate, *Un Documento*, 149.
48  Graciana's second daughter María de Yriarte was heard 'muchas vezes' to exclaim 'Joan Gaicoa, Joan Gaicoa' ['evil Lord, evil Lord'] during her interrogation, which was interpreted as the devil preventing her from speaking: AHN, Inq. libro. 835, fol. 388r.
49  *Tableau*, 382.
50  Henningsen, *The Witches' Advocate*, 170–1; Homza, *Village Infernos*, 38.
51  For example, AHN, Inq., Lib. 832, fol. 170v.
52  *Tableau*, 567–8. The exception was María de Zozaya from Errenteria, who had confessed but whose crimes were too notorious to be pardoned: Henningsen, *The Witches' Advocate*, 167. She passed away in prison, but her bones were still committed to the flames: *Relacion*, sig. A2v.
53  Henningsen, *The Witches' Advocate*, 150. For their sentences, see 198–9 (table 5).
54  On this engraving, see Swan, 'The "Preparation for the Sabbath"'.
55  The engraving included instructions for book binders to insert it 'au Discours 4. du 2. Livre, entre les pages 118 et 119'.
56  *Salazar Documents*, 115; AHN, Inq., Lib. 835, fols 386v, 388v. For the depiction of the devil 'en figura de cabron', see fol. 389r, or for the devil alternating between the two 'unas bezes parece de hombre y otras de cabron': fol. 390r.
57  *Tableau*, 72.
58  For the 'ymperio' of the queen of the Zugarramurdi sabbat, see AHN, Inq., Lib. 835, fol. 387r, according to which she 'siempre asiste allado del demonio'; on her being seated beside the devil, see fol. 398r. On the queen being at the devil's side, see also *Tableau*, 121.
59  *Tableau*, 125.
60  AHN, Inq., Libr. 835, fol. 387v, describes Miguel de Goiburu, the king of the sabbat, as 'el mas antiguo y primero de todos los bruxos barones'; see also Goiburu's own description on fol. 390v.

61  For example, Idoate, *Un documento*, 48, where several witches confess to having been introduced to the cult by their mother or father; AHN, Inq., Lib. 832, fols 170v–1r; AHN, Inq., Lib. 835, fols 388r, 389r, 396v–7r. For the term 'witches dynasties', see Idoate, *Un documento*, 35; Henningsen, *The Witches' Advocate*, 34–6.
62  *Salazar Documents*, 119; AHN, Inq., Lib. 832, fol. 173v.
63  Henningsen, *The Witches' Advocate*, 533.
64  For Ansugarlo, see *Tableau*, 131; see also 94, 209.
65  *Tableau*, 73; *Salazar Documents*, 117.
66  AHN, Inq. Libro 835, fol. 386v; *Tableau*, 72, 128, 133.
67  For examples of toads in the Zugarramurdi testimony: AHN, Inq., Lib. 835, fols 388v, 390r–v; AHN, Inq., Lib. 832, fol. 173r; *Salazar Documents*, 117. For French toads: *Tableau*, 75.
68  Idoate, *Un documento*, 103.
69  *Tableau*, 130, and also 136, 195. See similarly *Salazar Documents*, 125.
70  For children being taken to the sabbat until they reach the age of discretion: AHN, Inq., Lib. 835, fol. 390r. For them being admitted 'en la dignidad de hacer ponzoñas': *Salazar Documents*, 117. On the senior witches making potions in secret, see *Tableau*, 132. On the 'apprentissage' of witches, see also 131.
71  Millar, *Witchcraft, the Devil, and Emotions*, 56–9; Wilby, *Invoking the Akelarre*, 61–77, rather undersells the significance of the devil's role.
72  For example, AHN, Inq., Lib. 835, fols 388v, 389r, 389v, 390r; see also Lib. 832, fol. 171r.
73  *Tableau*, 135, and repeated on 491.
74  On receiving a toad the size of a pigeon or a chicken, see Idoate, *Un documento*, 103, 105. On children not being allowed to approach the 'gros' toads: *Tableau*, 131; on dancing with toads: 133, 210; on children being punished for mistreating toads: 114.
75  *Salazar Documents*, 117.
76  *Tableau*, 127, 137; *Salazar Documents*, 119, also 117, 127.
77  For the toad-finding expeditions, see *Salazar Documents*, 125; AHN, Lib. 835, fols 392r–v.
78  That Lapurdi witches also made potions at home can be deduced from a passing comment: *Tableau*, 132.
79  AHN, Inq., Lib. 835, fol. 397r; *Salazar Documents*, 123. For the Labourd, see the testimony of Jeannette de Belloc, or Atsoua: *Tableau*, 242.
80  AHN, Inq., Lib. 835, fol. 387r; *Tableau*, 460, 461.
81  *Salazar Documents*, 121.
82  *Tableau*, 126.
83  Idoate, *Un documento*, 164; *Salazar Documents*, 123; *Tableau*, 90, 462. On collections for witches, see 458.
84  See for example, AHN, Inq., Lib. 835, fol. 398r; and Inq., Lib. 832, fol. 171r.
85  *Salazar Documents*, 109.
86  *Tableau*, 128, 135.
87  *Tableau*, 90.
88  Idoate, *Un documento*, 137.
89  On the specific point of stronger teeth: AHN, Inq., Lib. 835, fol. 399v. For the digging up and consuming of witches: Idoate, *Un documento*, 139–40; *Salazar Documents*, 131; AHN, Inq., Lib. 835, fols 399r–v; AHN, Inq., Lib. 832, fols 171v, 173v.
90  *Tableau*, 196.

91 *Tableau*, 107–8. Rojas describes it as one of the two principal themes of witchcraft in Navarre: Rojas, 'Bad Christians and Hanging Toads', 245.
92 AHN, Inq., Lib. 835, fol. 397v; *Salazar Documents*, 121; *Tableau*, 90.
93 See the 1595 testimony excerpted in Rojas, 'Bad Christians and Hanging Toads', 198. For the identification, see Wilby, *Invoking the Akelarre*, 306–8.
94 For a fuller, heroic, but, in my view, not persuasive attempt at reconstructing the origins of Basque sabbat testimony, see Wilby, *Invoking the Akelarre*.
95 *Tableau*, 127, 207, 130.
96 *Tableau* (1613), 119.
97 *L'Incrédulité*, 111.
98 For an analysis of the intruder narrative, see Torquetti dos Santos, 'Demonologia e a narrativa do intruso'.
99 *Tableau*, 89–90.
100 *Tableau*, 210.
101 Idoate, *Un documento*, 85; AHN, Inq., Lib. 835, fol. 388v.
102 AHN, Inq., Lib. 835, fol. 391r.
103 Idoate, *Un documento*, 85.
104 AHN, Inq., L. 1679, image 118; for another example, see AHN, Inq., Lib. 835, fol. 397r.
105 Rojas, 'Bad Christians and Hanging Toads', 213; *Tableau*, 108; Patlapin, *Sorginak*, 41–2.
106 Idoate, *Un documento*, 85; AHN, Inq., Lib. 835, fol. 391r identifies the girl as coming from 'Trapaça en Francia'.
107 Idoate, *Un documento*, 162–3.
108 Idoate, *Un documento*, 157–62.
109 *Tableau*, 58, 214–15, 226–32.
110 See the examples given in *Tableau*, 100–5.
111 *Tableau*, 134, 223, 232.
112 Idoate, *Un documento*, 144–7; Henningsen, *The Witches' Advocate*, 400, 402 (case no. 45, 46, 74).
113 *Tableau*, 71, 76, 73.
114 *Tableau*, 217, 225, 217, 224. As stables were rare, even bestiality with animals was a surprisingly public crime.
115 *Tableau*, 223, 134, 224, 225
116 *Tableau*, 206, 207–8. Emphasis added.
117 *Tableau*, 208, 202. On these dances, see also Zika, 'The Transformation of Sabbath Rituals'.
118 *Tableau*, 210, 211.
119 Homza, 'When Witches Litigate'.
120 Henningsen, *The Witches' Advocate*, 175–80; and chap. 11.
121 *Tableau*, 223; see also 403.
122 *Tableau*, 216.
123 *Salazar Documents,* 125.
124 *Tableau*, 217.
125 They both mention each other: AHN, Inq., Lib. 832, fols 171v, 173v.
126 AHN, Inq., Lib. 832, fols 170v, 171v, 173v; Inq., Lib. 835, fol. 398v; Idoate, *Un documento*, 143. See also Henningsen, *The Witches' Advocate*, 154, for a later homosexual encounter with the devil.
127 *Tableau*, 115.

# Chapter 9

1. The girl's name is given in *Salazar Documents*, 107.
2. Griffiths, 'Crime and Disorder'.
3. Idoate, *Un documento*, 59.
4. According to another source, María was a member of the witches' sect for eighteen months and left the sect in the summer of 1608: *Salazar Documents*, 107, 109.
5. Idoate, *Un documento*, 75.
6. The exception is Jeanette d'Abadie.
7. For instance, Abadie was 'transportee' to the sabbat by a witch called Gratiane for four years: *Tableau*, 94.
8. For a historiographical survey, see Maza, 'The Kids Aren't All Right'. For a good introduction to early modern childhood, see French, *Early Modern Childhood*.
9. McGowan, 'Pierre de Lancre's *Tableau*', 192.
10. See for example, French, *Children of Wrath*.
11. Homza, *Village Infernos*, 99.
12. *Tableau*, sig. ã3v.
13. La Fontaine, *Speak of the Devil*, 115.
14. See for example, *Tableau*, ed. Scholz Williams, xxxv.
15. *Tableau*, 563.
16. *Tableau*, 306, although the warning originally comes from President Daffis.
17. La Fontaine, *Speak of the Devil*, ix–x, 116–18.
18. Cheit, *The Witch-Hunt Narrative*.
19. Harris, *Child Psychology in Twelve Questions*, esp. 190.
20. Crouzet, *Les enfants bourreaux*; Goswami, *Child Psychology*, 70–2.
21. *Tableau*, sig. ẽ3v, ẽ3r.
22. The number of 'plus de' six hundred persons was already reported by René Veillet (1639–1713), which drew on de Lancre's *Tableau*; Veillet, *Recherches sur la ville et sur l'église de Bayonne*, 190.
23. *Tableau*, sig. ã3v.
24. Homza, 'When Witches Litigate'.
25. Idoate, *Un documento*, 73.
26. Homza, *Village Infernos*, 31.
27. Idoate, *Un documento*, 54.
28. *Tableau*, 189. The unnamed teacher had fled to Lower Navarre ahead of the commission's arrival.
29. *Tableau*, 195, 96, see also the estimate on 120.
30. *Tableau*, 94, 134.
31. *Tableau*, 195.
32. *Tableau* (1613), 217.
33. *Tableau*, 73.
34. AD-33, 1 B 19, fols 123v–24v.
35. *Tableau*, 116.
36. *Tableau*, 141. The two girls, seventeen or eighteen years of age, were Margueritte and Lisalde, respectively, no last names given.
37. *Tableau*, 116, 126.

38 Two of the three priests executed, Arguibel and Migalena, were in their late sixties or seventies; Petry d'Aguerre was seventy-three years old; the unnamed father from Villefranque was eighty. In Zugarramurdi, Graciana de Barrenechea was in her eighties, as was Estevania de Navarcorena, who was part of the first group taken to Logroño: *Salazar Documents*, 133.
39 *Tableau*, 185–6.
40 *Tableau*, 135.
41 *Tableau*, 115.
42 *Tableau*, 126.
43 Barkham, *Aspects of Life*, 19.
44 *Tableau*, 223; for her execution, see 459.
45 *Tableau*, 66, 76.
46 *Les coustumes generalles de la ville et cité de Bayonne*, 46, 13. The minimum age to make a will applied to emancipated minors only.
47 The minimum testamentary age in the Labourd was fifteen for emancipated minors, and eighteen for others: *Les coustumes generalles*, 22. The rules governing the sale of property were considerably more restricted still.
48 *Tableau*, 551, 552.
49 For example, *Tableau*, 114, 422, 430, 562.
50 *Tableau*, 115, 179, 551.
51 See *Tableau* (1613), 364, for one rare exception.
52 *Tableau*, 429–30. De Lancre is referring to the two Ciboure priests.
53 Henningsen, *The Witches' Advocate*, 130–1.
54 BnF, Dupuy 42, fols 63r, 55r.
55 Communay, *Le Conseiller Pierre de Lancre*, 53 (appendix III).
56 *Tableau*, 461.
57 BnF, Dupuy 42, fols 56r, 62v.
58 BnF, Dupuy 42, fol. 66v.
59 *Tableau*, 72.
60 BnF, Dupuy 42, fols 54r, 60v.
61 Communay, *Le Conseiller Pierre de Lancre*, 53.
62 *Tableau*, 69, 142.
63 *Tableau*, 461–2.
64 *Tableau*, 91.
65 *Tableau*, 92, 57.
66 *Tableau*, 403, 400, 405–6.
67 *Tableau*, 399–400, 39, 402, 216, 403.
68 Henningsen, *The Witches' Advocate*, 135–6; *Salazar Documents*, 75; Homza, *Village Infernos*, 64, 102, 133.
69 AHN, Inq., Lib. 795, fol. 16v. Logroño, 13 November 1610.
70 According to de Lancre, the appointment was approved by the Bishop of Bayonne acting as the priest's diocesan bishop: *Tableau*, 405, 406, whereas Hualde would have been subject to the bishop of Pamplona. Hualde's appointment as an Inquisition commissioner also places him in Vera in late September/early October 1609, well before the commission's term ended: Henningsen, *The Witches' Advocate* 486n121.
71 *Tableau* (1613), 349.
72 *Tableau*, 186.

73 *Tableau*, 186, 187, 186. On the witch's or devil's mark, see Dauge-Roth, *Signing the Body*, chap. 1. Acupuncture may form a helpful parallel. While its needles provoke the release of natural opioids, they also stimulate receptors that drown out other pain sensations. I would like to thank Prof. Ann Taylor of the Cardiff University's School of Medicine for discussing this passage with me.
74 Beam, 'Local Officials and Torture', 78–80; Soman, 'La justice criminelle aux XVIe–XVIIe siècles', 38–49.
75 *Tableau*, 406, 430.
76 *Tableau*, 184, 185.
77 Goodare, 'The Scottish Witchcraft Panic of 1597', 58–60.
78 Rojas, 'Bad Christians and Hanging Toads', 72, 101.
79 *Salazar Documents*, 157, 159.
80 AHN, Inq., Lib. 835, fol. 356r.
81 *Tableau*, 185.
82 *Tableau* (1613), 364.
83 Henningsen, *The Witches' Advocate*, 249.
84 *Tableau*, 38, 39, 38.
85 *Tableau*, 190.
86 *L'Incrédulité*, 35.
87 *Salazar Documents,* 151.
88 Homza, *Village Infernos*, 21–3.
89 *Tableau*, 73, 190; for concrete examples, 100–1 and 102.
90 *L'Incrédulité*, 110.
91 *Tableau*, 76.
92 *Tableau*, 114, 68.
93 *Tableau*, 68, 114; on the number of witnesses, see 96.
94 *Tableau*, 97–8, 96, 98.
95 *L'Incrédulité*, 547.
96 *Salazar Documents*, 151.
97 See de Lancre's praise for Catherine d'Arreioüaque: *Tableau*, 96.
98 *Salazar Documents*, 109.
99 *Tableau*, 130.
100 De Lancre lists thirteen witnesses against the older priest, Migalena, and ten against Bocal: *Tableau*, 423. For Abadie's testimony, see 135.
101 Sabbats were held in two 'Eglises ou chappelles': *Tableau*, 60, including 'l'Eglise de Dordach', tellingly located on the border with Spain: 69.
102 *Tableau*, 60, 419.
103 *Tableau*, 462.
104 *Tableau*, 471.
105 *Tableau*, 96, 97.
106 *Tableau*, 106 (Marie de Marigrane), 143 (Marie de la Rat), 108, 66 (Marie and Catherine de Naguille), 71, 73 (Marie and Johannès d'Aguerre).
107 *Tableau* (1613), 117.
108 *Tableau* (1613), sig. ĩ4r.
109 *Tableau* (1613), sig. ĩ4v.

# Chapter 10

1. Henningsen, *The Witches' Advocate*, 393.
2. For example, Labat, *Sorcellerie?*, 35.
3. *Tableau*, 117.
4. Delorme, 'Les Récollets de l'Immaculée-Conception', 651.
5. *Tableau* (1613), sig. õ1r–v.
6. *Tableau*, 141.
7. *Tableau* (1613), sig. ĩ4v–õ1r; as well as *Tableau*, 141.
8. *Tableau*, 142.
9. See the added detail in *L'Incrédulité*, 547.
10. *Tableau*, 142–3.
11. The same claim was made for the similarly inviolate King James VI of Scotland: *Newes from Scotland*, sig. C4v.
12. *Tableau*, 141, 140.
13. *L'Église de Saint-Pée-Sur-Nivelle*, 6.
14. *Tableau*, 141.
15. *Tableau*, 196.
16. Henningsen, *The Witches' Advocate*, 250.
17. *L'Incrédulité*, 547. De Lancre may well have meant Ségure.
18. *Tableau*, 141.
19. *Tableau* (1613), sig. õ1r, sig. ĩ4v.
20. *Tableau*, 458, 70.
21. Rare examples are *Tableau*, 91, 114.
22. The Chateau du Ha discussed above.
23. *Tableau*, 143–5.
24. *Tableau*, 144; see also *L'Incrédulité*, 43–4, which paradoxically took her testimony as proof of the fact that the devil could not conjure up fake innocents at the sabbat (because these statues did not move).
25. *Tableau*, 144–5.
26. *Tableau*, 116–17.
27. Behringer, *Witchcraft Persecutions in Bavaria*, 189–90, 192, 205, 228–9.
28. AD-64, Bayonne FF 58, doc. 84; transcribed in Bordes, 'Recherches sur la sorcellerie', 223–5 (appendix XI).
29. Bordes, 'Recherches sur la sorcellerie', 223.
30. AD-64 Bayonne, BB 18, fol. 70.
31. Marie would place the visit 'environ cincq sepmaines' before the date of her testimony, which would put it around 21 September: Bordes, 'Recherches sur la sorcellerie', 223.
32. Bordes, 'Recherches sur la sorcellerie', 106.
33. *Tableau*, sig. ã3v.
34. Bordes, 'Recherches sur la sorcellerie', 223.
35. Bordes, 'Recherches sur la sorcellerie', 224.
36. Bordes, 'Recherches sur la sorcellerie', 225.
37. Roper, *Witch Craze*.
38. AD-64, Bayonne FF 58, doc. 85, which gives the two sisters' names as Marie and Marthe de Lalande.
39. AD-64, Bayonne FF 58, doc. 79, fol. 2r, a pleading on behalf of two of the suspected witches, notes that Jeanne Mondens did not make these accusations

when interrogated either by the local judges or by the commissioners. This likely refers to her original trial and confession and should not be taken as a sign that she is still alive.

40 AD-64, Bayonne FF 58, doc. 85.
41 AD-64, Bayonne FF 58, doc. 78.
42 *Tableau*, sig. ã3v–4r.
43 AD-64, Bayonne FF 58, doc. 82bis.
44 Homza, *Village Infernos*, 20–1, 109–21.
45 AD-64, Bayonne FF 58, doc. 79, fol. 1r.
46 AD-64, Bayonne FF 58, doc. 79, fol. 4r; Saint-Jean-de-Luz CC 2/1, Liasse 7, fol. 9r, where Romatet is already described as 'n[ot]re conseil'.
47 AD-64, Bayonne FF 58, doc. 79, fols 1r, 2r, 4r.
48 AD-65, Bayonne FF 58, doc. 82bis, fols 3v–4r.
49 I am not alone in detecting 'une certitude de ton bien moindre, une argumentation moins assurée' in this section: Hée, 'Les rapports ambigus', 146.
50 *Tableau*, 417, 569.
51 *Tableau*, 569.
52 *Tableau*, 514, 461.
53 *Tableau*, 521, 419.
54 Bernou, *La chasse aux sorcières*, 300, described him 'dans un état voisin de l'idiotisme'; Zintzo-Garmendia, *Histoire de la sorcellerie*, 241, diagnosed him with Alzheimer's. De Lancre's claim that his 'vieillesse' could not excuse him is certainly telling: *Tableau*, 418.
55 *Tableau*, 419, 450, 492.
56 *Tableau*, 420, 422, 523, 449–50. De Lancre ambiguously refers to Bocal's confession but then contradicts himself: compare 421 and 429.
57 *Tableau*, 452.
58 *Tableau*, 448–9.
59 *Tableau*, 450–1.
60 *Tableau*, 451.
61 *Tableau*, 523, 522.

# Chapter 11

1 AHN, Inq., Lib. 794, fol. 459r, where Valle comments on the 'mucha caridad y buena Boluntad' he received from 'el padre abbad' and the convent. Urdax, 20 [August] 1609. The abbot would officially apply for the position on 8 September in an audience with Valle: AHN, Inq., Lib. 794, fol. 434r.
2 AHN, Inq., Lib. 795, fol. 75r. Urdax, 4 October 1610.
3 AHN, Inq., Lib. 795, fol. 75v.
4 Henningsen, *The Witches' Advocate*, 173–5.
5 Homza, *Village Infernos*, 43–8, 99–100.
6 Zintzo-Garmendia, *Histoire de la sorcellerie*.
7 Monter, 'Witchcraft Trials in France', 223; Pearl, *The Crime of Crimes*, 136, describes the Parlement as 'not very interested in the notion of a demonic sect'.
8 Communay, *Le Conseiller Pierre de Lancre*, 29, 37.
9 For example, Pearl, *The Crime of Crimes*, 136; more nuanced is Dusseau, *Le juge et la sorcière*, 168–9.

## Notes

10  AD-64 Bayonne FF 563, doc. 128.
11  AD-64, Bayonne BB 18, fol. 397.
12  AD-64, Bayonne FF 563 doc. 94.
13  *Tableau*, 94–5.
14  Landemont, 'Procès de sorcellerie', 54. I have not been able to locate this document.
15  Arzadún, 'Las brujas de Fuenterrabía', 175, 177.
16  Arzadún, 'Las brujas de Fuenterrabía', 176, 360–1, 372.
17  AHN, Inq., L. 1679, image 213; see also Homza, *Village infernos*, 149.
18  AHN, Inq., L. 1679, image 214.
19  AHN, Inq., L. 1679, image 471.
20  *Tableau*, 143.
21  For the length of the period, see *L'Incrédulité*, 816.
22  Champeaud, *Le Parlement de Bordeaux*, 132n2.
23  See the four cases listed in Zintzo-Garmendia, *Histoire de la sorcellerie*, 755.
24  *Tableau*, 190, 143–5. Catherine was interrogated on 3 September 1610. De Lancre does not provide her date of execution.
25  *Tableau* (1613), 363.
26  *L'Incrédulité*, 649–50. The date of Catherine's original interrogation, 13 September 1609, coincides with the commission's presence in Ciboure and Saint-Jean-de-Luz. Why or how she escaped de Lancre's hands originally is not clear.
27  AD-64, Saint-Jean-de-Luz, CC 2, Liasse 1/14, fols 1r, 2r. Their names were Marie Marchant, Jeanne D'Aguerre, Joaneta Motharena and Catherine de Sonsac. For mention of the priests' imprisonment: fol. 2v.
28  For the banishment of Jeanne d'Aguerre, see AD-64, Saint-Jean-de-Luz, CC 2, Liasse 1/14, fol. 3v. There are additional payments for her travel back to Saint-Jean-de-Luz, see fol. 4r (presumably so that she could be formally punished there).
29  AD-64, Saint-Jean-de-Luz, CC 2, Liasse 1/15, fol. 2v.
30  These are Magdeleine de Haurgues and Marie Ourdin: Saint-Jean-de-Luz, CC 2, Liasse 1, item 15, fols 4r, 5v; for Ourdin's banishment, see: Saint-Jean-de-Luz, CC 2, liasse 1, item 14, fol. 6v.
31  AD-64, Saint-Jean-de-Luz, CC 2, Liasse 1/15, fol. 3v.
32  For the group of 'vingt trois tesmoignes', see Saint-Jean-de-Luz, CC 2, Liasse 1/14, fol. 2v; for the groups of nineteen and sixteen, see Saint-Jean-de-Luz, CC 2, Liasse 1/14, fol. 5r.
33  AD-64, Saint-Jean-de-Luz, CC 2, Liasse 1/14, fol. 5r.
34  *Tableau*, 514.
35  AD-64, Saint-Jean-de-Luz, CC 2, Liasse 1/14, fol. 5r.
36  *Tableau*, 514–22. AD-64, Saint-Jean-de-Luz, CC 2 Liasse 1/14, fol. 1r; *Tableau*, 514–22.
37  On the emergence of this so-called appel comme d'abus, see Bonzon and Galland, *Justices croisées*.
38  AD-64, Saint-Jean-de-Luz, CC 2, Liasse 1/14, fol. 4v.
39  AD-64, Saint-Jean-de-Luz, CC 2, Liasse 1/14, fol. 7v, lists a payment for his return to Saint-Jean-de-Luz.
40  AD-64, Saint-Jean-de-Luz, CC 2, Liasse 1/14, fol. 9r.
41  AD-64, Saint-Jean-de-Luz, CC 2, Liasse 1/15, fols 4v (expert from San Sebastian), 6v (cleaning of the fountain), 8v.
42  AD-64, Saint-Jean-de-Luz, CC 2, Liasse 1/14, fol. 11v.

43  AD-64, Saint-Jean-de-Luz, CC 2, Liasse 1/15, fols 11r, 14r.
44  AD-64, Saint-Jean-de-Luz, CC 2/14, fol. 9r.
45  Her imprisonment in the Parlement's conciergerie can be confirmed from a payment dated 16 September 1610: AD-64, Saint-Jean-de-Luz, CC 2/1(14), fol. 03v.
46  AD-64, Saint-Jean-de-Luz, CC 2/1(14), fols 3v, 4r.
47  See Chapter 1.
48  This family tree of the Haraneder family online is particularly helpful: http://www.auribat.com/documents/hommes/familles/haraneder.htm. Last accessed 31 July 2023.
49  Lamant-Duhart, *Saint-Jean-de-Luz*, 173, 175.
50  See for example, AD-64, Saint-Jean-de-Luz CC 2, Liasse 2/3, fol. 6r; Saint-Jean-de-Luz CC 2, CC 2, Liasse 2/4, fol. 4r. The nature of the allegations against Sanson are not revealed.
51  AD-64, Saint-Jean-de-Luz, CC 2, Liasse 1/14, Saint-Jean-de-Luz CC 2, Liasse 2/3, fol. 1r.
52  *Discours prodigieux et espouventable*, 10–11.
53  For de Lancre's role as 'rapporteur', see *Tableau* (1613), 89; for the number involved: 357. The names of some of the witches are reported on 171, 187, 360.
54  *Tableau*, 361.
55  See de Lancre's discussions of the trials of François de la Bosviale and Estevene d'Audebert, executed in 1615 and 1619, respectively: *L'Incrédulité*, 38, 355, 818–29.
56  AHN, Inq., Lib. 795, fol. 16v. Logroño, 13 November 1610.
57  For modern descriptions of the event, based on the Mongastón pamphlet, see Henningsen, *The Witches' Advocate*, 184–97; Fernández de Moratín and Alonso, *Quema de brujas en Logroño*; Homza, *Village Infernos*, 40–1.
58  *Relacion*, sig. A2r; Fonseca, *Relacion*, fol. 1r.
59  AHN, Inq., Lib 795, fols 16v–17r.
60  *Relacion*, sig. A2r; Fonseca, *Relacion*, fol. 1r.
61  On the honour, see Pérez, *The Spanish Inquisition*, 161.
62  *Relacion*, sig. A2r.
63  Flynn, 'Mimesis of the Last Judgment'; Homza, *Village Infernos*, 202n86.
64  The pamphlets, discussed below, put their number at fifty-three, but the inquisitors only identified fifty-two by name in their report: AHN, Inq., Lib. 835, fols 349r–51v (partially published in *Salazar Documents*, 132–40). This list also included two witch-priests who were punished in private and therefore did not participate. A comparison between the pamphlets and the list suggests that the latter omittedr three blasphemers.
65  The higher estimate comes from a contemporary Inquisition official who linked the turn-out to the presence of the witches: Henningsen, *The Witches' Advocate*, 184. For the 'more than' 20,000 estimate, see Fonseca, *Relacion*, fol. 2v.
66  AHN, Inq., Lib. 835, fols 348v–51v; partly reproduced in *Salazar Documents*, 132–41.
67  Henningsen, *The Witches' Advocate*, 186.
68  Fonseca, *Relacion*, fol. 3v.
69  *Relacion*, sig. A2v.
70  *Relacion*, sig. A3r.
71  *Relacion muy verdadera*. The ballad also singled out María de Zozaya, a witch from Errenteria, who had passed away in prison. Her ashes were still burnt because her crimes were deemed too notorious.

72 Fonseca, *Relacion*, 42v.
73 *Relacion*, sig. A15v; Henningsen, *The Witches' Advocate*, 195.
74 Alamay, *Marci Antonii Gourguei ... parentalia ... celebrata*, 12.
75 AHN, Inq., Lib. 795, fols 16v–17r. Logroño, 13 November 1610.
76 Herrera and Pons, 'The Moriscos Outside Spain', esp. 221–2.
77 *L'Incrédulité*, 470, 463.
78 AGS, Estado K 1453, doc. 96. Dated Bera, 25 July 1612.
79 *Scaligerana*, 2:484. Scaliger mockingly noted that Gourgue adored it as if it had been the body of a saint.
80 Courbin, 'Marc-Antoine de Gourgue', 50.
81 Cruseau, *Chronique*, 1:97.
82 Le Mao, *Parlement et parlementaires*, 363.
83 Courbin, 'Marc-Antoine de Gourgue', 4.
84 Barbiche, *Les institutions de la monarchie*, 121–3.
85 AD-64, Bayonne BB 18, fol. 228. 3 October 1611.
86 Harvey, *Muslims in Spain, 1500 to 1614*, 296.
87 For the phrase, see Lomas Cortés, *El procesc de expulsión*, 59. For Philip III's motives, see esp. 27–8.
88 Vincent, 'The Geography of the Morisco Expulsion', 28; Cardaillac, 'Le passage des Morisques en Languedoc', 268. For the Morisco presence in France, see also Alaoui, 'The Moriscos in France'.
89 La Grange, *Mémoires de ... Duc de La Force*, 2:11.
90 'Expulsion des Morisques en Espagne.'
91 Ravenez, *Histoire du cardinal François de Sourdis*, 260.
92 La Grange, *émoires de ... Duc de La Force*, 2:297 (Pau, 6 August 1610), 2:303 (Pau, 11 September 1610).
93 AD-64, Bayonne BB 18, fol. 228.
94 AD-64, Bayonne BB 18, fol. 229.
95 AD-64, Bayonne BB 18, fol. 282 (25 June 1612); for the link with disease, see fol. 211 (29 August 1611). See also fols 103 (21 February 1610) and 373 (10 June 1613).
96 AD-64, Saint-Jean-de-Luz CC 2, Liasse 2/4, fol. 5r.
97 *Tableau*, 348, 350.
98 Echegaray, '¿Se establecieron los Moriscos en el país vasco de Francia?'
99 Richelieu, *Mémoires*, 24. See also Alaoui, 'The Moriscos in France', 240–4.
100 Alamay, *Marci Antonii Gourguei ... parentalia ... celebrata*, 24.
101 Al-Ḥajarī, *Kitab Nasir Al-Din*, 140.
102 See the biographical sketch in Al-Ḥajarī, *Kitab Nasir Al-Din*, 22–66.
103 Al-Ḥajarī, *Kitab Nasir Al-Din*, 154–5, 158.
104 In Bordeaux, two monks (Jesuits?) visiting the 'Judge of the Andalusians' also attempted to convert him.
105 BnF, Clairambault 362, fol. 309r. Arnéguy, 19 May 1613.
106 La Force, *Le maréchal de la Force*, 1:159–77.
107 *L'Arrivee de la royne*, 5.
108 Caro Baroja, 'Cuatro relaciones', 141.
109 *Lettre contenant av vray le discours*, 12; *Lettre du Roy*, 4; *L'Ordre prescripte des ceremonies*, 11.
110 Chabagno, 'Bertrand d'Etchauz et les problèmes de la frontière'.
111 BnF, Clairambault 362, fol. 45r.

112 Jaurgain, *La maison de Gramont*, 1:373.
113 Cruseau, *Chronique*, 84.
114 Jaurgain, *La maison de Gramont*, 1:375.
115 BnF, Clairambault 373, fol. 138r.
116 Haristoy, *Recherches historiques*, 341, who unfortunately does not cite any sources on this point. The account is, however, consistent with a declaration Gourgue himself signed on 5 October 1610: Jaurgain, *La maison de Gramont*, 1:376.
117 Paris, BnF, Clairambault 1132, fols 41r, 44r–v.
118 Jaurgain, *La maison de Gramont*, 1:379, 380–1.
119 Cruseau reports that Roquelaure visited the court in April 1611 to accuse Gramont: Cruseau, *Chronique*, 2:102.
120 Gramont, *Memoires du marechal de Gramont*.
121 AHN, Inq., L. 1679, exp. 2, image 175.

# Chapter 12

1 AHN, Inq., L. 1679, exp. 2, image 89.
2 A letter from the Logroño tribunal to Madrid, dated 25 May 1619, makes clear that the inquisitors had forwarded Isasti's 'petición' on 10 April: AHN, Inq., L. 1679, exp. 2, image 63.
3 Caro Baroja, 'Cuatro relaciones', 145.
4 Caro Baroja, 'Cuatro relaciones', 131–2.
5 Caro Baroja, 'Cuatro relaciones', 132–6. Isasti's descriptions often make it difficult to determine whether Isasti is speaking from personal experience or relating hearsay.
6 The passage forms the opening quotation of Henningsen, *The Witches' Advocate*, and the conclusion of Idoate, *La Brujería en Navarra*, 242.
7 Rilova Jericó, *Historia nocturna de Hondarribia*, 150–4.
8 Rilova Jericó, *Historia nocturna de Hondarribia*, 212; see also Rilova Jericó, 'Las últimas brujas de Europa'.
9 On 14 September 1615, the Inquisition commissioner in Bilbao sent the Logroño tribunal 'las declaraciones de dos niños de diez años' (which do not appear to have survived); a second letter, dated 26 September, informed the inquisitors that the local corregidor had obtained confessions from four adult witches. Both letters were passed on to the Suprema on 9 October: AHN, Inq., Lib. 796, fols 263–5.
10 For Salazar's role, see Homza, *Village Infernos*, 188–90; for the role of the secular courts, Zabala, *Brujería e inquisición en Bizkaia*, 81–104.
11 AGG-GAO, JD IM 4/1/15, fol. 1v. Iraeta, 18 February 1621, although it seems that an inquisitor did visit in response: AHN, Inq., Lib. 798, fol. 288r. Logroño, 24 May 1621.
12 Idoate, *La Brujería en Navarra*, 357. The letter is dated 8 April 1595; quoted in Monter, *Frontiers of Heresy*, 255.
13 Haristoy, 'Le monastère de Notre-Dame de la Paix', 17. Haristoy provides a full transcription of a 'procès-verbal' that he (dubiously) describes as the monastery's 'charte de fondation'. I have not been able to locate the original.

14 AHN, Inq., Lib. 333, fol. 147r.
15 Delorme, 'Les Récollets de l'Immaculée-Conception', 652.
16 See the inventory in Besse, *Abbayes et Prieurés* 3:30–1. Bayonne was home to several medieval monasteries; the Labourd's only foundation, the Premonstratensian Abbey of Lahonce, was still further inland.
17 For the later history, see Haristoy, 'Le monastère de Notre-Dame de la Paix', 51. Haristoy's hope that the towns of Saint-Jean-de-Luz and Ciboure would work together and transform the building into 'une belle maison d'enseignement' is only coming to fruition now.
18 Fialetti, *Briefve histoire de l'institution des ordres religieux*, 43.
19 Delorme, 'Les Récollets de l'Immaculée-Conception', 643, 647.
20 The Recollects organized themselves in 'nations', with the French 'nation' absorbing neighbouring provinces as the boundaries of France expanded under Louis XIV: Meyer, 'Pour faire l'histoire des Récollets en France'.
21 Meyer, *Pauvreté et assistance spirituelle*, 20–1, 31.
22 Haristoy, 'Le monastère de Notre-Dame de la Paix', 18 (who mentions the arrival of five friars); Delorme, 'Les Récollets de l'Immaculée-Conception', 652 (who claims Gourgue 'obtained' six friars)
23 Delorme, 'Les Récollets de l'Immaculée-Conception', 652–3.
24 Haristoy, 'Le monastère de Notre-Dame de la Paix', 18.
25 Martin, *Voyages faits en divers temps*, 22.
26 Delorme, 'Les Récollets de l'Immaculée-Conception', 652, 653.
27 Haristoy, 'Le monastère de Notre-Dame de la Paix', 19. Gourgue's 'procès-verbal' does not provide a date for the disturbance.
28 Gourgue drew up the 'procès-verbal' documenting the turbulent founding of the convent on 13 December 1612 at the request of Saint-Jean-de-Luz officials. The town's account books record the purchase of a 'barrique de vin pour bailler a Monsieur de Gourgue' on 18 December: AD-64, Saint-Jean-de-Luz CC 2, Liasse 2/3, fol. 6r.
29 Rillot, 'La noblesse labourdine', 212.
30 Nogaret, *Saint-Jean-de-Luz*, 20.
31 Delorme, 'Les Récollets de l'Immaculée-Conception', 651–2.
32 Delorme, 'Les Récollets de l'Immaculée-Conception', 651. For 'Martin de Abbas', being a 'natural desta dha villa', see Ortiz, 'El proceso inquisitorial', 569. This source also identifies Habas as being sixty years old in 1632, so Lissalde also overstated his age in the early 1610s.
33 Ortiz, 'El proceso inquisitorial', 569. A source from Saint-Jean-de-Luz, dated 29 April 1711, described Habas as the 'fondateur de ce couvent' and as a Franciscan Observant who, when he could not attract his order to Saint-Jean-de-Luz, switched to the Recollects instead: Daranatz, 'Le couvent des Récollets de Ciboure-Saint-Jean-de-Luz', 353.
34 Nelson, *The Jesuits and the Monarchy*, 31–5, 53–5.
35 ARSI, Tolos. 17, fol. 130r; *Briefve refutation*, 7.
36 ARSI, Tolos. 17, fol. 127v; *Briefve refutation*, 2.
37 AD-64, Ustaritz GG 2–9, fols 125–6.
38 ARSI, Aquit. 15-I, fol. 103r.
39 ARSI, Aquit. 15-I, fols 120r–v.
40 ARSI, Aquit. 15-I, fol. 120r.
41 One of the printing licenses by Materre's superiors is dated 12 December 1616.

42 Materra, *Doctrina Christiana*, 11–16, 107–8.
43 Materra, *Dotrina Christiana* (1623), 354–63.
44 ARSI, Francia 3, fols 67r–v. Rome, 13 August 1613.
45 ARSI, Aquit. 2-I, fol. 16r. Rome, 18 June 1613.
46 Courbin, 'Marc-Antoine de Gourgue', 101–2; Alamay, *Marci Antonii Gourguei … parentalia … celebrata*.
47 ARSI, Gal. 46-I, fol. 6r (13 August 1613), fol. 9v (5 November 1613), fol. 10v (3 December 1613); for Pierre Bienassis's admission to the Society, see Rom. 172, fol. 168v.
48 ARSI, Aquit. 2-I, fol. 1v (6 November), 13r (23 April 1613); Gal. 46-I, fol. 10v.
49 ARSI, Gal. 46-I, fol. 25v (20 May 1615).
50 *Tableau* (1613), sig. ã2v, ã3v–4r, ẽ1v–2r. Unfortunately, neither the edition nor the letter can be more precisely dated.
51 The 1603 Edict of Rouen specified that Jesuits operating in France should be citizens: Nelson, *The Jesuits and the Monarchy*, 78.
52 ARSI, Arag. 7-I, fol. 55v.
53 ARSI, Castel. 34, fols 190r–2v; Henningsen, *The Salazar Documents*, 55–6.
54 The various catalogues disagree on his age: in 1606, he was '38 or thereabouts'; in 1614, he was 48: Aquit. 9-I, fols 222r, 273r.
55 ARSI, Vitae 149, fol. 323r. That Boucher did not speak Basque is made clear by a comment in *Annuae litterae*, 521–2.
56 ARSI, Tolos. 5, fol. 42.
57 *Annuae litterae*, 522.
58 *Annuae litterae*, 523–4.
59 *Annuae litterae*, 520.
60 ARSI, Aquit. 15-I, fols 136r, 145r.
61 ARSI, Aquit. 18, fol. 155r. Bordeaux, 22 August 1616.
62 ARSI, Vitae 149, fol. 323r.
63 ARSI, Tolos. 5, fol. 65. Members who left the Society were only permitted to enter the Carthusians, a contemplative order known for its strict vow of silence: Martin, *The Jesuit Mind*, 25.
64 ARSI, Aquit. 18, fol. 191r.
65 ARSI, Castel. 8, fol. 136r.

# Chapter 13

1 AD-64, Bayonne BB 18, fol. 557. The accused were called Saucy Darrotiz and a certain 'la Malansau bearnoise', respectively.
2 AD-64, Bayonne BB 18, fols 545, 559. De Lancre reports the arrival in Bayonne of a witch from Béarn in 1618, so more may well have arrived even after this attempted expulsion: *L'Incrédulité*, 108.
3 AD-64, Bayonne BB 18, fol. 564.
4 AHN, Inq., Lib. 794, fol. 416r. Logroño, 26 July 1609. See also their earlier (misfiled) letter, which cited testimony making similar claims: AHN, Inq., Lib. 796, fols 81–2. Logroño, 22 June 1609.
5 See AHN, Inq., Lib., 794, fol. 405r, where the inquisitors endorsing Aranibar's appointment mention 'los portugeses'. Logroño, 15 September 1609.

6 See the copy of the letter that the Logroño tribunal sent their commissioner in San Sebastián: AHN, Inq., Lib. 794, fols. 419r–20r. Logroño, 28 July 1609. Ylumbe does not feature in Hugon, *Au service du Roi Catholique*.
7 AHN, Inq., Lib. 794, fol. 418r. Saint-Jean-de-Luz, 15 July 1609. The unidentified 'un buen viejo hombre de buena vivienda y catolico', writing against the Portuguese, was likely one of the few 'good' Portuguese mentioned by Ylumbe in his final Inquisition interview: AHN, Inq., Lib. 1103, fols 531r–3v.
8 AHN, Inq., Lib. 795, fols 91r–v. San Sebastián, 31 October 1609, reported to Logroño that Ylumbe had been denounced to Gramont as a Spanish spy. Ylumbe later dates his arrest to 29 September: AHN, Inq., Lib. 1103, fol. 536r.
9 AD-64, Bayonne FF 563, doc. 73 (9 October 1609), doc. 78 (1 November 1609).
10 AHN, Inq., Lib. 1103, fol. 42v; partially edited as Wilke, 'Le rapport d'un espion', 136.
11 AHN, Inq., Lib. 795, fol. 85v. Bayonne, 13 April 1610.
12 AGS, Estado K 1453, doc. 96. Bera, 25 July 1612. The precise date of Ylumbe's release is unknown, but he testified to the Logroño tribunal about his French experiences on 22 January 1611, shortly before his death: AHN, Inq., Lib. 1103, fol. 525r.
13 On these trading privileges, see Nahon, 'Communautés espagnoles et portugaises', 47.
14 Trivellato, *The Promise and Peril of Credit*, esp. chap. 4.
15 Israel, *Diasporas within a Diaspora*, 191. See also the classic Roth, *A History of the Marranos*.
16 Israel, *Diasporas within a Diaspora*.
17 Melammed, *A Question of Identity*, vii, 87, 114. See also Graizbord, *Souls in Dispute*, 8–12; Wilke, 'Un judaïsme clandestin', 281.
18 Graizbord, *Souls in Dispute*.
19 Graizbord, 'Becoming Jewish in Early Modern France', 169.
20 Aulnoy, *Relation du voyage d'Espagne*, 8.
21 Nahon, 'Communautés espagnoles et portugaises', 118.
22 Wilke, 'Un judaïsme clandestin', 283.
23 Bodian, *Hebrews of the Portuguese Nation*, chap. 5. See also Bodian's study of the four Jewish 'dogmatista' martyrs executed by the Inquisition: Bodian, *Dying in the Law of Moses*, all of whom had performed self-circumcision.
24 Zink, 'Être juif à Bayonne en 1630'. On the latter point, see Graizbord, 'Becoming Jewish in Early Modern France', 154.
25 AHN, Inq., Lib. 795, fols 337r–45v ('Relacion de veinte personas Portugueses testifiados por Judios Judayzantes … Residentes en San Ju[an] de Luz'). The letter accompanying the memo (AHN, Inq., Lib. 795, fol. 336r) is dated Logroño, 11 August 1612.
26 AHN, Inq., Lib. 795, fol. 343v.
27 Mexico City, AGN, Inquisición, vol. 378, exp. 1, fol. 287r.
28 Roth, 'Quatre lettres d'Elie de Montalte', 165.
29 AD-64, Saint-Jean-de-Luz FF 12, Liasse 3, fol. 2r.
30 Wilke, 'Le rapport d'un espion', 129.
31 Révah, 'Autobiographie d'un marrane', 68.
32 Hourmat, *Histoire de Bayonne*, 196. The years 1602 and 1610 appear to have been other flashpoints: Lamant-Duhart, *Saint-Jean-de-Luz*, 55–6.
33 Lamant-Duhart, *Saint-Jean-de-Luz*, 57.

34 Tavim, 'Amesterdão em Terras de França?', 333; these arrivals are not included in the figures included in Swetschinski, *Reluctant Cosmopolitans*, 80.
35 AD-64, Saint-Jean-de-Luz CC 2, Liasse 2/5, fols 6r, 11r.
36 Kertanguy, *Léonora Galigaï*, 15.
37 Dubost, *Marie de Médicis*, 489–93; Mongrédien, *Léonora Galigaï*, 100.
38 Horsley, *Libertines and the Law*, 205–6.
39 Mongrédien, *Léonora Galigaï*, 8. On Leonora's suffering from 'un syndrome dépressif': Dubost, *Marie de Médicis*, 479.
40 Dubost, *Marie de Médicis*, 472–4; Horsley, *Libertines and the Law*, 208.
41 Kettering, *Power and Reputation*, 63, 77.
42 Kertanguy, *Léonora Galigaï*, 209.
43 Montalto's death in February 1616 spared him from any charges. His embalmed body was transported to Amsterdam for burial, as there were no Jewish cemeteries in France.
44 Kertanguy, *Léonora Galigaï*, 204.
45 *L'Incrédulité*, 14–15 ('Advertissemens'), 491–8.
46 AD-64, Saint-Jean-de-Luz, FF 12, Liasse 3, fol. 8v; *L'Incrédulité*, 492. The two accounts differ about her age: the first describing her as 'cinquante ans ou environ', the second as 'aagée de 60. ans'. The two sources call her 'Catherine de Fernandes' and 'Catherine de Fernandos' respectively. The printed pamphlet identifies her as 'Catherine Fervandes, aagee de soixante ans': *Horrible Iugement de Dieu*, 6. A later witness puts her age at 'mas de setenta años': AHN, Inq., L. 171, exp. 4, fol. 61r.
47 *Horrible Iugement de Dieu*. This pamphlet curiously post-dates the incident by one day, putting Catarina's death on 20 March, perhaps in order to position her 'sacrilege' on 19 March, the feast of 'S. Ioseph espoux de nostre Dame': *Horrible Iugement de Dieu*, 6.
48 *L'Incrédulité*, 492.
49 AD-64, Saint-Jean-de-Luz, FF 12, Liasse 3, fol. 11r; *L'Incrédulité*, 492. The two accounts slightly differ on the length of Catarina's stay prior to the incident: twenty days or a month.
50 Doihadard's longer statement has been printed three times: Webster, 'Hebraizantes Portugueses de San Juan de Luz en 1619'; Haristoy, 'Une juive brulée'; Haguenauer, 'Un autodafé à Saint-Jean-de-Luz'. All are rare and are problematic for different reasons.
51 *L'Incrédulité*, 492, acknowledges the Paris news pamphlet and produced the letter because it offered 'plus de certitude'. The letter could have circulated only in manuscript. The officials of Saint-Jean-de-Luz paid to have two copies made of the 'la l[ett]re que M[onsieur] le Vicaire G[e]n[er]al avoict escrit a M[onsieur] l'evesque sur le faict de la Portugaisse': AD-64, Saint-Jean-de-Luz, CC 2, Liasse 2/6, fol. 6r.
52 *L'Incrédulité*, 492–3.
53 AD-64, Saint-Jean-de-Luz, FF 12, Liasse 3, fol. 1v.
54 See the entries in AD-64, Saint-Jean-de-Luz, CC 2, Liasse 1/14, fols 2v, 8v, 9r.
55 AD-64, Saint-Jean-de-Luz, FF 12, Liasse 3, fol. 1v.
56 AD-64, Saint-Jean-de-Luz, FF 12, Liasse 3, fols 6v–7r. The assistant's name is reported differently in both versions, see *L'Incrédulité*, 493.
57 AD-64, Saint-Jean-de-Luz, FF 12, Liasse 3, fol. 7r.
58 On the blood libel, see in particular: Teter, *Blood Libel*. For de Lancre's comment: *L'Incrédulité*, 462.

59 AD-64, Saint-Jean-de-Luz, FF 12, Liasse 3, fol. 9r; *L'Incrédulité*, 495.
60 Zika, 'Hosts, Processions and Pilgrimages'.
61 AD-64, Saint-Jean-de-Luz, FF 12, Liasse 3, fols 5r, 7v, 11v.
62 The account books of Saint-Jean-de-Luz make it clear that the messengers were sent on foot, with money set aside for the town's Bayonne lawyer to rent a horse: AD-64, Saint-Jean-de-Luz, CC 2, Liasse 6, fol. 5v
63 Madrid, Museo Naval, Collection Vargas Ponce, vol. IX, doc. 47. San Sebastián, 29 March 1619.
64 AD-64, Saint-Jean-de-Luz, FF 12, Liasse 3, fol. 3r; *L'Incrédulité*, 494.
65 Madrid, Museo Naval, Collection Vargas Ponce, vol. IX, doc. 47.
66 AD-64, Saint-Jean-de-Luz, FF 12, Liasse 3, fols 4r, 5v.
67 Madrid, Museo Naval, Collection Vargas Ponce, vol. IX, doc. 47.
68 Bayonne, AD-64, Saint-Jean-de-Luz, FF 12, Liasse 3, fol. 5r.
69 *Horrible iugement de Dieu*, 12. This scene is set slightly later during the day and seems designed to further justify Catarina's death as 'un sacrifice à Dieu'.
70 AD-64, Saint-Jean-de-Luz, FF 12, Liasse 3, fol. 8r.
71 *Tableau*, 92.
72 Nahon, 'Communautés espagnoles et portugaises', 115. A rabidly anti-Semitic report by the Spanish spy Francisco Díaz de Medrano, from Bera, dated 25 July 1612, claimed that the Portuguese would have been killed if it had not been for the *doblones* (golden coins) they paid to Gramont 'cada dia': Simancas, Estado K 1453.
73 AD-64, Saint-Jean-de-Luz, FF 12, Liasse 3, fol. 9v.
74 *L'Incrédulité*, 496.
75 AD-64, Saint-Jean-de-Luz, FF 12, Liasse 3, fol. 10r.
76 AHN, Inq., L. 171, exp. 4, fol. 61v; partially reproduced in Ortiz, 'El proceso inquisitorial', 569.
77 AD-64, Saint-Jean-de-Luz, FF 12, Liasse 3, fol. 10v.
78 *L'Incrédulité*, 496.
79 AD-64, Saint-Jean-de-Luz, FF 12, Liasse 3, fol. 10v.
80 Madrid, Museo Naval, Collection Vargas Ponce, vol. IX, doc. 47.
81 *L'Incrédulité*, 496.
82 AD-64, Saint-Jean-de-Luz, FF 12, Liasse 3, fols 12r, 10v.
83 *Horrible iugement de Dieu*, 12.
84 *L'Incrédulité*, 496.
85 AD-64, Saint-Jean-de-Luz, FF 12, Liasse 3, fol. 11v; *L'Incrédulité*, 496.
86 *L'Incrédulité*, 496, 497.
87 *Horrible Iugement de Dieu*, 13–14, 10.
88 *L'Incrédulité*, 497–8.
89 AD-64, Saint-Jean-de-Luz, CC 2, Liasse 2/6, fols 7r, 6v.
90 AD-64, Bayonne, BB 19, fols 519, 520.
91 The witness was a certain Pedro de Echaverría: AHN, Inq., L. 171, exp. 4, fol. 64v.
92 AHN, Inq., Lib. 797, fols 496r–v.
93 AGS, Est., L. 2862. Unnumbered folio, dated 25 May 1619.
94 Zink, 'L'émergence de Saint-Esprit-lès-Bayonne'; Zink, 'Une niche juridique'.
95 The Inquisition witness discussed below suggested that some moved to 'Holanda y Zelanda': Mexico City, Archivo General de la Nación, Inquisición, vol. 378, exp. 1, fol. 293r.
96 Teter, *Blood Libel*; Rubin, *Gentile Tales*, esp. chap. 1.

97 *Mercure françois*, vol. 5 (1619), 66, 68. The pagination restarts at the beginning of each year.
98 AHN, Inq., L. 171, exp. 4, fol. 62v.
99 Lamant-Duhart, *Saint-Jean-de-Luz*, 118.

# Epilogue

1 Waters, *Cursed Britain*.
2 Chollet, *In Defence of Witches*.

# Bibliography

## Archives

Abbreviations used in the notes are indicated in brackets [ ].

### Austin, Texas, USA

*Harry Ransom Center*
   Medieval and Early Modern MS 230

### Bayonne, France

*Pôle d'archives de Bayonne et du Pays basque* [AD-64]
   Bayonne BB 17
   Bayonne BB 18
   Bayonne CC 306
   Bayonne FF 563
   Bayonne FF 58
   Ciboure, FF 2
   Saint-Jean-de-Luz CC 2
   Saint-Jean-de-Luz CC 7
   Saint-Jean-de-Luz III E 9744
   Saint-Jean-de-Luz III E 9745
   Saint-Jean-de-Luz FF 12
   Saint-Jean-de-Luz GG 2
   Saint-Jean-de-Luz GG 3
   Ustaritz GG 2–9
   1J 160/39

## Bordeaux, France

*Archives départementales de la Gironde* [AD-33]
    1 B 19
    1 B 485
    C 3813
    C 3814
    C 3891
    C 3977

*Archives de Bordeaux Métropole*
    2 S 160

## Brussels, Belgium

*Koninklijke Bibliotheek/Bibliothèque royale* [KBr]
    MS 21678

## Hondarribia, Spain

*Archivo municipal* [AMH]
    A-1-25
    A-1-26
    A-13-II-2-1
    B-1-I-5-2
    E-6-VI-6-16
    E-6-VI-6-20
    E-7-II-4-21

## London, UK

*British Library* [BL]
    Cotton MS Caligula E XI

*National Archives* [NA]
    State Papers [SP] 94/9
    SP 78/51

## Madrid, Spain

*Archivo Histórico Nacional* [AHN]
    Inq. [=Inquisición],
    l[egajo] 171, exp. 4
    l. 1679, exp. 2[1]
    lib. 333
    lib. 794
    lib. 795
    lib. 796
    lib. 797
    lib. 798
    lib. 835
    lib. 1103

*Museo Naval*
    Collection Vargas Ponce, vol. IX

## Mexico City, Mexico

*Archivo General de la Nación*
    Inquisición, 378

## Nuremberg, Germany

*Germanisches Nationalmuseum*
    MS 22474

## Pamplona, Spain

*Archivo Real y General de Navarra* [AGN]
    029603

## Paris, France

*Archives Nationales* [AN]
    MC/ET/CV/297

---

[1] Available online on PARES: https://pares.mcu.es:443/ParesBusquedas20/catalogo/description/2340978. Last accessed 1 August 2023.

*Bibliothèque de l'Institut de France*
    Godefroy 266
    Godefroid 273

*Bibliothèque nationale de France* [BnF]
    Clairambault 362
    Clairambault 1132
    Dupuy 42
    Dupuy 219
    Français 16,138

## Pau, France

*Archives départementales des Pyrénées-Atlantiques* [AD-64 (Pau)]
    C 1542
    C 1543

## Rome, Italy

*Archivum Romanum Societatis Iesu* [ARSI]
    Arag. 7-I
    Aquit. 2-I
    Aquit. 9-I
    Aquit. 15-I
    Castel. 8
    Castel. 34
    Francia 3
    Gal. 46-I
    Gal. 71
    Lugd. 18-II
    Roma 172
    Tolosa 5
    Tolos. 17
    Vitae 149

## Simancas, Spain

Archivo General de Simancas [AGS]
    Estado [Est.]
    K 1608
    K 1453
    L[egajo] 215
    L. 363
    L. 2862
    Guerra y Mar
    L. 721
    L. 725

## Tolosa, Spain

Archivo General de Gipuzkoa [AGG-GAO]
    JD IM 1/13/9
    JD IM 4/1/15
    JD IM 2/21/16

## Valladolid, Spain

Archivo de la Real Chancillería de Valladolid [ARCHV]
    pleitos civiles, Alonso Rodríguez (dep.), 241-1

## Venice, Italy

Archivio di Stato
    Senato, Dispacci, Spagna 42

# Printed sources

## Pierre de Lancre's writings (in chronological order)

*Tableau de l'inconstance et instabilité de toutes choses.* Paris: Abel L'Angelier, 1607 [*Tableau* (1607)]; 2nd edn. Paris: Abel L'Angelier, 1610 [*Tableau* (1610)].

*Tableau de l'inconstance des mauvais anges et démons où il est amplement traité des sorciers et de la sorcellerie.* Paris: Nicolas Buon, 1612; 2nd edn. Paris: Nicolas Buon, 1613.

*Modern French edition #1:* Edited by Nicole Jacques-Chaquin [Jacques-Lefèvre]. Paris: Aubier-Montaigne, 1982 [*Tableau*, ed. Jacques-Lefèvre].
*Modern French edition #2:* Edited by Jean Céard. Geneva: Droz, 2022 [*Tableau*, ed. Céard].
*German translation: Wunderbanrliche Geheimnussen der Zauberey.* s.l.: s.n., 1630.
*English translation: On the Inconstancy of Witches: Pierre de Lancre's Tableau de l'inconstance des mauvais anges et demons (1612).* Edited by Gerhild Scholz Williams. Tempe: Arizona Center for Medieval and Renaissance Studies, 2006.
*Spanish translation: Tratado de brujería vasca: Descripción de la inconstancia de los malos angelos o demonios.* Tafalla, Spain: Txalaparta, 2004.
*Le livre des princes.* Paris: Nicolas Buon, 1617.
*L'incrédulité et mescreance du sortilège plainement convaincue.* Paris: Nicolas Buon, 1622 [*L'incrédulité*].
*Du sortilège, où il est traicté, s'il est plus expedient de supprimer et tenir soubs silence les abominations et malefices des sorciers, que les publier et manifester.* s.l.: s.n., 1627.

## Other printed primary sources

Al-Ḥajarī, Aḥmad ibn Qāsim Ibn. *Kitab Nasir Al-Din Ala l-Qawm al-Kafirin = The Supporter of Religion against the Infidels.* Edited and translated by P. S. van Koningsveld, Q. Al-Samarrai and G. A. Wiegers. 2nd edn. Madrid: Consejo Superior de Investigaciones Científicas, 2015.
Alamay, Leonard. *Marci Antonii Gourguei, in supremo Burdigalensium senatu principis, parentalia in collegio burdigalensi Societatis Jesu celebrata.* Bordeaux, France: P. de La Court, 1629.
*Annuae litterae Societatis Jesu ad patres et fratres eiusdem Societatis.* Lyon, France: Claude Cayne, 1619.
Arles y Andosilla, Martin de. *Tractatus de superstitionibus, contra maleficia seu sortilegia quae hodie vigent in orbe terrarum.* Rome: Vincenzo Luchini, 1559.
Aulnoy, Marie Catherine La Mothe. *Relation du voyage d'Espagne.* The Hague, the Netherlands: Henri van Bulderen, 1691.
Automne, Bernard. *La Conférence du droict francois avec le droict romain.* Paris: Nicolas Buon, 1610.
Bacon, Francis. *Sylva Sylvarum: Or a Naturall Historie in Ten Centuries.* London: John Haviland & Augustine Mathewes, 1626.
Barakat, Robert A., ed. *The Willoughby Papers: An Historical Record of Newfoundland's First English Colony, 1610–1631.* Hopkinton, MA: s.n., c.1995.
Baroja, Pío. *La Dama de Urtubi.* Madrid: Alianza Editorial, 1993.
Bayle, Pierre. *Dictionaire historique et critique.* 4 vols. Rotterdam, the Netherlands: Reinier Leers, 1697.
Berger de Xivrey, M., ed. *Recueil des lettres missives de Henri IV.* 9 vols. Paris: Imprimerie royale, 1843–76.
Béthune, Maximilien de. *Mémoires de Maximilien de Béthune, duc de Sully.* Edited by Pierre-Mathurin de L'Ecluse des Loges. 8 vols. London: s.n., 1745.
Brunel, Antoine de. *Voyage d'Espagne: Contenant entre plusieurs particularitez de ce royaume, trois discours politiques sur les affaires du protecteur d'Angleterre, la reine de Suede, et du duc de Lorraine.* Cologne [=Amsterdam?]: Pierre Marteau, 1667.

*Calendar of the Manuscripts of the Most Hon. the Marquis of Salisbury*. Vol. 24: Addenda, 1605–1668. London: HMSO, 1976.

Caro Baroja, Julio, ed. 'Cuatro relaciones sobre la hechicería vasca'. *Anuario de la Sociedad de Eusko-Folklore* 13 (1933): 87–145.

Cell, Gillian T., ed. *Newfoundland Discovered: English Attempts at Colonisation, 1610–1630*. London: Hakluyt Society, 1982.

Chesnaye-Desbois, François Alexandre Aubert de La. *Dictionnaire de la noblesse, contenant les généalogies, l'histoire et la chronologie des familles nobles de France*. 2nd edn. Vol. 12. Paris: Antoine Boudet, 1778.

*Codex Calixtinus*. For an English translation, see https://codexcalixtinus.es/the-english-version-of-the-book-v-codex-calixtinus/. Last accessed 28 April 2024.

Coras, Jean de. *Arrest memorable du Parlement de Tolose*. Lyon, France: Antoine Vincent, 1561.

Cotgrave, Randle. *A Dictionarie of the French and English Tongues*. London: Adam Islip, 1610. http://www.pbm.com/~lindahl/cotgrave/. Last accessed 28 April 2024.

Cruseau, Étienne de. *Chronique d'Étienne de Cruseau*. Edited by Jules Delpit. 2 vols. Bordeaux, France: G. Gounouilhou, 1879.

Delorme, P. F. 'Les Récollets de l'Immaculée-Conception en Guyenne'. *Études Franciscaines* 48 (1936): 639–710.

*Discours prodigieux et espouventable de trois Espaignols et une Espagnolle, magiciens et sorciers qui se faisoient porter par les diables de ville en ville*. Paris: s.n., 1610.

*Discours tres-veritable d'un insigne voleur qui contre-faisoit le diable lequel fut pris et pendu à Bayonne au mois de decembre dernier mil six cens huict*. Troyes, France: Jean Oudot, 1609.

Échaux, Bertrand d'. *Trois lettres inédites de Bertrand d'Échaus, évêque de Bayonne*. Edited by Philippe Tamizey de Larroque. Auch, France: Félix Foix, 1879.

Espagnet, Jean d'. *La philosophie naturelle rétablie en sa pureté suivi de l'ouvrage secret de la philosophie d'Hermès*. Edited by Didier Kahn. Grez-Doiceau, Belgium: Beya, 2007.

Espagnet, Jean d'. *Le rozier des guerres, composé par le feu Roy Lois XI*. Paris: Nicolas Buon, 1616.

Espagnet, Jean d'. *The Summary of Physics Restored: The 1651 Translation with D'Espagnet's Arcanum (1650)*. Edited by Thomas Willard. New York: Garland, 1999.

'Expulsion des Morisques en Espagne (1610)'. *Études historiques et religieuses du Diocèse de Bayonne* 8 (1899): 520.

Fialetti, Odoardo. *Briefve histoire de l'institution des ordres religieux*. Paris: Adrien Menier, 1658.

Fonseca, Luis de. *Relacion summaria del auto de la fe*. Burgos, Spain: Juan Baptista Varesio, 1611.

Frommeling, Henningus. *Les mémoires de Henningus Frommeling, 1601–1614*. Edited by Charles Ruelens. Brussels: Charles Decq, 1861.

García Mercadal, José, ed. *Viajes de extranjeros por España y Portugal: desde los tiempos más remotos hasta comienzos del siglo XX*. Valladolid, Spain: Junta de Castilla y León, Consejería de Educación y Cultura, 1999.

Garibay, Esteban de. *Compendio historial de las chronicas y universal historia de todos los reynos de España*. Vol. 3. Barcelona: Sebastian de Cormellas, 1628.

Gaufretau, Jean de. *Chronique bordeloise*. Edited by Jules Delpit. 2 vols. Bordeaux, France: Charles Lefebvre, 1877–8.

Gaullieur, Ernest. *Histoire du Collége de Guyenne d'après un grand nombre de documents inédits*. Paris: Sandoz et Fischbacher, 1874.

Gramont, Antoine Charles de, III. *Memoires du Marechal de Gramont, Duc et Pair de France*. 2nd edn. 2 vols. Amsterdam: s.n., 1717.

Henningsen, Gustav, ed. *The Salazar Documents: Inquisitor Alonso de Salazar Frías and Others on the Basque Witch Persecution*. Leiden, the Netherlands: Brill, 2004.

*Horrible iugement de Dieu, tombé sur une femme juifve, pour avoir prophané le Sainct Sacrament de l'autel, Le 20. Mars 1619*. Paris: Abraham Saugrain, 1619.

Hoyarzabal, Martin de. *Les voyages aventureux du capitaine Martin de Hoyarsabal, habitant de Cubiburu, contenant les reigles et enseignemens nécessaires à la bonne et seure navigation*. Bordeaux [vere La Rochelle?]: Jean Chovin, 1579.

Idoate, Florencio, ed. *Un documento de la Inquisición sobre brujería en Navarra*. Pamplona, Spain: Editorial Aranzadi, 1972.

*Je vous écris de Saint-Jean-de-Luz et de Bidart, Guéthary, Ciboure, Socoa, Urrugne, Béoble, Hendaye, Ascain: récits et témoignages de voyageurs de 1526 à nos jours*. Urrugne, France: Pimientos, 20130.

*L'arrivee de la royne à Sainct Iean du Lud[=Luz]*. Paris: Sylvestre Moreau, 1615.

L'Estoile, Pierre de. *Mémoires-journaux*. 12 vols. Paris: Librairie des bibliophiles, 1875–99.

*L'ordre prescripte des ceremonies faictes et observees a S. Iean de Lus, à l'echange des infantes de France et l'Espagne*. Paris: Sylvestre Moreau, 1615.

La Grange, Édouard Lelièvre, ed. *Mémoires authentiques de Jacques Nompar de Caumont, duc de La Force, et de ses deux fils*. 4 vols. Paris: Charpentier, 1843.

*La puce de Madame Des-Roches: Qui Est vn Recueil de Diuers Poëmes Grecs, Latins et François*. Paris: Abel l'Angelier, 1583.

Larramendi, Manuel de. *Diccionario trilingue del castellano, bascuence, y latin*. San Sebastián, Spain: Bartholomè Riesgo y Montero, 1745.

*Le soldat navarrois*. s.l.: s.n., 1608.

*Les coustumes generalles de la ville et cité de Bayonne*. Bordeaux, France: Simon Millanges, 1576.

*Les coustumes generalles, gardees et observees au païs et bailliage de la Bourt, et ressort d'icelui*. Bordeaux, France: Simon Millanges, 1576.

*Lettre contenant av vray le discours de tout ce qui s'est passé en la ceremonie de l'eschange de la royne et de madame sur la riviere entre S. Jean de Lux et Fontarrabie*. Paris: Iean Sara, 1615.

*Lettre du Roy envoyee à messieurs les prevost des marchands et eschevins, tant sur l'eschange des infantes, qu'entree de la royne à Bayonne, et son arrivée à Bordeaux*. Paris: Sylvestre Moreau, 1615.

Martin, Barnardin. *Voyages faits en divers temps en Espagne, en Portugal, en Allemagne, en France, et ailleurs*. George Gallet, 1700.

Materra, Esteve [Materre], *Doctrina Christiana: Guiristinoac Iaquin behar dituen gauçen declaracinoa*. Bordeaux, France: Pierre de La Court, 1617. 2nd edn. *Dotrina Christiana*. Bordeaux, France: Jacques Millanges, 1623.

*Mercure françois*. 24 vols. Paris: Jean Richer and others, 1605–43. http://mercurefranc ois.ehess.fr/index.php?/categories.

Métivier, Jean de. *Chronique du Parlement de Bordeaux*. Bordeaux, France: G. Gounouilhou, 1886.

*Missale ad usum ecclesie cathedralis Baiocensis*. Paris: Regnault I Chaudière, 1543.

Montaigne, Michel de. *The Complete Works: Essays, Travel Journal, Letters*. Translated by Donald M. Frame. New York: Everyman's Library, 2003 [abbreviated as F].
Mornay, Philippe de. *Mémoires et correspondance*. Vol. 10: 1604–10. Paris: Treuttel et Würtz, 1824.
Navagero, Andrea. *Il viaggio fatto in Spagna, et in Francia*. Venice: Domenico Farri, 1563.
*Newes from Scotland Declaring the Damnable Life of Doctor Fian a Notable Sorcerer, Who Was Burned at Edenbrough in Ianuarie last. 1591*. London: William Wright, [1592].
Oihénart, Arnauld. *Les proverbes basques*. Paris: s.n., 1657.
Oihénart, Arnauld. *Notitia utriusque Vasconiae tum Ibericae, tum Aquitanicae*. Paris: Sébastien Cramoisy, 1638.
Orpustan, Jean-Baptiste, ed. 'Correspondance basque à la fin du XVI$^e$ siècle (1595–1598): 20 lettres de renseignements sur la politique de Henri IV et la fin des guerres contre la Ligue'. *Lapurdum: Euskal ikerketen aldizkaria*, no. 14 (2010): 137–62.
Pérès, Isaac de, *Chronique d'Isaac de Pérès, 1554–1611*, edited by A. Lesueur de Pérès. Agen, France: Impr. de F. Lamy, 1879.
Perrault, François. *L'anti-démon de Mascon*. 2nd edn. Geneva: Chouet, 1656.
Raemond, Florimond de. *L'Antichrist*. Lyon, France: Pillehotte, 1597.
*Recueil des choses notables, qui ont esté faites à Bayonne, à l'entreveuë du Roy treschrestien Charles Neufieme de ce nom, et la Royne sa treshonoree mere, avec la Royne Catholique sa soeur*. Paris: Vascozan, 1566.
*Relacion de las personas que salieron al auto de la fee*. [Logroño]: Juan Mongastón Fox, 1611.
*Relacion muy verdadera, donde se da larga cuenta del auto que la santa Inquisicion hizo en la cuidad de Logroño, a los ocho de Noviembre [1610], a donde fueron sacados treynta y tres bruxos y bruxas*. Logroño: Juan Mongastón, 1611.
Révah, Israël Salvator, ed. 'Autobiographie d'un marrane: Édition partielle d'un manuscrit de João (Moseh) Pinto Delgado'. *Revue des études juives* 119, no. 2 (1961): 41–130.
Richelieu, Armand Jean du Plessis, duc de. *Mémoires ... sur le règne de Louis XIII, depuis 1610 jusqu'à 1638*. Edited by Jean-Joseph-François Poujoulat. Nouvelle collection des mémoires pour servir à l'histoire de France depuis le XIII$^e$ siècle jusqu'à la fin du XVIII$^e$ siècle. Vol. 7. Paris: L'éditeur du commentaire analytique du code civil, 1837.
Roche-Flavin, Bernard de La. *Treize Livres des parlements de France*. Bordeaux, France: S. Millanges, 1617.
Rousseau, Jean-Jacques. 'Jugement sur la paix perpétuelle'. In *Collection complète des oeuvres*. Online edn (2012). http://www.rousseauonline.ch/Text/projet-de-paix-perpetuelle.php.
*Scaligerana, Thuana, Perroniana, Pithoeana, et Colomesiana, ou remarques historiques, critiques, morales et litteraires*. 2 vols. Amsterdam: Covens & Mortier, 1740.
Thou, Jacques-Auguste de. *Histoire universelle ... depuis 1543 jusqu'en 1607*. Translated by Jacques Adam et al. 16 vols. London: s.n., 1734.
Valencia, Pedro de. *Discurso acerca de los cuentos de brujas*. Obras completas. Vol. 7. Edited by Manuel Antonio Marcos Casquero and Hipólito B. Riesco Álvarez. León, Spain: Universidad de León, 1993.
Valois, Noël, ed. *Inventaire des arrêts du Conseil d'État (règne de Henri IV)*. 2 vols. Paris: Imprimerie nationale, 1886–93.

Voltaire. 'Petit commentaire de l'ignorant sur l'éloge du Dauphin de France'. In *The Complete Works*. Vol. 60c: Writings of 1766 (I), edited by James Hanrahan et al., 117–24. Oxford: Voltaire Foundation, 2013.

## Unpublished dissertations

Bordes, François. 'Recherches sur la sorcellerie dans le Béarn, les Landes, et le Labourd sous l'Ancien Régime'. École nationale des chartes, 1977.
Courbin, Elsa. 'Marc-Antoine de Gourgue, de l'héritage d'Ogier de Gourgue à la première présidence du parlement de Bordeaux'. Ecole nationale de chartes, 2010. http://www.chartes.psl.eu/fr/positions-these/marc-antoine-gourgue-heritage-ogier-gourgue-premiere-presidence-du-parlement.
Dravasa, Etienne. 'Les privilèges des Basques du Labourd sous l'ancien régime'. Université de Bordeaux, 1950.
Hawkins, Daniel B. '"Chimeras that Degrade Humanity": The Cagots and Discrimination'. Kings College London, 2014. https://www.academia.edu/15057536/Chimeras_that_degrade_humanity_the_cagots_and_discrimination.
Powis, Jonathan. 'The Magistrates of the Parlement of Bordeaux, c. 1500–1563'. University of Oxford, 1975.
Rojas, Rochelle E. 'Bad Christians and Hanging Toads: Witch Trials in Early Modern Spain, 1525–1675'. Duke University, 2016.
Torquetti dos Santos, Lívia. 'Demonologia e a narrativa do intruso: do *De la démonomanie des sorciers* ao *Tableau de l'inconstance des mauvais anges et démons*, a França e suas ficções diabólicas (1580–1613)'. Universidade Estadual de Campinas, 2021.

## Secondary literature

Alaoui, Youssef El. 'The Moriscos in France after the Expulsion: Notes for the History of a Minority'. In *The Expulsion of the Moriscos from Spain*, edited by Mercedes García-Arenal and Gerard Albert Wiegers, 239–68. Leiden, the Netherlands: Brill, 2014.
Arnold, Paul. *Le Mystère basque dévoilé*. Monaco: Éditions du Rocher, 1982.
Arzadún, Juan. 'Las brujas de Fuenterrabía: Proceso del siglo XVII; El 6 de mayo de 1611 en Fuenterrabia'. *Revista internacional de los estudios vascos* 3, no. 2 (1909): 172–81.
'Azurmendi disecciona el caso de las brujas de Zugarramurdi'. *El País*. 7 December 2013, sec. País vasco. https://elpais.com/ccaa/2013/12/07/paisvasco/1386420921_624000.html.
Azurmendi, Mikel. *Las Brujas de Zugarramundi: La historia del aquelarre y la Inquisición*. Córdoba, Spain: Almuzara, 2013.
Babelon, Jean Pierre. *Henri IV*. Paris: Fayard, 1982.
Bailey, Michael D., trans. *Origins of the Witches' Sabbath*. University Park: Pennsylvania State University Press, 2021.
Bakewell, Sarah. *How to Live, or, a Life of Montaigne: In One Question and Twenty Attempts at an Answer*. London: Chatto & Windus, 2010.
Bakker, Peter. 'Amerindian Tribal Names in North America of Possible Basque Origin'. In *'Erramu Boneta': Festschrift for Rudolf P. G. de Rijk*, edited by Xabier Artiagoitia, Patxi Goenaga and Joseba Andoni Lakarra, 105–16. Bilbao, Spain: Universidad del País Vasco, 2002.

Balsamo, Jean, and Michel Simonin, *Abel L'Angelier et Françoise de Louvain, 1574–1620*. Geneva: Droz, 2002.
Barandiarán, José Miguel de. *Brujería y brujas: Testimonios recogidos en el País Vasco*. 9th edn. San Sebastián, Spain: Txertoa, 2012.
Barbiche, Bernard. *Les institutions de la monarchie française à l'époque moderne, XVI<sup>e</sup>–XVIII<sup>e</sup> siècle*. Paris: Presses universitaires de France, 1999.
Barkham, Michael. 'French Basque "New Found Land" Entrepreneurs and the Import of Codfish and Whale Oil to Northern Spain, c. 1580 to c. 1620: The Case of Adam de Chibau, Burgess of Saint-Jean-de-Luz and "Sieur de St. Julien"'. *Newfoundland Studies* 10, no. 1 (1994): 1–43.
Barkham, Michael. 'La industria pesquera en el País Vasco Peninsular al principio de la edad moderna: ¿Una edad de ora?' *Itsas Memoria: Revista de Estudios Marítimos Del País Vasco* 3 (2000): 29–75.
Barkham, Michael. 'New Documents Concerning the French Basque Pilot, Martin de Hoyarsabal, Author of the First Detailed Rutter for the "New Found Land" (1579)'. *Newfoundland and Labrador Studies*, 2003.
Barkham, Michael. *Aspects of Life Aboard Spanish Basque Ships during the 16th Century, with Special Reference to Terranova Whaling Voyages*. [Canada]: Parks Canada, 1981.
Beam, Sara. 'Local Officials and Torture in Seventeenth-Century Bordeaux'. In *Social Relations, Politics, and Power in Early Modern France: Robert Descimon and the Historian's Craft*, edited by Barbara B. Diefendorf and Michael Wolfe, 61–86. Kirksville, MO: Truman State University Press, 2016.
Beguerie, Pantxika. *Le Pays basque de la superstition à la religion: Sanctuaires, dévotions et pèlerinages au Pays basque français depuis le Moyen Age*. Bidart, France: Ekaina, 1982.
Behringer, Wolfgang. *Witchcraft Persecutions in Bavaria: Popular Magic, Religious Zealotry and Reason of State in Early Modern Europe*. Translated by J. C. Grayson and David Lederer. Cambridge: Cambridge University Press, 1997.
Beiderbeck, Friedrich. *Zwischen Religionskrieg, Reichskrise und europäischem Hegemoniekampf: Heinrich IV. von Frankreich und die protestantischen Reichsstände*. Berlin: Berliner Wissenschafts-Verlag, 2005.
Beik, William. 'The Absolutism of Louis XIV as Social Collaboration'. *Past and Present* 188 (2005): 195–224.
Beik, William. 'The Violence of the French Crowd from Charivari to Revolution'. *Past and Present* 197 (2007): 75–110.
Bélanger, René. *Les Basques dans l'estuaire du Saint-Laurent, 1535–1635*. Montreal: Presses de l'Université du Québec, 1971.
Bély, Lucien. 'Conclusion des travaux: La paix de Vervins; fille d'Enger ou fille de Dieu?' In *Le traité de Vervins*, edited by Jean-François Labourdette, Jean-Pierre Poussou and Marie-Catherine Vignal, 557–68. Paris: Presses de l'Université Paris-Sorbonne, 2000.
Bendall, Sarah. *Shaping Femininity: Foundation Garments, the Body and Women in Early Modern England*. London: Bloomsbury, 2021.
Bergin, Joseph. *The Making of the French Episcopate, 1589–1661*. New Haven, CT: Yale University Press, 1996.
Bernou, Jean. *La chasse aux sorcières dans le Labourd (1609): étude historique*. Agen, France: Impr. Calvet & Célérié, 1897.

Besse, Jean-Martial. *Abbayes et prieurés de l'ancienne France*. Vol. 3: Provinces ecclésiastiques d'Auch et de Bordeaux. Ligugé, France: Abbaye Saint-Martin, 1910.

Blaÿ de Gaïx, Gabriel-François de. *Histoire militaire de Bayonne: De l'origine de Bayonne à la mort d'Henri IV*. Bayonne, France: Lamaignère, 1899.

Blécourt, Willem de. 'Sabbath Stories: Towards a New History of Witches' Assemblies'. In *The Oxford Handbook of Witchcraft in Early Modern Europe and Colonial America*, edited by Brian P. Levack, 84–100. Oxford: Oxford University Press, 2013.

Bodian, Miriam. *Dying in the Law of Moses: Crypto-Jewish Martyrdom in the Iberian World*. Bloomington: Indiana University Press, 2007.

Bodian, Miriam. *Hebrews of the Portuguese Nation: Conversos and Community in Early Modern Amsterdam*. Bloomington: Indiana University Press, 1999.

Bonzon, Anne, and Caroline Galland, eds. *Justices croisées: Histoire et enjeux de l'appel comme d'abus, XIVe–XVIIIe siècle*. Rennes, France: Presses universitaires de Rennes, 2021.

Boscheron des Portes, Charles. *Histoire du Parlement de Bordeaux depuis sa création jusqu'à sa suppression, 1451–1790*. 2 vols. Bordeaux, France: C. Lefebvre, 1877.

Bost, Jean, et al. *La Rhune: Pays basque*. Anglet, France: Éditions du Mondarrain, 1996.

Boureau, Alain. *Satan the Heretic: The Birth of Demonology in the Medieval West*. Chicago, IL: University of Chicago Press, 2006.

Boutcher, Warren. *The School of Montaigne in Early Modern Europe*. 2 vols. Oxford: Oxford University Press, 2015.

Boutruche, Robert. *Bordeaux de 1453 à 1715*. Bordeaux, France: Fédération Historique du Sud-Ouest, 1966.

Braudel, Fernand. *The Mediterranean and the Mediterranean World in the Age of Philip II*. Translated by Sian Reynolds. 2 vols. London: Fontana/Collins, 1972.

Briggs, Robin. 'Witchcraft and the Local Communities: The Rhine-Moselle Region'. In *The Oxford Handbook of Witchcraft in Early Modern Europe and Colonial America*, edited by Brian P. Levack, 200–16. Oxford: Oxford University Press, 2013.

Briggs, Robin. *The Witches of Lorraine*. Oxford: Oxford University Press, 2007.

Briggs, Robin. *Witches and Neighbours: The Social and Cultural Context of European Witchcraft*. 2nd edn. Oxford: Blackwell, 2002.

Brunet, Serge. *Les prêtres des montagnes: La vie, la mort, la foi dans les Pyrénées centrales sous l'Ancien Régime (Val d'Aran et diocèse de Comminges)*. Aspet, France: PyréGraph, 2001.

Busson, Henri. 'Montaigne et son cousin'. *Revue d'histoire littéraire de la France* 60, no. 4 (1960): 481–99.

Callard, Caroline. *Le temps des fantômes: Spectralités de l'âge moderne, XVIe–XVIIe siècle*. Paris: Fayard, 2019.

Cardaillac, Louis. 'Le passage des Morisques en Languedoc'. *Annales du Midi* 83, no. 103 (1971): 259–98.

Caro Baroja, Julio. 'Witchcraft and Catholic Theology'. In *Early Modern European Witchcraft: Centres and Peripheries*, edited by Bengt Ankarloo and Gustav Henningsen, 19–44. Oxford: Clarendon Press, 1990.

Caro Baroja, Julio. *The World of the Witches*. Translated by O.N.V. Glendinning. Chicago, IL: University of Chicago Press, 1988.

Carroll, Stuart. *Blood and Violence in Early Modern France*. Oxford: Oxford University Press, 2006.

Castell Granados, Pau. 'Sortilegas, divinatrices et fetilleres: Les origines de la sorcellerie en Catalogne'. *Cahiers de Recherches Médiévales et Humanistes* 22 (2011): 217–41.

Chabagno, Albert. 'Bertrand d'Etchauz et les problèmes de la frontière'. In *Autour de Bertrand d'Etchauz: Évêque de Bayonne, fin XVIe–début XVIIe siècle*, edited by Pierre Hourmat and Josette Pontet, 165–72. Bayonne, France: Société des sciences, lettres et arts de Bayonne, 2000.

Champeaud, Grégory. *Le Parlement de Bordeaux et les paix de religion, 1563–1600: Une genèse de l'Edit de Nantes*. France: Éditions d'Albret, 2008.

Charpentier, Josane. *La sorcellerie en Pays basque*. Paris: Librairie Guénégaud, 1977.

Charpentier, Louis. *Le mystère basque*. Paris: R. Laffont, 1975.

Chavarría Múgica, Fernando. 'Justicia y estrategia: Teoría y práctica de las leyes de la guerra en un contexto fronterizo; El caso de la jornada de San Juan de Luz (1558)'. *Mélanges de la Casa de Velázquez*, new series, 35, no. 1 (2005): 185–215.

Cheit, Ross E. *The Witch-Hunt Narrative: Politics, Psychology, and the Sexual Abuse of Children*. Oxford: Oxford University Press, 2014.

Chollet, Mona. *In Defence of Witches: Why Women Are Still on Trial*. Translated by Sophie Lewis. London: Picador, 2023.

Clark, Stuart. *Thinking with Demons: The Idea of Witchcraft in Early Modern Europe*. Oxford: Clarendon Press, 1997.

Cohen, Paul. 'Torture and Translation in the Multilingual Courtrooms of Early Modern France'. *Renaissance Quarterly* 69, no. 3 (2016): 899–939.

Communay, Arnaud. *Le Conseiller Pierre de Lancre*. Agen, France: Lamy, 1890.

Crouzet, Denis. *Les enfants bourreaux au temps des guerres de Religion*. Paris: Albin Michel, 2020.

Cursente, Benoît. *Les Cagots: Histoire d'une ségrégation*. Morlaàs, France: Cairn, 2018.

Daranatz, Jean-Baptiste. 'Le couvent des Récollets de Ciboure-Saint-Jean-de-Luz'. Bulletin de la *Société des Sciences, Lettres et Arts de Bayonne* 14 (1934): 351–66.

Dardano Basso, Isa. *Il diavolo e il magistrato: Il trattato Du sortilege di Pierre de Lancre, 1553–1631*. Rome: Edizioni di storia e letteratura, 2011.

Dardano Basso, Isa. *L'ancora e gli specchi: Lettura del Tableau de l'inconstance et instabilité de toutes choses di Pierre de Lancre*. Rome: Bulzoni, 1979.

Daston, Lorraine, and Katharine Park. *Wonders and the Order of Nature, 1150–1750*. New York: Zone Books, 1998.

Daston, Lorraine. 'The Nature of Nature in Early Modern Europe'. *Configurations* 6, no. 2 (1998): 149–72.

Dauge-Roth, Katherine. *Signing the Body: Marks on Skin in Early Modern France*. London: Routledge, 2019.

Davies, Surekha. *Renaissance Ethnography and the Invention of the Human: New Worlds, Maps and Monsters*. Cambridge: Cambridge University Press, 2017.

Davis, Natalie Zemon. 'On the Lame'. *American Historical Review* 93, no. 3 (1988): 572–603.

Davis, Natalie Zemon. 'The Silences of the Archives, the Renown of the Story'. In *Historical Knowledge: In Quest of Theory, Method and Evidence*, edited by Susanna Fellman and Marjatta Rahikainen, 77–96. Newcastle upon Tyne, UK: Cambridge Scholars, 2012.

Davis, Natalie Zemon. *The Return of Martin Guerre*. Cambridge, MA: Harvard University Press, 1983.

Davis, Natalie Zemon. *Trickster Travels: A Sixteenth-Century Muslim between Worlds*. London: Faber, 2007.

Delooz, Pierre. 'Towards a Sociological Study of Canonized Sainthood'. In *Saints and Their Cults: Studies in Religious Sociology, Folklore, and History*, edited by Stephen Wilson, 189–216. Cambridge: Cambridge University Press, 1983.

Delpit, Jules. 'Pierre de L'Ancre et la sorcellerie: À propos d'une rareté bibliographique'. *Bulletin du bibliophile et du bibliothécaire* 28 (1885): 81–9.

Delprat, Carole. 'Savoirs et déboires d'un juriste, Bernard de La Roche Flavin (1552–1627)'. *Histoire, économie and société* 19, no. 2 (2000): 163–84.

Desan, Philippe. *Montaigne: A Life*. Princeton, NJ: Princeton University Press, 2019.

Descimon, Robert. 'The Birth of the Nobility of the Robe: Dignity versus Privilege in the Parlement of Paris, 1500–1700'. In *Changing Identities in Early Modern France*, edited by Michael Wolfe, 95–123. Durham, NC: Duke University Press, 1997.

Desplat, Christian. 'D'un bucher à l'autre: La sorcellerie satanique avant et après l'Edit de 1682; quelques réflexions'. *Revista internacional de los estudios vascos* 9 (2012): 116–39.

Desplat, Christian. 'Henri IV et la Navarre française'. In *Provinces et Pays du Midi au temps d'Henri de Navarre, 1555–1589*, 65–90. Pau, France: Association Henri IV, 1989.

Dillinger, Johannes. 'Germany: "The Mother of the Witches"'. In *The Routledge History of Witchcraft*, edited by Johannes Dillinger, 94–112. London: Routledge, 2019.

Dop, Henry. *Les Seigneurs de Saint-Pée*. Bayonne, France: Darracq, 1965.

Douglass, William, and Jon Bilbao. *Amerikanuak: Basques in the New World*. Reno: University of Nevada Press, 1975.

Dravasa, Etienne. 'Problèmes de sorcellerie dans un pays frontalier: La mission du Conseiller Pierre de Lancre en Labourd'. In *La Frontière des origines à nos jours: Actes des journeées de la société internationale d'histoire du droit*, edited by Maïté Lafourcade, 425–44. Bordeaux, France: Presses Universitaires de Bordeaux, 1998.

Dubost, Jean-François. *Marie de Médicis: La reine dévoilée*. Paris: Payot, 2009.

Duplá, Antonio. *Presencia vasca en América, 1492–1992: Una mirada crítica*. San Sebastián, Spain: Tercera Prensa, 1992.

Dusseau, Joëlle. *Le juge et la sorcière*. [Bordeaux, France]: Editions sud ouest, 2002.

Eamon, William. *Science and the Secrets of Nature: Books of Secrets in Medieval and Early Modern Culture*. Princeton, NJ: Princeton University Press, 1994.

Echegaray, Bonifacio de. '¿Se establecieron los Moriscos en el país vasco de Francia?' *Bulletin hispanique* 47, no. 1 (1945): 92–102.

Egaña, Iñaki. 'Las brujas vascas y Lancre'. In *Tratado de Brujería Vasca: Descripción de la inconstancia de los malos ángeles o demonios*. Tafalla, Spain: Txalaparta, 2004.

Einarsson, Trausti. 'La trágica muerte de Martín de Villafranca'. In *Itsasoa: El mar de Euskalerria, la naturaleza, el hombre y su historia*, edited by Selma Huxley Barkham. Vol. 3: Los vascos en el marco Atlántico Norte: Siglos XVI y XVII, 289–94. San Sebastián, Spain: Eusko kultur eragintza etor, 1986.

Fernández de Moratín, Leandro, ed. *Quema de brujas en Logroño*. Valencia, Spain: Ediciones La Máscara, 1999.

Findlen, Paula. 'Natural History'. In *The Cambridge History of Science: Volume 3: Early Modern Science*, edited by Katharine Park and Lorraine Daston, 435–68. Cambridge: Cambridge University Press, 2006.

Findlen, Paula. *Possessing Nature: Museums, Collecting, and Scientific Culture in Early Modern Italy*. Berkeley: University of California Press, 1996.

Finlay, Robert. 'The Refashioning of Martin Guerre'. *American Historical Review* 93, no. 3 (1988): 553–71.
Flynn, Maureen. 'Mimesis of the Last Judgment: The Spanish Auto de Fe'. *Sixteenth Century Journal* 22, no. 2 (1991): 281–97.
Fogel, Michèle. *Marie de Gournay: Itinéraires d'une femme savante*. Paris: Fayard, 2004.
French, Anna, ed. *Early Modern Childhood: An Introduction*. Abingdon, England: Routledge, 2020.
French, Anna. *Children of Wrath: Possession, Prophecy and the Young in Early Modern England*. Farnham, England: Ashgate, 2015.
Gardère, J. *Les Seigneurs de Bonnut et Arsague; La Maison noble d'Amou et la famille des Caupenne*. Dax, France: Hazael Labèque, 1892.
Ginzburg, Carlo. *Ecstasies: Deciphering the Witches' Sabbath*. Translated by Raymond Rosenthal. New edn. London: Penguin, 1992.
Goodare, Julian. 'The Scottish Witchcraft Panic of 1597'. In *The Scottish Witch-Hunt in Context*, edited by Julian Goodare, 122–45. Manchester, England: Manchester University Press, 2022.
Gorosábel, Pablo de. *Noticia de las cosas memorables de Guipúzcoa o descripción de la provincia y de sus habitadores: Exposición de las instituciones, fueros, privilegios, ordenanzas y leyes*. Vol. 1. 6 vols. Tolosa, Spain: E. López, 1899.
Goswami, Usha C. *Child Psychology: A Very Short Introduction*. Oxford: Oxford University Press, 2014.
Goyhenetche, Manex. *Histoire générale du Pays basque*. 5 vols. San Sebastián, Spain: Elkarlanean, 1998–2005.
Graizbord, David. 'Becoming Jewish in Early Modern France: Documents on Jewish Comunity-Building in Seventeenth-Century Bayonne and Peyrehorade'. *Journal of Social History* 40, no. 1 (2006): 147–80.
Graizbord, David. *Souls in Dispute: Converso Identities in Iberia and the Jewish Diaspora, 1580–1700*. Philadelphia: University of Pennsylvania Press, 2004.
Greengrass, Mark. *France in the Age of Henri IV: The Struggle for Stability*. 2nd edn. London: Longman, 1995.
Green-Mercado, Mayte. *Visions of Deliverance: Moriscos and the Politics of Prophecy in the Early Modern Mediterranean*. Ithaca, NY: Cornell University Press, 2019.
Griffiths, Paul. 'Crime and Disorder'. In *Early Modern Childhood: An Introduction*, edited by Anna French, 181–96. Abingdon, England: Routledge, 2020.
Habasque, Francisque. 'Épisodes d'un procès de sorcellerie dans le Labourd au XVIIme siècle, 1605–1607'. In *Congrès de Biarritz-Bayonne: IVe congrès de l'Union Historique et Archéologique du Sud-Ouest*, 52–9. Biarritz, France: E. Soulé, 1912.
Habasque, Francisque. 'Les traités de bonne correspondance entre le Labourd, la Biscaye et le Guipuzcoa'. *Bulletin historique et philologique*, 1894, 560–74.
Haguenauer, P. 'Un autodafé à Saint-Jean-de-Luz en 1619'. *Annuaire des archives israélites*, 1902, 37–52.
Hamilton, Tom. *Pierre de L'Estoile and His World in the Wars of Religion*. Oxford: Oxford University Press, 2017.
Hamscher, Albert N. *The Royal Financial Administration and the Prosecution of Crime in France, 1670–1789*. Newark: University of Delaware Press, 2014.
Haristoy, Pierre. 'Fondation de la paroisse et de la commune de Ciboure (Basses-Pyrénées) aux XVIe et XVIIe siècles'. *Bulletin de la Société de Borda* 27 (1902): 181–92, 201–22.

Haristoy, Pierre. 'Le monastère de Notre-Dame de la Paix de Saint-Jean-de-Luz-Ciboure'. *Études historiques et religieuses du diocèse de Bayonne* 2 (1893): 16–21, 49–51.

Haristoy, Pierre. 'Les paroisses du Pays basque pendant la période révolutionnaire'. *Études historiques et religieuses du Diocèse de Bayonne* 4 (1895): 15–32.

Haristoy, Pierre. 'Les sorciers au Pays basque'. *Études historiques et religieuses du diocèse de Bayonne*, 1892, 517–25, 577–9.

Haristoy, Pierre. 'Une juive brulée par le peuple de St-Jean-de-Luz en 1619'. *Études historiques et religieuses du diocèse de Bayonne* 1 (1892): 307–19.

Haristoy, Pierre. *Recherches historiques sur le Pays basque*. 2 vols. Bayonne, France: E. Lasserre, 1883–4.

Harris, Paul L. *Child Psychology in Twelve Questions*. Oxford: Oxford University Press, 2022.

Harrison, Peter. 'Curiosity, Forbidden Knowledge, and the Reformation of Natural Philosophy in Early Modern England'. *Isis* 92, no. 2 (2001): 265–90.

Harvey, Leonard Patrick. *Muslims in Spain, 1500 to 1614*. Chicago, IL: University of Chicago Press, 2005.

Harvitt, Helen J. 'Gestes des solliciteurs: A Sixteenth Century Metrical Account of the Abuses of Law Courts, by Eustorg de Beaulieu'. *Romanic Review* 2, no. 3 (1911): 304–19.

Hée, Arnaud. 'Les rapports ambigus d'un évêque et d'un magistrat face a la sorcellerie dans le Labourd: Bertrand d'Etchauz et Pierre de Lancre'. In *Autour de Bertrand d'Etchauz: Évêque de Bayonne, fin XVIe–début XVIIe siècle*, edited by Pierre Hourmat and Josette Pontet, 139–52. Bayonne, France: Société des sciences, lettres et arts de Bayonne, 2000.

Henningsen, Gustav. 'El invento de la palabra aquelarre'. *Riev Cuadernos* 9 (2012): 54–65.

Henningsen, Gustav. *The Witches' Advocate: Basque Witchcraft and the Spanish Inquisition, 1609–1614*. Reno: University of Nevada Press, 1980.

Henrard, Paul Jean Joseph. *Henri IV et la Princesse de Condé, 1609–1610: Précis historique*. Brussels: Société de l'histoire de Belgique, 1870.

Herrera, Jorge Gil, and Luis F. Bernabé Pons. 'The Moriscos Outside Spain: Routes and Financing'. In *The Expulsion of the Moriscos from Spain*, edited by Mercedes García-Arenal and Gerard Albert Wiegers, 217–38. Leiden, the Netherlands: Brill, 2014.

Homza, Lu Ann, ed. and trans. 'Deliberations on the Reality and Heresy of Witchcraft, 1526'. In *The Spanish Inquisition, 1478–1614: An Anthology of Sources*, 153–63. Indianapolis, IN: Hackett, 2006.

Homza, Lu Ann. 'An Expert Lawyer and Reluctant Demonologist: Alonso de Salazar Frías, Spanish Inquisitor'. In *The Science of Demons: Early Modern Authors Facing Witchcraft and the Devil*, edited by Jan Machielsen, 299–312. London: Routledge, 2020.

Homza, Lu Ann. 'When Witches Litigate: New Sources from Early Modern Navarre'. *Journal of Modern History* 91, no. 2 (2019): 245–75.

Homza, Lu Ann. *Village Infernos and Witches' Advocates: Witch-Hunting in Navarre, 1608–1614*. University Park: Pennsylvania State University Press, 2022.

Horsley, Adam. *Libertines and the Law: Subversive Authors and Criminal Justice in Early Seventeenth-Century France*. Oxford: Oxford University Press, 2021.

Houdard, Sophie. *Les sciences du diable: Quatre discours sur la sorcellerie, XVe–XVIIe siècle*. Paris: Cerf, 1992.

Houllemare, Marie. *Politiques de la parole: Le Parlement de Paris au XVIe siècle*. Geneva: Droz, 2011.

Hourmat, Pierre. *Histoire de Bayonne*. Bayonne, France: Société des sciences, lettres et arts de Bayonne, 1987.

Hugon, Alain. *Au service du Roi Catholique: 'Honorables ambassadeurs' et 'divins espions'; Représentation diplomatique et service secret dans les relations hispano-françaises de 1598 à 1635*. Madrid: Casa de Velázquez, 2004.

Huxley Barkham, Selma. *The Basque Coast of Newfoundland*. Plum Point, Newfoundland: The Corporation, 1989.

Huxley Barkham, Selma. 'Documentary Evidence for 16th Century Basque Whaling Ships in the Strait of Belle Isle'. In *Early European Settlement and Exploitation in Atlantic Canada*, edited by G. M. Story, 53–95. St. John's, NL: Memorial University of Newfoundland, 1982.

Huxley Barkham, Selma. 'Los vascos y las pesquerias transatlanticas, 1517–1713'. In *Itsasoa: El mar de Euskalerria, la naturaleza, el hombre y su historia*. Vol. 3: Los vascos en el marco Atlántico Norte: Siglos XVI y XVII, edited by Selma Huxley Barkham, 27–164. San Sebastián, Spain: Eusko kultur eragintza etor, 1986.

Idoate, Florencio. *La Brujería en Navarra y sus documentos*. Pamplona, Spain: Diputación foral de Navarra, Institución Príncipe de Viana, 1978.

Iglesias, Hector. 'Recherche sur la situation linguistique de Biarritz au XVIII[ème] siècle'. *Bulletin du Musée Basque* 145 (1996): 109–50.

Israel, Jonathan. *Diasporas within a Diaspora: Jews, Crypto-Jews, and the World of Maritime Empires, 1540–1740*. Leiden, the Netherlands: Brill, 2002.

Jacques-Chaquin [Jacques-Lefèvre], Nicole. 'Nocturnes sorciers: Symboliques de la nuit chez quelques démonologues, XV[e]-XVII[e] siècles'. In *La Nuit*, edited by François Angelier and Nicole Jacques-Chaquin [Jacques-Lefèvre], 177–94. Grenoble, France: Jérôme Millon, 1995.

Jaurgain, Jean B. E. de. *La maison de Gramont, 1040–1967*. 2 vols. Lourdes, France: Les amis du Musée Pyrénéen, 1968.

Jones, Ann Rosalind. 'Contentious Readings: Urban Humanism and Gender Difference in La Puce de Madame Des-Roches (1582)'. *Renaissance Quarterly* 48, no. 1 (1995): 109–28.

Kahn, Didier. *Alchimie et Paracelsisme en France à la fin de la Renaissance, 1567–1625*. Geneva: Droz, 2007.

Kenny, Neil. *Born to Write: Literary Families and Social Hierarchy in Early Modern France*. Oxford: Oxford University Press, 2020.

Kertanguy, Inès de. *Léonora Galigaï*. Paris: Pygmalion, 2005.

Kettering, Sharon. *Power and Reputation at the Court of Louis XIII: The Career of Charles D'Albert, Duc de Luynes*. Manchester, England: Manchester University Press, 2008.

Knecht, R. J. *Francis I*. Cambridge: Cambridge University Press, 1984.

Koch, John. 'Is Basque an Indo-European Language?' *Journal of Indo-European Studies* 41, nos. 1–2 (2013): 255–67.

Kurlansky, Mark. *Cod: A Biography of the Fish That Changed the World*. London: Cape, 1998.

Kurlansky, Mark. *The Basque History of the World: The Story of a Nation*. London: Cape, 1999.

*L'Église de Saint-Pée-Sur-Nivelle. Buruxkak*. Vol. 4. Saint-Pée, France: Culture Patrimoine Senpere, 2014. https://www.cultureetpatrimoinesenpere.fr/buruxkak/images/buruxkak4.pdf.

La Fontaine, Jean Sybil. *Speak of the Devil: Tales of Satanic Abuse in Contemporary England*. Cambridge: Cambridge University Press, 1998.

La Force, Auguste de Caumont. *Le maréchal de La Force: Un serviteur de sept rois, 1558–1652*. 2 vols. Paris: Éditions de la Table Ronde, 1950–2.

Labat, Claude. *Sorcellerie? Ce que cache la fumée des bûchers de 1609*. San Sebastián, Spain: Elkar, 2009.

Laborde, Pierre. *Histoire du tourisme sur la côte basque, 1830–1930*. Biarritz, France: Atlantica, 2001.

Labourdette, Jean-François, Jean-Pierre Poussou and Marie-Catherine Vignal, eds. *Le traité de Vervins*. Paris: Presses de l'Université Paris-Sorbonne, 2000.

Lamant-Duhart, Hubert, ed. *Ciboure*. Bayonne, France: Ekaïna, 1987.

Lamant-Duhart, Hubert, ed. *Urrugne*. Bayonne, France: Ekaïna, 1989.

Lamant-Duhart, Hubert. *Saint-Jean-de-Luz: Histoire d'une cité corsaire*. Saint-Jean-de-Luz, France: Ekaldia, 1992.

Landemont, L'abbé. 'Procès de sorcellerie en Basse-Navarre'. *Revue de Béarn, Navarre et Lannes: Partie historique de la revue des Basses-Pyrénées et des Landes* 12 (1883): 49–54.

Larsen, Aaron. 'Darkest Forests and Highest Mountains: The Witches' Sabbath and Landscapes of Fear in Early Modern Demonologies'. *European Review of History* 31, no. 1 (2024): 157–74.

Larsen, Anne R. 'On Reading "La Puce de Madame Des-Roches": Catherine Des Roches's "Responces" (1583)'. *Renaissance and Reformation/Renaissance et Réforme* 22, no. 2 (1998): 63–75.

Le Bouëdec, Gérard. *Activités maritimes et sociétés littorales de l'Europe atlantique, 1690–1790*. Paris: Armand Colin/Masson, 1997.

Le Mao, Caroline. *Parlement et parlementaires: Bordeaux au grand siècle*. Seyssel, France: Champ Vallon, 2007.

Legrand, Théodoric. *Essai sur les différends de Fontarabie avec le Labourd du XV$^{me}$ au XVIII$^{me}$ siècle*. Pau, France: Impr.-Stéréotypie Garet, 1905.

Linden, Stanton J. '"By Gradual Scale Sublim'd": Jean d'Espagnet and the Ontological Tree in Paradise Lost, Book V'. *Journal of the History of Ideas* 52, no. 4 (1991): 603–15.

Loewen, Brad, and Claude Chapdelaine, eds. *Contact in the 16th Century: Networks among Fishers, Foragers and Farmers*. Ottawa, ON: University of Ottawa Press, 2016.

Lomas Cortés, Manuel. *El proceso de expulsión de los moriscos de España, 1609–1614*. [Valencia, Spain]: Universitat de València, 2012.

Machielsen, Jan. 'Lancre, Pierre de, 1556–1631'. In *Dictionnaire des philosophes français du XVIIe siècle: Acteurs et réseaux du savoir*, edited by Luc Foisneau and Élisabeth Dutartre-Michaut, 984–8. Paris: Classiques Garnier, 2015.

Machielsen, Jan. 'The Making of a Teen Wolf: Pierre de Lancre's Confrontation with Jean Grenier (1603–10)'. *Folklore* 130, no. 3 (2019): 237–57.

Machielsen, Jan. 'Thinking with Montaigne: Evidence, Scepticism and Meaning in Early Modern Demonology'. *French History* 25, no. 4 (2011): 427–52.

Machielsen, Jan. *The War on Witchcraft: Andrew Dickson White, George Lincoln Burr, and the Origins of Witchcraft Historiography*. Cambridge: Cambridge University Press, 2021.

Machielsen, Jan, and Thibaut Maus de Rolley. 'The Mythmaker of the Sabbat: Pierre de Lancre's *Tableau de l'inconstance des mauvais anges et démons*'. In *The Science of Demons: Early Modern Authors Facing Witchcraft and the Devil*, edited by Jan Machielsen, 283–98. London: Routledge, 2020.

Maclean, Ian. *Interpretation and Meaning in the Renaissance: The Case of Law*. Cambridge: Cambridge University Press, 1992.

Maclean, Ian. *Montaigne philosophe*. Paris: Presses universitaires de France, 1996.

Malvezin, Théophile. *Michel de Montaigne: Son origine, sa famille*. Bordeaux, France: Charles Lefebvre, 1875.

Mandrou, Robert. *Magistrats et sorciers en France au XVIIe siècle: Une analyse de psychologie historique*. Paris: Éditions du Seuil, 1980.

Martijn, Charles A., Selma Huxley Barkham and Michael Barkham. 'Basques? Beothuk? Innu? Inuit? Or St. Lawrence Iroquoians? The Whalers on the 1546 Desceliers Map, Seen through the Eyes of Different Beholders'. *Newfoundland Studies* 19, no. 1 (2003): 187–206.

Martin, A. Lynn. *The Jesuit Mind: The Mentality of an Elite in Early Modern France*. Ithaca, NY: Cornell University Press, 1988.

Martin, Julian. *Francis Bacon, the State, and the Reform of Natural Philosophy*. Cambridge: Cambridge University Press, 1992.

Maus de Rolley, Thibaut. 'Of Oysters, Witches, Birds, and Anchors: Conceptions of Space and Travel in Pierre de Lancre'. *Renaissance Studies* 32, no. 4 (2018): 530–46.

Maza, Sara. 'The Kids Aren't All Right: Historians and the Problem of Childhood'. *American Historical Review*, 125, no. 4 (2020): 1261–85.

McGowan, Margaret. 'Pierre de Lancre's *Tableau de l'inconstance des mauvais anges et demons*: The Sabbat Sensationalized'. In *The Damned Art: Essays in the Literature of Witchcraft*, edited by Sydney Anglo, 182–201. London: Routledge & Kegan Paul, 1977.

Melammed, Renee Levine. *A Question of Identity: Iberian Conversos in Historical Perspective*. Oxford: Oxford University Press, 2004.

Merchant, Carolyn. ' "The Violence of Impediments": Francis Bacon and the Origins of Experimentation'. *Isis* 99, no. 4 (2008): 731–60.

Mettam, Roger. 'France'. In *Absolutism in Seventeenth-Century Europe*, edited by John Miller, 43–68. Houndmills, UK: Macmillan, 1990.

Meyer, Frédéric. 'Pour faire l'histoire des Récollets en France, XVIe–XIXe siècles'. *Chrétiens et sociétés. XVI$^e$–XXI$^e$ siècles* 2 (1995): 83–99.

Meyer, Frédéric. *Pauvreté et assistance spirituelle: les franciscains récollets de la province de Lyon aux XVII$^e$ et XVIII$^e$ siècles*. Saint-Etienne, France: Université de Saint-Etienne, 1997.

Michelet, Jules. *La sorcière*. Paris: E. Dentu Libraire-Editeur, 1862.

Millar, Charlotte-Rose. *Witchcraft, the Devil, and Emotions in Early Modern England*. Abingdon, England: Routledge, 2017.

Mongrédien, Georges. *Léonora Galigaï: Un procès de sorcellerie sous Louis XIII*. Paris: Hachette, 1968.

Monteano Sorbet, Peio J. *El iceberg navarro: Euskera y castellano en la Navarra del siglo XVI*. Arre Navarra, Spain: Pamiela, 2017.

Monter, William. 'Toads and Eucharists: The Male Witches of Normandy, 1564–1660'. *French Historical Studies*, 20, no. 4 (1997): 563–95.
Monter, William. 'Witchcraft Trials in Continental Europe'. In *Witchcraft and Magic in Europe: The Period of the Witch Trials*, edited by Bengt Ankarloo and Stuart Clark, 1–52. London: Athlone, 2002.
Monter, William. 'Witchcraft Trials in France'. In *The Oxford Handbook of Witchcraft in Early Modern Europe and Colonial America*, edited by Brian P. Levack, 218–31. Oxford: Oxford University Press, 2013.
Monter, William. *Frontiers of Heresy: The Spanish Inquisition from the Basque Lands to Sicily*. Cambridge: Cambridge University Press, 1990.
Mousnier, Roland. *L'Assassinat d'Henri IV: 14 mai 1610*. Paris: Gallimard, 2008.
Mousnier, Roland. *Les institutions de la France sous la monarchie absolue: 1598–1789*. 2nd edn. Paris: Presses universitaires de France, 1992.
Mulsow, Martin. 'Ambiguities of the Prisca Sapientia in Late Renaissance Humanism'. *Journal of the History of Ideas* 65, no. 1 (2004): 1–13.
Nahon, Gérard. 'Communautés espagnoles et portugaises de France, 1492–1992'. In *Les juifs d'Espagne: Histoire d'une diaspora, 1492–1992*, edited by Henry Méchoulan, 111–44. Paris: Liana Levi, 1992.
Nelson, Eric. *The Jesuits and the Monarchy: Catholic Reform and Political Authority in France, 1590–1615*. Aldershot, England: Ashgate, 2005.
Newman, William. *Newton the Alchemist*. Princeton, NJ: Princeton University Press, 2018.
Newman, William. *Promethean Ambitions: Alchemy and the Quest to Perfect Nature*. Chicago, IL: University of Chicago Press, 2004.
Nogaret, Joseph. *Saint-Jean-de-Luz des origines à nos jours*. Bayonne, France: Imprimerie du Courrier, 1925.
Nordman, Daniel. *Frontières de France: De l'espace au territoire, XVI$^e$–XIX$^e$ siècle*. Paris: Gallimard, 1998.
Ogilvie, Brian W. *The Science of Describing: Natural History in Renaissance Europe*. Chicago, IL: University of Chicago Press, 2008.
Orpustan, Jean-Baptiste. *Nouvelle toponymie basque: Noms des pays, vallées, communes et hameaux de Labourd, Basse-Navarre et Soule*. New edn. Pessac, France: Presses universitaires de Bordeaux, 2006.
Ortiz, Antonio. 'El proceso inquisitorial de Juan Núñez Saravia, banquero de Felipe IV'. *Hispania* 15, no. 61 (1955): 559–81.
Ospital, Jacques. *La chasse aux sorcières au Pays basque en 1609*. Urrugne, France: Pimientos, 2009.
Ostling, Michael 'Babyfat and Belladonna: Witches, Ointment and the Contestation of Reality'. *Magic, Ritual, and Witchcraft* 11, no. 1 (2016): 30–72.
Ostorero, Martine. *Le diable au sabbat: Littérature démonologique et sorcellerie, 1440–1460*. Florence, Italy: SISMEL, 2011.
Parker, David. *The Making of French Absolutism*. London: Hodder Arnold, 1983.
Patlapin, Juan. *Sorginak: Sorcières en Pays basque; Contes et légendes des sept provinces*. Translated by André Gabastou. Urrugne, France: Pimientos, 2011.
Pearl, Jonathan L. *The Crime of Crimes: Demonology and Politics in France, 1560–1620*. Waterloo, ON: Wilfric Laurier University Press, 1999.
Pérez, Joseph. *The Spanish Inquisition: A History*. New Haven, CT: Yale University Press, 2005.

Piant, Hervé. *Une justice ordinaire: Justice civile et criminelle dans la prévôté royale de Vaucouleurs sous l'Ancien Régime.* Rennes, France: Presses universitaires de Rennes, 2015.

Pitts, Vincent J. *Henri IV of France: His Reign and Age.* Baltimore, MD: Johns Hopkins University Press, 2009.

Pontet, Josette. 'Le choix de Gramont comme gouverneur de Bayonne à la fin du XVI$^e$ siècle'. *Bulletin de la Société des Sciences, Lettres et Arts de Bayonne* 171 (2016): 23–40.

Pontet, Josette. 'Le gouverneur et l'évêque: Deux pouvoirs rivaux dans la ville, deux personnalités irréconciliables; Antoine II de Gramont et Bertrand d'Etchauz'. In *Autour de Bertrand d'Etchauz: Évêque de Bayonne, fin XVI$^e$–début XVII$^e$ siècle* edited by Pierre Hourmat and Josette Pontet, 187–208. Bayonne, France: Société des sciences, lettres et arts de Bayonne, 2000.

Poumarède, Jacques. 'De l'*Arrêt mémorable* de Coras (1561) à l'*Histoire tragique* (1613) de Ségla: L'invention de la chronique criminelle'. *Annales du Midi* 120, no. 264 (2008): 503–34.

Prétou, Pierre. *Justice et société en Gascogne à la fin du moyen âge, 1360–1526.* Rennes, France: Presses universitaires de Rennes, 2010.

Rampling, Jennifer M. *The Experimental Fire.* Chicago, IL: University of Chicago Press, 2020.

Rappoport, Angelo S. *Superstitions of Sailors.* London: Stanley Paul, 1928.

Ravenez, Louis-Waldemar. *Histoire du cardinal François de Sourdis.* Bordeaux, France: G. Gounouilhou, 1867.

Rectoran, Pierre. *Corsaires basques et bayonnais du XVe au XIXe siècle: Pirates, flibustiers, boucaniers.* Bayonne, France: Plumon, 1946.

Ribard, Dinah. 'Sur plusieurs frontières: Le président d'Espagnet, 1564–après 1637'. *Les Dossiers du Grihl*, special issue no. 1 (2022; original publication date 2005).

Ricau, Osmin. *Histoire des Cagots: Race maudite de Gascogne, Béarn, Pays basque et Navarre Franco-Espagnols, Asturies et Province de Léon.* Bordeaux, France: Osmin Ricau, 1963.

Richards, John F. *The Unending Frontier: An Environmental History of the Early Modern World.* Berkeley: University of California Press, 2003.

Rillot, Nathalie. 'La noblesse labourdine, 1610–1630'. *Bulletin de la Société des Sciences, Lettres et Arts de Bayonne* 166 (2011): 207–22.

Rillot, Nathalie. 'Portrait d'un noble labourdin au XVII$^e$ siècle'. *Bulletin de la Société des Sciences, Lettres et Arts de Bayonne* 165 (2010): 73–94.

Rilova Jericó, Carlos. 'Las últimas brujas de Europa: Acusaciones de brujería en el País Vasco durante los siglos XVIII y XIX'. *Vasconia: Cuadernos de historia-geografía* 32 (2002): 369–93.

Rilova Jericó, Carlos. *Historia nocturna de Hondarribia, 1611–1826: Brujería en el entorno de una ciudad marítima vasca entre el antiguo régimen y la revolución industrial.* Hondarribia, Spain: Hondarribiko Udala, 2011.

Roberts, Penny. 'French Historians and Collective Violence'. *History and Theory* 56, no. 4 (2017): 60–75.

Roberts, Penny. 'Review of "Blood and Violence in Early Modern France"'. *Reviews in History*, no. 572 (2007). https://reviews.history.ac.uk/review/572. Last accessed 28 April 2024.

Roper, Lyndal. *Oedipus and the Devil: Witchcraft, Sexuality and Religion in Early Modern Europe*. London: Routledge, 1994.
Roper, Lyndal. *Witch Craze: Terror and Fantasy in Baroque Germany*. New Haven, CT: Yale University Press, 2004.
Roth, Cecil. 'Quatre lettres d'Elie de Montalte: Contribution à l'histoire des Marranes'. *Revue des études juives* 85, no. 169 (1928): 137–65.
Roth, Cecil. *A History of the Marranos*. 3rd edn. New York: Meridian Books, 1959.
Roussel, Théophile. 'Cagots et lépreux'. *Bulletins et mémoires de la Société d'Anthropologie de Paris* 4 (1893): 148–60.
Rowland, Ingrid D. *From Pompeii: The Afterlife of a Roman Town*. Cambridge, MA: Harvard University Press, 2014.
Rowlands, Alison. 'Witchcraft and Old Women in Early Modern Germany'. *Past and Present* 173 (2001): 50–89.
Rubin, Miri, *Gentile Tales: The Narrative Assault on Late Medieval Jews*. Philadelphia: University of Pennsylvania Press, 2004.
Ruff, Julius R. *Crime, Justice and Public Order in Old Regime France: The Sénéchaussées of Libourne and Bazas, 1696–1789*. Abingdon, England: Routledge, 2015 (1984).
Sahlins, Peter. *Boundaries: The Making of France and Spain in the Pyrenees*. Berkeley: University of California Press, 1989.
Saint Bris, Gonzague. *Henri IV et la France réconciliée*. Paris: Club France Loisirs, 2009.
Sainz Varela, José Antonio, and Eloísa Navajas Twose, eds. *¡Brujas! Sorginak! Los archivos de la Inquisición y Zugarramurdi*. Madrid: Ministerio de Cultura, 2008.
Satrústegui, José María. 'Relectura de los textos vascos de espionaje del siglo XVI'. *Fontes linguae vasconum* 64 (1993): 443–76.
Sawyer, Jeffrey K. *Printed Poison: Pamphlet Propaganda, Faction Politics, and the Public Sphere in Early Seventeenth-Century France*. Berkeley: University of California Press, 1990.
Schalk, Ellery. *From Valor to Pedigree: Ideas of Nobility in France in the Sixteenth and Seventeenth Centuries*. Princeton, NJ: Princeton University Press, 2014.
Schiff, Stacy. *The Witches: Salem, 1692*. New York: Little, Brown, 2015.
Scholz Williams, Gerhild. *Defining Dominion: The Discourses of Magic and Witchcraft in Early Modern France and Germany*. Ann Arbor: University of Michigan Press, 1999.
Scott, Amanda L. *The Basque Seroras: Local Religion, Gender, and Power in Northern Iberia, 1550–1800*. Ithaca, NY: Cornell University Press, 2020.
Serjeantson, Richard. 'Francis Bacon and the "Interpretation of Nature" in the Late Renaissance'. *Isis* 105, no. 4 (2014): 681–705.
Soman, Alfred. 'Decriminalizing Witchcraft: Does the French Experience Furnish a European Model?' *Criminal Justice History* 10 (1989): 1–22.
Soman, Alfred. 'Deviance and Criminal Justice in Western Europe, 1300–1800: An Essay in Structure'. In *Sorcellerie et justice criminelle: Le Parlement de Paris, 16$^e$–18$^e$ siècles*. Aldershot, England: Variorum, 1992, chapter 4.
Soman, Alfred. 'La justice criminelle aux XVI$^e$–XVII$^e$ siècles: Le Parlement de Paris et les sièges subalternes'. In *Sorcellerie et justice criminelle: Le Parlement de Paris, 16$^e$–18$^e$ siècles*. Aldershot, England: Variorum, 1992, chapter 7.
Soman, Alfred. 'La justice criminelle, vitrine de la monarchie française'. *Bibliothèque de l'École des chartes* 153, no. 2 (1995): 291–304.
Soman, Alfred. 'Les procès de sorcellerie au Parlement du Paris, 1565–1640'. *Annales: Economies, sociétés, civilisations* 32 (1977): 790–814.

Soman, Alfred. 'The Parlement of Paris and the Great Witch Hunt, 1565–1640'. *Sixteenth Century Journal* 9, no. 2 (1978): 31–44.

Soman, Alfred. 'Witch Lynching at Juniville'. *Natural History* 95, no. 10 (1986): 6–15.

Swan, Claudia. 'The "Preparation for the Sabbath" by Jacques de Gheyn II: The Issue of Inversion'. *Print Quarterly* 16, no. 4 (1999): 327–39.

Swetschinski, Daniel M. *Reluctant Cosmopolitans: The Portuguese Jews of Seventeenth-Century Amsterdam*. Liverpool, UK: Liverpool University Press, 2000.

Szajkowski, Zosa. 'Population Problems of Marranos and Sephardim in France, from the 16th to the 20th Centuries'. *Proceedings of the American Academy for Jewish Research* 27 (1958): 83–105.

Tabernero, Cristina, and Jesús M. Usunáriz. 'Bruja, brujo, hechicera, hechicero, sorgin como insultos en la navarra de los siglos XVI y XVII'. In *Modelos de vida y cultura en Navarra (siglos XVI y XVII): Antología de textos*, edited by Mariela Insúa, 381–429. Pamplona, Spain: Servicio de Publicaciones de la Universidad de Navarra, 2016.

Tamizey de Larroque, Philippe. *Essai sur la vie et les ouvrages de Florimond de Raymond, conseiller au Parlement de Bordeaux*. Paris: Auguste Aubry, 1867.

Tavim, José Alberto Rodrigues da Silva. 'Amesterdão em Terras de França? Judeus de Marrocos em Saint-Jean-de-Luz'. In *D'Aquém, d'Além e d'Ultramar: Homenagem a António Dias Farinha*, edited by Francisco Contente Domingues, José da Silva Horta and Paulo David Vicente, 1:319–35. Lisbon: Centro de História, Faculdade de Letras da Universidade de Lisboa, 2015.

Teter, Magda. *Blood Libel: On the Trail of an Antisemitic Myth*. Cambridge, MA: Harvard University Press, 2020.

Tinsley, Barbara Sher. *History and Polemics in the French Reformation: Florimond de Raemond, Defender of the Church*. Cranbury, NJ: Susquehanna University Press, 1992.

Trevor-Roper, Hugh R. *The European Witch-Craze of the 16th and 17th Centuries*. Harmondsworth, England: Pelican Books, 1969.

Trivellato, Francesca. *The Promise and Peril of Credit: What a Forgotten Legend about Jews and Finance Tells Us about the Making of European Commercial Society*. Princeton, NJ: Princeton University Press, 2019.

Tuke, Hack. 'The Cagots'. *Journal of the Anthropological Institute of Great Britain and Ireland* 9 (1880): 376–85.

Ugartechea y Salinas, J. M. 'La pesca tradicional en Lequeitio'. *Anuario de Eusko-Folklore* 22 (1967): 9–155.

Veillet, René. *Recherches sur la ville et sur l'église de Bayonne*. Edited by Victor Pierre Dubarat. Bayonne, France: L. Lasserre, 1910.

Veyrin, Philippe. *Les Basques de Labourd, de Soule et de Basse-Navarre, leur histoire et leurs traditions*. 2nd edn. [Grenoble, France]: Arthaud, 1955.

Villeneuve, Roland. *Le fléau des sorciers: La diablerie basque au XVII$^e$ siècle*. [Paris]: Flammarion, 1983.

Vincent, Bernard. 'The Geography of the Morisco Expulsion: A Quantitative Study'. In *The Expulsion of the Moriscos from Spain*, edited by Mercedes García-Arenal and Gerard Albert Wiegers, 17–36. Leiden, the Netherlands: Brill, 2014.

Viton de Saint-Allais, Nicolas. *Nobiliaire universel de France, ou Recueil général des généalogies historiques des maisons nobles de ce royaume*. Vol. 17. Paris: Bachelin-Deflorenne, 1874.

Vivo, Filippo de. *Information and Communication in Venice: Rethinking Early Modern Politics*. Oxford: Oxford University Press, 2009.

Waters, Thomas. *Cursed Britain: A History of Witchcraft and Black Magic in Modern Times*. New Haven, CT: Yale University Press, 2019.
Webster, Wentworth. 'Hebraizantes portugueses de San Juan de Luz en 1619'. *Boletín de la Real Academia de la Historia* 15, no. 4 (1889): 347–60.
Wilby, Emma. *Invoking the Akelarre: Voices of the Accused in the Basque Witch-Craze, 1609–1614*. Brighton, England: Sussex Academic Press, 2019.
Wilke, Carsten Lorenz. 'Le rapport d'un espion du Saint-Office sur sa mission auprès des crypto-juifs de Saint-Jean-de-Luz (1611)'. *Sigila: Revue interdisciplinaire franco-portugaise sur le secret* 16 (2006): 127–41.
Wilke, Carsten Lorenz. 'Un judaïsme clandestin dans la France du XVII siècle: Un rite au rythme de l'imprimerie'. In *Transmission et passages en monde juif*, edited by Esther Benbassa, 281–312. Paris: Publisud, 1997.
Wing, John T. *Roots of Empire: Forests and State Power in Early Modern Spain, c. 1500–1750*. Leiden, the Netherlands: Brill, 2015.
Yturbide, Pierre. 'Le Bilçar d'Ustaritz au Pays de Labourd'. *Revue internationale des études basques* 1 (1907): 74–83.
Zabala, Mikel. *Brujería e inquisición en Bizkaia*. Bilbao, Spain: Ekain, 2000.
Zika, Charles. 'Hosts, Processions and Pilgrimages: Controlling the Sacred in Fifteenth-Century Germany'. *Past and Present* 118 (1988): 25–64.
Zika, Charles. 'The Transformation of Sabbath Rituals by Jean Crépy and Laurent Bordelon: Redirecting Emotion through Ridicule'. In *Emotion, Ritual and Power in Europe, 1200–1920: Family, State and Church*, edited by Merridee L. Bailey and Katie Barclay, 261–84. Cham, Switzerland: Springer International, 2017.
Zink, Anne. 'Être juif à Bayonne en 1630'. *Annales du Midi* 108, no. 216 (1996): 441–60.
Zink, Anne. 'L'émergence de Saint-Esprit-lès-Bayonne: La place d'une ville nouvelle dans l'espace juif à l'époque moderne'. *Archives juives* 37, no. 1 (2004): 9–27.
Zink, Anne. 'Une niche juridique: L'installation des Juifs à Saint-Esprit-lès-Bayonne au XVIIe siècle'. *Annales* 49, no. 3 (1994): 639–69.
Zintzo-Garmendia, Beñat. *Histoire de la sorcellerie en Pays basque: Les bûchers de l'injustice*. Toulouse, France: Privat, 2016.

# Index

Acquaviva, Claudio 93, 214–15
adolescents *see* teenagers
Age of Enlightenment 208
*akelarre see* witches' sabbat
alchemy 78, 81, 83–5
Aldrovandi, Ulisse 78
Al-Ḥajarī, Ahmad Ibn Qasim 203
Aliaga Martínez, Luis de 207
Americas 12, 32, 223
    *see also* Newfoundland
Amou (village) 196
Amou, Jean-Paul de Caupenne, Lord of
    23–6, 45, 62, 63, 64, 101, 103,
    114, 174
  attacked by the devil 169–72
Amou family 23
Ansó valley 99
anti-Judaism 224–5, 232, 284n
Araitz 160
Aranībar, León de 187–9, 197, 206, 221
Arguibel 117, 182–3, 265n
Ascain 17, 123, 135, 136
  witch-trials in 114, 117, 165,
    171–2, 182
*auto de fe* 90, 111, 122, 160, 188,
    196–8, 236
  ballad about 198
  de Lancre's discussion of 4, 71
  visitors to 157, 198, 210 *see also*
    Logroño tribunal
Azkoitia 209

Bacon, Francis 78–9
  *Sylva Sylvarum* 78
Baroja, Pío 11, 24
*barrabam*, Basque for devil 155, 169–70
  *see also* devil

basilisk 78
Basque Country 2
  barren and sandy 29
  culture 8
  diet 29
  inhabitants 22, 26, 41, 43, 89, 93–4,
    103, 105, 111, 122, 156
  merchants and financiers 32, 47–8
  monoglots 19–20
  proverbs 32, 39
  provinces 9
  smoking in 38
  treaties of good relations 22, 29
  women wearing traditional headgear
    36–7; *see also* sailors
Battle of Pavia 10
Bayle, Pierre 83–4
Bayonne 3–4, 9, 28, 29, 47, 50, 63,
    74, 96, 97, 98, 101, 110, 113,
    117, 118, 152, 175, 189, 190,
    194, 206, 212, 213, 215–16,
    226, 228–9
  aldermen of 62, 109, 114, 155, 179,
    182, 184, 219–20, 232
  castles of 17
  cathedral of 157, 176, 178, 180,
    182–3
  conspiracies against 49, 96–7,
    175–6, 180
  decisions 220
  distinct from the Labourd 24
  envoy 95–6
  executioner of 114, 159
  law courts 46, 48, 62
  merchants 19, 32, 222
  missal of 1543 35
  Moriscos in 202–3

New Christians in 199, 222–3, 229, 232
prison 50, 51, 62, 109, 192
surgeon of 151, 157, 159–60
visit by Charles IX 30
Béarn 11, 20, 60, 99, 202
    Jesuit preaching in 214, 215, 217
    witches banished from 190, 219, 281n
Beaulieu, Eustorg de 72
Becerra Holguín, Alonso 122, 136, 137, 145, 191, 198
Bera 18, 157, 162, 197
Biarritz 29, 50, 114, 203, 232
    future seaside resort 1
    witches from 42, 73, 114, 156, 159, 165, 229
Bidache 101, 205–6, 222, 232
Bidasoa river 17, 18, 98, 99, 211
    exchange of the princesses on 204
Bienassis, Pierre 93
Big Barbe 175, 176, 179
Bilbao 9, 17, 29, 32
    witchcraft in 209
Biltzar 22–3, 63, 207, 236
Biron conspiracy 97
Black Mass *see* witches' sabbat
Bocal, Pierre 118, 165, 183, 273n
Bohemians 20, 60
    dance 140; *see also cagots*
Bologna 78
Bordeaux 10, 32, 38, 44, 50, 51, 110, 210, 214, 215, 216, 222
    Basque witches and teenagers in 55, 56, 75, 116, 132, 135, 146, 153, 163, 172, 176, 180, 192, 194–6, 256n
    executions in 52, 57, 73–4, 193–4, 196
    lion in 77
    literary culture of 70, 94
    witch priests in 182
Bordeaux Parlement *see* Parlement of Bordeaux
Bosdeau, Jeanne 73–4, 132
Boucher, Jean 215–17, 281n
Braudel, Fernand 15, 42

*cagots* 20, 140, 171–2, 224; *see also* Bohemians
Cambo-les-Bains 114, 154, 192
Capuchins 210
catechism 213
Chateau du Ha, Bordeaux 192, 193
Chibau, Adam de 32, 50, 55–9, 61, 104, 116, 195
Chibau, Pierre de 47, 189
children 1, 21, 38, 43, 44, 161, 162, 187–91, 191, 214
    accusing relatives 165–6
    as the commission's spies 84–5, 111–12, 116, 117, 146, 149, 153–5, 159–60
    dedicated to the devil 2, 150, 165–6, 207
    mental world of 148
    sleeping in churches 45, 161–4
    testimonies 173, 190, 208; *see also* teenagers
Christianity 21, 25, 122, 173, 213, 215, 216, 222, 223, 225
    renunciation of 129–30, 215
church 26, 36, 45, 50, 58, 59, 171, 198, 211, 212, 216, 226, 228
    assemblies in 54, 56, 123, 154–5, 231
    bricked-in doors in 10, 20
    children sleeping in 45, 161–4
    votive objects in 35
Ciboure 1, 24, 28, 32, 33, 45, 50, 64, 99, 101, 102, 114, 123, 164, 171, 203, 211
    part of Urtubie's domain 26–7
    tensions with Saint-Jean-de-Luz 27–8, 61, 211
    witch-priests of 118, 164–5, 182–3, 210
    witches' sabbat at 28, 123, 135, 145–6
Concini, Concino 224
*conversos see* New Christians
Coras, Jean de 71, 72
Cornau Marie du 175–6, 178
Coton, Pierre 22, 214, 215, 217
Cruseau, Étienne de 49–50, 69–70, 73, 102, 200, 204

Daffis, Guillaume 69–71
Davis, Natalie Zemon 71, 72
deforestation 29
Della Porta, Giambattista 79
  *Magia naturalis* (1558) 78
demonology 79, 136, 207 see also Lancre, Pierre de
devil 4, 15–17, 35, 69, 75, 82, 109, 128, 131, 133, 137, 145, 161, 163, 166, 169–70, 183, 193, 199, 216–17, 229
  a communications provider 39
  deceptions of 28, 38, 91, 150, 164, 173, 176
  a goat 73–4, 82, 127, 208
  on a golden throne 127, 155, 171, 190
  heterosexuality of 141–2
  a linguist 21, 190
  sex with 2, 81, 85, 91, 129, 139, 142, 151
  sheep thief pretending to be 3, 62
  a tree trunk 138–43
  vampirism of 2, 11, 120, 130–1, 134, 171–2; see also devil's mark; witches' sabbat
devil's (or witch's) mark 148, 150–1, 156, 158–61
Doihadard, Michel 226–8, 230, 231

Echaux, Bertrand d' 25, 104, 204, 216, 230
  against try-out marriages 38
  conflict with Antoine de Gramont 26, 109, 210, 226
  interdict by 49–50, 58
  opponent of de Lancre 180–4
Edict of Grace 52, 162, 191, 210, 216
Elizondo, José de 232
England 9, 12, 19–20, 21, 30, 32, 69, 83, 96–7, 122, 130–1, 198
*épices* 46
epilepsy (caused by witchcraft) 177, 219
Errenteria 207, 268n, 277n
Espagnet, Jean d' 1, 2, 43, 84, 92, 93, 101, 109, 169, 179, 187
  addition to the witchcraft commission 102, 104, 110–11
  author of *Arcanum* 83

inspection of the border 102, 114, 154–5, 169, 199
poetry 4, 119, 267n; see also witchcraft commission
ethnography 6, 8, 15, 38, 82, 89, 156
execution, executions 4, 41, 53, 68, 110, 114, 152, 159, 166, 168, 192, 193, 196
  in Bayonne 3
  in Bordeaux 52, 57, 73–4, 193–4
  methods of 46
  number of 110, 116–17, 148–9
  of witch-priests 182–3; see also *auto de fe*

Fernandes, Catarina 225–33
1582 witchcraft commission 42, 73, 74
1598 Treaty of Vervins 96
France 22–3, 25, 41–2, 152, 187, 192, 199, 210, 215, 222–3
  in crisis 92, 95, 122, 189, 224
  foreign policy 59, 96–9, 158, 204, 211
  justice in 4, 23–4, 45–7, 63, 67, 70, 72, 103, 183, 194
  monarchy of 10, 26, 67–8, 97, 200
  refuge for the suffering 203
  source of bad things 61, 188; see also French-Spanish border
French Revolution 10, 24, 43, 95, 101, 206
French-Spanish border 4, 17–18, 21–2, 84, 97, 98, 104, 116, 123, 134, 190, 199, 210, 220–1, 229, 236
  disappearing act 10, 18, 42
  disputes at 99–101, 204
  empowerment by 10, 16, 23–6, 111, 205
  Moriscos crossing at 189, 202–3

Gajén, Inesa de 61–2, 190
Galigai, Leonora Dori 224
Garonne river 87, 188
Gascon dialect 10, 19, 190, 229
Gaudin, Luís Pascual 77
gender 17, 35–9, 92–3, 152, 156, 161
Germany 45, 97
  witch-hunts in 2, 15, 174
Gipuzkoa 17, 41, 115, 191, 207–9

Goiburu, Juanes de 128–9, 141–2
Goiburu, Miguel de 123, 130, 142, 149
Gourgue, Marc-Antoine de 192, 196–206, 210–11
Goyetche, Jean de 48, 49, 51–3, 55–7, 62
Gramont, Antoine de 96, 98, 111, 158, 160, 202, 206, 228
  conflict with Bishop Echaux 26, 109, 210, 226
  mayor of Bayonne 24–5
  prince of Bidache 101, 205, 232
  protection of New Christians 203, 221, 229–30, 232
Grenier, Jean 74, 79, 82, 90, 147
Guerre, Martin 71, 73, 102

Habas, Martin 212, 224, 233
Haitze, Bertrand de 44, 57, 118, 213, 217
Hammer of the Witches see *Malleus maleficarum*
Haraneder, Jehan de 21, 195
Haristeguy, Françoise 51, 52
Haristeguy, Jean de 48, 255n
Haristeguy, Marie de 47, 49, 57, 253n
Haurgues, Martissans de 48, 253n
Hendaye 10, 60, 63, 101, 113, 119, 155, 164, 182
  execution in 114
  part of Urtubie's domain 26–7, 62, 64, 101
  sabbats in 28, 99, 129
Henry II, King of France 46, 222
Henry III, King of France 42
Henry IV, King of Castile 41
Henry IV, King of France 3, 20, 24, 43, 57, 95, 214
  as King of Navarre 9, 96, 101
  murder of 189, 203–4, 206
  relation with Bordeaux Parlement 68, 72, 96
  scheming by 97–8
Hondarribia 18, 24, 61, 98–9, 113, 122, 190, 207
  witchcraft in 21, 190–1, 238
*Horrible iugement* 229, 231
Hoyarsabal, Martin de 30

Hualde, Lorenzo de 18, 157, 162, 197–8, 272n

incubi and succubi 3, 136–7
Isasti, Lope Martínez de 31, 39, 207–8

Jesuits 93, 160, 212–17; see also Acquaviva, Claudio; Boucher, Jean; Solarte, Hernando de
Judaism 222, 230, 232
  in Venice 223; see also New Christians
Jülich-Cleves-Berg 98
Jureteguía, María de 123, 198
justice 67, 122, 174–80, 224, 229, 235–6
  alternate image of 72
  faithful exercise of 67–8
  high cost of 45–6
  like a palm tree 67
  shadow of 174–80; see also France, justice in; vigilantism

L'Angelier, Abel 70
La Masse, Catherine de 51, 53–8, 63, 116, 124, 146, 162, 194–5, 212
*La Puce de Madame Des-Roches* (1582) 70
La Roche Flavin, Bernard de 67
Labourd, Pays de 9, 21, 39, 43–4, 50, 95, 96, 104, 115, 172, 188–9
  as a border region 10, 18, 35, 96, 101–2, 104
  as a mini-New World 38
  (democratic) institutions of 22, 23, 63, 207, 236
  fishing and whaling in 29–33, 89, 93
  population of 16, 71, 156
  privileges of 22–3, 25, 97, 111; see also Basque Country
Lancre, Pierre de
  analysis of failing patriarchy 39
  attempt to join the Society of Jesus 214
  Basque origins 87
  coat of arms 87, 88
  death 189
  *Du sortilège* (1627) 6, 81
  efforts to visit the sabbat 119
  embodiment of constancy 87
  ethnography 15, 38

as 'gleeful executioner' or 'butcher' 7
*Le livre des princes* (1617) 92
*L'incrédulité et mescreance du sortilège plainement convaincue* (1622) 89, 119, 225–6
marriage 89, 93
relationship with Bordeaux colleagues 102–3, 110, 147, 188–9
relationship with Jean d'Espagnet 84
relationship with Michel de Montaigne 21, 85, 89–91, 94
relationship with Tristan d'Urtubie 64, 103–4, 171, 172, 179
retirement 89, 92, 119, 188–9
sleeps through witches' sabbat 169–70
*Tableau de l'inconstance et instabilité de toutes choses* (1607, 2nd ed. 1610) 87, 89–91, 97; *see also* Tableau de l'inconstance des mauvais anges et démons
Lapurdi *see* Labourd, Pays de
Lasse, Boniface de 41–2
*lettres de jussion* 103, 105
Limousin 73
Lissalde, Mathias de 44, 56, 57, 111, 124, 168, 210–3
Logroño tribunal 20, 113, 117, 121–5, 157, 187–8, 196–7, 209, 221; *see also* auto de fe; Spanish Inquisition
Louis XIII, King of France 26, 29, 92, 95, 98, 202, 204, 224
Louis XIV, King of France 10, 25, 72

MacRedor, Andrew 75
*Magia naturalis* (Della Porta) 78
male and female sex demons *see* incubi and succubi
*Malleus maleficarum* 207, 227
Materra, Esteve 213–4
*Mercure françois* 3, 4, 232–3
Mexico City 223, 232
Migalena 183, 273n
Mons, Jehanne de 89, 93
Mondens, Jeanne 175–6
Montaigne, Catherine Eyquem de 103
Montaigne, Michel de 21, 73–4, 85, 87, 94, 103

*Essays* (1580) 70, 74, 87, 89, 90–1
Montmorency, Charlotte-Marguerite de 98–9
Moriscos
  conspiracies involving 97–8
  expulsion of 189, 198–9, 202–3, 206
Morguy 160
Mornay, Philippe de 3
Mutriku 113

natural history 77–80, 83
natural magic 78–9
Navarre 9, 17–20, 24, 30, 60, 115, 212, 214, 232
  French claims to 96–9
  witch-hunting in 40–2, 63, 115, 134, 146, 179, 188, 190, 208; *see also* Bera; Zugarramurdi
Necato 152, 156, 163
*negativos* 125, 197, 198
New Christians 20–11, 25, 199, 222, 229–31
Newfoundland 29–33, 161, 168, 179, 202, 231, 233; *see also* whales/whaling
Nivelle river 1, 26, 47, 63, 211

Oriotz, Martin d' 50–52, 55, 58, 254n, 256n
Our Lady of the Peace (convent) 206, 209–12, 233

Palais de l'Ombrière 69
Parlement of Bordeaux 2, 6, 46, 50, 90, 93, 94, 200, 231
  and witchcraft 42, 43–4, 48, 51, 53, 58, 63–4, 73–5, 96, 101–3, 105, 110, 114, 135, 147, 182–4, 189, 192–6, 206, 210
  high self-regard of 67–72, 103
  positive assessment of 45, 72–3
Parlement of Paris 45, 73, 79, 97, 224–5
Parlement of Rouen 73
Parlement of Toulouse 69, 71
Pasquier, Étienne 70, 71
*Paulette* 68
Pays de Labourd *see* Labourd, Pays de
Philip III, King of Spain 196, 204, 232
philosophers' stone *see* alchemy

Pliny the Elder 77, 79
Portuguese 20, 221–5; *see also* New Christians
priests 18, 24, 31, 39, 44, 50, 61, 63, 155, 164, 207–8, 212, 216, 223, 225–8, 231
    as interpreters 157; *see also* Haitze, Bertrand de; Hualde Lorenzo de; witch-priests
prince de Condé 98
*prisca theologia* 80
Pyrenees 8, 89, 96, 101
    primitive cruelty of 15
    witch-hunting in 40–2

Raemond, Florimond de 73–4
Recollects 57, 210–2
refugees 63, 111, 115, 117, 182, 191, 199; *see also* Moriscos; New Christians
*retentum* 117
Rols, Bertrande de 71
Rome 93, 214–15, 217
Rosteguy, Bertrand de 87
Rousseau, Jean-Jacques 95

sailors 28–35, 38–9, 124, 135, 161, 211, 214, 232–3
    and lynching of Catarina Fernandes 225–31
    wishful thinking about 110, 168; *see also* whales/whaling
Sainte-Croix-du-Mont 89
Saint-Jean-de-Luz 10, 19, 37, 57, 122, 124, 162, 193, 208, 233
    and the sea 29, 102, 123
    children of 1
    merchants of 21
    officials of 45, 47–50, 52–4, 58, 60, 104, 154, 195–6, 228, 231
    Portuguese community of 20, 199–200, 221–32
    pillaged by Spanish forces 17, 233
    priests of 182–4, 194, 210, 216, 226, 229
    privileges of 22, 101
    tensions with Ciboure 27–8, 61, 211
    witch-trials at 47, 114, 116–17, 168, 174
Saint-Pée 24, 50, 62, 113, 116, 163, 188, 235–6
    witch-trials at 114, 117, 154, 163, 169–71
Salazar Frías, Alonso de 8, 52, 116, 121, 141, 145, 167, 171, 190, 208, 217
*sambenitos* 197
San Sebastián 17, 33, 113, 190, 195, 207, 208, 221, 228
Sansin, Juanes de 141–2
Sanson, Guiraud de 48, 50, 53–6, 116, 194
Sanson, Joannes de 193–5
Santiago de Compostela 8, 16
Sare 114, 117, 138, 150, 163, 188
Satan *see* devil
Scotland 38, 75, 159–60
Ségure, Auger de 62, 155, 170, 175, 179, 256n
seroras 39, 134, 164
smoking 38
Socoa 99, 102, 104, 211, 263n
Solarte, Herrando de 160, 162, 163, 215, 217
Sorhaindo, Charles de 109, 114, 175, 179, 180, 182
Sourdis, Cardinal de 77, 202
Spain 1, 4, 8, 10, 32, 98–9, 189, 204, 221
    conquest of Navarre 9
    espionage for 25, 199, 200, 221
    war with France 17, 22–4, 96
    witchcraft in 44–5, 52, 63, 120, 122–3, 131, 146, 190–1, 196–9 *see also* French-Spanish border; Moriscos; New Christians; Spanish Inquisition
Spanish Inquisition 17, 33, 41, 52, 110–11, 113, 117, 120–3, 125, 136, 137, 141, 160, 187, 197–9, 207, 210, 222–4, 232; *see also auto de fe*; Logroño tribunal

*Tableau de l'inconstance des mauvais anges et démons* (1612; 2nd ed. 1613) 11, 90, 111, 168, 171, 192–3
  as empirical investigation 78, 81, 85
  as ethnography 8, 38, 89
  as a legal text 68, 70, 79
  description of the devil 138, 141
  emotions in 81–3
  engraving included in 7, 33–4, 125
  inclusion of Logroño pamphlet 4, 198
  intended audience 68
  obsession with the sabbat 50–51, 119, 133
  on werewolves 70–71, 74
  structure of 6, 44, 89–90, 112–13, 121, 180
  use of testimony 9, 112, 116, 117, 152, 153, 164, 168, 172, 194
  title page 5, 198, 215
teenagers 44, 51, 116, 146–53, 170–1, 194, 213; *see also* children
Toulouse 69, 215
treaties of good relations 22, 29

Urdax 25, 113, 122, 189, 221, 232
Urrugne 17, 26, 50, 61–4, 103, 104, 172, 211
  privileges of 101–2
  witchcraft commission in 114, 150, 152, 161, 163; *see also* Urtubie, Tristan de Gamboa d'Alzate d'
Urtubie, Tristan de Gamboa d'Alzate d' 64, 101, 111
  agent of chaos 24, 26, 53, 59, 211
  attacked by the devil 169, 172
  involvement in witch-hunting 62–3, 114, 169–72, 191
  marriage of 103
  not a witch 61
  relationship with Pierre de Lancre 64, 103–4, 171, 172, 179
Ustaritz 44, 57, 117, 118, 191, 192, 213, 217
  capital of the Labourd 45, 47, 114, 189, 228

Valle Alvarado, Juan de 113, 121, 136–7, 141, 145, 187, 191; *see also* Spanish Inquisition

vigilantism 17, 52–7, 157, 168, 187–9, 191, 212, 229–30
Vitelleschi, Mutio 93

Welles, Orson 220
whales/whaling 9, 20, 28–33, 89, 93
witch families 128, 165–6
witch-finders 2, 159–60, 202, 216
witch-priests 3, 38, 73, 113, 116–18, 125, 132, 153, 170, 173, 210
  defended by Bishop Echaux 180–84, 195; *see also* Arguibel; Bocal, Pierre; Migalena
witchcraft commission
  authorization of 22, 29, 43, 49, 58, 72, 96, 98, 105, 110, 150, 155
  in Ascain 114, 117, 165, 171–2, 182
  in Bayonne 109, 110
  in Saint-Jean-de-Luz 114, 116–17, 168, 174
  in Saint-Pée 114, 117, 154, 163, 169–71
  in Urrugne 114, 150, 152, 161, 163
  route of 114–15
  sponsors of 16, 24, 62, 103
  opposition to 167–85
witchcraft scepticism 7, 45, 64, 72–5, 91, 93, 94, 112, 173, 181, 189, 196, 224; *see also* Salazar Frías, Alonso de; Solarte, Hernando de
witches
  as teachers 128, 149, 151, 190
  causing harm 17, 44, 171, 177
  dancing 81, 91, 135, 139–40, 155
  flying 6, 84–5, 120, 131, 179
  having sex 2, 6, 81, 85, 91, 129, 139, 142, 151
  giving birth to toads 137
  looking for toads 124
  raising storms 28, 33, 35, 204, 213
witch's mark *see* devil's mark
witches' sabbat 40, 73, 80, 111
  black masses at 3, 73, 118, 132, 164–5, 170, 183, 216
  child-care at 2, 150, 153, 216
  collective imagination 142
  innocent people at 173–4
  intruders at 136

queens at 124, 127, 134, 152
  sources for 120–5
  toads at 125–34, 216–17
witnesses *see* teenagers

xenophobia 224, 225
Ximildegui, María de 45, 62, 123, 132, 145, 146, 149, 157, 162, 164

Ylumbe, Marcos de 18, 221, 223, 282n
Yriarte, María de 123

Ziarnko, Jan 7, 125
Zugarramurdi 20, 45, 62, 145, 165, 198
  caves of 40
  sabbat testimony from 122–37, 141–2, 152